Behavioral Corporate Governance in Practice

New Models for Leadership and Oversight

Jan Stolker

Routledge
Taylor & Francis Group
LONDON AND NEW YORK

First published in English 2026 by Routledge
4 Park Square, Milton Park, Abingdon, Oxon OX14 4RN

and by Routledge
605 Third Avenue, New York, NY 10158

Routledge is an imprint of the Taylor & Francis Group, an informa business

Published in Dutch as 'Het spel in de boardroom' by Boom 2023

British Library Cataloguing-in-Publication Data
A catalogue record for this book is available from the British Library

ISBN: 978-1-041-03593-0 (hbk)
ISBN: 978-1-041-03591-6 (pbk)
ISBN: 978-1-003-62440-0 (ebk)

DOI: 10.4324/9781003624400

Typeset in Univers LT Std
by Apex CoVantage, LLC

Access the Support Material: www.routledge.com/9781041035916

"For our shared prosperity, corporate social responsibility and good governance are indispensable. This calls for a constructive yet critical dialogue between supervisors and executives—growing together with an eye for new opportunities. This book compellingly demonstrates how that can be done, and how it can be done better."

Prof. Dr. K. (Kim) Putters, *Chair of the Social and Economic Council of the Netherlands and Professor of Broad Prosperity, Tilburg University, The Netherlands*

"Supervision is people's work. Rules, codes, and compliance are, of course, essential. But insight into the organization you oversee—its psychological processes, performance, integrity, and culture—is at least as important. That applies to every organization, in every sector, large or small. How do you achieve that? Fortunately, people can learn, and behavioral governance is finally receiving the attention it deserves."

M.J.A. (Maria) van der Hoeven, *Non-Executive Director and former Minister of Education and Minister of Economic Affairs, The Netherlands*

"Many non-executive directors ask how they—external and often distant—can overcome their information disadvantage and truly understand what is happening within the organizations they supervise. Jan Stolker's book provides answers by sharing practice-tested tools and interventions that offer insight into the behavior, performance, and dilemmas of organizations."

Prof. Patrick Reinmoeller, *Professor of Strategy and Innovation, IMD Business School, Switzerland*

"A must-read for all non-executive directors—and for executives as well. Rich in best practices and real-world case studies."

Dr. F.J.G.M. (Frans) Cremers, *Non-Executive Director at publicly listed companies; former CFO, VNU N.V. and Shell Group*

"Everything you wanted to know about boardrooms—or, put differently, this book answers all your questions about boardroom dynamics, including the ones you didn't know you had or didn't dare to ask."

Prof. Dr. G.W. (Goos) Minderman, *Non-Executive Director in civil-society organizations, Associate Professor at Stellenbosch University, South Africa, and Visiting Professor at the Erasmus Governance Institute, The Netherlands*

"At last, serious attention to what social transitions mean for management and supervision in companies. With solid grounding, vivid examples, and years of experience, Jan Stolker demonstrates how fundamental the shift in thinking and working must be—from managing risks to embracing societal goals and guiding one's own internal transition."

Prof. Dr. D.A. (Derk) Loorbach, *Professor of Socio-Economic Transition Science, Erasmus University Rotterdam, The Netherlands*

"Inclusive and moral leadership, combined with strategic insight, is indispensable for today's executive and non-executive directors. This book explains why."

Prof. Dr. A.L. (Annelien) Bredenoord, *Rector Magnificus, Erasmus University Rotterdam, and Non-Executive Director, The Netherlands*

Behavioral Corporate Governance in Practice

Behavioral Corporate Governance in Practice provides readers with a comprehensive understanding of corporate governance and its challenges.

While covering the key aspects of any board's agenda, this book goes a step further by deconstructing behavioral dynamics and balancing both leadership and oversight in its examination of governance. The book explores the psychological aspects of decision-making and boardroom dynamics, including ethics, morals, rationality, biases, and emotions. Building on these considerations, the author presents a new leadership model in reaction to the classic model of chief executive officer (CEO) narcissism, one based on strategic and empathetic leadership. A case is also made for the internally and externally balanced board, which exhibits an effective mix of behavioral dynamics and strategic sensitivity to the wider societal context beyond organizational interests. Topics covered include information management, finance, accounting, risk management, fraud and corruption, purpose, risk, strategy, and the role of the external auditor as an ally of the non-executive. Case studies and reflection questions throughout the book serve to enhance readers' understanding of the nuances of these topics.

This book is essential for postgraduates and practitioners interested in corporate governance, strategy, leadership, and oversight.

Online resources for instructors include slides for each chapter.

Jan Stolker serves as Director of Leadership and Governance at the Erasmus School of Economics/EURAC, Erasmus University Rotterdam, and is founder of the Erasmus Governance Institute. He advises boards and lectures internationally on governance, strategy, and risk.

CONTENTS

ABOUT THE AUTHOR

Jan Stolker studied economics at Erasmus University Rotterdam and began his career in international finance at Amro Bank in Amsterdam and New York. He later founded ABN AMRO Capital, expanding its private equity activities across 17 countries.

Since 2002, he has served as an independent advisor and executive director focused on restructuring and governance and has held non-executive directorships on more than 20 international boards.

In 2009, he founded the Erasmus Governance Institute (EGI), the university's executive education and research center, which he led until his retirement in 2024. He has lectured at CELAP, the China Executive Leadership Academy in Pudong, Shanghai, and Leeds Business School. His research focuses on boardroom dynamics, behavioral oversight, risk management, and the role of human behavior in shaping governance outcomes.

He serves as Director of Leadership and Governance at the Erasmus School of Economics, bridging academic research and boardroom practice. His work contributes to a growing understanding of governance as a function of human behavior, and of the capacity of boards to navigate societal, technological, and climate change.

PREFACE TO THE INTERNATIONAL EDITION

In boardrooms around the world, a small group of people carries a responsibility that cannot be delegated. They rarely seek the spotlight. Yet when corporate judgment fails—when warning signs are missed, risks are ignored, or difficult decisions are quietly avoided—it is their behavior that determines whether a company thrives, stumbles, or collapses.

These are the non-executive directors: those whose role is neither to lead nor to execute, but to oversee. And despite the weight of their responsibility, they remain among the least examined figures in business literature. Books abound on strategy, finance, and celebrated chief executive officers (CEOs). Corporate failures are meticulously analyzed with the benefit of hindsight. But the people tasked with appointing leadership and preventing failure? Their work unfolds largely in the shadows.

This book approaches governance from a behavioral perspective, guided by a simple but demanding conviction: formal structures, rules, and procedures are essential, but it is behavior that ultimately determines outcomes.

For that reason, this book centers on the people in the boardroom: their personalities, values, and interactions. It examines how judgments are formed, how power is exercised, and how responsibility is taken, or sidestepped, when decisions become difficult and the stakes are high.

When I began working on the international edition in early 2025, I could not have foreseen how rapidly the corporate and societal context would change. Was this a genuine surprise, or had warning signs been missed? Following the U.S. elections, political polarization intensified, and after decades of liberalization, politics reasserted its primacy over the business sector. Corporate boards around the world, which generally prefer stability, were suddenly forced to navigate deepening trade conflicts, rising geopolitical tensions, and, in some cases, the consequences of military confrontations.

As these developments unfolded, a pattern became difficult to ignore. The behavioral dynamics of the political arena—strongly personalized leadership and polarization—have increasingly entered corporate boardrooms. The result? A growing emphasis not only in politics but also in corporations, on short-term strategic thinking, self-interest over fiduciary judgment, loyalty over independence, and silence over intervention.

In this process, democratic values, including the rule of law governing relations among citizens, governments, and corporations, have come under pressure. The global marketplace has become more contested. Corporate strategies aimed at balancing economic performance with environmental and social responsibility increasingly face backlash.

This book invites reflection on organizations, values, and leadership, as well as on the ambiguities and dilemmas inherent in oversight systems. Written for those willing to take on that responsibility, it encourages readers to ask not only whether decisions are legal or compliant but also whether they are attentive, courageous, and worthy of society's trust, thereby contributing to the creation of sustainable value.

This book can offer no guarantees, but it hopes to offer recognition. In the case studies, readers may recognize moments of sound judgment, hesitation, and failure—sometimes quiet, sometimes spectacular. They show that governance can falter anywhere. They also shed light on how much depends on this group of people who rarely seek the spotlight yet carry a unique responsibility.

If this all sounds rather grim, rest assured that the book—with over 80 short case studies—also shows that the role of oversight can be meaningful and, at times, even quietly enjoyable.

ACKNOWLEDGMENTS AND LOOKING AHEAD

This book began as a translation of my Dutch textbook on behavioral governance: *Het spel in de boardroom*. During the writing process, it gradually evolved into a broader reflection on governance in an international context, marked by increasing complexity and uncertainty. Early research at Erasmus University and discussions with participants in my board programs shaped the perspective that governance is driven not only by rules and compliance but above all by behavior, character, and values. This is a global phenomenon across times of stability and disruption.

As these forces continue to shape companies, economies, and communities, behavioral governance has moved to the top of the board agenda. This book is finished, yet in many ways it remains a work in progress.

This book could only have been written with the support of many people: executive and non-executive board members, entrepreneurs, auditors, lawyers, regulators, civil servants, and—importantly—people outside the governance world, advisors, and NGOs, all offering perspectives on what good oversight should look like. After all, governance affects us all.

This book draws on the experiences of participants in the programs of the Erasmus Governance Institute (EGI), including insights from hundreds of boardroom cases they developed. Their contributions underscore not only how challenging the work of non-executives and executives can be but also how dilemmas can be addressed through shared reflection.

I am grateful for the insights exchanged with academics at home and abroad, across disciplines including economics, behavioral sciences, strategic leadership, psychology, neurology, law, and sociology. In the Netherlands, I benefited greatly from discussions with non-executive associations and colleagues at the Erasmus School of Economics (ESE).

THANK YOU

My sincere thanks go to Harry Commandeur (Erasmus University), co-initiator of the EGI program, for many inspiring conversations, and to Cees van Halem (Erasmus University), who first encouraged the idea of a "small book" and later engaged with many of its now larger chapters. Martin Hoogendoorn and the late Hans Gortemaker (both Erasmus School of Accounting and Assurances), Hans Strikwerda (University of Amsterdam), and Jatinder Sidhu (Leeds University) supported me with their unrivaled scientific knowledge of accounting, governance, and strategic thinking. Frans Cremers stood out among many non-executive directors willing to share his experience in international corporate governance. Frans van de Meché (Erasmus MC) and Han Bleichrodt (University of Alicante) provided insights on neurology and behavioral economics. Maria van der Hoeven, former minister and EGI alumna, shared her insights on governance and the dynamics of international boards. Carel Stolker, my brother and former rector magnificus of Leiden University, read several drafts with a critical and encouraging eye. Patrick Reinmoeller

(IMD Business School, Lausanne) and Winfried Ruigrok (University of St. Gallen), specialists in corporate governance, generously shared their global governance experiences. Marnix Holtzer, lawyer at DLA Piper, shared valuable insights on sustainable governance in the EU.

During the translation and internationalization of this book, I had the invaluable professional support of Steffi Gande, ensuring a smooth and consistent reading of the manuscript.

A special thank-you goes to the EGI community: the speakers, program facilitators, non-executives, governance experts, and especially the many alumni I've spoken with over the past 20 years. Their experiences brought this book to life.

PERSONAL NOTE

This book was encouraged by the new generation: my children *Marlyne, Floor,* and *Thomas*; their partners *Merve* and *Fabian*; and the next generation—*Sam, Ella, and Mila*. They reminded me that good governance must always be viewed through the eyes of those who follow us.

Last but not least, my deepest thanks go to my wife, Trea, economist, psychotherapist, co-reader, and sparring partner. She helped me keep the human and psychological dimensions of governance firmly in view, and above all, she patiently endured the long period of living with an often-absent author.

DISCLAIMER AND ENCOURAGEMENT

Despite careful research, extensive case material, and the insights of many co-readers, governance remains a complex and evolving field. The interpretations in this book reflect the context and best judgment available at the time of writing. Others may view the same situations differently. New insights—or errors of the author—may shed new light on cases and governance matters, and that is both inevitable and valuable.

This book does not claim to offer definitive answers. On the contrary, the reflection questions at the end of each chapter are meant to encourage continued thinking and ongoing dialogue—particularly about one's own role in oversight and the behavioral dynamics of governance.

As is customary in the EGI's programs, I warmly invite your reflections, suggestions, and critiques. New insights are always welcome.

CHAPTER 1

Introduction: Oversight under pressure

CONTENTS

EVERYTHING EVERYWHERE ALL AT ONCE

Picture this: you're a non-executive board member, tasked with oversight. You're sipping your coffee, quietly reviewing the quarterly reports. Everything seems to be under control. Suddenly, your phone buzzes. Your organization is front-page news—for all the wrong reasons. What happened? Where did things go wrong, and most painfully, how could your board not have seen it coming?

It's 2022, the aftermath of the coronavirus crisis. Chaos is erupting in Schiphol, the Netherlands' main airport. This international hub is overwhelmed by travelers: lost suitcases, endless queues, frustrated passengers, exhausted employees, and outraged airlines. Outside the terminal, residents are protesting against noise pollution, while grandparents voice their concerns about the climate legacy they are leaving for their grandchildren. The chief executive officer (CEO) looks on helplessly as his organization unravels. The newly appointed independent board chair must remain calm and lead the response. Meanwhile, the outside world has no clue what the company is up against.

FROM CONTEXT TO RESPONSIBILITY

As long as an organization is successful, the CEO takes the credit. The non-executive directors remain comfortably invisible. But when things fall apart, they're pulled into the spotlight, held accountable by shareholders, stakeholders, and the public at large. The inevitable question arises: who was responsible for oversight?

DOI: 10.4324/9781003624400-1

Oversight is about people. Psychology shapes how boards function—not just through individual character, but through subtle power games, sharp questioning, silence, loyalty, and fear of conflict. Under pressure, these dynamics can be as decisive as any strategy or spreadsheet. Authority can harden into dominance—like a *Sun King* unchecked by institutional power—turning the boardroom itself into a source of pressure, where power, ego, and silence shape how directors act.

And then, there is the outside world. More than ever, it is a turbulent place. Geopolitical tensions, climate disruption, shifting regulatory expectations, and political polarization all collide at boardroom doors. Political bullying risks spilling over into the business sector. Environmental, social, and governance (ESG) principles, originally intended to guide businesses responsibly and sustainably into the twenty-first century, have come under intense pressure.

BEYOND THE JOB DESCRIPTION: MEETING PUBLIC EXPECTATIONS

In corporate governance literature, executive leadership often takes center stage. Yet far less attention is paid to non-executive directors, who carry a different kind of responsibility. What exactly is expected of them? How do the expectations placed upon them align with the realities they face? And where does the red line between execution and oversight lie?

The role of non-executive directors on the board is defined in laws, codes, and a company's bylaws. These individuals are responsible for ensuring that effective leadership is in place and overseeing strategy, integrity, and values. As organizations increasingly shape public life, directors must also earn public trust. In this arena, oversight and ethics are inseparable.

Once focused mainly on compliance, the non-executive's role has broadened over the years: they are now expected to balance performance with integrity and to integrate an awareness of society's evolving expectations into their judgment.

A MAGNIFYING GLASS ON THE BOARDROOM CHARACTERS AND DYNAMICS

One way to look at the boardroom is as a high-stakes game where two sides meet: the executives who run the company day to day and the non-executive directors who bring oversight. The overall purpose, mission, and goals of the company are shared. Yet each side holds different information, faces different pressures, and plays different roles.

This book asks a critical question: if boardrooms are filled with accomplished, thoughtful people, why do they so often get things so right—and other times, as case studies in this book illustrate, so predictably wrong? Is it really a case of bad luck when things go awry?

The explanation sits squarely in human behavior. We like to believe that boardroom decisions emerge from careful rational analysis. However, Nobel Prize winners such as Herbert Simon, Daniel Kahneman, and Richard Thaler have shown us something different: even brilliant individuals make flawed decisions when biases, blind spots, and group dynamics take over.

Boardrooms are not just arenas of logic—they are human theaters. Subtle power games, status anxieties, and personality traits play out around the table. Narcissistic tendencies can distort dynamics: when confidence tips into dominance, when charisma suppresses dissent, and when directors hesitate to challenge the person at the head of the table. This is what this book refers to as behavioral governance: governance shaped not only by rules, but by human behavior in practice.

WHEN SILENCE BECOMES RISK

You have probably been in a meeting where everyone seemed to agree, but you sensed something was wrong. Did you speak up? Often, people don't. That silence, multiplied across countless boardrooms, explains more governance failures than any technical analysis. In the executive programs at Erasmus University and in my own board experience, I have seen seasoned directors struggling with this very dilemma. I have struggled with it myself. Directors often describe the pressure to remain collegial, the fear of appearing obstructive, and the difficulty of questioning a charismatic CEO without concrete evidence to support their concerns. But I have also seen boards that get it right: fostering *psychological safety*, encouraging dissent, and knowing where to draw the line between supporting management and challenging bad decisions where it matters.

CENTRAL QUESTION

That leads to the central question for any non-executive board member: *How do you truly understand what is happening in your organization when you operate as a part-timer, far from the heartbeat of daily decisions? How do you exercise real oversight when power, information, and time are not on your side?*

Old patterns, new risks, greater responsibility

For decades, governance reform has followed a predictable cycle: crises lead to reform, but new failures emerge. Since the corporate scandals of the early 2000s, such as Enron and Parmalat among others, reforms have followed, yet they failed to prevent the near collapse of the global financial system in 2008. Serious failures persist, and structural reforms continue to lag behind the realities of a free-market system. Wirecard, Credit Suisse, and even the world's most prestigious consultancy firms, in cases of misconduct, remind us that overconfidence and unethical behavior remain significant threats, even in an era of heightened compliance.

Some organizations lack professionalism. Others lack a moral compass. Governance failures aren't confined to large corporations. They also occur in family businesses, social enterprises, schools, hospitals, churches, and NGOs.

New laws and regulations will inevitably arise in the wake of public scandals. But history shows they rarely arrive in time—and even when they do, rules alone are not enough. Laws can set boundaries, but they can't shape judgment, courage, or ethics. Without attention to human behavior, culture, and the broader impact of corporate decisions, rules are easily bypassed. Too much focus on procedure blinds us to deeper issues.

WHY THIS BOOK FOR NON-EXECUTIVE DIRECTORS?

Most governance literature focuses on what executives should do. This book takes a different approach: it examines oversight from the perspective of those who must challenge, question, and ultimately hold executives accountable.

What does the world look like when you're responsible for asking difficult questions but only meet eight times a year, reading the room as a charismatic CEO pitches an ambitious strategy, and something feels off?

This book applies behavioral science to the practice of oversight. It doesn't just describe *what* went wrong in boardroom failures, but it also explains *why* intelligent, experienced non-executive directors missed the warning signs. By understanding the psychological forces at play, the biases, group dynamics, and personality traits that shape boardroom behavior, directors can better recognize these patterns in real time and intervene before small problems become crises.

This book draws on real cases from both sides of the table: the executives accountable for execution and the non-executive exercising oversight. This dual perspective reveals the information asymmetries, competing pressures, and human dynamics that make governance so challenging—and so critical to get right. Three converging fields underpin this analysis: corporate governance theory, behavioral economics, and organizational psychology.

This book is written for board members and oversight professionals, but it also addresses those who work in and around the boardroom, including external auditors, lawyers, bankers, regulators, consultants, and journalists. For students of business administration, leadership, behavioral sciences, accounting, and control, this is an accessible introduction to the practice and theory of behavioral sciences in business and nonprofit organizations. Finally, this book calls on anyone curious about what happens behind the closed doors of boardrooms. Oversight is no longer just an insider's concern. It shapes the decisions that affect us all.

How to read this book?

Including this introduction, this book is divided into six chapters, all of which are enriched with short real-world cases that bridge theoretical insights with practical applications. Reflection questions at the end of each chapter offer a useful tool for individual learning or board evaluation.

Chapter 2 examines the human aspects of leadership and oversight, providing the conceptual framework for the chapters that follow. What personality traits and ethical dispositions shape the behavior of those at the top? It introduces the *dark triad*—narcissism, *Machiavellianism*, and antisocial behavior—as key behavioral risks in leadership. Why do charisma and competence sometimes coexist with dominance or moral blind spots? The chapter concludes by examining how these traits play out in boardroom dynamics.

Chapter 3 demonstrates how ownership shapes governance: the board of a listed company emerges as distinctly different from that of a private equity firm, a family business, or a nonprofit organization. Each plays by its own rules, logic, and culture. This chapter examines how strategy, control, and accountability shift in relation to ownership, purpose, and institutional logic.

Chapter 4 examines how boards rely on information, but not all information yields insight. Biases, blind spots, and behavioral traps influence what directors perceive, overlook, or misinterpret. The chapter transitions from fraud and corruption to the role of external auditors, concluding with the challenge of incorporating integrity into board decision-making.

Chapter 5 considers strategy as more than just analysis, arguing that behavior, culture, and purpose shape strategy. Boards face storms of uncertainty, geopolitical shocks, climate disruption, and technological volatility. Internally, they must guard against pitfalls such as *groupthink* and *tunnel vision*. *Pre-mortems*, scenario planning, and culture scans can strengthen strategic and ethical risk management, supporting resilience and purpose.

Chapter 6 turns to leadership, oversight, and the balanced board: how to appoint and support the all-important CEO and the executive team. Organizations operate within a complex stakeholder context, with global impact. This calls for tough choices coupled with a clear moral stance. The chapter presents a new model of strategic and empathetic leadership. It concludes with a provocative question: *how can a board achieve the right balance, both in the boardroom and in its wider relationship to society?*

About this book

This book is written for a global audience and is built on international experience. It draws on insights from the executive programs for non-executive directors at the Erasmus Governance Institute (EGI), part of Erasmus University Rotterdam. For over two decades, participants in these programs have worked through hundreds of real-life boardroom cases spanning listed companies, private equity firms, family businesses, NGOs, schools, and hospitals.

The cases featured in this book go well beyond personal experience. They are drawn from major international governance failures and successes, selected for their broader relevance. Some appear anonymously; others are based on publicly available information from court rulings, parliamentary inquiries, and investigative journalism, with clear source attribution.

It's important to note that the cases presented in this book are not final verdicts. Governance stories evolve: new developments may surface years after a case first comes to light, and new insights may reshape our understanding. The goal here is to offer meaningful lessons, not definitive conclusions.

Notes for the reader

- **Focus:** this book concerns the people in the boardroom and their behavior, culture, and dynamics, seen through the lens of oversight.
- **Oversight:** in this book, the term "oversight" refers to the central governance role of non-executive directors and regulators. It is characterized by strategic distance, independent judgment, and accountability.
- **Board types in this book:** legal structures matter. Yet, to maintain legibility and ease of reading, in this international edition we use the one-tier board model as our base reference. Where relevant, differences between the one-tier, two-tier or hybrid systems are noted.
- **One-tier board model**: executive and non-executive directors serve together on the same board. This system is standard in most of the Anglo-Saxon corporate world—for example, the United Kingdom and the United States—as well as in India and Japan.

- **Two-tier board model:** non-executive directors tasked with oversight sit in their own body—the supervisory board—while management has its own executive board. This is also called the "Rhineland model." It is present in many countries in continental Europe, such as Germany, and in China.
- **Board of executive directors:** this is the top organizational level, typically led by the CEO and including the chief financial officer (CFO) and the chief operating officer (COO).
- **Executive management/committee:** the day-to-day leadership team, with titles varying by country and by sector.
- **Boardroom:** the physical meeting space and the forum for oversight and decision-making.
- **Stakeholders:** individuals or groups with direct or indirect interests in the organization, including shareholders—often highlighted separately—employees, suppliers, customers, and communities affected by environmental and social impact.

CHAPTER

2

Oversight in the boardroom: The human side

CONTENTS

§2.1—WHY OVERSIGHT MATTERS

Introduction

Oversight is everywhere. Or is it nowhere at all? It all depends on who you ask. In today's society, the oversight of businesses and social organizations takes many forms, ranging from supervisory boards and non-executive directors to auditors and government-appointed inspectors. There is a flood of rules, regulations, and audits. Most of the time, this system works. But when things go wrong, the question rings out loud and clear: Was nobody watching? Where was the oversight?

This book makes the case that answering these questions requires a shift from traditional governance thinking to *behavioral governance*. This approach recognizes oversight as fundamentally shaped by human psychology, emotions, power dynamics, and social interaction. While laws and codes define what boards *should do*, behavioral governance examines how human factors determine what boards *actually do*.

The challenge is structural. Non-executive directors operate as part-timers, at a distance from daily operations, dependent on information filtered by the very executives they oversee. They hold formal authority but face practical limits: incomplete information, uncertain judgment, and the social pressures inherent in any group dynamic.

DOI: 10.4324/9781003624400-2

Success breeds confidence—sometimes too much. Organizations may disappoint, sometimes structurally. So, what is going wrong? Are the rules unclear? Do we have the right people? Are we getting too little or expecting too much from those tasked with oversight? Scholars have long noted that governance doesn't unfold in a vacuum; it reflects the social dynamics among those who hold and exercise power in and around the boardroom.

Reliance on oversight

The focus on executive leadership often overshadows the purpose of oversight. Before introducing the role of the non-executive director, we consider the broader landscape in which they operate. Viewed from above, like a drone scanning society, we see a world in which people rely on businesses, nonprofit organizations, and civic institutions for the necessities of life. This deep reliance underscores the importance of people being able to trust those they depend on.

Young people receive education at institutions ranging from elementary schools to universities. Consumers purchase a wide range of products and services, including healthcare, food, housing, energy, and vacations. They seek assurance that those products and services are safe and reliable. Beyond consumers, investors, employees, and suppliers also rely on these qualities, making trust a crucial concern across industries.

Yet it is becoming increasingly complex to assess the quality of all these products and services, let alone how they are produced. A consumer can figure out whether a cell phone works. However, they are hardly in a position to know whether that phone is safe, doesn't catch fire easily, guarantees their privacy, or is produced sustainably. Supply chains are long and often opaque. Production processes can harm the environment and exploit workers. For the average consumer, the amount of information needed to make an informed judgment about product and service quality is simply overwhelming.

Power imbalances and geopolitical pressures

Power imbalances shape the relationship between organizations and their stakeholders. A "small fish in a big pond" effect is at play: consumers and citizens can feel powerless, while companies loom large. Conflicting interests are everywhere: consumers want quality at low prices; companies aim for low costs and maximize profits.

Tensions also run inside organizations. Employees seek good working conditions but may hold back, fearing for their jobs, while companies focus on efficiency and low wages, yet can't ignore their workers' loyalty. Investors face their own squeeze, torn between financial returns and the growing pressure to invest responsibly. Society and the planet have no seat at the table, even as sustainability becomes urgent.

Layered on top of these factors is political pressure. Politicians are eager to prove their mettle through economic intervention. Governments prioritizing their own interests impose regulations, tariffs, and trade measures, reshaping global markets. In 2025, major power blocs—the United States, China, and the EU—intensified their battle, using economic policy as a geopolitical weapon. U.S. tariffs on steel, aluminum, and other goods triggered global trade disputes, forcing companies to rethink their supply chains. Such interventions distort competition, heighten uncertainty, and increase pressure on leadership.

All these forces weave a tight web of economic and social tensions, shaping how organizations decide and act. For non-executive directors, the task isn't to manage these forces directly but to ensure organizations are ready to face their impact.

The role of oversight: internal, external

This is where oversight comes into play. To strengthen public trust and protect citizens, governments have built an ecosystem of checks and balances to keep powerful organizations under control. It includes laws, mandatory disclosure, auditors, and non-executive directors monitoring the boards of larger organizations. At its core, the system seeks to address power imbalances and safeguard the public interest.

Governments fulfill this role through two main oversight systems: external and internal. Inspection services and regulatory authorities carry out external oversight. Internal oversight happens within organizations, through boards of non-executive directors. Both systems are enshrined in law, and serious failures can lead to personal liability for both executives and non-executives. Yet, despite these formal structures, the reality is far from perfect. The concept of oversight is often foggy and subjective. While the law's intent is clear, its interpretation varies widely, as the case studies in this book will reveal.

External oversight

Government inspections have a long history because quality and reliability are vital to both the economy and society. Oversight bodies aim to guarantee the quality of products and services and promote transparency. One historic example from the Netherlands is the Calibration Office, which has been checking weights and measures since the Middle Ages to ensure fair treatment for citizens and businesses—a reminder that market trust has always rested on basic guarantees: that a kilogram is a kilogram. Today, inspections monitor sectors such as education, healthcare, and environmental impact. Beyond inspections, regulatory authorities such as central banks and financial market regulators supervise markets and safeguard systemic stability.

Internal oversight

For large organizations in both the business and nonprofit sectors, internal oversight isn't optional—it is the law. Non-executive directors are responsible for oversight and advising the executive board. They may not always be fully independent, but they are expected to act as such, balancing a wide range of sometimes competing interests inside and outside the organization. They also act as the employer of the executive board, appointing executives, evaluating performance, and determining remuneration. This dual role creates inherent ambiguity.

What non-executive directors actually do to monitor executive management is largely invisible to the outside world, as board members seldom speak outside the boardroom. Shareholders and other stakeholders often only notice governance failures when it is too late. International savers looked on helplessly as prominent banks collapsed in 2008 or, more recently, as Silicon Valley Bank and Credit Suisse fell, taking their money down with them.

This problem extends far beyond banking. Some industries create substantial profits for shareholders even as their legal products, such as vapes, tobacco, and gambling, cause well-documented harm. Likewise, numerous production processes have proven harmful for the environment; sometimes the damage is uncovered only in hindsight, but often the risks are already known and deliberately kept from view. These cases highlight how oversight is not just a matter of market stability but also one of public health, safety, and trust.

At its core, effective oversight means more than just formal checks and balances. It is about ensuring quality, protecting trust, and weighing up the interests of investors, employees, customers, and society at large. To be meaningful, oversight must have teeth: boards are empowered to intervene when necessary, correct executive leadership, or, as a last resort, dismiss it.

Part-timers at a distance

Non-executive directors must make do with a limited understanding of the organization they oversee. They function as part-timers, at a distance from the day-to-day operations of the workplace, hereafter also referred to as the "primary process," and must navigate an environment of uncertainty. Their oversight role relies on information provided by the very entity they are overseeing. But is that information sufficient, clear, and complete? Can they make sound judgments based on it? In practice, psychology tends to push in the opposite direction: it is easier to trust information than to challenge it.

Non-executive directors bear a formal responsibility, but they cannot sit in the CEO's chair. Meanwhile, the CEO, busy running the business, is hardly waiting around for their advice. As long as things are going well, the non-executives often have little choice but to trust the CEO's motives and integrity.

The secret of the boardroom

For most people, the boardroom remains a mystery, and when it comes to the quality of oversight by non-executive directors, the fog thickens. The outside world does not see records of what's actually said in meetings between executives and non-executives. In a sense, this is logical; directors need a safe space for open, candid discussion.

On paper, the division of roles looks neat and tidy: executives run the company, and non-executives keep them in check. Laws, governance codes, and board charters outline the boundaries. But here's the catch: while the "what" of oversight is broadly prescribed, the "how" is left almost entirely to personal interpretation. Each non-executive director relies on judgment, habits, and prior experience. Oversight, then, doesn't follow a single playbook—it is more like a free-format game where the players write their own rules.

Secrecy can feed the perception that non-executives and executives aren't holding each other accountable; they are closing ranks. And whether or not this is the case in a given boardroom is almost irrelevant. When transparency is absent, suspicion becomes the default, compounded by the behavioral twist: when outsiders see so little, they often assume the worst.

When oversight breaks down

From society's point of view, oversight is an invisible function, one that lacks transparency. Yet, from time to time, information emerges about the way non-executive directors operate, for example through parliamentary inquiries, court investigations into corporate disputes, or disclosures by insiders. Several examples are presented in the following pages.

Harold Geneen, the influential chair and CEO of the industrial conglomerate ITT Corp, served on many boards in the 1960s and 1970s. He stated as an insider: "I would estimate that approximately 95% of boards of directors are not fully doing what they are legally, morally and ethically supposed to do. They are not doing their jobs."[1] He was referring to non-executive directors' high degree of dependence on the CEO: "They serve at the pleasure of the chief executive." That seems like a long time ago, but even in the subsequent decades history appeared to repeat itself.

An example from the Netherlands highlights systemic failure of external oversight: in a disillusioned letter, Pieter van Vollenhoven, former chair of the Dutch Safety Board, warned that ministries are often allowed to tamper with rules, without timely correction by internal and external watchdogs.[2] He attributes this failure to a deeper problem: oversight has become too much an extension of ministerial management, shielding political leadership from its responsibility. In some cases, ministries can delete unwelcome passages from inspectorates' reports. Van Vollenhoven describes this as "extremely undermining to the functioning of society." A similar collapse of independence in oversight occurred in the United States, where the overly close relationship between aircraft manufacturer Boeing and its external regulator proved to be part of a disastrous governance cocktail (as we will explore later in a case study in Chapter 6, Section §6.2).

In fact, Geneen and Van Vollenhoven convey the same message. People who are active in oversight often fail to meet the expectations of the outside world, because they lack sufficient independence. They can only fulfill their role objectively if they are free from dependence on the organization's management and willing to confront when necessary. Good oversight requires non-executive directors to be directly accountable to shareholders and stakeholders. However, we see very little of this. If any information is communicated to the outside world, it almost always comes from the executive management. From the non-executive directors, a vague boilerplate statement in the annual report is usually all that appears.

Under pressure, but not beyond repair

Is it all going wrong? With numerous books on scandals and the media spotlight on corporate and nonprofit failings, it is easy to conclude that governance and oversight are under par. As the saying goes, if you only have a hammer, you tend to see every problem as a nail. But a more nuanced view is needed, one that takes concerns seriously without exaggerating them. Many companies and civil society organizations function well, demonstrate clear accountability, and learn from their mistakes.

Just as failing directors often remain invisible to the outside world until a scandal breaks out, the same is true of those who perform well in successful organizations. Their contribution rarely makes headlines. On balance, the successes of business and civil society organizations have led to high levels of prosperity in our society. Yet prosperity has its own shadow side. In some areas, it now threatens to collapse under the weight of its own success. One only has to consider the global climate and environmental crisis. That's why enduring prosperity demands not only ambition but also unrelenting vigilance.

SUMMARY AND CONCLUSION

Oversight is essential because executives hold more power and information than those they are meant to serve, yet oversight mechanisms are often weak. On paper, non-executive directors are tasked with overseeing, advising, and holding management accountable. In practice, they operate as part-timers, far from the day-to-day "primary process," and dependent on information supplied by the very executives they must oversee.

This creates an environment of uncertainty, where it is easier to trust than to challenge. Laws and governance codes define roles but provide little guidance on how oversight should be exercised, leaving directors to rely on their own judgment, habits, and experience. The result is inconsistency, opacity, and suspicion from the outside world.

In most cases, transparency is limited: board compositions are public, but meaningful details about directors' backgrounds, interests, and potential conflicts are rarely disclosed. Meeting records between executives and non-executives remain secret, reinforcing the perception that directors and management close ranks rather than hold each other accountable.

Oversight, then, is both vital and fragile—dependent on independence, transparency, and the willingness of non-executives to push back when necessary. Without these, oversight risks becoming an illusion, eroding the very trust on which companies and society depend.

§2.2—THE TABLE OF POWER

Introduction

Oversight shapes trust and defines how organizations are held accountable. Around that polished Table of Power in the boardroom, where decades of collective experience gather, policies are debated and decisions are made.

An unsettling but straightforward question hovers over every meeting and crisis: *who truly holds the power in the boardroom?* Behind the formal structures, a subtle—and at times hardball—game unfolds between executive and non-executive directors. Authority and power are distinct mechanisms of influence: power can impose decisions; authority earns followership. Without balance, one corrodes the other.

Across corporate governance models worldwide, most decision-making power rests with executives and shareholders. At the same time, companies and civil society organizations are expected to consider the interests of their broad range of stakeholders. Yet customers and communities, those most affected by boardroom choices, lack direct representation where key decisions are made. When their voices are absent, oversight risks becoming incapacitated, making it blind to the very interests it is meant to safeguard.

This section examines how that imbalance plays out through the lens of behavioral governance: specifically in the boardroom, in its meeting rituals, and in the dynamics between those who hold formal power and those who claim authority, where formal structures alone cannot explain how decisions are actually made.

Surveillance from a tower

For citizens, oversight is an invisible function. This is not only due to its abstract nature but also because of the exclusive setting where supervisors typically meet: the boardroom. Boardrooms, especially those of large multinationals, are literally elevated, positioned on the top floor of the company's headquarters. They appear to radiate power and exclusivity. Even for non-executives, gaining access to the boardroom is not automatic; it requires an introduction. First, you must check in at the reception desk, identify yourself—since in a large organization, people don't necessarily know you—have your bag scanned, and then be directed to the elevator.

Unless you are a director or non-executive director, you can't enter the boardroom of a multinational company. Occasionally, young managers are invited to the Table of Power to give a presentation or assist a director in securing approval for a strategic plan. The sense of executive power at that table is inescapable. Simply sitting at the table confers a sense of status. And yet, this appearance of authority doesn't guarantee responsible decision-making, as we will explore later.

The artist's view

Artists' opinions are often the very last thing directors in a boardroom want to hear. Their work may, at best, decorate the walls. For her book *The Table of Power* (1996), Jacqueline Hassink (1966–2018) photographed the meeting rooms of the 40 largest companies in Europe. There are no people in the photos; only the rooms and furniture are visible. The pictures reflect the abstract, formal world of corporate decision-making, which is far removed from the daily lives of citizens. Notably, 19 companies refused to cooperate and were represented by a black page—a negative space in which power remained unseen. What were the reasons for not participating? "Photography in the boardroom is strictly prohibited," "security is at stake," and "the company does not understand the point of taking pictures of the boardroom." However, one company, British oil giant BP (after its initial refusal in 1995), was willing to participate in the second edition of the book. After the Deepwater Horizon drilling rig disaster, BP wanted to chart a new course with greater transparency.

Power has a history

In the world of international corporate governance, English is the universal language of business. The word "board" calls to mind the seventeenth-century boardrooms where governors—such as the Gentlemen Seventeen of the Dutch East India Company (VOC)—convened to direct their multinational enterprise. Dutch Golden Age paintings capture the scene: dark-paneled rooms, the sheen of polished wooden plank tables, and men in black robes and white collars exuding wealth, authority, and deliberation. Today, the board comprises both executive and non-executive directors. They meet periodically in the *boardroom* to discuss strategic plans, review reports, and make key decisions.

But prestigious boardrooms and headquarters are not a business invention. Throughout history, power has been expressed through monumental buildings—from the imposing façades of city halls and courts to the grand halls of universities and even hospitals. These structures have long symbolized authority and distance, placing rulers, administrators, or governors far from the daily realities of work. Headquarters radiate success and often reflect periods of unchecked expansion. Yet history also suggests that the construction of grand new edifices can just as easily foreshadow decline.

Room with a view?

The boardroom's position raises fundamental questions about the role and effectiveness of this body. Can non-executive directors in this setting truly fulfill their responsibility to the organization? The spreadsheets with financials usually add up. But do non-executive directors have a deep enough understanding of the organization's culture, norms, and values? Are they sufficiently connected to its societal operating context, and do they grasp the interests of all its stakeholders? When their position is too elevated and distant, non-executive directors risk focusing solely on high-level strategy, lose touch with the organization's realities, and become a group lacking a central focus.

Whereas the boardrooms of large multinationals and some civil society organizations exude power, the contrast with the "boardroom" of family-owned businesses can be striking. Here, decisions may well be made around the kitchen table. In family-owned businesses, the owner and chief executive are often one and the same individual, operating in proximity to the primary, core process, meeting customers in person. Here, the guiding principle is: "We keep things normal." By contrast, in companies owned by private equity investors, efficiency and cash flow are paramount. Luxury offices are sold off, and the board meets at a canteen table.

Balance of power in the boardroom

Power and authority shape the game of oversight and executive leadership in the boardroom. This ongoing interplay involves the non-executive directors, the executive board, shareholders, and stakeholders, each with their own interests and respective levels of influence. Non-executive directors often believe—or at least hope—that they are appreciated for their talent, insights, and reputation. That may well be true. But where executive directors may tolerate the oversight of the non-executive directors, they do not always welcome their vision or involvement. In some cases, they view the board's oversight function as ceremonial, a bureaucratic hurdle, or a body that, on balance, is too detached to fully grasp the organization's real opportunities and challenges.[3]

The formal and practical power relationships between non-executive and executive directors at the top of the organization differ widely across types of organization—whether a listed company, family business, private equity firm, or civil society organization. Formal non-executive power is derived from its statutory position, laws, codes, and formal agreements between stakeholders. In companies, non-executive directors can appoint and dismiss the executive management, subject to shareholder approval. In civil society organizations, in the absence of shareholders, the non-executive board members have an even greater responsibility. They are often formally empowered to approve or reject major strategic decisions, shaping the organization's long-term direction.

When formal power meets practical limits

However, the power of the non-executive directors is far from absolute: it is constrained by uncertainty and doubt. Their informational position is structurally limited. They lack a complete and accurate picture of the organization's actual condition—how positive or serious is the situation in reality? Is their perspective even correct, given that they must rely on information filtered by executive management? This setup makes blind spots not just possible but also likely, as we will explore in Chapter 4.

Complicating matters, the CEO may enjoy deep employee loyalty, making intervention by the non-executive directors difficult. While, in theory non-executive directors have the authority to suspend executives or reject a strategic plan, in practice they rarely intervene in the "heat of the moment." Instead, the executive management will typically ease concerns, assert its own position, and push forward with its decisions, while oversight hesitates.

The non-executive directors hold formal statutory authority and power. However, in practice, the executive board occupies the strongest position. By virtue of its management mandate and day-to-day control of the organization, it directs operations, takes strategic, tactical, and operational decisions, and maintains a monopoly on information. As a result, it can, at times, present the non-executive directors with a fait accompli. There are situations in which they are retrospectively confronted with an investment, acquisition, or strategy change without having had the opportunity to review the business case beforehand.

Once non-executive directors conclude that a change in executive leadership is necessary, many prefer to delay an uncomfortable confrontation whose outcome is far from certain. Instead of acting decisively, they often postpone the moment of truth, hoping the problem will somehow resolve itself. Many dislike performance reviews with management, and outright conflict even more. After all, such disputes can drain energy within the board and cause damage to the reputation of the company and its board alike. In hindsight, many admit: "We acted a year too late." But in boardrooms, hesitation has consequences: for individuals, for trust, and for the organization's long-term future.

Moral authority in the boardroom

Power and authority are distinct forces that shape how both non-executive and executive directors influence boardroom dynamics, from decision-making to interpersonal relations. Power stems from hierarchical position, and physical and mental force. Authority, by contrast, rests more on moral credibility, respect, and empathy (see Figure 2.1).

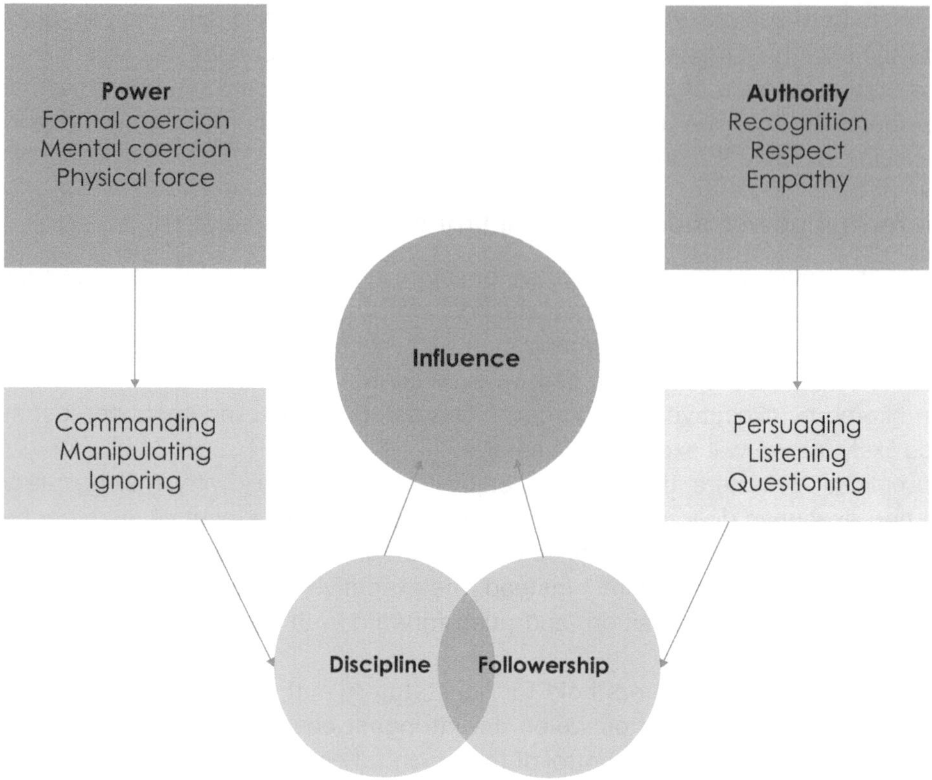

Figure 2.1
Power and Authority

Authority, is only partly positional. Non-executive directors hold formal status as the organization's highest body, yet true authority lies in experience, sound judgment, and, above all, moral integrity. People follow leaders not out of obligation but out of trust that doing so serves both them and the organization.

Nelson Mandela, while on Robben Island, held no formal power, yet his moral authority commanded universal respect. Authority is not about subordination but about followership and service.[4] When exercised effectively, it fosters teamwork, allowing both executives and non-executive directors to bring out the best in each other.

The rise of the Sun King

Vision, self-confidence, empathy, and the ability to inspire and work with others are often cited as essential leadership qualities. However, leaders who start with genuine authority can, over time, become overly self-assured. Their ability to listen fades, and their leadership style shifts toward top-down communication and command. In such cases, acquired authority turns into raw power. A sense of conceit and arrogance takes hold.

Case Study: You are not born a Sun King; you become one

You are not born a Sun King; you become one. In his youth, the French monarch Louis XIV (1638–1715) was a timid, conflict-averse young man.[5] Cardinal Mazarin, his key mentor, shaped his education with a fundamental lesson: *trust no one.* He styled himself the "Sun King" (*Roi Soleil*), choosing the sun as his emblem. All of France revolved around him. As Louis amassed victories, surrounded by a subservient and uncritical court, his royal authority hardened into absolute power—a power that, in time, strained France's finances and set the stage for future unrest, including the French Revolution (in 1789). In modern boardrooms, the "Sun King" has become shorthand for a leader whose unchecked dominance overwhelms collective oversight.

A successful CEO who never faces criticism risks turning into a leader whose authority has become absolute. Non-executive directors can unintentionally contribute to this metamorphosis through excessive praise. A widely published example comes from the Netherlands, where former Ahold CEO Cees van der Hoeven, after being named "Businessman of the Year" five times, evolved into just such a phenomenon. The impressed board chair even suggested cloning him. Today, Elon Musk stands as an even more prominent case. His dominance as CEO of not only Tesla, Inc., but also X Corp. and SpaceX, combined with his political reach, made the Tesla board concerned about his commitment to leading Tesla, as we will see in Chapter 3, Section §3.3. With millions of followers, Musk raises urgent questions about the concentration of executive power and the limits of effective oversight.

As Dutch writer Annie M.G. Schmidt wisely puts it: "He who is praised too much gets a bad character." To keep such power in check, it is essential that the non-executive directors, in both their composition and the way they function, offer a strong and credible response, a form of what John Kenneth Galbraith termed "countervailing power." This balance ensures the necessary equilibrium between oversight and executive authority. Brilliant leaders, in particular, are vulnerable to slipping into dominant behavior when left unchallenged—which is why they require most of all structured dissent.[6]

Who do we not see in the boardroom?

Non-executive directors need to recognize who, by default, is missing from their Table of Power. Employees, suppliers, customers, local residents—despite being fundamental to the organization's survival and success, are conspicuously absent. Instead, their voices are filtered through departments: human resources, purchasing and sales, and customer service, the help desk with its waiting time. In listed companies even shareholders have to resort to investor relations.

Beyond these key stakeholders lies another large gap. Nowhere in the boardroom do we find representatives of the wider world—those who stand up for the climate, justice, the environment, and future generations. How can organizations make truly responsible decisions when some of the most urgent voices are not even in the room?

If non-executive directors are serious about responsible oversight, they must ensure that these absent voices are at least heard, considered, and built into decision-making. This is especially urgent in an era where short-term profits dominate decision-making. Long term corporate survival depends on striking a balance between financial returns and societal values (see Chapter 5, Section §5.2). When the voices and interests of absent, distant or directly impacted stakeholders are not considered, the consequences can be severe.

Case Study: Grenfell Tower—the fire that exposed a system

The Grenfell Tower fire in London (2017), which claimed 72 lives, showed how oversight can collapse when safety concerns raised by residents were repeatedly ignored, passed along, and minimized. Despite detailed safety regulations and formal responsibilities, no institution took ownership of the obvious fire risks.

The official inquiry concluded that residents "were badly let down" by a system marked by complacency and diffusion of responsibility—each party assuming someone else would act but, in fact, acting carelessly. Grenfell is a stark reminder that governance is ultimately about protecting people who are not in the room, whose well-being depends on decisions taken far above their heads.[7]

SUMMARY AND CONCLUSION

In the boardroom, power is rarely perfectly balanced—a dynamic tension at the heart of behavioral governance. CEOs and executive boards, chosen for vision, decisiveness, and the ability to navigate complexity, do not always welcome scrutiny. Yet effective oversight requires countervailing power.

Non-executive directors face inherent challenges. As part-timers, they meet only periodically and often remain too distant from the organization's daily operations. Information provided by executives may be incomplete or filtered, leaving directors unaware of emerging risks. Loyalty to a dominant CEO can discourage dissent, creating a culture of silence in the boardroom. When a CEO begins to act like a Sun King, oversight should not be passive; it demands an explicit assertion of power.

The most effective non-executives combine their statutory authority with personal credibility, grounded in experience, independence, and moral clarity. This balance builds trust within the board and enhances decision-making.

Today's corporations and civil society organizations exert immense influence on economies and societies. Their boards cannot ignore the voices absent from the table—stakeholders, communities, and future generations. Responsible governance requires making those perspectives part of every decision.

§2.3—THE PLAYERS IN THE BOARDROOM

Introduction

When organizations fail, the inevitable question arises: why did no one act? But the deeper question is: who should have seen the risk coming? Oversight depends not on abstract structures but on the people in the room, their awareness, their autonomy of judgment, and their willingness to challenge assumptions. The answer doesn't just lie in someone's skills or CVs. It lies in their character and courage.

Traditionally, non-executive directors have been homogeneous: drawn from similar elite backgrounds, overwhelmingly male, and lacking ethnic and socioeconomic diversity. While that is slowly changing, for example, with more women taking up non-executive roles on boards, a critical question remains: *how does diversity actually translate into better governance?*

The real power of diversity lies in its ability to challenge: to bring fresh perspectives that question norms, flag emerging risks, open debate, and reframe problems. But this only works when independence of mind, psychological safety, active inclusion, and a shared understanding of how biases distort judgment are present. Without these, even the most diverse boards will miss early warning signs.

Characters in the boardroom

At the center of the Table of Power sits the chair of the board, sometimes literally on a chair with a higher back or in a different color. Across the table sits the executive board, which usually consists of just the CEO, CFO, COO, and these days the Chief Technology Officer (CTO). From the outside, the boardroom resembles a theater, a space where roles are played, lines delivered, and silence speaks as much as words—a stage where similarities and differences stand out. Consider age, gender, cultural background, and stature. Are these merely the external characteristics of such individuals, or do they reveal something deeper about how they think and act?[8] When it comes to non-executive directors, not only does their expertise matter; their personalities and temperaments also shape the dynamics at the table.

Recognizing the different characters in the boardroom is hardly a modern exercise. The Greek scholar Theophrastus, a disciple of Aristotle, was a keen observer of human nature.[9] He outlined 30 troublesome character traits of citizens in ancient times with a touch of cynical humor. Times change, but people remain the same. Among his character descriptions, the following appear strikingly relevant today: omnipotence (I can do it all), the scandalous pursuit of profit (greed), recklessness, paranoia, deceitfulness, arrogance, flattery, and vanity.

From schoolyard to boardroom

We may remember some of these traits from the schoolyard: the quiet thinker sitting alone, the loud extrovert, the work-shy, the high achiever, the bragger, the caring empathy, and the hyperactive rule-breaker with boundless energy and a short attention span, often sent to the principal's office. Even as children, we instinctively assessed who we clicked with, who we avoided, and who we even excluded. Fast-forward 50 years, and many of these personalities sit together in the boardroom. Education, career paths, and friendships have refined their character, amplifying some traits, while others have faded or disappeared.

Some of the less desirable traits described by Theophrastus still surface in leadership circles. Smart careerists excel at hiding these facets or, alternatively, at convincing others that they are vital. Over time, people develop behavioral patterns shaped by their character.

In moments of crisis, both their strengths and weaknesses become more visible. Some leaders withdraw into deep reflection, others jump to conclusions, some methodically weigh their options, while others react with open frustration, becoming grumpy.

The ideal leader in an organization is someone who remains flexible, yet in charge, adjusting their behavioral style to the needs of any given situation. They stay calm in stressful circumstances and know how to unite warring factions. They have empathetic qualities but are also resolute. To what extent are we able to discover those qualities in ourselves, in others on the board, and in the broader leadership team?

The chair should not be a pushover

Among these personalities, one role stands apart: the chair. In this pivotal role, the chair sets the agenda, leads meetings, and wields significant influence over executive and non-executive appointments. Until the 1990s, the president of the executive board in many countries was often seen as a *primus inter pares*. With the rise of the Anglo-Saxon CEO model, however, this role evolved into that of a commander-in-chief. As executive boards today often consist of only one or two executive members, non-executive directors must shoulder greater responsibility for checks and balances. The independent chair, together with other non-executives, forms a countervailing force against a potentially overbearing CEO, assuming the two roles are not held by the same person, as remains common in the United States.

Self-insight is essential for any chair. Without a clear understanding of their own capabilities, blind spots, and impact, even experienced leaders can unsettle board dynamics. Every chair, like every CEO, brings strengths and vulnerabilities to the table; the question is: which? How those qualities play out depends heavily on context. Sometimes the chair and CEO are natural leaders who instinctively navigate social dynamics; at other times, a chair is appointed to restore balance after the failure of a dominant CEO, a role that may require a very different leadership profile. In the end, the test of a chair lies not in their credentials but in how they perform under pressure. Are they truly effective leaders, or are they merely riding the momentum of past success? Do they display a sense of entitlement or vanity that erodes trust and creates toxicity? A chair must combine calm authority with the courage to act when it matters.

Servant leadership, a concept first articulated by Robert Greenleaf, is particularly valuable for board chairs, whose roles depend more on influence than on hierarchical command. Unlike a CEO, a chair's power lies in creating the conditions in which the board performs at its best. By listening, encouraging constructive dissent, and ensuring all voices are heard, a servant-leader chair strengthens oversight, balances executive power, and builds trust. This sharpens decision-making, makes the organization more resilient under pressure, and keeps the chair-CEO relationship balanced and constructive. Servant leadership does not imply passivity; it requires a chair who combines openness with the readiness to stand firm and act decisively when circumstances demand it.[10]

Competencies and profiles of the non-executive

Having the right competencies on the board is a no-brainer, yet in practice, some essentials are too often missed. This may stem from sloppiness or complacency in the hiring process ("we know someone we can work with") or from disagreement about which competencies truly matter. Attempts to please everyone may lead to broad, vague profile descriptions. The new non-executive director is expected to be an all-rounder—collaborative, independent, strategic, and hands-on. The result is that candidates who tick a few boxes, rather than the most critical competences, are accepted by default. Boards must cut through the noise and define what genuinely matters.

Key competencies for non-executive directors are relatively easy to outline. Entrepreneurial experience builds understanding of what it takes to lead an organization. Functional expertise in areas such as technology, finance, strategy, and risk adds depth. Equally important are interpersonal and communication skills: active listening, asking sharp questions, analytical thinking, and having the courage to make tough calls. This combination turns a group of non-executive directors into a cohesive, high-performing board.

Selecting people based on their competencies and personal attributes requires thorough preparation and a sharp eye for bias. Too often, résumés on platforms such as LinkedIn present candidates as experts in an unrealistically wide range of fields or as possessing the full spectrum of exceptional competencies. But how true are these claims? Someone praised for their vision may, on closer inspection, prove to be a smooth talker lacking real strategic substance. An ex-politician expected to bring useful government connections may end up as an outcast, evoking negative associations with politics. Likewise, a person known for "connecting people" may, under pressure, shy away from confrontation instead of taking a firm stand.

Relationships or independence

The appointment process aims to select people who can build trust with the CEO and their fellow non-executive directors. That is why many businesses and nonprofit organizations recruit from their existing networks, sometimes with the help of headhunters who know their circles well. In some cases, the CEO may even put forward their own preferred candidate. While close ties can foster familiarity and ease, they also open the door to subtle biases. Humans are naturally prone to loyalty and favoritism. While strong relationships can foster collaboration, they can just as easily weaken the objectivity required for effective oversight.

An organization's annual reports and website list who serves on its board. But what the public sees tells only part of the story and rarely reveals the backgrounds, informal networks, personal interests, or potential conflicts that shape behavior behind the scenes. Across jurisdictions, effective board oversight hinges on the independence of non-executive directors. Leading regulatory and governance frameworks, including those issued by central banks, ethics boards, and corporate governance codes, tend to converge around three core dimensions of independence:

- Independence in status, or formal independence: no direct ties to the director or company. Ensuring freedom from embedded loyalties or obligations.[11]
- Independence of mind, or being able to judge autonomously, to voice dissent when necessary, and to weigh competing interests without deferring to dominant personalities or group pressures.[12]

- Independence in appearance concerns how a director is perceived. Even without an actual conflict of interest, any relationship or circumstance that might cause a reasonable observer to question the director's objectivity should be avoided.[13]

True independence is never absolute. The requirement for non-executive directors to maintain constructive relationships with executive management inhibits their independence. This makes it likely that non-executive directors, consciously or unconsciously, allow personal relationships to influence their oversight. Non-executives also have a vested interest in their role, not only because they hold the position, but also because it is a paid and prestigious role. (see also Chapter 6).

As James D. Westphal and Edward J. Zajac emphasize, corporate governance is never enacted in a social vacuum. It is embedded in relationships, networks, shared norms, and informal exchanges that can give rise to corporate elites. These hidden ties can quietly reinforce or undermine formal oversight, often in ways invisible to outsiders.

That said, interdependence can be beneficial. In companies undergoing restructuring, a strong foundation of trust between the non-executive directors, management board, and shareholders can contribute to effective oversight. It enables the fast exchange of viewpoints and strengthens the commitment of all parties involved.

For this reason, private equity-owned companies often select proven non-executive directors from their immediate network. In a family business, appointing a family member as a non-executive director can reinforce the crucial bond between the family and the company, fostering a deeper level of involvement. What matters most is ensuring independence in the oversight function and eliminating obstacles that could compromise the non-executive director's objectivity.

The *beast in the boardroom*

Ensuring a constructively collaborative board is crucial—especially in times of crises, which are often unforeseen. Non-executive directors must be able to rely on one another and speak the same language. Research has shown that teams with a broad mix of perspectives are more effective.[14] In this context, "diverse" goes beyond experience, gender, one's international, professional, and cultural background, or age; it also includes behavioral traits and ways of thinking. In practice, the latter dimensions are often overlooked when composing the non-executive board.

When filling vacancies, boards often favor individuals who align with existing non-executive directors in thinking, behavior, and style, or those perceived as a good team fit: flexible, adaptable, and skilled at building connections. People who resemble the group are quickly seen as reliable, while those with a critical, independent attitude are viewed with suspicion. Even when their presence would strengthen the board, they are often overlooked.

Overly harmonious relationships come at the expense of critical analysis and sharp decision-making. The best decisions are made when issues are examined from multiple perspectives. A non-executive director at a publicly traded company once complimented a new colleague: "She dares to ask the question that the rest of us are only thinking about." This is both fair and troubling, as a reluctance to ask critical questions in the boardroom results in a weak, ineffective board. Lucy Kellaway, former *Financial Times* columnist and mathematics teacher, advocates for "the beast in the boardroom": a non-executive director who speaks candidly and is not afraid to challenge the chair.[15]

SUMMARY AND CONCLUSION

Paradox defines the boardroom: the trust and familiarity that make a team cohesive can also weaken its vigilance. Effective governance depends on the people around the table, the chair, the CEO, and the non-executive directors, as well as on how they interact. Boards often hire for comfort, choosing trusted candidates from their own networks. Cohesion grows, but so can complacency. Oversight demands discomfort and diversity. When competencies and character are not scrutinized, groupthink follows, and oversight weakens.

A broad perspective and board autonomy are therefore essential. An independent chair safeguards integrity, oversees management, and ensures that non-executives act both as a cohesive team and as a countervailing power to the executive board.

The most valuable directors speak openly and challenge when needed. Yet dissent only works when the board protects it. *The question isn't whether a board has different faces around the table, but whether it has different voices in the room and whether those voices can safely dissent when it matters most.* A lone beast is no beast. What counts is a culture that welcomes challenge and draws strength from difference.

Only when competence, independence of mind, and open debate are actively fostered can boards stay awake, effective, and trusted by the stakeholders they serve.

§2.4—EMOTIONS IN THE BOARDROOM

Introduction

A CEO slams his hand on the table. "This deal happens, period." Some non-executives exchange glances; some nod. They are familiar with this behavior. Only once they are at home do they realize the questions that were left unasked: Who reviewed the assumptions? Why the urgency? Directors are expected to be rational. Calm. Analytical. Yet in that moment around the table, with hearts racing and social pressure mounting, their rationality vanishes. This is not weakness. It is neuroscience.

And it is a problem. This board lacks the countervailing power needed to challenge its dominant CEO. Understanding why our brains react in this way is the first step; building structures to compensate for those reactions is a necessary second.

Executive and non-executive directors bring their own histories, temperaments, and emotions to the table. Although they are expected to make rational and balanced decisions, reality proves otherwise. Emotions influence boardroom decision-making more than we care to admit. Leaving emotions at home is an illusion.

Why are emotions so often ignored when we need them most? Psychology and modern neuroscience help us understand which primal guiding forces are at work.

The myth of the rational director

Classic economic theory assumes that rational decision-making predominates in the boardroom. Logic predicts that capable leaders, those who can provide ambitious but responsible direction for the organization, are selected for the executive board. Non-executive directors, in turn, are selected for their independent judgment, their ability to judge complex issues and their willingness to hold management to account. Schooled in rational thinking, often with long-standing experience as executive directors or experts, they are expected to possess a keen ability to discern a strategy's strengths and weaknesses. They are assumed to be fluent in spreadsheets and board assessment. If that were true, it would be almost impossible *not* to have a capable board.

Despite their experience and intelligence, non-executive directors frequently make irrational choices. Think of appointing a CEO who lacks the right competencies, approving poorly thought-out investment decisions, misjudging markets, or accepting situations where the personal interests of management are prioritized over those of the organization. *Are we not individually competent, or are we failing as a team in the boardroom?* This question goes to the heart of boardroom dynamics and will resurface when exploring structured decision-making in Chapter 5, section § 5.4 later.

The brain in the boardroom

Numerous organizational scientists and psychologists have studied decision-making and conducted experiments to find out what can go wrong in these processes. Neuroscientist Frans van der Meché has examined the role our brain plays in the boardroom. He draws on the work of Daniel Kahneman, whose research revealed systematic biases in human decision-making.[16] Kahneman popularized the distinction between *thinking fast* and *slow*: the fast, almost unconscious form of decision-making versus the slow, considered, and judiciously conscious way. Van der Meché explains these two systems from an evolutionary perspective. He distinguishes between the *rational* brain and the *social-emotional* brain.[17]

The human brain has evolved unique capacities, making us the earth's dominant life form. Our rational brain draws on everything we've learned through childhood, education, and work. For non-executive directors, their accumulated experience is invaluable. They have learned how to place an issue in context, ask the right questions to gain insight, and spot opportunities and possible problems. With this foundation, the rational brain can make decisions smoothly and logically.

Our more primitive, social-emotional brain is rooted in an older evolutionary development. Think of early humans: hunting and gathering in tall grasses, seeking food and mates, then retreating to a weatherproof cave for safety. This brain constantly colors our choices and decisions, determining whether something feels right or wrong. These feelings are understandable but not necessarily rational. Past experiences shape them but may not rest on an accurate analysis of the present situation.

In prehistoric times, survival depended on forming groups. Hunting became more effective, and the protection against threats grew stronger when people acted together. Group formation fostered empathy, connection, and mutual protection—emotions that generated positive outcomes. However, negative emotions also took root, particularly a fear of rejection or exclusion. The same dynamics surface today in the boardroom when someone stands alone in opposing a decision. Disagreement can feel uncomfortable, making conformity the easier path, even when it comes at the cost of better decisions. Power, status, and competition for resources, often labeled as greed, are other evolutionary drivers that can still trigger harmful behavior, even aggression.

When feelings take the floor

Van der Meché suspects that such factors also shape boardroom dynamics. In reality, both rational and social-emotional thinking play a role, but emotions can easily overpower rationality—especially under pressure, when we feel threatened, or when recognition is withheld. In these moments, people may lose self-control, becoming angry, raising their voices, threatening opponents, or withdrawing.

Emotions are easy to misread. A smile, for instance, may be meant as encouragement but perceived as arrogance. Pride in accomplishments can energize an organization, yet it can just as easily slip into overconfidence or boasting. A more varied mix of perspectives in the boardroom can help in recognizing and interpreting such signals; research shows that women are more adept at identifying and naming emotions.

Boardroom dynamics are about relationships and the tensions they create. Deliberations are never based solely on rational arguments—the social-emotional brain plays a leading role. Consider the independent chair who insists on speaking first on every agenda item, stifling group discussion; the CEO who presents the board with a fait accompli; or the directors who, out of misplaced loyalty, protect a once-successful but now failing CEO.

In times of tension and uncertainty, the rational brain is helpful but fragile. Numbers in a spreadsheet can be checked, but sound judgment depends on understanding how those numbers were derived, who verified them, and what alternatives were considered. Without that scrutiny, negative emotions can take over and drive irrational decisions that harm the organization. Similar dynamics can be seen in public life—for example, in the 2007 Dutch decision to build coal-fired power plants despite growing concerns about CO_2 emissions. Although not publicized internationally, the case reflects a broader pattern: climate-related decisions and blind spots are often shaped less by facts than by emotions, optimism, and groupthink (see Case: Framing climate change).

Case Study: Framing climate change—why facts alone don't drive change

In 2007, former U.S. Vice President and climate advocate Al Gore warned that it would be completely irresponsible to build new coal-fired power plants unless they were equipped with the still undeveloped technology for CO_2 capture and storage. Political and corporate leaders in the Netherlands were aware of this, yet the argument failed to sway their decision, as they were driven by an unshakable belief in new coal gasifier technology.

The minister and the power company pressed ahead; counterarguments no longer carried weight, swept aside by the triumphant feeling that often accompanies major innovative investment decisions. In the years that followed, the technology proved commercially unviable. The CO_2 capture never materialized, leaving the country with costly plants and rising emissions that were known, even at the time, to be incompatible with long-term climate targets; a reminder of how overconfidence and groupthink can override rational scrutiny.[18]

Thinking fast and slow in the boardroom

Long before neuroscience provided detailed insights into how the brain functions, behavioral psychologists and economists have been experimenting and seeking explanations for human behavior since the 1950s. Daniel Kahneman showed that human judgment and decision-making differ fundamentally from the rational model we often assume. He is best known for his powerful distinction between two systems of thinking, which we elaborate on below.

System 1 is the rapid, instinctive way of thinking. Ideal for routine tasks such as driving a car or recognizing patterns, it operates almost entirely unconsciously. This allows quick decisions, and explains why most people rely on it by default; we drive our car on autopilot, so to speak. Yet this same speed of decision-making also makes System 1 prone to cognitive biases, subtly shaping the choices we make.

When decisions engage System 2, slow thinking, we take time to consider the complexity of the issues at play. In doing so, we draw on the full capacity of our rational brain. Rather than relying on routines, we follow structured procedures where arguments and alternatives are exchanged and tested through discussion, a process that lies at the heart of boardroom decision-making under uncertain conditions.

Yet even well-reasoned decisions are not immune to bias. One of the most common is hindsight bias—the "I've always known" effect, where outcomes seem obvious only after the fact. This bias can lead people to overestimate their judgment and create overconfidence in their abilities in future decisions. It can also strain board dynamics, as the feeling of "knowing better" by some may make others feel dismissed or belittled. That is why non-executive directors are cautioned not to decide too quickly; instead of cruising ahead on autopilot, they need a broader, reflective perspective.

Rationalizing versus emotions, head versus heart

In System 1, the world looks clear, predictable, and under control. We seek simple stories to explain complex outcomes. This leads to what is known as the *"success phenomenon"*: the tendency to attribute positive results to personal talent and failure to external forces. In the boardroom, this bias favors overconfident CEOs, who are often judged by short-term outcomes, such as share price, growth, and acquisitions, rather than by the long-term, sustainable quality of their decisions. Past achievements then serve as a shield against scrutiny, regardless of the extent to which luck or timing played a role. Success is credited to talent; failure, to bad luck. The result is a feedback loop that inflates reputations and reduces critical oversight.

Kahneman's experiments show that major success often stems from a combination of moderate talent and a hefty dose of luck. Yet boards rarely interpret it that way. Instead, they may reinforce the CEO's aura of competence—because doing so validates their own earlier choice to appoint them. This rationalization feeds a loop: past success justifies future approval. Scrutiny fades; critical oversight erodes.[19]

The concept of rationalization brings us back to how the brain works. Lans Bovenberg emphasizes the importance of recognizing the emotional and relational side of human beings. He argues that the emotional and relational side of humans operates through fast System 1 processes, where emotions rise quickly to the surface, making us instantly enthusiastic or causing us to fall in love. In contrast, slower System 2 thinking provides the space to reflect on the emotional and ethical dimensions of our choices, beyond initial impulses.

This awareness enables a more balanced approach to handling emotions in leadership and governance. To capture this distinction, Bovenberg coined the idea of *feeling and loving in both fast and slow ways.*[20]

SUMMARY AND CONCLUSION

The "rational" board member of traditional economic theory does not exist. In reality, our brains are wired to prioritize social and psychological needs such as safety and belonging—instincts that once kept us alive but can mislead us in complex decision-making.

Kahneman's fast, intuitive System 1 operates by default, running on routine and feeling. It drives quick judgments, where predictable biases easily creep in. Yet boardroom decisions are rarely simple. They involve uncertainty, high stakes, and long-term consequences—conditions that demand System 2: slow thinking. This requires careful analysis, reflection, and deliberate consideration of alternatives rather than instinctive reactions.

Emotions are deeply rooted and exert a powerful influence on judgment. While System 1 reacts swiftly and intuitively, System 2 creates the space to step back, analyze, and place both thoughts and feelings into perspective.

Non-executive directors need to be alert to how emotions shape board dynamics and decision-making. Making emotions openly discussable, especially in reflective moments such as board evaluations, should become a natural and valued part of governance practice. Effective boards are not those that suppress emotion but those that understand and integrate it, turning awareness into better decisions, stronger relationships, and more sustainable leadership.

§2.5—BEHAVIOR IN THE BOARDROOM

Introduction

The boardroom can be a fertile ground for bad decisions. Pressures to make quick decisions, coupled with uncertainty and conflicting interests, create a high-risk environment. And our brains don't always help: emotions and fast, intuitive thinking often overpower calm, rational analysis.

Even directors who recognize emotional triggers face another challenge: the systematic biases that operate below conscious awareness, quietly distorting judgment. These aren't occasional lapses; they're hardwired shortcuts in the way we think and decide.

Group processes are designed to enhance decision-making, but they can just as easily undermine it. What cognitive and ethical mechanisms drive this, and how can non-executive directors steer group dynamics toward better decision-making in the boardroom?

Settling for "good enough"

Faced with complexity, time pressure, and competing interests, directors often *satisfice*—settling for decisions that feel *good enough* rather than truly optimal. Herbert Simon, the psychologist, economist, and Nobel Prize winner (1978), observed that people struggle to process all the available information and alternatives when making decisions.[21] He calls this *bounded rationality*. The term reflects the built-in limits of human decision-making. We can only perceive, process, and incorporate so much. Stress, distraction, and cognitive overload can all distort judgment and introduce bias.

This is not surprising—after all, who can fully grasp every aspect and consequence of a decision? More striking is that many executives, even though they are aware of these limits, tend not to question their choices. They proceed under the belief that they are being fully rational. Yet rationality is always filtered through what we assume to be true — our beliefs about how the world works, what counts as evidence, and whose judgment to trust. Because we cannot oversee everything and often take comfort in past decisions, we risk falling into *tunnel vision*, a state in which only one conclusion seems possible. When satisficing meets ambition and a culture that silences dissent, rationalization can become dangerous.

Beyond rationality: how real people make choices

Executives who consistently achieve their budgets can become complacent. Being human, they sometimes opt for low-risk, satisficing solutions that are adequate in the short-term, rather than optimal. For shareholders and stakeholders, this can be frustrating: they seek stable cash flows and dividends combined with growth and long-term value creation.

Traditional economic theory assumes that decision-makers always maximize utility: a pension fund selects the highest-yielding investment, parents choose the school offering the best education, and patients seek treatment at the best hospital. Reality, however, is more nuanced. Pension funds may prioritize sustainability even if that means accepting lower short-term returns.

Case Study: Volkswagen—the psychology behind Schummelsoftware

Few companies have been brought to their knees by a failing corporate culture as dramatically as Volkswagen (VW).

A key component of its strategy was VW's bet on "clean diesel" engines as the company's unique selling point, a bold move at a time when hybrids were already on the market. But this fixation on diesel performance and efficiency, combined with an authoritarian leadership style and a culture that discouraged dissent, created the conditions for what followed.

Under relentless pressure to deliver on ambitious goals, engineers and managers developed the infamous "Schummelsoftware" to disguise excessive emissions during testing. What began as a technical workaround gradually normalized deception. Although many felt uneasy, they rationalized the manipulation as necessary to compete: *Everyone's doing it this way*, and *it doesn't really hurt anyone*. Obedience to authority, fear of contradicting leadership, and a shared belief in the larger mission dulled ethical judgment.

The consequences were enormous: VW faced €30 billion in damage claims, had to hand over 480 million documents to authorities, and was held in a regulatory stranglehold for years. The company's reputation collapsed, and it missed the opportunity to lead in electric vehicles—a market decisively seized by U.S. Tesla and Chinese BYD, both, unencumbered by legacy investments.

For non-executive directors, *satisficing behavior* creates a dilemma. They must judge whether the outcomes pursued by the CEO are truly sufficient for the organization and its stakeholders. A CEO may settle for an "easy" option that minimizes personal risk, or present ambitious plans that they know will be immensely difficult to implement. Non-executives, meanwhile, must weigh these tendencies against stakeholder expectations. This is a difficult task, since their oversight role limits direct stakeholder engagement and leaves them reliant on management narratives.

These tensions do not stop at the boardroom door. As long-term stakeholders, ESG-oriented investors and broader society can clash with short-term financial goals of companies they invest in. In the current political climate, particularly in the United States, companies and investor groups are being pressured to retreat from explicit ESG commitments. Investor preferences and board priorities are as always shaped by shifting social and political dynamics. Bounded rationality hasn't left the boardroom; it has simply moved to the political arena, where electoral incentives, limited attention to externalities and polarized framing shape strategic choices.

The bounded mind of the non-executive director

We have seen that the human brain, although capable of remarkable achievements, is not designed for perfect decision-making. As Herbert Simon argued, we must temper our expectations about the robustness of our rationality. Building on this, Dolly Chugh and Max Bazerman showed that we are not nearly as rational as we like to believe.[22] Even when information is available, cognitive blind spots and biases can prevent us from recognizing early warning signs. In the famous "invisible gorilla" experiment, participants are asked to watch a basketball game and count the number of passes between players. In doing so, they fail to notice a person in a gorilla suit walking across the court. This experiment illustrates the fact that our attention is selective—we miss what's right in front of us.[23]

The same dynamic plays out in the boardroom. Truly rational decision-making requires having all relevant information and the capacity to process it fully. In practice, non-executive directors face the dual challenge of data overload and limited time. Meeting papers are often voluminous, with appendices so dense they are practically unreadable. And even then, directors can never be certain they have been given all the information they need.

This isn't theoretical. This gap between perceived and actual rationality is a behavioral constant, not an individual failing—one for which boards must actively compensate, rather than ignore. When bounded awareness meets financial complexity, and a CEO who knows exactly how to exploit both, the risks can be devastating.

Non-executive directors often believe that their expertise will equip them to make sound decisions. In practice, bounded rationality and bounded awareness interfere. Directors rely on heuristics—mental shortcuts that facilitate quick conclusions but can cloud judgment. Some focus narrowly on calculation: if spreadsheets add up, the proposal gets approved; others rely on personal trust, reading the CEO's confidence as a substitute for verification.

When faced with data overload, non-executives have to simplify reality to make their task manageable. This speeds up decision-making but, as Karl Weick warns, carries serious

Case Study: Too good to check—hubris and blind spots at Vestia

Though more than a decade old, the Vestia case remains strikingly relevant—and its impact is still felt today. In 2010, the supervisory board of Vestia, the largest housing corporation in the Netherlands, reviewed audited financial statements so complex that even the external auditor became buried in the details and failed to see the bigger picture: a €23 billion derivatives position, many times the value of the housing portfolio.

The CEO reassured the non-executive directors that sophisticated instruments such as swaptions, swaps, caps, and floors represented a rational strategy to minimize financing costs—and even generate profits. Other housing corporations, he claimed, were mere amateurs. The auditor, confident in its review, issued unqualified opinions for years. In the annual report, the CEO proudly described another successful year. Overwhelmed by short-term success and financial complexity, the non-executive directors felt no need to push back. Seasoned as they were, they trusted the system. With praise from an uncritical housing ministry in its pocket, the year closed in apparent peace of mind.

Just one year later, the illusion collapsed. Vestia's interest rate bets proved reckless as market rates fell into negative territory. Behind the scenes, the one-person executive board operated without checks and balances, while the treasury manager had been bribed by bankers eager to expand their derivatives business. The misconduct went unnoticed in an uncritical boardroom filled with non-executives recruited from the CEO's network. Vestia narrowly avoided bankruptcy, surviving only through a sector-wide bailout.[24]

risks: by reducing complexity to neat categories, they may miss both environmental impact and internal organizational complexity.[25]

Bounded ethicality: blind spots in the mirror

As guardians of shareholder and stakeholder interests, non-executive directors play a key role in setting and monitoring an organization's ethical compass. This is no easy task. Ethics, norms, and values are neither absolute nor always clearly defined in law. Many organizations lack a clear internal framework for standards and values.

What one person sees as fraud may appear acceptable, even desirable, to another. Norms and values evolve and can reverse course, both within companies and across society. Until 2006, foreign bribes in the Netherlands, for example, were openly recorded as tax-deductible business expenses. More recently, in 2024, the U.S. administration, citing concerns about an *uneven playing field* in international markets issued an executive order instructing the Department of Justice to halt prosecutions of Americans accused of bribing foreign officials to win business. At the same time, supported by the anti-woke movement, the government encouraged companies to revisit their compliance, diversity, and ethics programs.

As a result, business practices once deemed unacceptable, such as silent gender discrimination or negligence toward climate impacts, may once again be normalized. For non-executive directors, these shifting standards can create ethical blind spots: the very essence of bounded ethicality.

Bounded ethicality in action—Fastow and de Vries

- Andrew Fastow, Enron's CFO, who was later convicted of fraud, explained after his release from prison how ordinary the misconduct felt to him at the time: *"I thought I was helping shareholders, and was convinced I was playing the game by the rules. If I didn't, somebody else would. That's just how the system worked in my eyes. With every transaction, my brain said I was getting richer."*
- Marcel de Vries, Treasury Manager of Vestia, told the 2014–2015 Dutch Housing Corporation Parliamentary Inquiry how easily he rationalized bribery: *"It started with Oppenheim* [a representative of his bank Sal. Oppenheim]. *He offered me money. I justified it to myself."*

The stories of both men illustrate how ethical boundaries can shift gradually and internally, rather than through sudden, deliberate choices. What looks like fraud in hindsight often felt normal and justified in the heat of the moment—a classic hallmark of bounded ethicality.

Bazerman and Chugh distinguish between *bounded awareness* and *bounded ethicality*: the former concerns factors that we fail to notice, while the latter concerns failures to act ethically, even when we do notice them.

In the boardroom, discussions often begin on the implicit assumption of colleagues' integrity. But how ethical are those colleagues in reality? Bounded ethicality explains how individuals tend to see their own actions as more ethical and competent than they actually are.[26]

This self-perception is often reinforced by *positional rationalization:* directors interpret their appointment as confirmation of their competence, thereby strengthening their belief that their decisions, and generous compensation, are fully justified. The testimonies of Andrew Fastow at Enron and Marcel de Vries at Vestia illustrate how ethical boundaries can erode from the inside out. Both men believed they were acting within the rules, even as they crossed clear ethical and legal lines.

Due to our cognitive and ethical limitations, we risk developing an overly positive self-image that blinds us to our own shortcomings. Recognizing these patterns—among non-executive directors and in their interactions with executives—is the starting point for any meaningful discussion about ethics.

A good relationship between executives and non-executives is crucial and often facilitates smoother cooperation on the board. Therefore, boards consciously or unconsciously nurture ties by exchanging compliments, fostering informal interactions, and arranging outings.

Conflicts: the ones we see and the ones we excuse

Conflicts of interest, both minor and significant, arise wherever people work together. In smaller societies, individuals and organizations often encounter one another across multiple settings. While cooperation and networking can create opportunities for mutual benefit, they can also blur boundaries and give rise to tensions. The line between legitimate opportunity and conflict is often indistinct. Consider a nephew or a former colleague who, through personal ties, can quickly perform a task or solve a problem within an organization without much explanation. This is, where the word "nepotism" originates.

A visible conflict of interest occurs when personal interests directly collide with those of the organization. Think of an M&A consultant who advises on strategy but earns a success fee when a proposed takeover goes through; or an auditor who, faced with a client representing a large share of their firm's consulting revenue, hesitates to issue a negative opinion.

In such cases, people often convince themselves they can remain objective despite the conflict. Non-executive directors may hesitate to "split hairs," believing they can neutralize any bias. Yet behavioral research tells a different story: in a 1998 series of surveys, 85% of participants rated themselves as more objective than others—a statistical impossibility. Most overestimate their own ethical integrity, underlining just how invisible such biases can be to those who harbor them.[27]

The hidden conflict: when bias disguises itself as fit

More challenging still is identifying what Chugh calls an *invisible conflict of interest*—one that is not even recognized as such.[28] These conflicts arise from conscious or unconscious bias in decision-making. A director may favor a candidate simply because they resemble them in background, appearance, or demeanor, even when a more qualified candidate exists. Such biases feel like "a good fit" rather than favoritism, which makes them all the more deceptive.

Reciprocity dynamics shape another subtle form of hidden conflict. As Westphal describes, non-executive directors who engage in flattery and excessive praise toward executives often gain favor and inclusion.[29] Those who are more critical and independent-minded, by contrast, risk being excluded from informal networks, missing out on invitations to social gatherings, access to inside information, and visibility for future board appointments. For those who cannot afford to lose their position, independence becomes fragile. When stepping down is not an option, the invisible conflict of interest quietly takes hold.

When dissent fades and trust goes unquestioned, boards can slip into ethical blind spots. Evaluation questions can cut through that silence, such as: "Name one thing we're doing that, if leaked to the press, would embarrass us."

SUMMARY AND CONCLUSION

As human beings, we are limited in what we can perceive and process—*bounded awareness* plays tricks on us. In the boardroom, decision-making unfolds within the constraints of *bounded rationality*: directors must act on information that is often excessive, incomplete, or biased.

To cope with this complexity, individual non-executive directors rely on *unconscious heuristics*, simple rules of thumb that help them navigate difficult choices but can also cloud their judgment. While opposing views may complicate deliberations, they should be welcomed as a source of richer insight.

A core responsibility of non-executive directors is to identify, prevent, and resolve conflicts of interest, both visible and hidden. Their mandate is to ensure that the company's decisions serve its long-term interests and those of its stakeholders.

Yet in practice, even the most principled directors are shaped by the relationships around them. Consciously or unconsciously, personal interests, friendships, and social ties can influence judgment. This is *bounded ethicality* in action, when people sincerely believe they are acting ethically, yet unknowingly fall short.

The result is seldom deliberate wrongdoing but a gradual erosion of integrity. Only sustained awareness of these hidden dynamics, and the courage to challenge, can stop that slide and restore true boardroom accountability.

§2.6—THE MEETING AS A SERIOUS ILLUSION

Introduction

Is a board meeting a form of top-level sport—or merely a routine? Around the table sit individuals with experience, expertise, and authority, yet these qualities alone do not guarantee sound decisions. In the previous sections, we examined how behavioral factors shape governance at the individual level.

Sometimes, a board meeting is little more than a formality, its outcome predetermined before discussions even begin. Effective oversight, by contrast, demands alert, engaged non-executive directors who can stay attentive and interpret the flood of information quickly and critically during deliberations.

Teamwork at the board table can be a source of strength—but also of risk. Social conformity, status dynamics, and groupthink can distort even the best-intentioned decision-making. How vulnerable are non-executive directors in these settings? How do such biases creep in? And, perhaps most importantly, how can they be recognized, prevented, and countered in the boardroom?

Two meetings, one outcome

From a distance, a board meeting appears to be a structured process governed by clear rules and procedures. There is an agenda; laptops are open, displaying the relevant documents. The chair opens the session, information is exchanged, opinions are voiced, decisions are made, and everything is recorded in the minutes. It all looks orderly, but experienced board members know that there are always at least two meetings.

The first one begins days earlier, with phone calls between the CEO and the chair, and may continue right up to the moment the official board meeting starts. The CEO seeks to build support for key proposals by aligning with the chair on how to frame difficult issues and anticipate board reactions. This isn't necessarily manipulation, but uncertainty, a search for reassurance and tactical guidance on how the discussion might unfold.

Non-executive directors often hold pre-meetings of their own—informal phone calls or scheduled sessions without the CEO present. Since they meet only a few times a year, these moments help them reconnect, strengthen relationships, and exchange insights.

They may also offer early signals about the tone of upcoming discussions or about CEO–chair alignment. Sometimes, even a meeting strategy emerges: a coordinated "good cop, bad cop" routine, or agreements on who will ask the difficult questions.

While pre-meetings can be valuable for preparation and cohesion, they also carry risks. A chair who aligns too closely with the CEO risks losing independence, while a well-intentioned effort to maintain harmony can make it harder to challenge the CEO's position. Likewise, private discussions among non-executives may lead to predetermined outcomes, eroding trust among executive directors who are excluded from those conversations.

The *sleep paradox* in the boardroom

Experienced non-executive directors are often seasoned players in board meetings, skilled at timing their interventions. Yet despite their expertise, not everyone is fully present when the meeting begins. Global executives flying in from different time zones may struggle with jet lag. Sleep deprivation, though rarely discussed, has a measurable impact on governance: even a one-hour nightly deficit can significantly impair cognitive performance.

Take, for example, a veteran venture-capital director flying in for a meeting. At 80, he may still deliver a sharp one-liner at the right moment—but does he still play a truly valuable role? And who will tell him that?

Neuroscientist Els van der Helm has shown how lack of sleep undermines judgment, distorts interpretation, and weakens learning.[30] The Dutch Brain Foundation likewise finds that fatigue reduces self-awareness and dulls sensitivity to group dynamics.

When major failures occur, the media often blames an "asleep at the wheel" board. But are the non-executives really the sleepers? More often, it's the insomniac CEO or overworked auditor. Many CEOs take pride in 80-hour work weeks, convinced they need little rest. This is the sleep paradox: the less they sleep, the more the brain convinces them that they are functioning well—until exhaustion or burnout takes hold. Yet in the boardroom, sleep remains taboo. Fatigue is seen as weakness, and "sleep is for losers."

Long-serving non-executive directors face another risk: routine dulls alertness. Over time, vigilance fades, and key details go unnoticed. Others struggle with attention deficits, the restless director who slips out mid-meeting for a conveniently timed "emergency call."

Finally, overcrowded agendas further drain focus and the quality of discussions. In a three-hour meeting with ten agenda items, each topic averages just 18 minutes, barely enough for questions or reflection. Some boards spend an hour merely approving the minutes of the previous meeting, often relegating this task to the end of the agenda when attention is at its lowest.

Since the COVID-19 pandemic, virtual meetings have become routine, bringing a new challenge: how to sustain genuine engagement when participants are only half present on screen.

Words, words, words

Non-executive directors spend their lives in meetings. But even they can become distracted. Some drift into thoughts about their personal lives; others quietly check emails, or even exchange private messages while the discussion continues.

Words fly across the table, but each participant interprets them in a different way. Are they truly understood? When someone speaks of a "crisis," do they mean an immediate emergency or a long-term challenge? When a director insists an investment is "necessary," does that mean the company will collapse without it? And is the urgency for a new head-office really an operational need or a result of prestige-seeking and rivalry? On multilingual boards, the risk is even greater: crucial nuances may be lost in translation.

Beyond the interpretation of words, every board member brings preferences to the table—what might be called their hobby horse: short-term certainty, higher margins, innovation, thorough analysis. Under skilled leadership, these differences can spark constructive debate and deeper insight. But there's a catch: a seasoned CEO often knows these preferences and strategically tailors arguments to win support. The growth-focused director gets optimistic forecasts; the risk-averse director receives extensive data. Words become weapons of persuasion, not just vehicles of meaning.

The power of silence

Intimidation takes different forms in the boardroom—from strategic silence to subtle threats, raised voices, swearing, and, in extreme cases, physical aggression. Communication is not limited to words. Some of the most powerful messages are delivered without a single syllable being uttered. As psychologist and communication scholar Paul Watzlawick observed, every behavior carries a communicative element: *"You can't not communicate."* A person's silence at the table is therefore not neutral—it is a message in itself. The critical question is: what does it signify?[31]

Adapting observations of Desmond Morris and Paul Ekman, people communicate in different ways, and the boardroom's real debate can happen in silence: the CEO's steepled fingers projecting authority, the skeptical raise of an eyebrow, the impatient drumming on the table, and the defensive crossing of arms.[32] By doing so, they consciously or unconsciously exchange information about who they are, how they think about others, and whom they support to someone across the table.

There can be misunderstandings: a non-executive director may transmit concentration with their silence. But others may interpret that silence in a different way: the person is shy, does not dare to speak, is not interested, or agrees. There is also a natural, though undesired, form of silence: moments when directors sense something is wrong but choose not to speak up. This dynamic reflects what is called the *bystander effect*: individuals see a problem but remain silent, assuming that someone else will act. They may feel uncertain, concerned about making a foolish remark or mistake. In the boardroom, such passivity can quietly legitimize dominance, reinforce unhealthy dynamics, and erode effective oversight.

Lessons from the zoo

Consider the CEO who felt that a newly appointed non-executive director showed him insufficient respect. In the previous board, he had been accustomed to getting his own way, taking important decisions without prior discussion with the non-executive directors. When the new

Case Study: *Bokito* in the boardroom

Bokito, a gorilla raised in captivity, became infamous in the Netherlands for attacking a visitor who misread his non-verbal signals. Rejected by his mother at an early age, as if that were not enough, Bokito became an attraction at Blijdorp Zoo in Rotterdam, the Netherlands. As a potentially aggressive primate, he communicated through silence, stillness, and direct staring. One regular visitor to the Zoo believed she had a friendly relationship with him: "If I smile at him, he smiles back." But this turned out to be a serious misunderstanding. After a breakout, she was severely attacked. Bokito believed that his smiling fan disrespected him, a challenge to his dominance. For a gorilla, as for humans, staring can be a form of intimidation. In the Netherlands, Bokito has become a household shorthand for explosive dominance—even an insult in the Dutch language. But in fact, Bokito did not shout; he stared, using nonverbal signals to control a situation. Just as in the boardroom, where words matter, but silence often speaks louder.

director asked what seemed a critical question, the CEO responded with a forceful lecture, interpreting it as a challenge to his authority, much like Bokito. The chair remained passive, failing to intervene. As a result, the CEO's behavior was reinforced, and another crisis loomed.

In such situations, the new non-executive director is placed in an impossible position. To avoid being sidelined and disqualifying themselves as a board member, they have only two options: fight back or resign. Staying would mean enduring a difficult relationship with a dysfunctional chair and the fellow non-executives who allowed the incident to happen. How can a non-executive be expected to function under such conditions?

An effective chair must be able to read both spoken and unspoken signals and understand how intentional or unintentional behavior shapes the meeting. Does a non-executive director's communication style contribute positively or negatively to the discussion? Is the CEO using diversion tactics to manipulate the board? Occasional conflict is not necessarily harmful; it can surface hidden tensions and clarify misunderstandings. But a chair who fails to step in when conflict arises loses authority, and with it, control over the board's dynamics.

The pull of consensus: groupthink

A well-run meeting isn't just about efficiency; it's about drawing out different perspectives to reach better decisions. Yet one of the greater risks in governance is *groupthink*—the tendency for board members to conform to the majority view in order to avoid conflict.

In 1972, psychologist Irving Janis (1918–1990) studied a number of disastrous U.S. military decisions, such as the 1961 Bay of Pigs invasion. He then formulated his classic theory of groupthink, a phenomenon to which small groups of decision-makers can fall prey. He described groupthink as a deep-rooted condition in which people suppress their own opinions to maintain harmony.[33] A board member might think, *"I wasn't entirely comfortable with this decision, but I didn't want to be the killjoy."* Once harmony becomes the implicit goal, critical thinking quietly retreats.

Over time, this dynamic can slide into *confirmation bias*. When a group selectively focuses on information that supports its earlier conclusions—and no one brings in fresh insights—the illusion of having been right all along is quietly reinforced. A mix of overconfidence and selective perception can blind even intelligent groups to warning signs.

Groupthink is especially likely under domineering leadership, which discourages dissent. Other risk factors include time pressure and a homogeneous board composition. Board size and time pressure also matter: when there are more than five non-executive directors, plus executives, meetings can start to resemble a mini-congress, where genuine dialogue becomes difficult.

The remedy is simple in theory but challenging in practice: effective decision-making requires a board composition that fosters diversity of thought, a culture that encourages dissent rather than penalizes it, and a chair who ringfences enough time for what truly matters. Regular evaluations and limits to board tenure can help prevent stagnation and keep group dynamics healthy.

SUMMARY AND CONCLUSION

The board meeting is not just routine; it is a behavioral arena where cognitive biases and social dynamics collide. Pre-meetings may ease tension, but they risk predetermined outcomes. Language and interpretation shape understanding: words such as "crisis" or "necessary investment" can have different meanings for each participant. *Words, words, words* should give us pause: are we truly listening to one another, or just talking past each other?

Fatigue, the hidden variable, weakens alertness and judgment, reinforcing the illusion of control. *Groupthink* remains one of the greatest threats to oversight, allowing dominant leaders to shape consensus and silence dissent. The *bystander effect* adds another layer of risk: directors may sense something is wrong but stay silent, assuming others will act. Effective governance depends on diversity of thought, reflection, and the courage to voice minority opinions.

A vigilant chair must safeguard space for critical inquiry and psychological safety. A board culture that values independent thinking and deliberate dialogue is the only antidote to the behavioral traps that turn meetings into rituals rather than engines of oversight. A candid self-evaluation—a clear look in the mirror—can transform boardroom dynamics.

§2.7—NARCISSISM IN THE BOARDROOM

Introduction: the lure of power and praise

Power, prestige, and reward drive the CEO. To succeed, they must show courage, articulate a clear vision, and inspire those around them. With that short but powerful title, the CEO has assumed an increasingly dominant role in organizational leadership.

Narcissistic traits are, to some extent, necessary for effective leadership; they fuel confidence, ambition, and resilience. Yet when these traits grow unchecked, they can become destructive. In their most extreme form, this self-focus can slide into the manipulative and morally detached behaviors described as the "*dark triad.*"

In today's high-pressure environment, CEOs are expected to deliver not just steadily but also fast. But at the summit of the mountain, the air gets thin. What happens when confidence, once seen as strength, starts morphing into destructive narcissism?

For non-executive directors, this creates a delicate balance: embracing the drive and vision these traits can bring, while guarding against their potential to distort power. And central to this book, how can they recognize these psychological patterns early enough to exercise effective oversight in the face of leaders who thrive on admiration and control?

Narcissism: learned young, practiced old

Narcissism may sound like an unpleasant character trait, yet Sigmund Freud, the pioneer of psychoanalysis, argued that narcissism, or self-love, is a natural and universal part of the human psyche. Its intensity, however, varies.[34] Most psychologists trace its roots to the earliest stages of personal development.[35]

From an early age, children compete for attention and affirmation. Negative experiences—lack of affection, warmth, or recognition—can distort the development of self-worth. Over time, these early patterns shape how a person perceives the world and their relationships with others. Between the ages of two and five, as the emotional distance between parent and child grows, a healthy balance between independence and security ideally forms. When that balance fails, defensive self-enhancement can become deeply rooted.[36] Psychologists identify two developmental extremes: neglect and overindulgence.[37] Children deprived of attention may inflate their sense of self to regain control; those showered with admiration may internalize the illusion that they are exceptional. Both paths can produce adults who crave validation and struggle with empathy.

The narcissism spectrum

Because *narcissism* is used loosely, it's often misunderstood. It can evoke strong emotions: on the soccer field, referees may be called narcissists as an insult, while psychiatrists use it as a diagnostic term, defined in the *Diagnostic and Statistical Manual of Mental Disorders (DSM-5)*.[38] Manfred Kets de Vries, a leading psychoanalyst, was among the first to show how narcissistic tendencies shape both leadership and corporate culture.[39]

Narcissism exists on a spectrum. At one end, adaptive forms fuel ambition and creativity; at the other, the grandiose self-regard of dominant, yet vulnerable narcissism erodes accountability. Self-confidence turns into entitlement, empathy gives way to self-interest, and admiration replaces accountability. Organizations begin to destabilize.

Remember the Sun King dynamic from Chapter 2, Section §2.2? This is its psychological foundation. When unchecked narcissism meets boardroom power, Louis XIV's "L'État, c'est moi" becomes "The company is me." History shows that even absolute rulers were rarely constrained from within. Modern corporations face a similar risk when internal countervailing power is weak.

As discussed earlier, the Sun King dynamic illustrates how admiration and absolute control can merge into a spectacle of power. The same pattern plays out in modern corporations, where charismatic leaders bind others to their vision, demand loyalty, attribute a company's triumph to themselves and blame others when things go wrong. The outside world often rewards such leaders as visionaries and heroes. Being in the vicinity of such a leader allows others, including non-executive directors, to bask in the leader's reflected brilliance, sharing in the glow of success and prestige. This is visible when a Sun King is named "Entrepreneur of the Year." But non-executives must remain level-headed, objective, and independent.

The narcissist in the boardroom

Not unlike other people in power positions, such as politicians, strong narcissistic traits are common among top executives. Economist Kees Cools observed that CEOs of fraudulent firms were quoted far more often in the media than their peers. These CEOs often showcased photographs of themselves with world leaders, symbols of status and recognition.

As admiration grows, so does the risk of hubris and moral drift.[40] Psychologist Antoinette Rijsenbilt developed a set of five objective criteria in her research:[41]

- Evoking significant media attention
- A strong focus on personal rewards
- The pursuit of power
- An insatiable drive for more
- A tendency to seek additional financial emoluments

Because of these potentially destructive traits, narcissism rarely enjoys a positive reputation. So, why are so many CEOs with narcissistic traits appointed? Non-executive directors face a complex dilemma. They must select leaders with constructive qualities such as strategic vision, high energy, and the ability to inspire and connect people, as well as leaders who are unafraid to make tough decisions when needed. That's why candidates who admit to uncertainty or hesitate to act are avoided. Unwilling to step into the CEO's role themselves, many prefer confident, self-driving leaders who require little oversight.

The CEO with narcissistic traits thinks big, wants to lead and is willing to take risks. Such an individual stands out, exudes confidence, and often radiates what might be called a charming form of brutality. Extroverted and authoritative, these CEOs are valued for qualities such as independence, taking responsibility, and a problem-solving orientation. As Manfred Kets de Vries observes, such leaders can drive performance through vision and enthusiasm, but their volatility and grandiosity can just as easily create chaos.

Research shows that narcissistic CEOs are prone to overconfidence. This fuels high-risk behavior and sharp performance swings, underscoring why an effective counterbalance is critical.[42] When narcissism is combined with manipulation or a disregard for others, its impact on governance and organizational integrity can become far more dangerous. This is where the concept of the *dark triad* provides a powerful lens.

The dark triad of leadership

High-profile leaders with narcissistic traits inspire awe and even reverence, as can be seen in the political arena. Their power often remains unchecked, buoyed by the unwavering loyalty of their followers, regardless of their actions. In the corporate world, driven by power, money and prestige, such leaders are naturally drawn to sectors where excessive risks and rewards are the norm. When challenged, they may resist objectivity, constructing their own version of reality and gradually coming to believe it.

To understand the link between leadership and narcissism, it helps to look at what psychologists have called the *dark side of personality*. In 1990, personality psychologist Robert Hogan and his colleagues described the shadow side of charisma, the notion that the same traits that make someone an inspiring leader, such as confidence and charm, can also tip into arrogance, manipulation, and self-interest when taken to extremes.[43] Building on that idea, psychologists Delroy Paulhus and Kevin Williams (2002) introduced the *dark triad of personality*: three overlapping traits—narcissism, Machiavellianism, and psychopathy—that capture different shades of socially undesirable behavior.[44]

These traits exist on a spectrum, and while everyone shows them to some degree, they become more visible in competitive environments, particularly among people in leadership or high-power positions. Hollywood offers a vivid example in the HBO drama *Succession*, loosely inspired by the Murdoch family, owners of the media empire that includes publisher News Corp and broadcaster Fox. The series portrays a publicly traded family-run business where patriarchal, dominant leadership draws family members into a web of control, in which manipulation and deception are elevated to an art form.

Although a wealth of publications on *corporate psychopathy* have appeared in recent years, this book adopts a slightly different approach. We use a modified version of the triad: narcissism, Machiavellianism, and, instead of psychopathy, antisocial behavior (see Figure 2.2).[45] This fits better with the behavioral focus of this book and aligns with the new DSM-5 terminology, emphasizing patterns of conduct.

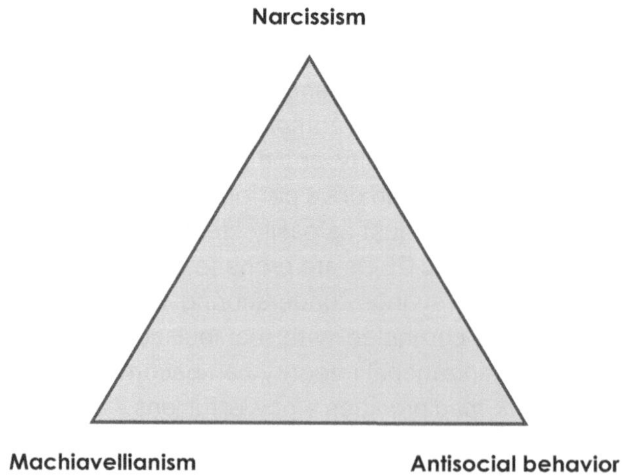

Figure 2.2
The Dark Triad of Leadership: Narcissism, Machiavellianism, and Antisocial Behavior

1. *Narcissism* is marked by an intense need for admiration and a tendency to project superiority. Leaders scoring high on the narcissism spectrum often hold an inflated self-image and a strong desire for power, convinced of their entitlement and others' inferiority, as if colleagues should feel lucky to work with them. At the same time, they radiate charm, optimism, and a "can-do" mentality, qualities that can make confidence seem inspiring rather than self-absorbed.

   On the darker side, because their self-worth depends on external validation, even mild criticism can feel like a personal attack. When an analyst at an Enron press conference challenged the company's practices, CEO Jeff Skilling snapped back, "asshole," unaware that his microphone was still on. In that moment, arrogance exposed the insecurity beneath the façade. Unchecked narcissism is also associated with moral and sexual boundary violations, as shown by the late Jeffrey Epstein. He cultivated an image of sophistication and philanthropy, surrounding himself with influential figures from business, politics, and royalty. Behind that façade, wealth, charm, and connections became tools of manipulation and exploitation, culminating in revelations of human trafficking and abuse.[46]
2. *Machiavellianism* is named after *Niccolò Machiavelli*, the Italian diplomat and philosopher who, in *Il Principe*, described cunning and manipulation as essential tools in the power struggle.[47] In psychology, it describes a personality style marked by strategic deceit and calculated manipulation in the pursuit of personal gain. Those high in Machiavellian tendencies excel at bending morality and prove useful to leaders when problems must be concealed, rivals neutralized, or conflicts managed discreetly.

   Machiavellians are hard to spot. They appear pragmatic, loyal, and trustworthy, quietly operating behind the scenes, knowing whom to flatter, isolate, or misinform to steer decisions in their favor. Often serving as "fixers" or informal power brokers, they rationalize their conduct as *just good practice*, seldom acknowledging the harm it causes. When power and wealth are at stake, moral boundaries become negotiable, and others may be pushed into choices against their own interests.

The rise and fall of Robert Maxwell—when power turns inward

Robert Maxwell rose to prominence as a flamboyant media mogul. He made three ambitious promises when he proposed to his wife: he would earn a military decoration for heroism, amass a fortune, and become the prime minister of England. Maxwell came remarkably close to achieving that vision, building a vast empire that included the Mirror Group and several other media companies.

After his death in 1991—he was found floating in the Atlantic near his yacht—investigations uncovered that he had misappropriated (embezzled) approximately £440 million from the Mirror Group pension funds to prop up his businesses. The sheer scale of the fraud, and the failure of oversight mechanisms to detect it, became a pivotal catalyst for finalizing the Cadbury Report, which went on to reshape corporate governance in the UK and beyond.

Maxwell left behind nine children and his wife, who meticulously compiled photo yearbooks filled with newspaper clippings about his career. Incidentally, Maxwell's yacht, the *Lady Ghislaine*, was named after his youngest and favorite daughter, who was arrested in New York in 2020 as a longtime "business associate" of Jeffrey Epstein.

3. *Antisocial behavior* (referred to by Paulhus and Williams as *psychopathy*) is marked by a blatant disregard for others. These leaders understand empathy cognitively but do not feel it emotionally. Skilled at reading emotional expressions and vulnerabilities, they use that insight to charm, dominate, and exploit. Willing to break rules and agreements, even engaging in criminal acts, they deny responsibility and ignore consequences.

   Every situation becomes an opportunity to advance their own agenda, regardless of the harm caused to others. Relationships are transactional, and loyalty lasts only as long as it is useful. At the extreme end of this spectrum, a near-total absence of conscience makes individuals with such traits destructive to organizations, people, and their environment.[48]

Different studies indicate that the psychopathy component of the dark triad is present during the lifetime of 1–3.3% of the general population. But the prevalence rises sharply in prisons (about 47% of their male population and 21% of the female population).[49] Research conducted in corporate settings reports that between 3% and 12% of senior managers display dysfunctional psychopathic traits, depending on the criteria used.[50]

In organizational life, individuals with such traits rarely resort to overt physical violence, though it can occur, for example, in predatory sexual behavior. Instead, they display more subtle and socially acceptable forms of aggression. Although it is not always illegal, this behavior can cause significant harm to colleagues, subordinates, clients, and the organization and its shareholders and stakeholders. Traits associated with antisocial behavior are evident in white-collar crimes such as insider trading, investment fraud, environmental violations, and human rights abuses.

A recent study found that middle managers with higher indicators of dark triad traits were less committed to social and environmental responsibility, suggesting that antisocial dispositions can undermine long-term ethical and sustainable business practices.[51]

Straight talk, hard fall—the Welch legacy at GE

On LinkedIn, Jack Welch (1935–2020), the former CEO of General Electric, was described as "one of the world's most respected and celebrated CEOs." But as Lucy Kellaway quipped in the *Financial Times*: "Bragging like this is not just flagrant, it is borderline fraudulent." Welch became famous for his rigorous performance system, in which the bottom 10% of employees were fired annually. His strategy sent GE's stock soaring but created a brittle, fear-driven culture.

His hand-picked successor, Jeff Immelt (CEO, 2001–2017), inherited Welch's empire and its blind spots. Immelt projected confidence, as a precaution even having a second private jet follow his own, symbolizing the era's excess. Beneath the polished surface, the stock price took a dive as the market recognized an overreliance on financial engineering and a failure to set priorities. Hubris and a culture that muted dissent hollowed out the company.[52] Immelt later admitted what went wrong: his board wasn't used to pushing him back hard enough, struggled to challenge his confidence and optimism, and became overwhelmed by complexity.[53] The Welch–Immelt era shows how charismatic leadership and unchecked ego can distort governance. When power is concentrated and dissent discouraged, performance may shine briefly—but trust, culture, and values eventually crack.

These dynamics are not just theoretical. They play out vividly in corporate history, where charismatic, high-performing CEOs have often been celebrated even as underlying risks grew. Jack Welch, former CEO of General Electric (1981–2001), exemplifies this phenomenon, as his leadership was praised even years after his departure.

For non-executive directors, pronounced narcissistic leadership poses a significant risk. In such environments, critical questions may be perceived as personal attacks, creating a bystander effect in which directors remain silent when vigilance is most needed. Recognizing manipulative or antisocial tendencies early is essential to maintaining effective countervailing power in the boardroom. In Chapter 6, Section §6.5, we will return to how organizations can balance ambition with accountability and ethical restraint.

SUMMARY AND CONCLUSION

Narcissistic leadership—especially when combined with *antisocial behavior*—often provokes disbelief: "That can't be true, can it?" Yet narcissism exists on a spectrum, and nearly everyone displays it to some degree. Narcissistic leaders often possess persuasiveness, courage, and vision; their charisma can easily win people over, including non-executive directors.

Alongside these assets, however, lie serious governance risks. Such leaders may disguise motives, conceal misconduct, and blur ethical lines, making them difficult to oversee, and even harder to confront. During CEO selection, nominating committees must ask: are they meeting a visionary entrepreneur, or a disruptive narcissist in disguise?

The Dark Triad (narcissism, *Machiavellianism*, and antisocial behavior) highlights distinct threats: Machiavellians thrive on manipulation and hidden agendas, while those high in antisocial traits pursue personal gain with little or no regard for others. Non-executives, conscious of their limited visibility, should stay alert to *ethical fading*: where admiration, loyalty, and dependence on the information supplied can quietly narrow moral awareness. They must also keep their eyes peeled to warning signs—reports of a toxic culture, reckless bets, and patterns of concealment—and ensure strong countervailing power when a CEO shows dominant narcissistic traits.

In the end, the board cannot escape accountability for oversight, whether failure stems from intent, negligence, or willful blindness.

§2.8—BOARDROOM DYNAMICS

Introduction

The boardroom is a strategic arena. The players—executives, non-executive directors, and advisors—collaborate, maneuver, and sometimes compete to influence outcomes. Characters, narcissism, and empathy determine the outcome. As discussed in Chapter 2, Section §2.6, communication in these settings is rarely neutral: power is conveyed not only through words but also through silence, posture, and timing. The players' communication style reveals whether they are sympathetic or antagonistic.

To fulfill their formal mandate, the art of oversight means striking a balance between an oversight role and active engagement. The executive management expects the support of the non-executive directors, but not one that crosses into execution. This creates a tension: non-executive directors must simultaneously support and critically assess the executive board.[54] Moreover, while independent judgment is key, their appointment is sometimes influenced by shareholders or, in some countries, the works council, raising doubts about their true independence.

Like any well-structured game, meetings often follow a familiar pattern of polite questions and carefully framed answers. However, when the stakes rise, such as in a takeover, a major investment, a change in incentive structures, a whistleblower report, or a leadership review,—the game intensifies. It can quickly escalate into a contest of influence and power.

In this section, we explore the rules and interactions in the boardroom game through the lens of communication theories. Where Chapter 2, Section §2.6, examined how these dynamics unfold moment by moment during meetings, here we view them strategically, as part of a broader game of influence and power. How can directors navigate these tensions?

Darwinian struggle

How people communicate and influence one another in groups has long fascinated psychologists. Kurt Lewin, Timothy Leary, and Donald J. Kiesler each revealed a piece of this puzzle.[55,56,57]

Lewin (1890–1947) showed that behavior reflects both inner motives and external pressures, and that personal judgment is shaped by group influence. Dynamics in the boardroom are defined by hierarchy, formality, and power. A CEO may project authority among directors, yet that aura can fade quickly in settings, such as the factory floor or an informal staff meet-up. From outside the boardroom, shareholders, stakeholders, and government exert pressure on executives and non-executives to protect and advance their specific interests.

The path to the top of an organization can resemble a Darwinian struggle, where internal candidates compete fiercely for the ultimate position: *survival of the fittest*. The executive environment can include other contenders for the top job; around them are players who may be supportive allies or subtle underminers. Careers, reputations, and legacies are at stake, encouraging strategic self-protection and careful image management.

Communication in a circle

Building on these ideas, Leary explored interpersonal dynamics, showing that individuals often see themselves as rational and cooperative while perceiving others as aggressive or dependent. His *interpersonal circumplex* mapped behavior along two key dimensions: warmth versus hostility, and dominance versus submission.

Kiesler later expanded this model, demonstrating how one person's behavior naturally pulls a complementary response from another. When someone acts dominant, cooperative,

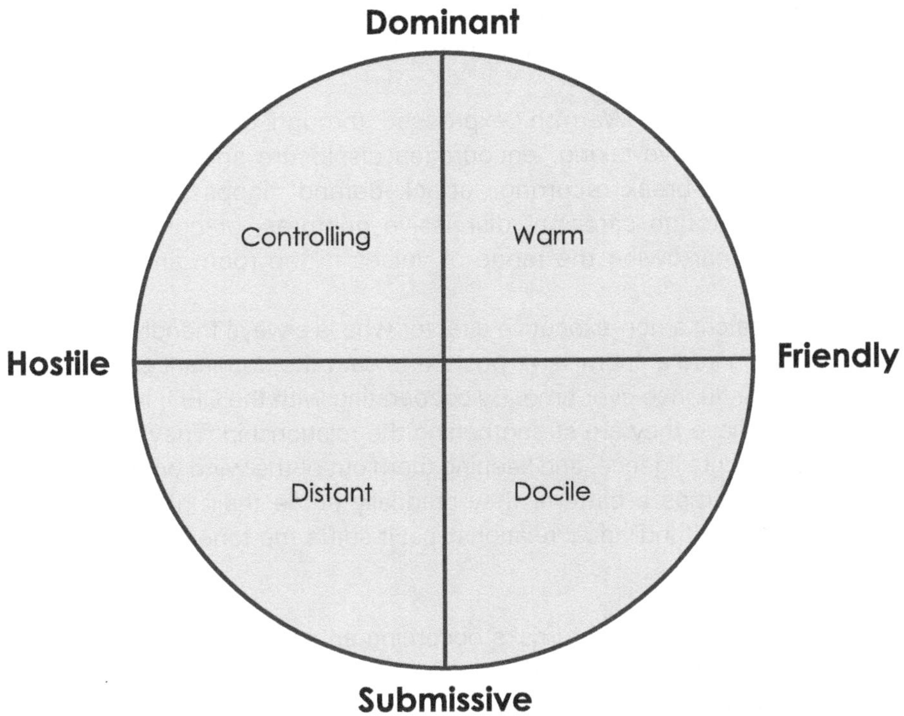

Figure 2.3
The Interpersonal Circle of Board Dynamics

warm, or hostile, they send out signals, inviting others to respond, completing the interpersonal circle (see Figure 2.3).

This model helps explain why communication patterns in boardrooms can so quickly become locked into predictable loops and power play. It offers insights into how interpersonal dynamics in the boardroom shape both the tone and the quality of decision-making, and how people adapt their behavior not only to the situation but also to the people they interact with.

- *Dominance versus submission.* Assertive or dominant behavior tends to provoke either compliance or counter-aggression, whereas cooperative behavior encourages openness and engagement. When dominance becomes excessive, it suppresses contributions from others. Board members may hesitate to speak up, anticipating social or even career consequences for dissent. Over time, this imbalance erodes open dialogue and pushes the group toward defensive or submissive postures. Research by Weck, Veltrop c.s. shows how a small number of individuals can dominate the discussion: their repeated opinions consolidate their status, disproportionately shape decisions, and pave the way for groupthink. Dissenting voices fade, and the board's collective intelligence narrows.[58]

- *Warmth versus hostility.* Warmth, expressed through curiosity, acknowledgment, and genuine perspective-taking, encourages disclosure and cooperation. It lowers defenses and helps break recurring "attack–defend" loops. By contrast, hostility, whether shown through sarcasm, dismissive gestures, or contempt, creates psychological threat, narrowing the range of voices in the room and amplifying power asymmetries.

  But there is a catch: a non-executive director who is always friendly and accommodating may risk sliding into a submissive posture toward the dominant CEO or fellow board members, losing influence over time. By cooperating with the CEO, non-executive board members may believe they are strengthening the relationship. They celebrate their success, praising their intelligence, and keeping them out of the wind when things get tough. But when this becomes a pattern, they gradually erode their influence and authority. This doesn't just affect individual relationships; it shifts the tone of the discussion in the boardroom.

As critical distance fades, the board risks becoming an echo chamber rather than a deliberative body. A dominant, narcissistic CEO may now feel unchecked, proceeding with their plans undisturbed. Herein lies a vital role for the independent chair: to ensure that all perspectives, opinions, and insights around the table are voiced and considered, bringing the right people into the discussion at the right time and maintaining balance and effective governance.

Trust: the fine line between confidence and complicity

Trust does not exist in a vacuum. It grows, or withers, within the interpersonal dynamics of the boardroom. The aforementioned patterns of dominance, warmth, and hostility shape whether board members trust each other's competence or trust each other as people. As Cools observes, as a tool of governance, control, alone has not prevented scandals in the past; he argues for a culture of trust that complements formal oversight.[59] But what does trust mean in this context?

Board members depend on one another, yet their individual interests may diverge. Trust allows them to cooperate despite these differences and work toward their shared goal: the organization's success. The relationship is mutual. Executives, whether they admit it or not, draw confidence from the trust of their non-executive counterparts. Reciprocal trust steadies the board in moments of uncertainty.

Two main forms of trust shape board dynamics. Competence-based trust reflects the non-executive directors' expectation that the executive board has the skill and judgment to design and execute strategy, and handle crises. This form of trust grows in climates where accountability, transparency, and procedural clarity are strong: actions match words and promises are kept.

Emotional trust, by contrast, arises from relational signals, warmth, and respect. It rests on the belief that colleagues act in good faith, that their intentions are honorable, and that vulnerability will not be exploited. When both executive and non-executive directors feel valued and heard, trust deepens into psychological safety—an assurance that every voice can be raised without fear or dismissal. Empathy is its foundation: by recognizing each other's pressures and constraints, board members create a climate where disagreement can coexist with respect. Under pressure, this trust becomes the social glue that holds a board together.

Well-founded trust, whether rational or emotional, benefits the organization. It reduces the need for micromanagement, lowers the costs of control and fosters more candid conversations. Research links trust to stronger team commitment, higher satisfaction, and better performance.[60]

SUMMARY AND CONCLUSION

Communication in the boardroom is never neutral. It is not just about information; it signals power, trust, hesitation, and resistance. Even silence speaks. A raised eyebrow, a sharp tone, a pause before responding, these moments shape relationships and influence who feels invited to speak and who withdraws.

Boardroom interaction follows patterns. Some voices dominate, others accommodate. Some directors create openness; others close it down. Kiesler's interpersonal circle helps make these dynamics visible, structured along two dimensions: dominance versus submission, and warmth versus hostility. Dominance can silence dissent or trigger counterforce. Warmth, expressed through genuine listening and curiosity, creates psychological safety. Hostility narrows the field of contribution.

The chair plays a decisive role. Not as a referee of procedure but as a guardian of the quality of the conversation. The chair sets the tone, balances airtime, invites dissent, and prevents alignment from turning into conformity.

Trust sits at the center of it all. Competence-based trust grows from structure, expertise, and accountability. Emotional trust grows from respect and openness. Both are necessary. Too little trust produces control and defensiveness. Too much trust produces blind spots and complacency.

When trust shifts into loyalty, and loyalty into unquestioned alignment, oversight weakens. Independence erodes quietly. Integrity becomes vulnerable. Non-executive directors risk moving from guardians of the organization to passive bystanders.

Sustainable governance requires balance. Trust must be paired with critical distance. Empathy must coexist with challenge. Loyalty should serve integrity, not undermine it.

REFLECTION QUESTIONS

Questions §2.1—Why oversight matters

1. Where does your board position itself on the spectrum from compliance and control to a broader stewardship of societal interests?
2. How do non-executive directors demonstrate accountability in practice?
3. Do the current conditions and relationships allow non-executive directors to act with genuine independence?

Questions §2.2—The Table of Power

1. How does your board—especially the chair—create countervailing power and balance formal power with moral authority in the organization?
2. How do you verify that information from the executive board is accurate and complete? How do you identify blind spots—what you are *not* receiving?
3. When key stakeholders are absent from the Table of Power, what concrete mechanisms ensure their interests are represented in decisions?

Questions §2.3—The players in the boardroom

1. Has the board systematically assessed how individual personalities and character traits influence its collective performance and decision-making?
2. How transparent and objective is the process of appointing new non-executive directors to the board, and what informal dynamics shape that process?
3. Who might be considered the "beast in your boardroom"? How does their presence affect board dynamics and independence?

Questions §2.4—Emotions in the boardroom

1. Which of *Kahneman's systems* dominates decision-making in your board: fast, intuitive System 1 thinking or slow, reflective System 2? Can you give concrete examples?
2. What role do emotions play in your boardroom decision-making? How are they surfaced or addressed in evaluations?
3. How does your board actively reflect on hindsight bias when reviewing past decisions and outcomes?

Questions §2.5—Behavior in the boardroom

1. Can you identify concrete examples of *bounded rationality* within your board?
2. How does your board address *bounded ethicality*, the risk of believing it acts ethically while overlooking blind spots?
3. Is the evaluation of potential visible and invisible conflicts of interest systematically included in your annual board agenda?

Questions §2.6—The meeting as a serious illusion

1. How effectively do your board's meeting dynamics foster openness and independence, and what role do pre-meetings and informal exchanges play in shaping decisions?
2. Does your board demonstrate the ability to observe, listen, and manage tensions between meeting participants?
3. Is your board structured and facilitated in a way that actively prevents groupthink?

Questions §2.7—Narcissism in the boardroom

1. Are there visible signs of dark triad traits in the behavior of your top managers?
2. Can you identify *Machiavellian behavior* or subtle white lies aimed at influencing the non-executive board?
3. How can your board support the CEO in their isolated job while still maintaining critical distance and independence?

Questions §2.8—Boardroom dynamics

1. How would you describe the communication style between your board and executive management: cooperative, oppositional, dominant, or dependent?
2. Has your non-executive board ever faced false or misleading information, and how did it respond?
3. How would you rate the level of trust between your non-executive board and the executive board? Is oversight truly independent?

NOTES

1 Harold Geneen (1985), *Managing*, New York: Avon Books.

2 Prof. Pieter van Vollenhoven (2020 June 30), *Naar onafhankelijk toezicht (Toward Independent Oversight).*

3 John A. Pearce II, Shaker A. Zahra (1991), *Relative power of CEOs and boards of directors: Associations with corporate performance*, Strategic Management Journal, 12.

4 A.C. Zijderveld (1998), *De samenleving als schouwspel (Society as a Spectacle. A Sociological Learning and Reading Book)*, Maarssen: Reed Business.

5 Georges Mongrédien (1938), *La Vie Privée de Louis XIV*, Paris: Hachette.

6 American economist John Kenneth Galbraith developed the concept of countervailing power as an institutional safeguard for representing consumer interests. See (1952), *American Capitalism: The Concept of Countervailing Power*, Boston: Houghton Mifflin Company.

7 Grenfell Tower Inquiry (2024 September), *Phase 2 Overview Report of the Public Inquiry into the Fire at Grenfell Tower on 14 June 2017.*

8 See, for example, George Herbert Mead (2015), *Mind, Self & Society*, Chicago: University of Chicago Press.

9 Theophrastus (373?—287? B.C.), *Characteres* (original in Greek: Ἠθικοὶ χαρακτῆρες).

10 R.K. Greenleaf (1977), *Servant Leadership: A Journey Into the Nature of Legitimate Power and Greatness*, Paulist Press.

11 Financial Reporting Council (FRC) (2018 July), *The UK Corporate Governance Code*, London: FRC.

12 International Ethics Standards Board for Accountants (IESBA) (2023), *Handbook of the International Code of Ethics for Professional Accountants (including International Independence Standards)*, 2023 Edition, New York: International Federation of Accountants (IFAC).

13 IESBA, *Handbook of the International Code of Ethics for Professional Accountants.*

14 David Rock, Heidi Grant (2016 November 4), *Why diverse teams are smarter, Harvard Business Review.*

15 Lucy Kellaway (2011 October 9), *Everyone benefits from a beast in the boardroom, FT Column.*

16 Daniel Kahneman (2012), *Thinking Fast and Slow*, London: Penguin Books.

17 Frans van der Meché (2012 November 6, December), *Van Neurowetenschap naar gedrag (From neuroscience to behavior)*, M&O Magazine.

18 See also Greenpeace Netherlands Foundation (2008 October), *The Economics of Coal-Fired Power Plants.*

19 M.H. Bazerman, A.E. Tenbrunsel (2011), *Blind Spots: Why We Fail to Do What's Right and What to Do About It*, Princeton University Press.

20 Lans Bovenberg, professor of relational economics, values and leadership (2019), *Where is the Love, on Value and Values*, Inaugural address, Rotterdam: Erasmus University.

21 H.A. Simon (1955), *A behavioral model of rational choice, The Quarterly Journal of Economics*, 69(1), 99–118.

22 D. Chugh, M.H. Bazerman (2007), *Bounded awareness: What you fail to see can hurt you*, Mind & Society, 6(1), 1–18.

23 D.J. Simons, C.F. Chabris (1999), *Gorillas in our midst: Sustained inattentional blindness for dynamic events*, Perception, 28(9), 1059–1074.

24 *Parliamentary Inquiry into Housing Corporations*, 2014–2015, The Hague, The Netherlands.

25 See interview *Harvard Business Review Sense and Reliability. A conversation with celebrated psychologist Karl E. Weick* (2003 May), Interview by Diane L. Coutu.

26 Dolly Chugh, Max H. Bazerman, Mahzarin R. Banaji (2005), *Bounded ethicality as a psychological barrier to recognizing conflicts of interest.* In: Conflicts of Interest: Challenges and Solutions in Business, Law, Medicine, and Public Policy. Cambridge University Press.

27 D.A. Armor (1998), *The Illusion of Objectivity: A Bias in the Perception of Freedom from Bias*, Ph.D., University of California.

28 Dolly Chugh, Max H. Bazerman, Mahzarin R. Banaji (2005), *Bounded Ethicality as a Psychological Barrier to Recognizing Conflicts of Interest*, Harvard University.

29 See also James D. Westphal, Edward J. Zajac (2013), *A behavioral theory of corporate governance: Explicating the mechanisms of socially situated and socially constituted agency*, The Academy of Management Annals, 7(1).

30 E. Van der Helm, M.P. Walker (2009), *Overnight therapy? The role of sleep in emotional brain processing*, Psychological Bulletin, 135(5), 731–748.

31 P. Watzlawick, J.H. Beavin, D.D. Jackson (1967), *Pragmatics of Human Communication*, New York: W.W. Norton & Company.

32 Desmond Morris (1977), *Manwatching: A Field Guide to Human Behaviour*, London: Jonathan Cape. Paul Ekman (2003), *Emotions Revealed: Recognizing Faces and Feelings to Improve Communication and Emotional Life*, 2nd ed., New York: Times Books.

33 Irving Janis (1972), *Victims of Groupthink: A Psychological Study of Foreign-Policy Decisions and Fiascoes*, Boston: Houghton Mifflin Company.

34 Sigmund Freud (1914), *Zur Einführung des Narzißmus*, Wien: Internationaler Psychoanalytischer Verlag.

35 Robert Greene (2018), *The Laws of Human Nature*, London: Penguin Random House.

36 Heinz Kohut (1971), *The Analysis of the Self: A Systematic Approach to the Psychoanalytic Treatment of Narcissistic Personality Disorders*, New York: International Universities Press; M.S. Mahler, F. Pine, A. Bergman (1975), *The Psychological Birth of the Human Infant: Symbiosis and Individuation*, New York: Basic Books; J. Piaget (1951), *The Child's Conception of the World*, London: Routledge & Kegan Paul.

37 Carolyn C. Morf, Frederick Rhodewalt (2001), *Unraveling the paradoxes of narcissism: A dynamic self-regulatory processing model*, Psychological Inquiry, 12(4).

38 DSM-5 (2022), *Diagnostic and Statistical Manual of Mental Disorders*, edited by the American Psychiatric Association.

39 Manfred Kets de Vries (2006), *The Leadership Mystique: A User's Manual for the Human Enterprise*, Prentice Hall UK and M.F.R. Kets de Vries; D. Miller (1985), *Narcissism and leadership: An object relations perspective*, Human Relations, 38, 583–601.

40 Kees Cools (2005), *Controle is goed, vertrouwen nog beter (Control is Good, Trust Even Better)*, Assen: van Gorkum.

41 Antoinette Rijsenbilt (2011), *CEO Narcisme Meting en Impact (CEO Narcissism: Measurement and Impact)*, Thesis; J.A. Rijsenbilt, H.R. Commandeur (2013), *Narcissus enters the courtroom: CEO Narcissism and fraud*, Journal of Business Ethics, 117(2), 413–429.

42 Arijit Chatterjee, Donald C. Hambrick (2007), *It's All about Me: Narcissistic Chief Executive Officers and Their Effects on Company Strategy and Performance*, Johnson Graduate School, Cornell University.

43 R. Hogan, R. Raskin, D. Fazzini (1990), *The dark side of charisma*. In: K.E. Clark, M.B. Clark (Eds.), *Measures of Leadership* (pp. 343–354). West Orange, NJ: Leadership Library of America.

44 D.L. Paulhus, K.M. Williams (2002), *The dark triad of personality: Narcissism, Machiavellianism and psychopathy*, Journal of Research in Personality, 36, 556–563.

45 P. Babiak, R.D. Hare (2006), *Snakes in Suits: When Psychopaths Go to Work*, New York: HarperCollins.

46 Bloomberg Newswire, Opinion September 27, 2019. *The Weird Narcissism of Jeffrey Epstein's Philanthropy*.

47 Niccolò Machiavelli (1469–1527) *Il Principe*. Firenze, (first published 1532).

48 See also Volker Lingnau, Florian Fuchs, Till E. Dehne-Niemann (2017), *The influence of psychopathic traits on the acceptance of white-collar crime: Do corporate psychopaths cook the books and misuse the news?* Journal of Business Economics, 87, 1193–1227.

49 J. Schnittker, S.H. Larimore, H. Lee (2020), *Neither mad nor bad? The classification of antisocial personality disorder among formerly incarcerated adults*, Social Science & Medicine, 264, 113288.

50 The measurement of corporate psychopathy involves a large number of characteristics attributed to psychopaths as well as advancing scientific understanding. This explains the wide range of this score. Literature: Paul Babiak, Craig S. Neumann, Robert D. Hare (2010), *Corporate psychopathy: Talking the walk*, Behavioral Sciences and the Law, 174–193; Catharina Fritzon, Nathan Brooks, Simon Croom (2020), *Corporate Psychopathy, Investigating Destructive Personalities in the Workplace*, Palgrave MacMillan.

51 Matthias Pelster, Stefan Schaltegger (2022), *The dark triad and corporate sustainability: An empirical analysis of personality traits of sustainability managers*, Business Ethics, the Environment & Responsibility, 31, 80–99.

52 Thomas Gryta, Ted Mann (2020), *Lights Out: Pride, Delusion, and the Fall of General Electric*, Boston: Houghton Mifflin Harcourt.

53 C.J. Prince (2021), *Former CEO Jeff Immelt, What I've Learned*, Corporate Board Member.

54 J. Roberts, T. McNulty, P. Stiles (2005), *Beyond agency conceptions of the work of the non-executive director: Creating accountability in the boardroom*, British Journal of Management, 16(S1), S5–S26.

55 Timothy Leary (1956), *Interpersonal Diagnosis of Personality*, Ronald Press Co.

56 Donald J. Kiesler (1996), *Contemporary Interpersonal Theory and Research: Personality, Psychopathology, and Psychotherapy*, New York: John Wiley & Sons.

57 Kurt Lewin (1936), *Principles of Topological Psychology*, McGraw-Hill.

58 M. Weck, D.B. Veltrop, J. Oehmichen, F. Rink, R. Krause (2023), *Towards a Configural Theory of Influence Patterns Within the Boardroom*, Academy of Management Proceedings.

59 Cools, *Controle is goed, vertrouwen nog beter (Control is Good, Trust Even Better).*

60 J.B. Smith, D.W. Barclay (1997), *The effects of organizational differences and trust on the effectiveness of selling partner relationships*, The Journal of Marketing, 61(1), 2–21; E. De Jong (2012), *Beyond shared perceptions of trust and monitoring in teams: Implications of asymmetry and dissensus*, Journal of Applied Psychology, 97(2), 391–406.

CHAPTER

3

Dynamic governance: How ownership shapes structures and culture

CONTENTS

§3.1—DIFFERENT GOVERNANCE FOR DIFFERENT PURPOSES: DEFINING OVERSIGHT

Governance begins with ownership. Whoever owns the company determines how power is exercised, how decisions are made, and which behaviors are rewarded. Each ownership model, whether that of a family business, listed corporation, private equity, cooperative, or state enterprise, creates its own governance logic. At the same time they all share a human dimension shaped by perception, incentives, and influence.

As organizations evolve from founder-led ventures to complex corporate entities, governance must adapt. Ownership transitions reconfigure authority, information flow, and trust under the pressure of competition and regulation.

This section introduces the dynamic triangle—a framework that highlights three forces driving governance behavior: financial interests, power dynamics, and reputational concerns. These forces interact constantly, often in tension with each other, revealing that the core question is not only *who governs* but also *how power is exercised and perceived.*

DOI: 10.4324/9781003624400-3

Across ownership forms, directors confront persistent conflicts: between managers and shareholders, among shareholders themselves, and between corporations and their stakeholders. Recognizing these structural tensions is essential to understanding governance as both a control system and a behavioral dynamic.

Creative destruction

Economist Joseph Schumpeter, one of the foremost thinkers on innovation and entrepreneurship, uses the term "the perennial gale of creative destruction" to describe the relentless storm of innovation that is reshaping the entrepreneurial landscape.[1]

His analysis shows how new entrants disrupt and ultimately replace old, legacy companies. Some examples of their destabilizing innovations:

- Bold ideas (think of Tesla's 100% electric and self-driving cars)
- New combinations of existing products and services (such as internet-based hotel reservations and real-time comparison via Booking.com)
- Lean, team-based production systems (as pioneered by Japanese Toyota)

This is surprising: why do established companies, despite their deep market knowledge, customer insights, and years of experience, fail to adapt and get outsmarted? One possible answer lies in the psychological phenomenon of "tunnel vision," another in conservatism bias, coupled with inflexible leadership. Conservatism bias plays down the threats posed by newcomers. The relentless drive, focus, and creativity of the innovator are another. Tesla was certainly not the inventor of the electric car but made electric cars desirable and got the timing right.

A striking illustration of *conservative bias* is Nokia, once one of the most successful companies in the world.

Case Study: Nokia—the visionary and the despot: how one man made and broke Nokia

Founded in 1865 as a pulp mill, Finland's Nokia became a global leader in mobile phones during the 1990s. Its devices were innovative, reliable, and iconic. Yet by 2012, the company's dominance had vanished. Nokia fell victim to *tunnel vision*—a belief in its own invincibility that blinded it to the disruptive force of internet-enabled smartphones. Management underestimated how Apple and Samsung would redefine competition through ecosystems of software and services rather than hardware design alone.

But strategic tunnel vision wasn't the only cause. Research based on 76 interviews revealed how CEO Jorma Ollila's autocratic leadership, strengthened by a track record of past success, created a culture of fear. Executives described him as "extremely temperamental," prone to shouting at subordinates "at the top of his lungs" during meetings.[2] This environment discouraged dissent, distorted reporting, and fostered overconfidence at the board level. The result was *authority bias*: bad news was filtered, innovation slowed, and decision-making became detached from market reality.

These behavioral dynamics led to over-optimistic reporting and a widening disconnect between top management and on-the-ground realities. Innovation stalled. By 2013, Nokia's phone production was effectively history. Yet the company did not disappear. Under new leadership, it reinvented itself by acquiring telecom giant Alcatel-Lucent, transforming into a major player in the network technology sector.

The Nokia case demonstrates not only how behavioral governance failures rooted in—overconfidence, deference, and fear can bring down even the strongest firms but also how renewal is possible when leadership and culture evolve.

The Table of Power (Chapter 2, Section §2.2) shows how boardrooms take shape across different types of companies and how cultural and ownership factors quietly determine who sits at the table, who speaks, and who truly decides. To the outside world, these ownership differences are largely invisible. Consumers rarely pause to consider whether the product or service they buy comes from a family business, a listed corporation, a private equity-owned firm, or a cooperative.

Internally, however, governance structures differ significantly, shaping both decision-making processes and broader corporate dynamics. At the core of formal governance sits the shareholder, the owner of the company's capital. The shareholder structure determines how power is distributed between the shareholders, the executive and the non-executive board members.

Different governance for different purposes

- Family firms concentrate power in the person of the owner-director (O/D), the person at the head of the table and at the heart of every strategic decision. Non-executives rarely challenge this center of gravity; they advise as far as the family allows. Common pitfalls are the belief that the O/D knows best in all matters. Success can reinforce the leader's confidence, reducing their openness to alternatives for management succession, a phenomenon known as *founder's syndrome.*
- Publicly listed companies operate according to a different script. Shareholders appoint non-executives to safeguard their interests, yet in practice power still drifts toward the executive team. Management holds the firm's information, and as ownership becomes fragmented among thousands of investors, oversight weakens—and executives quietly consolidate control.
- Private equity ownership flips this dynamic. Here, owners don't just monitor—they intervene. Fund partners take seats as non-executive directors, pushing strategy, targets, and discipline with notable intensity. Oversight is active but seldom independent; governance resembles that of a family business, but turbo-charged and tied to financial targets.
- Cooperatives have a different challenge: members are both owners of the cooperation and entrepreneurs. Their interests overlap but don't always align. What begins as a collective, designed to pool purchasing or marketing power, can evolve into a global business, drifting from its grassroots origins. Governance is democratic in principle but over time member interests can diverge or conflict.

- State-owned enterprises sit at the intersection of markets and politics. Some run essential services; others invest in regional development or innovation. But unlike private firms, they must answer to ministers and parliaments as well as to customers. Political preferences can seep into the boardroom, steering strategy, investment priorities, and leadership choices.

Case Study: Blokker—founder's syndrome and the fall of a retail empire

The Blokker story highlights how concentrated control, generational disengagement, and weak non-executive challenge can undermine a strong brand. It shows the behavioral risks of unchallenged leadership in family governance—where loyalty replaces objectivity and tradition outweighs adaptation.

Dutch retailer Blokker grew into one of Europe's best-known household goods chains under helmsman Jaap Blokker (1942–2011). Despite co-owning the firm with his brother, Ab Blokker dominated all major decisions. His leadership reflected *founder's syndrome*: deep personal identification with the business, mistrust of outsiders, and resistance to change. His children showed no interest in succeeding him, and in his eyes, no outsider, even those who had worked with him for years, was good enough to take up the reins.

Blokker's strength—his intuition for retail—became a weakness when consumer habits shifted online. Loyal to his stores and staff, he dismissed digital innovation, insisting the company's future lay in shop locations and purchasing power.

Non-executive directors, although experienced, lacked the authority to challenge Blokker or plan for his succession. Their oversight became symbolic. After his death, competitors such as discounter Action and online retailer Coolblue, both backed by private equity, seized market share. The company's structure and culture proved too rigid to adapt. Despite turnaround efforts, the company was unable to recover from cultural inertia and shifting consumer habits. In 2024, after 128 years, it ceased trading. Its collapse affected 394 stores and 3,500 employees.[3]

The dynamic ownership triangle

Business ownership is not static; it evolves over time, and its governance regime shifts accordingly (Figure 3.1). One key driver of change is the need for financing to support growth and development. Fresh capital can be raised through the stock market or private equity. Many of today's well-known listed companies have followed this route: software firms, such as Google, Microsoft, and Apple, as well as online travel agency Booking.com.

Succession is a common trigger for change, especially in family businesses. When no suitable heir is available, a sale becomes inevitable: often to private equity, sometimes alongside the existing management team in a management buyout. Yet ownership does not always move in one direction. Families sometimes return: a new generation steps up, founders intervene when strategy drifts, or attractive market conditions open a door to buy back what they once built. These reversals reflect a simple truth: emotional and strategic ties can outlast formal exits.

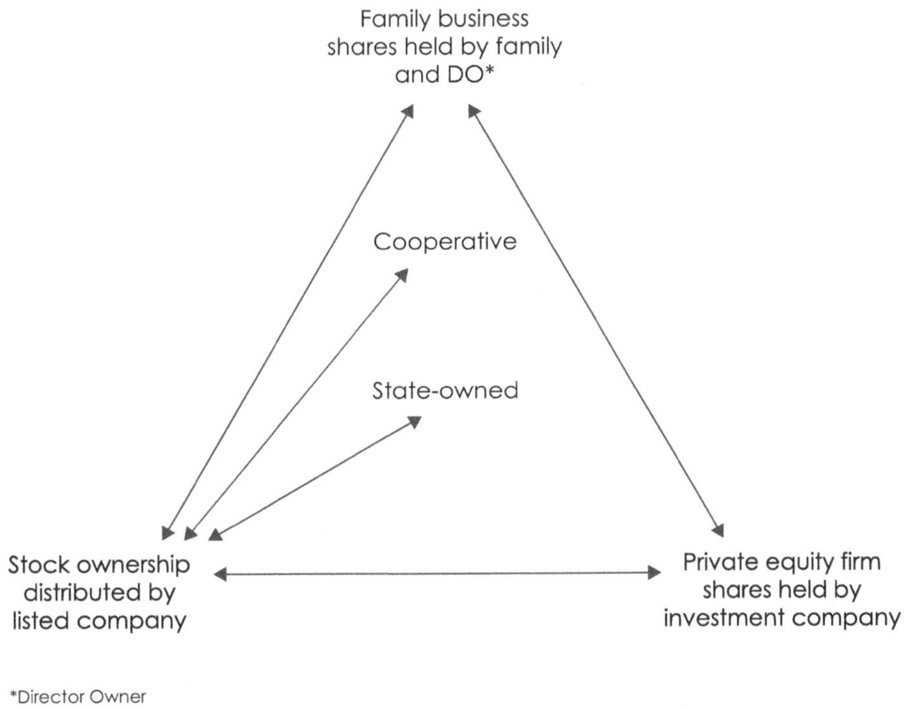

Figure 3.1
The Dynamic Triangle of Corporate Ownership

Case Study: Dell Technologies—strategic control through ownership

Michael Dell founded Dell Technologies in 1984 from his college dorm room, building a global reputation for efficiency and direct sales. After going public in 1988, the company thrived; but by the 2010s, the rise of smartphones, cloud computing, and shifting consumer preferences put pressure on Dell's traditional PC business.

To regain strategic freedom, Dell partnered with private-equity firm Silver Lake in 2013 to take the company private in a $24.9 billion leveraged buyout. Freed from quarterly market pressures, the company could now restructure and invest for the long term. Three years later, it acquired EMC Corporation for $67 billion, transforming itself into a leader in cloud and enterprise solutions.

In 2018, with renewed growth and a stronger financial position, Dell returned to the public market. Michael Dell retained significant ownership and control, ensuring its long-term vision. The Dell case illustrates strategic ownership control—combining founder leadership, private-equity partnership, and public-market access—and exemplifies the *dynamic triangle* in corporate governance.

Private equity ownership is inherently temporary; firms are typically sold after a five- to seven-year investment period. The buyer may be an independent competitor, or if the company is large and financially stable, it may be taken public via a stock market listing. Conversely, PE investors also take struggling public companies private to restructure and revitalize them outside the spotlight of the markets.

Cooperatives can shift, too. In the quest for fresh capital or to facilitate members wishing to sell their shares, some choose stock-market listings, as illustrated by New Zealand dairy exporter Fonterra and Dutch agriculture cooperative ForFarmers.

In such a hybrid structure, the cooperative remains intact and retains its position as a major shareholder, while its shares are listed on the stock exchange. However, the success of this model is not guaranteed. Hybrid structures can expose a tension between the members' desire for long-term stability and the public shareholders' appetite for short-term financial returns.

A similar dynamic plays out in the public sector. State ownership, too, is not fixed. Governments, even in market-dominated economies, have strategic interests, for example, in infrastructure or defense industries. In times of crisis, the state may step in as the owner of last resort, for example, during the 2008 financial collapse (see Chapter 3, Section §3.5). Public ownership is shaped by political preferences that support either free market or state-controlled activities.

While ownership structures set the formal boundaries of governance, it is the behavior around the boardroom table that ultimately drives decision-making, risk-taking, and leadership effectiveness. Therefore, in Chapters 4, 5, and 6, we shift our focus from structure to psychology. We will explore how information is filtered or ignored, how formal authority gives way to informal influence, how group dynamics shape strategic choices, and how perceptions of risk evolve across various settings.

Three conflicts of interest

Conflicts of interest are inherent in corporate governance. As organizations seek to balance the aims of owners, managers, and external stakeholders, tensions naturally arise. Non-executive directors, responsible for overseeing and protecting stakeholder interests, play a critical role in recognizing and managing these tensions. Three recurring conflicts are particularly relevant.

- Agency conflict

In 1776, economist Adam Smith observed that once managers are appointed to run a company, a new dynamic emerges: they may no longer act purely in the interest of the firm's owners.[4] After an IPO, shareholders become further removed from daily operations and must rely on the board for information about the company's performance. This distance creates a risk that executive management (as *agents*) prioritizes their own interests over those of shareholders. Filtering, framing, or withholding information define the classic *agency conflict*.[5]

- Shareholder conflict

Tensions can occur among shareholders themselves, especially between large and small investors. In family businesses, certain relatives may hold greater voting power, allowing one branch to dominate decisions. Disputes arise between those who seek to preserve independence and those pursuing higher dividends or an exit. Similar dynamics appear in listed companies, where large shareholders can steer outcomes simply because smaller investors fail to vote—a phenomenon known as *shareholder absenteeism*. Private equity firms typically address this issue through a shareholders' agreement that defines voting rights and limits unilateral control.

- Company–stakeholder conflict

A third, and increasingly visible, conflict lies between companies and the societies around them. External stakeholders—such as residents of areas near factories or airports—may lack a formal voice yet still bear the consequences of corporate activity. Environmental controversies, including those involving Ilva, 3M, and Chemours, show how corporate impact can erode public trust and legitimacy. These disputes often divide communities, with some valuing jobs and stability, while others prioritize health and safety. Balancing economic and social interests adds yet another layer of complexity to corporate decision-making.

Case Study: Ilva—when stakeholder interests collide

For decades, Southern Italy's Ilva steel plant in Taranto was both an economic lifeline and an environmental disaster. Europe's largest steel producer employed 15,000 people and sustained the local economy, yet its toxic emissions of heavy metals and dioxins turned Taranto into one of Europe's most polluted cities. Studies linked the plant to elevated cancer rates, respiratory disease, and premature death.

Directors faced an impossible dilemma. Workers and their families depended on Ilva's wages, while environmental groups and health advocates demanded closure to protect residents—especially children at heightened risk of illness. The community split apart. In 2012, judges ordered a partial shutdown and charged managers with environmental crimes. Workers protested, environmentalists countered, and the city became paralyzed.

The case revealed a governance failure rooted in silence. Non-executive directors reacted too late, constrained by narrow definitions of fiduciary duty and lacking mechanisms to include community concerns. The lesson is clear: environmental and social risks must be recognized and addressed early, before crisis forces false choices between livelihoods and lives. By 2024, Ilva remained open—under government control, still employing thousands, and still polluting. A warning frozen in time.

A global perspective on fiduciary models and board independence

Independence and stakeholder awareness are essential for effective board oversight, but the legal duty to consider shareholder and stakeholder interests varies widely across jurisdictions.

In stakeholder-oriented systems, such as Germany, the Netherlands, and France, boards are legally required to balance shareholder value with broader societal interests. For example: German co-determination law reserves half of the supervisory board seats for employee representatives.

By contrast, shareholder primacy models, such as those in the United States and Australia, assign fiduciary duties mainly from the shareholders' perspective. Though this framework has deep legal roots, the balance between market autonomy and state intervention—through industrial policy, and social regulation—continues to shift, testing the practical limits of shareholder primacy.

Hybrid approaches, including those of the UK and India, blend shareholder orientation with explicit social duties: the UK's Companies Act 2006 requires regard to employees and community impact, while India's Companies Act 2013 requires profitable firms to spend 2% of net profits on corporate social responsibility CSR.

In China, corporate governance reflects a distinctive model in which the state and the Communist Party are deeply intertwined. Party committees are embedded in major companies to align corporate strategy with national policy objectives. In Japan, long-term relationships, interlocking *keiretsu* networks, and lifetime employment traditions foster stakeholder alignment through trust-based practices.

What unites all countries is that non-executive directors are tasked to exercise sound, autonomous judgment, act in good faith, and serve the long-term interests of the company.

SUMMARY AND CONCLUSION

Companies take many forms: family firms, listed corporations, private equity ventures, cooperatives, and state-owned enterprises; each with its own governance logic. Ownership shapes how power is exercised, decisions are made, and oversight functions. Yet governance is equally, if not more, shaped by behavior than by frameworks.

As ownership structures evolve, governance frameworks must adapt. Within these shifting conditions, non-executive directors are expected to act with autonomy, managing conflicts of interest between managers, shareholders, and external stakeholders.

Across jurisdictions, board responsibilities differ: stakeholder-primacy models, shareholder-primacy regimes, and hybrid frameworks define fiduciary duties in distinct legal and cultural ways.

In an era of disruption and creative destruction, non-executive directors must safeguard continuity, while guiding renewal, protecting resilience without resisting change.

§3.2—ALL IN THE FAMILY: GOVERNANCE IN THE FAMILY BUSINESS

Introduction

The family business is the beating heart of most economies. It combines enterprise with identity, capital with kinship. Entrepreneurial families often think in terms of generations, not quarters, striving to hand over a thriving company, rather than just profits.

That long-term perspective may seem appealing, yet the reality of family business is riddled with paradoxes. Contrary to popular belief, most do not endure across generations. Many remain small, struggling with succession, emotional ties, and the weight of legacy—especially when the future of the firm is at stake.

When it comes to governance, attitudes differ widely. Larger family enterprises may appoint non-executive directors to bring an outside perspective, while smaller ones tend to rely on trusted advisors—or none at all. The Owner-Director (O/D) remains firmly in charge, balancing vision with control and often deciding how far external voices are allowed to reach.

How can oversight work as it should when ownership, leadership, and family are one and the same? This section explores the strengths and pitfalls of family governance, where trust and tradition can both empower—and constrain—the enterprise.

Entrepreneurship at your own risk

Dozens of Dutch Swinkels family cousins walk in a joyous procession alongside the Trappist fathers from the Koningshoeven Trappist brewery. It is owned by Bavaria, the Dutch Swinkels family company with roots dating back to 1680. They make their way to the dedication of a small chapel, a gift from the parent company. This scene reflects a broader truth: family businesses worldwide are deeply intertwined with both their economic and cultural heritage.

These businesses form the backbone of economies across Europe and beyond. In the European Union alone, family-owned companies make up more than 60% of all businesses, ranging from small enterprises to global corporations. They employ between 40% and 50% of the private sector workforce, making them a crucial driver of employment and economic stability.[6] But few grow as old as Bavaria. Long-term survival is a universal challenge. Under 30% survive into the third generation, a trend observed across Europe, North America, and Asia, where succession remains one of the greatest hurdles for family enterprises.[7]

However, when a family establishes strong governance and prepares for leadership succession in time, it can endure for generations. A prime example is Japan's Kongō Gumi, the oldest family business in the world, whose longevity proves that with the right foundation, such an enterprise can stand the test of time—regardless of geography.

Case Study: Kongō Gumi—homes for the gods

Specializing in wooden temple construction, Kongō Gumi has been around for more than 1,400 years. Founded by Shigemitsu Kongō, a Korean immigrant, it builds not ordinary houses but dwellings for the gods. Many of its prestigious and ancient commissions are still standing, including the Hōryū-ji temple (the temple of the "Flourishing Law") in Nara. The company operates under its own governance code, *Shokuke Kokoroe no Koto*, which emphasizes quality, customer satisfaction, respectful collaboration, and humility. A key figure within the family business holds the ceremonial title *sho daiku*—master carpenter. For centuries, Kongō Gumi thrived by staying true to its core expertise, with a notable yet somber deviation during World War II when it diversified into coffin production. In an unusual departure from Japan's traditionally male-dominated construction sector, the company made history in 1934. For the first time, it awarded the title of *master carpenter* to a woman, recognizing her vital role in sustaining the craft.

However, during the real estate boom of the 1980s, under new leadership, Kongō Gumi fell into the "herding" behavior trap, investing heavily in speculative real estate with borrowed funds, simply because others were doing the same. Insufficient risk management and a lack of internal countervailing power weakened oversight. When the economy slowed, both the temple construction sector and the broader real estate market suffered heavy losses, pushing the family business into financial turmoil. In 2006, the Takamatsu construction conglomerate stepped in to save Kongō Gumi from collapse.

Now operating under new ownership, the company continues to uphold its ancient traditions and values—albeit with modernized governance. A former Takamatsu executive has been appointed Chairman of the Board on behalf of the new shareholder, now overseeing a governance system designed to balance centuries-old heritage with the expectations of modern shareholders.

In large family businesses, decision-making is typically formal, relying on structured reporting. Risks are identified, documented, and systematically evaluated. Smaller companies make decisions around the kitchen table, driven by intuition and personal experience. Management leans on rules of thumb that have proven effective in the past. The O/D enjoys the benefits of success but also bears the full downside of failure, which reinforces a strong awareness of consequences.

Sustainability as legacy

Embedded in their local environment, family businesses often favor the *stewardship model*, which focuses on a long-term perspective and passing down of core values. The family not only shares in the company's success but also feels a deep sense of responsibility toward the community, customers, and long-standing employees. A recent survey found that an overwhelming majority of family business directors emphasize the strategic importance of sustainability, reflecting a strong focus on the interests of future generations. The younger the owner-directors, the more actively they embrace long-term environmental and social goals. A large majority aim to position their company as a leader in sustainability within their community, including a commitment to responsible employment practices.[8]

Non-executive director in the family business: a friendly favor?

Most owner-directors neither have nor want non-executive directors. For small business owners, oversight feels unnecessary. Power sharing rarely sits well with those who pride themselves on independence. Relying on their own judgment, they insist on calling the shots. That autonomy has brought them to where they are today. This is—and remains—their company. Appointing and consulting a non-executive director takes time and effort. And then there's the cost—how much do you want to pay someone to watch over your shoulder? Many prefer to draw on a network of specialists, an accountant, a notary, or a fellow entrepreneur, people they can call when needed.

If appointing a non-executive director becomes unavoidable, due to the company's size, a legal requirement, or a growing number of family shareholders, the entrepreneur typically chooses someone they trust. This often means a family member, a friend, or a long-time acquaintance, sometimes someone who is difficult to refuse due to family ties. Because friends and family rarely provide genuine countervailing power, the wise look for a strong, independent director, or at least an independent informal advisor, someone who keeps them sharp.

Future-proofing family business

Family businesses are often seen as enterprises with a long-term vision. Some of the largest have dominated their industries for generations. Yet, studies show that only half are truly future-ready, and in only one-third of families do members agree on the company's direction.[9] Leadership succession often triggers tensions, leading to internal divisions and emotional conflict, none of which serve the interest of the company.

Spouses, sometimes referred to in family-business language as "the cold side," can bring fresh energy to the firm but are often seen as outsiders. Sometimes, it is not the spouse who creates division but the family's own resistance to new voices and unfamiliar loyalties. Within the inner circle, influence is shared more easily, and mistakes are more readily forgiven.

The ideal external non-executive director combines boardroom experience with the *emotional intelligence* needed to navigate family dynamics. They spot early signs of trouble, help anchor the company through tough times, and know when to step in to defuse the conflicts that are characteristic of family-run businesses. Strong listening skills and the ability to connect people are essential traits, particularly when cohesion is at risk.

Non-executive directors also enhance the company's reputation and credibility. A family business with external directors is seen as more professional and mature—qualities that appeal to financiers. Finally, they act as a safeguard in case the entrepreneur is suddenly incapacitated by accident or illness. A visionary owner thus carefully considers the right mix of competencies and character.

Case Study: Interturbine—failing forward

"Failure as a route to success" was the motto of Bert Twaalfhoven (1928–2023). In the early 1960s, he founded the industrial holding company Indivers and launched more than 50 enterprises. Sixteen did not succeed—he took pride in these failures as lessons learned. In the post-war years, he launched a chain of self-service washrooms, tapping into the growing demand for modern washing machines before home ownership became widespread. He later shifted to technology and aluminum extrusion, and he founded Interturbine, which became an international player in the production and maintenance of turbine blades for aircraft engines.

Driven by his global ambitions and passion for venture capital, Twaalfhoven carefully selected his non-executive directors based on clear criteria: managerial experience in large industrial companies, scientific expertise, strong ties to technical universities, and a deep understanding of innovation and venture capital. His board reflected his worldview: diverse, international, connected, and innovation-driven.

The non-executive director as therapist

Psychoanalyst and economist Manfred Kets de Vries explored the emotional and psychological dynamics between entrepreneurs and their children.[10] His work examines key themes such as family values, loyalty versus autonomy, power struggles, and deep-seated fears.

In some families, a strong sense of duty, thrift, and modesty shapes the business culture. Here, children are expected to prioritize the company's interests over their own aspirations. In others, absent parents, neglected heirs, or overindulgent upbringings lead to conflicting visions for the company's future.

When family members with different stakes hold diverging views on succession, tensions can escalate quickly. The process often resembles a King Lear scenario where power, inheritance, and personal ambition collide, often with dramatic consequences.

In Shakespeare's King Lear, the aging monarch decides to divide his kingdom among his three daughters, granting the largest share to the one who flatters him most. What follows is a spiral of manipulation, rivalry, and betrayal—culminating in a tragic battle over inheritance.

Family business succession rarely ends in bloodshed, but emotional fallout, fractured relationships, and lasting divisions are all too common. The echoes of Lear's drama—clashing loyalties, unspoken expectations, and unmet needs—still haunt many boardrooms.

Even seasoned non-executives can find themselves sidelined or overwhelmed, as the McCain case illustrates. In the end, it is the founder and the family majority who decide whether external advice is followed—or ignored.

Case Study: McCain—splitting the potato: leadership, loyalty, and loss

In 1956, Harrison and Wallace McCain co-founded McCain Foods, building it into the world's largest producer of frozen fries. However, while their business thrived, a dispute about future leadership emerged—one that would eventually divide the family. By the 1990s, succession became unavoidable. Wallace insisted on keeping leadership within the family, naming his son, Michael, as his successor. Harrison, however, had no faith in him and believed an external leader with industry expertise would better serve the company's future. The disagreement escalated into a power struggle.

As tensions rose, family members sided with Harrison, leaving Wallace in the minority. In 1994, Wallace and Michael were forced out. But Wallace refused to accept defeat. He acquired a controlling stake in Maple Leaf Foods, one of Canada's largest food companies, and installed Michael as CEO. Under Michael's leadership, Maple Leaf became a major industry player, ensuring the McCain name remained influential—even if it was no longer tied to McCain Foods.[11]

Wallace's story shows how emotion and reason often intertwine in family business decisions. His resistance to external succession reflected loss aversion and identity threat—the pain of losing control over the company he co-founded and the challenge to his legacy. His subsequent acquisition of Maple Leaf Foods, though partly driven by a desire for vindication, also demonstrated sharp strategic judgment: recognizing an undervalued company and transforming it into a success. Emotion provided the drive; reason ensured execution. The case reveals how pride and logic often coexist in family governance, shaping outcomes that balance brilliance with behavioral risk.

DNA versus merit: the succession dilemma

Sometimes, succession in the family business carries a tinge of nepotism. Instead of asking who the best candidate is, the real question becomes: can one of the children take over? Decision-making revolves around ensuring the business stays within the family. One common challenge is the age and experience gap between the founder and their children. This can lead to positioning a young and inexperienced successor in a leadership role, someone who might only hold a middle management position in a different company. The family may underestimate the importance of leadership experience, overlooking ambitious non-family candidates who could be better suited to lead the company forward.

Many founders have high expectations for their children. They believe that having the right genes and growing up around the business will naturally lead them to succeed. While they are often aware of their children's limitations, it's still a case of "family comes first." With enough guidance, they hope the next generation will grow into the role, even when reason suggests otherwise. To ease the transition, a trusted advisor is sometimes brought in, while control remains firmly in family hands.

Founder's syndrome: when letting go becomes the hardest act

F*ounder's syndrome* arises when a founder, lacking confidence in their successor or convinced that no one else can lead the company as well as they do, refuses to step aside. What begins as devotion can turn into a serious governance risk, undermining both the authority of the incoming leader and the effectiveness of the board. When the founder keeps hanging around, the new leader may not have the necessary space to grow into the new role and lead. Internal debate is stifled, innovation slows, and employees, particularly those who identified strongly with the founder, may resist change. Worse, if an unqualified child is appointed, talented employees may leave, while only "yes-men" remain.

Family succession can be successful if it is thoroughly prepared, clearly communicated, and supported by the wider family. In some cases, multiple children with complementary skills form an ideal leadership team—one may lead product development, another sales, and a third, finance and administration. However, in many families, power struggles emerge. One dominant child may take control, sidelining siblings and creating internal divisions. If succession is poorly managed, disputes over leadership and strategy can spiral out of control, dividing generations. It is no coincidence that family disputes frequently escalate into legal battles. Family businesses may differ in formal governance structures across countries, yet certain dynamics remain universally recognizable.

A structured succession process is therefore essential. Ideally, it is led by independent directors who can assess candidates objectively and ensure that external options are considered alongside family members.

Case Study: Beaulieu—carpet kings and family feuds

Beaulieu International Group offers a vivid example of how personal ambition, informal norms, and family loyalties shape corporate governance. Under Roger De Clerck (1924–2015), the son of a flax farmer, Beaulieu grew into one of the world's largest carpet manufacturers. His success rested on the "democratization of the carpet," launched in 1962 when affordable wall-to-wall coverings began rolling off the looms in Lembeek, Belgium.

De Clerck expanded aggressively, keeping prices low through efficiency—and, as later revealed, questionable tax practices. He organized his empire around his six children, dividing the world into family fiefdoms. Known for his charismatic authority and flair for symbolic gestures, he celebrated his 75th birthday by inviting Margareth Thatcher, George Bush, and Michael Gorbachev to his farm in Wielsbeke, where the company's headquarters and boardroom were still located. During lunch, De Clerck himself served guests with a large ladle—a theatrical gesture symbolizing his hands-on control.

At the time, Belgium's business world thrived on tacit understandings that granted entrepreneurs informal privileges. De Clerck's longtime confidant, a local politician without a formal contract, quietly smoothed the way in local decision-making. "Ours was a relationship of trust," he later recalled, capturing the blurred line between business and politics that defined the era.[12] When Belgium tightened tax enforcement in the 1980s and 1990s, the climate changed. Beaulieu made headlines not for innovation but for financial misconduct, including VAT fraud and money laundering. Two of De Clerck's children served short prison sentences, while Roger himself—shielded, many believed, by wealth and influence—avoided jail.

The family fractured in 1998 when sons Jan and Dominique struck a deal with the tax authorities, a move that was seen within the family as a betrayal. They were ostracized, illustrating how loyalty norms can outweigh legal compliance. The family reconciliation took 23 years.

Despite the turmoil, Beaulieu survived. Today, it remains a major player in the carpet industry, run by external management under a formal governance structure. A new generation now sits on the board, marking a cultural shift from personal authority to professionalized leadership and institutional accountability.[13]

Large family firms, such as U.S. agri-giant Cargill, Dutch family holding company SHV, or French luxury goods powerhouse LVMH, have both the experience and financial muscle to pursue their strategic agendas independently. Smaller enterprises, by contrast, must choose between remaining independent or being taken over by an industry peer or a private equity investor. It is precisely at this inflection point that the non-executive director must step out of the owners' shadow and take on a more proactive advisory role. This requires experience in business transitions to assess which constellation offers the company the best path forward. Just as importantly, they must possess the authority and resolve to guide the family through a complex and emotionally charged exit process.

SUMMARY AND CONCLUSION

Family businesses are the backbone of the global economy. While some grow into legacy enterprises, most remain modest in size and struggle with intergenerational continuity. Their core strengths—low bureaucracy, hands-on management, and close customer relationships—enable agility and deep local rootedness. A long-term outlook often makes them early adopters of sustainability and active promoters of community stewardship.

However, there are pitfalls. Governance is frequently dominated by the owner-director and a close inner circle of family members, leaving little room for critical oversight. Many avoid appointing non-executive directors altogether. And when they do, the role is often symbolic, a friend, a cousin, or a trusted advisor brought in as a gesture, rather than as a true governance safeguard.

Truly independent directors face a delicate balancing act. They must navigate complex family dynamics and emotional loyalties while maintaining the distance required for effective oversight. Without the space to challenge decisions, they risk becoming symbolic—the Achilles' heel of governance, rather than its backbone.

Succession is often the most critical moment of all. It can trigger *founder's syndrome*, where the outgoing leader resists letting go. Here, the non-executive director must step up not only to guide the transition but also to protect the company's future. Serving on the board of a family business may seem appealing, but it is far from simple. It demands deep experience, emotional intelligence, and the courage to speak hard truths. In the end, it is not a favor among friends but a serious responsibility with real consequences.

§3.3—NAVIGATING BETWEEN SCYLLA AND CHARYBDIS: GOVERNANCE IN LISTED COMPANIES

Introduction

The stock market is a central pillar of our capitalist society. Investors, private individuals or pension funds, place their capital in shares and other securities, expecting solid returns. In doing so, they relinquish direct control over their capital to corporate executives and asset managers. To safeguard their interests, independent non-executive directors are appointed to ensure oversight, accountability, and a balance of power.

Due to these potential conflicts, stock markets worldwide are among the most heavily regulated of all financial markets. While governance laws vary by jurisdiction, this book focuses on the universal behavioral dynamics that influence directors, regardless of their legal framework.

Non-executives must navigate between two powerful forces. On one side, in their oversight role, they must consider the interests of a diverse group of shareholders and stakeholders. Each has different priorities—some may seek high short-term dividends, others may emphasize long-term, sustainable value creation. On the other side, they must work constructively with executive leadership teams that seek to maintain operational autonomy and often pursue their own strategic agenda.

What does it take for those responsible for oversight to align strategic autonomy with long-term accountability?

Going public: the power and the pitfalls

It is 9 a.m., and the stock market gong, struck by a beaming CEO, signals the market opening to newly issued shares. A new listing—an IPO. A new day on the trading floor. Behind the scenes, a vast industry works to ensure the IPO's success; each player with their own vested interests. Investment bankers set the valuation, lawyers draft the issuance documents, and securities dealers keep the market moving. All profit from the process and are highly motivated to keep the stock market game alive—an inherently uncertain market.

For successful companies that were once family or private equity-owned, an IPO is often the gateway to financing and expansion. Yet the stock market has always produced winners and losers. In the early days of capitalism, the winners were oil majors, railroads, and later, industrial conglomerates. Today, technology companies such as Google, Amazon, Microsoft, and Nvidia dominate the industry. Others—such as Eastman Kodak, Wirecard, and Steinhoff International—fell from grace through strategic missteps, poor governance, or outright fraud. Listed companies come and go. Of the 750 firms listed in 1970 on the Amsterdam Stock Exchange, the world's oldest stock market, only 23 remained in 2020; a textbook case of creative destruction. Yet, a company's disappearance from the stock exchange doesn't always mean it has ceased operations. Some are acquired; others return to private ownership.

Throughout this section, we'll see how directors, both executive and non-executive, play a decisive role in shaping a company's future.

Information asymmetry

Shareholders entrust their money to a board whose strategy they mostly learn about through the media. With an IPO, the problem of information asymmetry becomes clear. The company's board possesses detailed knowledge of its plans, direction, and key markets. Shareholders, by contrast, remain distant and must rely on the board's integrity, initiative, and judgment.

Institutional investors and bank analysts hold an advantage over retail investors through privileged access to company information. They gain insights via meetings with the board and investor relations officers, though their assessments remain influenced by inherent biases. Retail investors, as outsiders, must rely on an often opaque prospectus and wait for press releases or annual reports. Only at the Annual (Shareholder) Meeting can they pose a single question—one that may or may not receive a clear answer. Voting agencies aim to strengthen shareholders' influence by representing larger groups and ensuring their concerns are heard, yet the balance of power between shareholders and executives is never static—it shifts continually, a perpetual cycle of influence and resistance that is explored further in this section.

Real-world examples show how such an imbalance can lead to both success and failure. Dutch fintech Adyen, listed on the Amsterdam Stock Exchange in 2018, quickly met high expectations and joined the AEX index. Another fintech, German Wirecard, listed in 2000 and included in the DAX 30 in 2018, collapsed amid a scandal. These contrasting stories underscore the importance of transparency, governance, and trust in modern capital markets.

Case Study: Wirecard—a FinTech champion built on deception

In 2020, the Wirecard house of cards collapsed after an investigative team from the *Financial Times* had begun exposing one of the largest fraud cases in German corporate history. New shareholders were left empty-handed. Once seen as a rising star in fintech, Wirecard had built its early success processing high-risk online payments before expanding into other markets. Behind its rapid growth, however, lay an elaborate network of fictitious transactions and shell companies, some based in the Far East.

At its peak, Wirecard's reputation was so inflated that rumors suggested it might even acquire Deutsche Bank, the nation's financial cornerstone. Eager investors, lured by glossy prospectuses and grand promises, received little real information—and were left disillusioned when the truth emerged.

Failures in oversight became evident. Members of the supervisory board (Aufsichtsrat) admired CEO Markus Braun as a visionary, if dominant, leader. One dissenting voice, Anastassia Lauterbach, a board member known in governance circles for her tough approach, later reflected: "I joined the board too easily. Never again will I serve where a majority has been in office for more than a decade."[14] Her experience highlights how groupthink and deference to charismatic leadership can silence even seasoned directors.

Regulatory blind spots compounded the problem. Germany's financial regulator, BaFin, failed to act decisively and even went so far as to sue *Financial Times* journalists for alleged market manipulation. Some BaFin employees held Wirecard shares. Meanwhile, a Deutsche Bank board member with personal ties to COO Jan Marsalek urged Wirecard to "finish" the *FT* and bought more shares.

As of early 2026, Marsalek remains a fugitive, reportedly under the protection of Russian interests. Braun denies wrongdoing, while a Munich court has ordered him and two directors to pay €140 million in damages. Once worth over €24 billion, Wirecard has been dismantled, its assets sold off, its name erased from financial markets. Its legacy endures as a cautionary tale of unchecked ambition, regulatory failure, and corporate deception.[15]

Satisficing or *betting the farm*

The directors of listed companies must develop a balanced policy within the remit of their *fiduciary duty,* serving both shareholders and stakeholders. This requires a profitable strategy with an acceptable risk profile. But when is a strategy sufficiently profitable? What constitutes an adequate level of risk? Some investors demand maximum returns and dividends in the shortest possible time frame. Others, particularly long-term investors, prioritize sustainability—even at the expense of short-term profit. Corporate strategy often becomes a balancing act between conflicting strategic preferences.

That said, shareholders and stakeholders cannot expect the board to be omniscient or omnipresent. Executive leadership operates in a complex environment where decisions must be made in conditions of uncertainty and incomplete information about future markets, prices, regulations, technology, and competitors' strategies. Due to *bounded rationality* (as discussed in Chapter 1), they can never process all available data into a perfectly coherent policy. In addition, executive boards may consciously or unconsciously create smokescreens that obscure actual risks and trade-offs. This makes it difficult for non-executive directors to obtain a clear view of the company's true position and to exercise effective oversight.

Boardroom behavior spans a spectrum between two extremes, though most companies operate somewhere in the middle:

- Satisficing behavior (risk-averse approach): directors pursue conservative or familiar strategies, even if these do not maximize stakeholder value. This approach emphasizes stability and personal security; executives may focus on preserving compensation and minimizing threats to their position.
- Betting the farm (high-risk approach): at the other extreme, directors may adopt aggressive, high-stakes strategies that endanger the entire company. Unlike shareholders, executives may be shielded from the full consequences of failure, encouraging excessive risk-taking.

The challenge for non-executive directors is to assess where leadership sits on this spectrum and ensure that decisions align with long-term value creation. This requires recognizing that executives often exhibit multiple biases simultaneously. *Overconfidence bias* may lead them to overestimate their ability to forecast markets, while *anchoring bias* can cause them to fixate on initial assumptions. As a result, companies may drift toward short-term, self-serving goals rather than the sustainable interests of stakeholders.

Case Study: Strategy—a leveraged bet on Bitcoin, driven by conviction

In August 2024, U.S. software company MicroStrategy rebranded as "Strategy." CEO Michael Saylor was driven by his conviction that Federal Reserve policy would erode the dollar's purchasing power through inflation and monetary expansion. Strategy became the first publicly traded company to adopt Bitcoin as its principal treasury reserve asset, presenting this as a "dual strategy" of software and Bitcoin accumulation. From August 2020 through 2025, Saylor intensified his strategy, issuing convertible debt and new equity—totaling approximately $8 billion by October 2025—solely to acquire more Bitcoin.

This leverage deliberately made Strategy significantly more volatile than Bitcoin itself, with the stock often moving at multiples of Bitcoin's price swings. Saylor fully embraced this dynamic. As Bitcoin rises and falls, Strategy follows with amplified movement.

The governance question is clear: how should boards respond when a CEO's extreme, yet publicly deliberate and transparent bet delivers outsized volatility, challenging traditional risk principles?

For non-executive directors, success does not itself validate excessive concentration, as they have a fiduciary responsibility to the company and its shareholders and bondholders. Their task is to test the conviction behind the bet, ensure transparent risk communication to investors, and define clear boundaries around concentration and leverage so that their fiduciary duty is not displaced by the force of a CEO's belief.

Strategy's story is still unfolding—a real-time test of whether extreme concentration represents visionary leadership or a governance failure in waiting.

Case Study: Tesla—Betting on Genius—and Pay

Under Elon Musk's leadership, Tesla became the dominant electric vehicle producer, reaching a $1.3 trillion market capitalization by 2024—twice the combined value of its largest competitors. Tesla trades more like a technology company than a traditional automaker, reflecting Musk's expansive vision that extends from Tesla to SpaceX and his acquisition of Twitter (now X).

However, Musk's leadership also revealed major agency challenges when the board approved a $56 billion compensation package in 2018. These issues resurfaced when Musk sought to claim the reward after meeting all performance milestones. The approval process, tied to market capitalization growth, exposed classic conflicts where directors may prioritize personal ties or incentives over shareholder interests.

A Delaware court later ruled the process "deeply flawed," citing a lack of board independence. The judge noted that directors were "swept up by rhetoric" and "starry-eyed by Musk's superstar appeal." *Confirmation bias* may have led them to accept only supporting evidence, while the *halo effect* of Musk's past success likely clouded judgment and discouraged dissent.[16] Board chair Robyn Denholm was singled out for receiving a "life-changing" compensation that, according to Judge McCormick, undermined her independence. Denholm's total Tesla stock sales over the years exceeded $500 million.[17]

The case exposed tensions between majority and minority shareholders. Although 72% approved the package in 2024, the court sided with a minority investor, voiding it on procedural grounds. Tesla's appeal to the Delaware Supreme Court was successful, as the Court in December 2025 reversed the rescission of the compensation package, ruling that such a remedy was inequitable given that Musk had already performed under the plan and the parties could not be restored to their original position. In the meantime, Tesla reincorporated in Texas, adopting bylaws requiring 3% ownership to sue—curbing future minority challenges.

In November 2025, Tesla shareholders once and for all settled the dispute by approving—this time under Texas law—a new, historic $1 trillion bonus plan. Seventy-five percent voted in favor, betting on genius, while 25%, including several major institutional investors, voted against, citing dilution of existing shareholders and the deliberate concentration of key-person risk stemming from Musk's dominance.

Musk's growing political visibility in a divided United States has provoked backlash and, at times, eroded Tesla's brand loyalty. Yet the broader saga demonstrates how exceptional performance can blur governance boundaries: shareholders may embrace risks that courts deem unacceptable, exposing deep divisions over who ultimately defines fairness, accountability, and control.

The balancing act of the non-executive director

In listed companies, shareholders usually remain distant from daily operations, while the board is entrusted with setting and overseeing corporate strategy. In most countries, shareholder rights are explicitly enshrined in law, yet in practice, shareholders are typically consulted only on major matters such as mergers, share issues, or dividend distributions, and on the appointment of non-executive directors.[18]

Non-executives are expected to ensure that the management board acts in the interests of all stakeholders. This expectation raises a critical question: do they possess sufficient information to fulfill this responsibility? Their ability is constrained by structural information asymmetries: the executive board has far greater access to operational and strategic detail, particularly regarding internal processes, culture, risk exposure, emerging developments, and the impact on external stakeholders. Even executives themselves lack full visibility into the complexities of day-to-day operations. Chapter 4 explores these asymmetries in greater detail.

In their oversight role, non-executive directors must balance competing expectations: delivering shareholder returns, safeguarding broader societal interests, and giving executives sufficient space to manage the business effectively. Excessive scrutiny can erode trust, while too little oversight may invite pressure from activist investors—whether financially or sustainability-driven—who seek greater influence or direct board representation.

Beyond monitoring, non-executive directors also hold crucial levers of governance. They oversee executive appointments and remuneration, evaluate performance, and, when necessary, may intervene—up to and including executive dismissal. Though rare, such actions underline the weight of fiduciary responsibility in a complex and often ambiguous governance environment.

The Unilever case illustrates how non-executive directors can serve as both mediators and participants in this struggle, as activist investors and long-term funds seek to influence strategy from both inside and outside the boardroom.

Case Study: Unilever—when activists step inside

In 2022, activist investor Nelson Peltz, whose Trian Fund held a roughly 1.3% stake in Unilever, joined the board as a non-executive director. His entry alone marked a turning point: the stock jumped 9.3% on the announcement, signaling investor anticipation of a more profit-driven agenda. It also underscored the strategic weight non-executives can carry, particularly when they represent activist capital. Over the following three years, Unilever underwent two CEO transitions as the board responded to mounting investor pressure for sharper execution, a leaner structure, and stronger financial discipline.

Other investors took a contrasting view. Dutch pension fund ABP, which held 0.25% of Unilever within its €520 billion globally diversified portfolio, voted against the company's 2024 remuneration report and climate transition plan, citing diluted climate ambition. Roughly 28% of shareholders opposed the remuneration report—an unusually high level of dissent for a blue-chip company. While this symbolic protest drew public attention, it had little visible impact on the company's strategic course.

By 2025, Unilever had spun off several business lines, reflecting not only a sharper focus on profitability but also a reassessment of the commercial limits of its green ambitions. This shift contrasted with the priorities of sustainability-focused investors. In this landscape, the non-executive director becomes a mediator of competing capital logics, translating activist urgency and sustainability ambition into a coherent strategic course.

SUMMARY AND CONCLUSION

Nearly 250 years after Adam Smith, the holy grail of balancing interests in publicly listed companies remains elusive. Non-executive directors hold fiduciary duties to both shareholders and stakeholders, yet they must rely on information filtered through the executive board. This structural information asymmetry limits effective oversight and can cloud judgment (see Chapter 4).

Strategic decision-making in listed companies is rarely straightforward. Boards operate along a spectrum—from *satisficing*—sticking with familiar, low-risk strategies—to *betting the farm* through bold moves with uncertain outcomes. Both behaviors carry risks, especially amid increasingly vocal and polarized expectations between visionary, growth-oriented shareholders and sustainability-driven stakeholders (see Chapter 5).

Non-executive directors must walk a behavioral tightrope: staying close enough to understand and guide management decisions, yet sufficiently distant to preserve independent oversight. As the cases show, excessive trust can enable misconduct, while shareholder activism and board composition can decisively reshape a company's trajectory.

In today's capital markets, there are no easy answers. Ultimately, the oversight role demands constant calibration—a modern-day navigation between *Scylla and Charybdis*: between trust and control, long-term value and short-term pressure, and competing visions of what a company should stand for.

§3.4—REWARD, RISK: THE CEO PAY DEBATE

Introduction

Boards of listed companies often chase the same dream: hire a star CEO, reward them handsomely, and watch value soar. Yet when performance disappoints, an uncomfortable truth emerges: generous rewards do not necessarily cause exceptional outcomes.

Performance-based incentives have ballooned in size and complexity, often outpacing actual results. While a compelling package is seen as essential, behavioral economists warn that such incentives can backfire—encouraging excessive risk-taking, short-term thinking, or even misconduct.

In the aftermath of the 2008 financial crisis, aggressive incentive schemes fueled public distrust. The debate has since become as much about business risk as it is about fairness and reputation. Excessive pay can erode both performance and credibility, both internally and in the eyes of society.

Remuneration consultants and headhunters cite fierce competition for talent and short CEO tenures as justification for rising pay. Non-executive directors face a difficult dilemma: in their often-vulnerable relationship with the CEO, they must assess what truly drives performance while explaining to shareholders and stakeholders how pay balances market pressure with broader expectations of responsibility and fairness.

This section sets the stage for the broader discussion of the role of remuneration in leadership and governance.

Beyond ball games: the illusion of objectivity

CEO compensation is often compared to the market-driven rewards of elite athletes. Both hold star status, yet fans rarely object to a footballer's extraordinary income. In sports, an individual's performance is visible and measurable: we see who scores, who defends well, and who delivers that decisive assist. Data analytics instantly quantify value, and underperformers are quickly dropped. Popularity also counts, reflected in shirt sales and sponsorships. On the field, value creation—and reward—are transparent, even if luck plays its part.

In corporate life, the CEO may appear just as central a figure, but measuring individual impact is far less precise. Results unfold over the years and depend on teamwork, market conditions, and, a quieter kind of luck. Shareholders and non-executive directors must rely on judgment, not scoreboards. Performance attribution to one person thus becomes speculative, while pay remains concrete.

In family-owned, cooperative, and private-equity firms, owners exert direct influence on pay, keeping remuneration generally lower. Exceptional rewards occur only after a successful exit, when value is realized through the sale of a company. In listed companies, by contrast, dispersed ownership and market pressure separate pay from performance, rendering the reward process itself a test of governance.

Top pay and shareholder value: a paradox

In the 1990s, Harvard Finance Professor Michael C. Jensen (1939–2024) proposed a solution to the agency problem, the misalignment between executives and shareholders.[19] He observed that executives in the 1990s were less generously compensated than their 1920s counterparts, which he believed weakened performance.

Jensen's remedy was to align executive and shareholder interests through generous stock-based compensation. Stock options, he argued, were ideal: they required no immediate cash outlay, offered high upside potential, vested over time, and justified lower base salaries. His model also assumed that CEOs should hold a substantial, long-term personal stake in their company's shares. Underperformance would then directly affect their own wealth—provided they were not shielded by golden parachutes.

This compensation model, now known as the Long-Term Incentive Plan (LTIP), typically pays out over a five- to seven-year horizon. It was rapidly adopted by publicly traded companies and remains dominant today. With booming stock markets, executive pay soared. Yet, the very mechanisms designed to align executive and shareholder interests failed to deliver the promised results. Studies in the United States and Europe show no compelling evidence that stock options or equity-based pay alone improve long-term performance. Since the 1990s bull market, variable compensation has been driven more by overall market conditions than by company-specific results.[20] After a string of accounting scandals associated with companies such as Enron and WorldCom, the system came under fire.

Jensen later acknowledged shortcomings in how incentive schemes were implemented. In *Executive Pay* (2005), he admitted that poorly designed incentive systems not only failed to link compensation with genuine performance but also encouraged executives to pursue growth and market optimism at the expense of long-term value and organizational integrity.[21] The idea that CEOs should have real skin in the game never quite took off as bonus schemes drifted away from accountability, giving executives plenty of upside but little real risk. As a result, many pay structures pushed leaders to focus on how things looked rather than how they really were, managing perceptions instead of performance.[22]

Extrinsic and intrinsic motivation

Economist Alexander Pepper (London School of Economics) has raised questions about what really drives executives.[23] According to Pepper, they aren't primarily motivated by big bonuses or other *extrinsic* motivators, though they certainly don't turn them down. What truly matters are *intrinsic* motivators, such as satisfaction, pride, recognition, and appreciation from clients and colleagues. Prestige, visibility, autonomy, and power also play a key role. Pepper points out that financial rewards can lose their impact when they are uncertain or lie too far in the future. His research found that executives would be willing to sacrifice 30% of their pay in exchange for a more personally fulfilling role. Jeroen van der Veer, former CEO of Shell and one of the highest-paid Dutch executives of his time, echoed this view. In an interview, he said that it would have made no difference to him if he had been paid 50% more or less, and that companies should rethink their policies. However, he didn't offer any concrete solutions.[24] The notion of the "level playing field" can also come into play here: executives may be open to lower pay, as long as it doesn't put them below their peers at similar companies.

Reward and the dark side of leadership

While executive compensation is often designed to be a tool for alignment and motivation, it can also create blind spots. The prospect of high rewards can encourage high risk—even reckless—behavior. Leaders high on the narcissism spectrum may be especially prone to excessive risk-taking, particularly when they are incentivized through large variable compensation packages.[25] Their fixed salary and short-term incentives provide a secure baseline income, ensuring financial stability. If their aggressive strategies succeed, long-term incentive plans can become extremely valuable. If they fail, they face only limited personal risk. Even when leaders are forced to step down, they often receive generous golden parachutes—the severance packages that undercut the principle of executive accountability.

Incentive structures may also create opportunities for manipulation. Executives whose compensation is tied to stock price may be tempted to inflate performance figures to maximize personal gain. Common tactics include prematurely recognizing revenue, deferring expenses, or postponing impairment charges.[26] In many listed companies, bonus schemes reward annual milestones. When results disappoint, performance targets are quietly recalibrated.

Meanwhile, non-executive directors often overestimate their ability to detect or prevent risky or unethical behavior from the executives they oversee. The banking crises in 2007 and 2023 underscore this vulnerability. The collapses of Silicon Valley Bank in the United States and Credit Suisse in Switzerland were partially driven by high-stakes variable pay structures that failed to account appropriately for risk (see also Chapter 5, Section §5.4).

The pay debate: survival on the remuneration committee

Serving on a remuneration committee is no easy task. Its members walk a tightrope: offer too little and risk losing a strong CEO or damaging a good relationship; offer too much and they may end up rewarding a risk-laden future. Industry benchmarks intensify the pressure, steadily pushing pay upward. This creates a classic *prisoner's dilemma*: if all firms restrained CEO pay, as many non-executive directors would prefer, no one would lose this critical talent. Acting alone feels too risky in today's environment of escalating bonuses, so committees follow the trend, even when they privately doubt its merits.

Prominent business leaders have long raised concerns. Warren Buffett and Charlie Munger of Berkshire Hathaway, the legendary investment conglomerate, have criticized pay structures that reward luck over skill. The challenge remains: how to balance competitive compensation with accountability and long-term alignment between executives, shareholders, and society.

To maintain a good relationship with their CEO, non-executive directors often rely on remuneration consultants (the specialists hired to advise on CEO compensation). Each year, these advisors update complex bonus structures using sophisticated formulas and multiple performance targets, despite evidence that executives can only realistically focus on one or two key objectives.

Remuneration consultants: guardians of fairness or architects of inflation?

Remuneration consultants operate within the very system they help sustain. In a world where high executive pay has become normalized, their role is often framed in procedural rather than normative terms: producing defensible pay packages rather than questioning underlying trends. Their financial dependence on corporate clients further complicates claims of independence.[27]

A key driver of rising CEO pay is *peer benchmarking*. Boards and their consultants assemble a peer group of "comparable" CEOs, yet selection bias often tilts the peer set upward. Higher-paid peers raise the benchmark, making median or upper-quartile positioning the implicit target rather than the ceiling. As a result, few CEOs are ever positioned below average. It's a self-reinforcing cycle that does not merely reflect the market: it gradually resets it.

The assumption that only "star CEOs" justify market-leading pay often goes untested. What remains underexplored is the availability of internal or non-star candidates who may combine competence with more modest pay expectations; a factor rarely considered in benchmarking, even though it could help temper the upward drift.[28]

Pay decisions, behavior, and *interlock*

Beyond benchmarking, three structural dynamics, each tied to the role and independence of non-executive directors, shape how CEO compensation is set. For example, social dynamics influence the independence of remuneration committees, as explored by governance experts Zajac and Westphal. Interlocking (overlapping) networks contribute to the problem: executives and non-executives often circulate in the same elite circles, creating subtle pressure to avoid conflict. Board members may hesitate to question pay proposals, as doing so can create a risk of reputational fallout or reduce the possibility of future board appointments.[29] Larger committees add to these issues: more voices can mean less challenge, paradoxically diluting accountability rather than strengthening it.

A second force is the concentration of ownership. When major shareholders (or independent directors representing them) are on a board, the tone changes. Research shows that when investors hold more than 5% of shares, oversight and financial discipline increase, narrowing the agency gap and putting natural pressure on pay levels.[30]

A third influence lies in the parallel upward drift of executive and non-executive compensation. This frequently occurring alignment creates a subtle mutual incentive: weakening the willingness of those responsible for oversight to challenge the generous pay proposals of those they oversee.[31]

Trust inside and outside the enterprise

The moral dimension of escalating executive pay ultimately lies with the board of directors. In 1984, management guru Peter Drucker (1909–2005), drawing on the insights of Dutch Nobel laureate Jan Tinbergen, proposed that a CEO's salary should not exceed 20 times the average employee's pay. He warned that excessive pay gaps could undermine teamwork and organizational cohesion.[32] Despite his prominent name, Drucker's influence on the debate remained limited. Over time, thanks to stock-based incentives, the CEO-to-employee pay ratio in the S&P 500 companies has spiraled to 268.[33] As markets are interconnected, the culture of high executive pay, originating in the United States, has since spread to Europe.

Harvard governance expert Jay Lorsch (1932–2015) observed that for most of the twentieth century, corporations weren't seen purely as profit machines. They were social institutions with obligations to employees, communities, and society. To regain trust inside and outside the organization, Lorsch calls on boards to treat executive pay not merely as a contract but as a reflection of corporate purpose and public legitimacy.[34]

Politicians, trade unions, and stewardship-oriented institutional investors, acknowledging the pay gap as a symptom of growing inequality, and hoping to put moral pressure on companies, responded by requiring companies to disclose internal pay ratios, the so-called *say-on-pay* vote, and publish the level of shareholder support for their remuneration policies.[35] However, making these figures public produced an unintended consequence. Instead of curbing escalation, the disclosures intensified peer-group comparisons: once executives could see how their pay ranked against that of competitors, boards often felt compelled to "keep up," treating median or upper-quartile benchmarks as targets rather than limits. The result? Transparency, meant to restrain excess, quietly became another engine of upward drift.

The wider public, meanwhile, is growing impatient with the widening gap between reward and responsibility. When Jamie Dimon, Chairman and CEO of JPMorgan Chase, was asked about his own compensation, he responded, "The board sets mine; I have nothing to do with it." The remark landed poorly. During a 2019 House hearing, U.S. Congresswoman Katie Porter confronted him with the monthly budget of a JPMorgan employee who could not make ends meet despite working full time. Her question—"How should she manage this budget shortfall?"—went viral, capturing growing public frustration with executive pay disparities.

The moment highlighted a deeper behavioral tension: as long as boards and executives treat compensation as an internal matter, insulated from societal norms, external scrutiny will only intensify.[36] Similar scenes have played out in Europe: at Dutch retailer Ahold Delhaize's 2015 shareholder meeting, a young employee appeared half-dressed before the board to protest the gulf between his wages and the CEO's millions; a stark image of inequality that the board chair dismissed as "inappropriate for the AGM."

Top earners often deflect accountability, while non-executive directors hesitate to challenge the system. Restoring trust—both within the company and with society—demands shared accountability: executives owning their rewards and boards showing real independence and restraint.

SUMMARY AND CONCLUSION

Executive pay remains a persistent challenge. Designed to align incentives with performance, remuneration has soared without clear evidence of proportional performance benefits. Leaders are motivated not only by money but also by purpose, reputation, and professional recognition—factors often overlooked in purely financial incentive models.

Stock-based incentives, intended to reward long-term success, can unintentionally encourage short-termism, risk-taking, and strategic manipulation. Peer benchmarking may mirror market trends more than individual performance, rewarding luck as much as leadership.

Non-executive directors face a structural paradox: their oversight role requires independence, yet compensation norms, social ties and benchmarking practices can limit their willingness to challenge excess. Professional ties among board members, known as *the Westphal effect*, may further reinforce conformity and reduce the inclination to question excess. Restoring confidence in executive pay depends less on ever more complex formulas and more on disciplined judgment and clarity of purpose. These are principles essential to rebuilding trust in corporations, and the markets they serve.

§3.5—GUARDIANS AND GAMBLERS: GOVERNANCE IN BANKING

Introduction

Banks are built on promises and the trust that those promises will be kept. Because their stability underpins the wider financial system, bank governance deserves separate attention in this book. While banks attract and allocate money via loans, their work is not only about keeping funds safe but also about taking calculated risks and managing loan portfolios.

Banking demands prudence, transparency, and responsibility. Yet it also attracts ambitious people who are drawn to the excitement of large transactions. Some prioritize growth and profitability over caution. This creates a persistent tension between risk-taking and financial security, posing a challenge for both regulators and non-executives responsible for oversight.

The tension is not only structural but also psychological: behavioral factors such as overconfidence, *moral hazard*, and *groupthink* often undermine effective oversight, even in highly regulated institutions.

For good reason, banking has become one of the most heavily regulated sectors of the economy. Yet vulnerabilities remain. After the 2008 global financial crisis, governments had to intervene again in 2023 to stabilize failing banks. What, then, can non-executive directors do to reduce the likelihood of future crises?

Managing other people's money

Sitting on the board of a bank is no small task. It means overseeing an institution that moves vast sums of other people's money through systems that few fully understand. Modern banks are sprawling, data-driven organizations whose risks are often buried deep in models and markets. Their activities span three broad domains:

- Lending and credit: Banks finance everyday life as well as large-scale ambitions: from family homes to billion-dollar infrastructure projects. Their lending decisions fuel growth across sectors. In energy, for instance, they may support both fossil fuel producers and windmill farms, revealing the strategic and ethical trade-offs that boards must weigh.
- Payments and settlements: Behind every card payment or international transfer lies a vast banking infrastructure.
- Investment banking: Banks advise on mergers, acquisitions, and public listings—transactions that can reshape industries and test the boundaries of judgment, risk awareness, and integrity at its highest level.

At its core, banking is the management of other people's money. This rests on a continuous exercise of trust requiring technical competence, ethical judgment, and the courage to uphold integrity even when unobserved. A true test of judgment for non-executive directors.

Risk and reward

At the heart of these activities lies a concept that is both fundamental and elusive: risk versus reward. In sectors such as automotive or IT, production processes are complex, and the risks can be high, yet the outcomes are tangible—physical products or digital services that generate immediate revenue upon sale.

Banking is fundamentally different. Money is raised from savers and investors and then issued as loans, creating long-term exposure to risk. A bank's profitability depends on whether the rewards adequately offset those risks. Unlike selling a car or a software license, a bank's main product—credit—remains on its balance sheet for years, carrying inherent uncertainty. A borrower's financial situation can change at any time, turning a once-profitable loan into a liability.

Banks also face another persistent threat: *liquidity mismatch*. Since they primarily operate with borrowed funds, such as customer deposits or bonds, any loss of confidence can trigger instability. If too many depositors rush to withdraw their money at once, a bank run can follow, threatening the institution's survival.

Beyond lending and financing, banks serve as the backbone of the global payments system. The scale is staggering: in 2023, the global payment industry processed 3.4 trillion transactions and generated $2.4 trillion in related revenues, underscoring the centrality of payments in the financial ecosystem.[37] Yet not all transactions involve honest actors. Banks can be exploited for tax evasion, corruption, and illicit financial flows, making the detection and prevention of financial crime a continuous challenge for boards and regulators alike.

Doing God's work: a short history of investment banking

Investment banking focuses on advising corporate clients and acting as an intermediary in mergers and acquisitions. Banks also manage the issuance of shares and bonds and trade financial instruments, including complex derivatives. Banking is a service industry at the heart of the capitalist system.

The bonus culture that defines modern banking took root in the United States during the 1970s. By the 1980s, it had spread across Europe. High rewards made it tempting to take risks with the bank's capital—yet this meant working with other people's money. No wonder the 2007–2008 financial crisis was a turning point: banking, once viewed as a pillar of economic growth, turned into a source of public anger and political distrust.

Even as Lehman Brothers' bankruptcy dominated rescue meetings among central banks, Goldman Sachs came to symbolize Wall Street's aggressive investment culture. Although not the main culprit behind the 2008 collapse, the bank's role in creating and trading complex mortgage derivatives—often while betting against its own clients—made it a defining face of financial excess. After receiving emergency support, then-CEO Lloyd Blankfein famously declared he was "just a banker, doing God's work." Whether careless or calculated, his words captured the ethical distance that had taken hold across the industry.[38] As discussed in See § 2.7, executives high on the narcissism spectrum often show a strong appetite for wealth-driven risk. Investment banking is a business that tends to reward it, as several cases in Chapter 4 will show.

To escape the low margins of traditional lending, many European banks entered investment banking in the 1990s. Non-executive directors, often unfamiliar with this new risk culture, relied heavily on consultants, who promised growth and shareholder value.[39] To foster unity and to emphasize the importance of higher stock prices, banks granted generous stock awards to employees; some even displayed real-time share prices in staff canteens.

Case Study: ABN AMRO—€71 billion domino run

At the turn of the century, ABN AMRO aimed to become one of the world's top five investment banks. However, when operational costs continued to outpace profits, the vulnerability of the investment banking model became apparent. In 2007, in a bold attempt to outdo ABN AMRO's ambitions, Fortis, Royal Bank of Scotland (RBS), and Banco Santander took over the large struggling bank at an inflated price. The transaction proved disastrous: within a year, Fortis and RBS had collapsed under the weight of the €71 billion deal. Hubris played a central role. Fortis signed first and then failed to secure sufficient and timely financing, leaving it exposed to a liquidity crunch when markets turned. RBS, driven by aggressive expansionism, chose to bypass proper due diligence on ABN AMRO's portfolio.

As systemically essential banks, ABN AMRO, RBS and Fortis had to be rescued by their respective states. Queen Elizabeth, at the London School of Economics, asked about the roots of the financial crisis: "Why did nobody see it coming?" Amid expectations of unlimited growth and a culture of executive arrogance, even the central banks receded into the background. All were captivated by visionary bankers and failed to serve as a countervailing power. They only resurfaced, shocked and unprepared, when it was too late. Rob Hazelhoff, former Chairman of ABN AMRO, was widely regarded as a representative of traditional, responsible banking, an emblem of integrity. Deeply disheartened by the fiasco, he refused to drive his car through the Vijzelstraat in Amsterdam, his old headquarters. His motto was simple: a bank should manage other people's money with care and integrity.[40]

Too big to fail?

What of the external regulators, the central banks? Remarkably, they appeared impressed by the risk management systems in the sector. In mid-2007, just before the crisis, the chairman of De Nederlandsche Bank confidently enumerated the benefits of the new bank regulatory framework, Basel II. It promised "greater operational efficiencies, better capital allocation and greater shareholder value through the use of improved risk models and reporting capabilities."[41]

This confidence revealed a classic pattern: regulators sought evidence that validated their existing beliefs about effective oversight; a textbook case of *confirmation bias*. Meanwhile, the banks' sophisticated technical presentations created a powerful *halo effect*. Impressive risk dashboards and complex models generated an aura of control and competence that obscured the risk-taking that lay beneath.

Yet the regulators had missed a fundamental shift. Through waves of mergers since the 1980s, the big banks had become too big to fail; and the bankers knew it. This knowledge fundamentally altered their relationship with risk. When failure means rescue rather than ruin, the normal constraints dissolve. The underlying psychological dynamic was one of *moral hazard*: bankers could pursue aggressive strategies confident that, should things go wrong, the state would be compelled to step in and prevent systemic collapse.

The regulators' response, Basel III, came in 2010—too late to prevent the crisis it was designed to address. More troublingly, the 2023 state bailouts of Switzerland's Credit Suisse and California's Silicon Valley Bank serve as stark reminders that little has changed. The psychological patterns that enabled the 2008 crisis, including overconfidence in risk models, deference to technical complexity, and the comfort of knowing rescue is assured, remain firmly intact.

Swimming with sharks: the shadowy world of money laundering

For decades, managing foreign capital has been a central pillar of the financial sector of small, open economies like Switzerland, Luxembourg, the Netherlands, and the British Isles.[42] Promising discretion and financial stability, banks attracted both legitimate clients and tax-sensitive investors through numbered accounts that offered privacy but limited transparency. The banking system projects an image of precision and civility, leading society to expect both financial safety and ethical integrity.

Facilitating multinationals with tax structures however, entails inherent risks. As noted in a 2021 Dutch government report, complex legal and financial arrangements can obscure beneficial ownership and complicate the tracing of cross-border money flows.[43] The infrastructure of aggressive tax planning also creates vulnerabilities attractive to criminal organizations.

Bounded ethicality helps explain why governments support the conduit function: just as individuals overestimate their morality, so do nations. While preaching transparency, governments often turned a blind eye to money streams, hoping to siphon local tax revenues and benefit from legal and tax consultancy, even if other countries suffer tax losses.

Few bank executives or board members recognized that these financial flows could also attract predatory actors. Networks around the trust sector were exploited by oligarchs and organized crime cartels. Anticipating stricter EU anti-money-laundering rules, many shifted their assets elsewhere. Danske Bank played a major role, but other European banks—including Deutsche Bank, ING, ABN AMRO, NatWest, and Morgan Stanley (Switzerland)—were also implicated.

These cases show how financial systems can grow desensitized to ethical limits. A 2012 survey of U.S. and UK financial professionals found that 24% believed unethical or even illegal conduct might be necessary for success, revealing how peer behavior can normalize rule-bending even in heavily regulated environments.

Danske Bank's experience illustrates how deeply embedded institutions can become exposed to illicit flows moving through the wider financial system.[44]

Case Study: Danske Bank—profits, signals, and silence

Danske Bank, at the time Denmark's largest, became central to one of the biggest money-laundering scandals in modern history. Following its acquisition of the Finnish bank Sampo in 2007, Danske inherited a subsidiary in Tallinn, Estonia.

There, a small team processed over €200 billion, primarily from Russia and former Soviet states, routing funds through major institutions such as Deutsche Bank.[45] Certain anomalies should have raised red flags: despite representing only 0.5% of Danske's assets in 2011, the Tallinn branch contributed 11% of the group's profits, 99% of which came from non-resident clients. Internal memos showed *mild* concern over "Russian customers again," ironically flagged by Russian Central Bank staff. Weakness in governance was compounded by the fact the bank's Estonian branch operated IT systems separate from its headquarters, which delayed effective oversight and detection.

In 2013, a whistleblower reported suspicious payments linked to politically exposed Russian families. A critical internal audit followed in 2014. Yet Thomas Borgen, the bank's respected CEO, dismissed the concerns. He argued that it would be financially unwise to exit the offshore business prematurely. The supervisory board failed to intervene, later claiming there was "no basis" to challenge management. Warning signals were met with reassurances in a pattern of willful blindness where information was available, but ignored. Only in 2018, when the reputational damage became irreversible, was Borgen dismissed.

This case raises the question: how can non-executive board members improve the quality and independence of their information flow?

Fighting money laundering is not as easy as it seems

According to the UN Office on Drugs and Crime, between 2% and 5% of global GDP is laundered each year—equivalent to anything from $715 billion to $1.87 trillion.[46] Banks are caught in the middle. Everyone in the developed world should have access to a bank account, and institutions cannot exclude customers solely on the basis of suspicion. Besides black money looks just like white money, once it is in the system.

This regulatory ambiguity left frontline employees uncertain and inconsistent. Some turned a blind eye to dubious clients; others quietly reduced compliance alerts by disabling irritating anti-money-laundering warnings. Within this culture, money laundering was treated less as a crime and more as an administrative inconvenience. Yet it is through banks that money—whatever its color—enters the system, carrying with it a broader societal responsibility.

For non-executive board members to act effectively, insight into the bank's primary processes—how it actually operates—is essential. Understanding the "know-your-customer" principle has today become just as critical for oversight as familiarity with loan books and trading activities.

Guardians and gamblers: governance in banking

Most European banks employ a two-tier governance structure: an executive board for daily management and a supervisory board for control and accountability. The design aims to ensure distance, objectivity, and balance. In the United Kingdom and the United States, banks typically follow a one-tier model, where executives and non-executives serve on the same board.

In practice, neither system has proven superior. Repeated bank crises on both sides of the Atlantic show that structure alone cannot ensure stability. Bankers and their overseers operate within dense webs of regulation—Basel standards, capital ratios, liquidity rules, and compliance frameworks—yet effectiveness depends less on design than on the behavior of those applying them. Governance in banking is, therefore, not about who sits where but how they think and act when prudence is required.

Formal oversight can also create *expert bias*: the illusion that a thick layer of non-executives, auditors, and supervisors guarantees control. In reality, layered oversight often diffuses responsibility—everyone trusts the system, yet no one feels personally accountable. Investors and customers, meanwhile, can be lulled into complacency, focusing on returns rather than risk. Many sign contracts for complex products they barely understand. Today non-executive board members face often over 1,000 pages of reports and filings per month.

Compliance has expanded into an industry of its own. Non-executives spend increasing time analyzing risk reports, allowing less attention to be paid to culture and strategy—the very areas where the gravest threats often arise. Despite billions in fines and layers of new controls, illicit money flows persist. The CumEx case illustrates that: governance cannot rely on regulation alone but must rest on sound judgment, curiosity, and moral courage.

Case study: CumEx—just another day with eyes closed

Between 2001 and 2011, a network of traders, banks, tax and law specialists orchestrated the *CumEx* and *CumCum* schemes—widely regarded as one of Europe's largest dividend tax fraud. Exploiting legal ambiguities and complex share-trading structures, they enabled multiple reimbursements of a single dividend tax payment. The schemes were extremely profitable for banks but cost taxpayers an estimated €55–€150 billion across Europe, including more than €35 billion in Germany alone. Due to their cross-border design and legal ambiguity, they were difficult to uncover and prosecute. In recent years, several major banks have reached settlements after authorities confirmed their involvement in facilitating these trades, even as executives and non-executives claimed they had not seen the practices develop. The scandal exposed the influence of financial lobbying, regulatory inertia, and *bounded ethicality*—a culture where participants rationalized the trades as legitimate "tax optimization," while prosecutors ultimately classified key elements as fraud.

The risk committee: the paradox of control

Non-executive directors share the same cognitive limits as the managers they oversee. Confident in their expertise, many navigate endless reports yet still overestimate their grasp of risk—a classic case of *bounded rationality*. After the 2008 crisis, the U.S. Dodd-Frank Act (2010) required large banks to form risk committees, a model now adopted worldwide. But a paradox soon emerged: committee members, though diligent, appear to lose objectivity as their committees grow too close to risk managers, sometimes inclined to present optimistic, easily digestible views. Boards then defer to their committees, scarcely challenging their conclusions, if at all.

Beyond this oversight fatigue lies another concern: the soaring cost of compliance. In some banks, over a fifth of staff now work in control functions. The bureaucracy has become so heavy that legitimate clients struggle to open accounts. Banks risk discarding honest customers along with the money launderers.

The future of finance

Tougher regulations on fraud prevention and anti-money laundering, combined with higher capital requirements imposed by central banks, have triggered a wave of regulatory disintermediation. As traditional banks face billions in fines and stricter oversight, two forms of migration have emerged: criminal money flows shift into unregulated, instruments such as cryptocurrencies, while legitimate credit moves toward unregulated shadow banks.

The collapse in 2025 of First Brands and Tricolor, companies that transitioned from manufacturing and car finance into aggressive subprimelending to vulnerable borrowers, illustrates the risks when credit activity migrates beyond the regulatory perimeter. Operating outside the scrutiny applied to deposit-taking banks, both groups expanded rapidly before funding pressures and loan losses exposed fragile business models.

For traditional banks, the outcome is sobering: high compliance costs and reputational repair, while risk itself has largely relocated. For society, the uncomfortable truth remains: when regulation pushes activity into the shadows, risk flows to those least equipped to understand them. When oversight weakens, the public ultimately bears the cost.

SUMMARY AND CONCLUSION

Oversight of banks is one of the most complex tasks in corporate governance. Banks operate intricate business models in a densely regulated environment, where interconnected markets amplify spill over, and increase the burden on boards.

These threats are significant and persistent. The cultural tension in banking persists. Investment banking's incentives, with its appetite for high-stakes deal making, risk-taking, and performance pay, often clash with banking's core principles: prudence and responsible risk management. For non-executive directors, the challenge becomes acute when authority and narrative control are concentrated in a dominant chief executive, where information is asymmetric, and complexity favors insiders.

A further challenge lies in the often-overlooked connection between banking and illicit finance. While banks are indispensable to economies, they remain vulnerable to abuse.

Risk committees and endless reporting provide structure, but too often they become pitfalls rather than solutions. To ensure long-term resilience, the central governance task is not simply more compliance, but better judgment, balancing regulatory discipline with strategic understanding, and ensuring risk is confronted rather than displaced.

§3.6—UNICORNS AND LOCUSTS: GOVERNANCE IN PRIVATE EQUITY

Introduction

Private equity (PE) is one of finance's most powerful ownership models. It is also one of the most polarizing and least understood. Admired for reviving struggling companies and delivering strong returns, it is equally criticized for operating behind closed doors.

At one end of the PE spectrum, venture capital (VC) backs young startups, fueling growth and occasionally producing unicorns. At the other end, management buyout (MBO) investors take control of mature or underperforming firms, driving performance through operational pressure, tight targets, and disciplined timelines.

Intensity is the defining feature. PE rewards speed, discipline, and measurable results. But its heavy use of debt, playbook of deep restructuring, and aggressive recapitalization and cash extraction can impose real social costs on employees, suppliers, and communities. These pressures make strong internal oversight essential.

Non-executive directors in private equity are usually not independent, but they are meant to provide that counterweight. Their effectiveness varies widely. To be credible, they must understand the behavioral engine that drives PE: the culture of urgency, the relentless cash focus in leveraged transactions, the expectations of investors, and the power dynamics that shape how boards actually work. These forces set the boundaries for challenge, accountability, and ethical restraint.

This section explores what society can realistically expect from oversight in one of capitalism's most high-octane, behavior-driven arenas.

Venture capital, a risky gamble?

Venture capital (VC) is the classic form of early-stage private equity, and especially the United States is the most developed VC market. Silicon Valley investors, from the 1970s onward, helped founders fuel the exponential growth of their high-tech start-ups from humble beginnings in garages and college dorms. Examples include Apple, Microsoft, Amazon, and Nvidia. Today, these companies are the most valuable in the world.

VCs do far more than provide funding. They help build founding teams, sharpen strategic focus (market positioning and organizational design), and open doors to international networks of suppliers, customers, and academic partners. They also provide the non-executive directors and expert advisors to guide a firm's early governance and assure hands-on support during its critical primary growth stages.

Despite the term "venture capital," the activities of these firms are a far cry from simple gambling. The professional venture capitalist is highly selective and works on the assumption that every investment must have a credible path to success. The underlying logic is behavioral: spreading a portfolio too widely risks diluting attention, commitment, and oversight. Instead, focused involvement, sector specialization, and hands-on engagement are essential levers, from the initial idea to maturity.

MBO: smart strategy or self-deception? Behavioral drivers

Entire industries have been reshaped by management buyouts (MBOs), ranging from underperforming divisions carved out of larger firms to publicly listed companies taken private. MBO investors typically target companies with strong fundamentals that are underperforming within their existing holding structure. Particularly attractive are firms with solid or high-potential cash flows, operating in stable or growing markets. Occasionally, PE will seize an opportunistic deal on the edge of collapse when the upside looks irresistible.

MBOs fundamentally alter incentives. Managers become co-owners through equity participation, hence the term *management buyout*. Unlike executives at publicly traded companies, their rewards depend almost entirely on a successful exit. *Satisficing behavior*, characterized by settling for "good enough" outcomes, as evident in underperforming listed companies, gives way to a keener focus on operations and goals.

Underperforming publicly traded companies have long been a favorite hunting ground for PE. The iconic RJR Nabisco transaction—taken private by KKR in 1988—became one of the first true megadeals and a symbol of PE's capacity to drive restructuring, efficiency and strategic renewal. PE also invests in family-owned businesses that lack a successor, such as the Italian eyewear chain Vision Group and the fashion group Hugo Boss. Equally significant are the many corporate spin-offs, such as that of Unilever's margarine division. Much of PE's edge lies in focus: tighter governance, operational discipline, and in the case of leveraged buyouts, the amplifying effect of debt.

For non-executive directors, this brings a distinct set of risks to monitor. Fresh leadership can sharpen focus and discipline, yet when overconfidence meets ambitious targets, it can create a false sense of control. A narrow financial focus may foster short-termism and increase pressure to extract value, including balance sheet items such as corporate pension reserves. Cost-cutting can be unavoidable, but its impact on employee morale and long-term cohesion requires careful attention. Financial optimism combined with heavy leverage can prove disastrous when results fall short or interest rates rise—as the collapses of the large LBOs (Leveraged Buyouts) such as TXU, Debenhams, and Hertz have shown.

As governance shifts from public to private, so does the balance between oversight and operational execution. In public companies, executive directors typically operate independently or at arm's length from shareholders, providing only periodic updates to a diffuse group of these. By contrast, MBO executives work under the direct and intensive oversight of the investor-shareholder. The PE fund holds ultimate control, usually as a majority shareholder, and often through non-executive board representation.

Closer PE shareholder involvement in executive decisions need not be troublesome. As one executive of a Philips division recalled after it was taken private: "Once under PE ownership, I never missed the slow-moving bureaucracy of my former parent. Budget decisions no longer had to pass through layers of approval."[47]

Case study: Philips divest and regret—when private equity captures the upside

From 1990 to 1996, CEO Jan Timmer of Philips gained recognition for steering the faltering Dutch electronics firm through "Operation Centurion," an intensive effort to divest non-core activities and restore profitability. He had inherited a culture marked by complacency and weak entrepreneurship. In his biography, he later criticized his successors for allowing those same tendencies to return. Rather than pursuing strategic renewal, they relied on divestments.

In 2006, this approach proved costly to shareholders when Philips sold its semiconductor division to a PE consortium led by KKR. By the end of 2024, the spin-off—renamed NXP—was worth more than twice Philips' market capitalization. A similar pattern emerged with ASML: instead of cultivating long-term innovation internally, Philips felt forced to divest the business for a fraction of its eventual value, as ASML later became one of Europe's most valuable technology companies.

These outcomes show how organizations can revert to familiar routines after the departure of reforming leadership. Faced with uncertainty, boards, including their non-executives, tend to favor strategies that feel easy, such as divestments, whereas long-term renewal demands sustained investment and tolerance for risk. The private equity governance model operates differently: with concentrated ownership and shorter reporting lines, they impose discipline and pursue focused strategies to unlock potential. In hindsight, the value created at NXP and ASML highlights how governance structure and strategic time horizon can materially influence outcomes.

PE firms are typically bound by agreements with their financial sponsors, such as pension funds and institutional investors, to exit their investments within roughly five to seven years period while delivering substantial returns. To meet this compressed timeline, value-creation plans are often already drafted during the due diligence phase—the comprehensive pre-acquisition review. During this stage, PE teams identify operational improvements, cost reductions, and growth opportunities that will bring future returns.

This creates a fundamental governance tension. While speed and decisiveness are essential for capturing "low-hanging fruit" in the early years, PE firms must also balance these short-term gains with a credible long-term strategy. Ultimately, a company's future exit valuation depends more on its future growth potential than on its current performance.

The financial trapeze

In the MBO model, PE investors pursue a clear value creation agenda. Competition among PE firms has intensified over the last two decades, pushing acquisition multiples higher. Leverage has become essential to meet ambitious return targets—hence the term "Leveraged Buyout" (LBO). Leverage boosts returns on invested equity when performance improves. But when performance weakens, debt can quickly turn from a tool into a trap, amplifying losses and financial strain.

The 2005 buyout of Toys "R" Us illustrates this risk. Burdened with more than $5 billion in debt, the toy retailer collapsed in 2018. Critics, citing asset stripping, argued its capital structure left too little room to adapt to declining sales. Roughly 30,000 employees lost their jobs, many initially without severance pay. A cautionary tale about leverage in cyclical businesses.[48]

The leverage-intensive strategy has flourished since the mid-2000s, as abundant credit flowed into private equity. Central banks in the United States and Europe have for years provided a solid floor for leveraged finance by maintaining historically low interest rates, even dipping into negative rates in Europe between 2014 and 2022. Borrowing costs fell sharply and exit valuations benefited from abundant liquidity.[49]

The result was a long period of exceptional growth of PE, as illustrated by Figure 3.2—showing private equity investments in MBOs since 1996 in relation to the benchmark

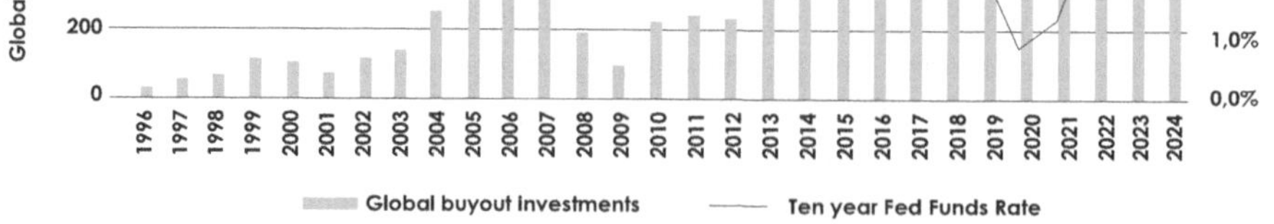

Figure 3.2

Relationship Between Long-Term (Ten Years) Interest and MBO Investments

Source: St Louis FED, Long-term Federal Reserve Board 10-Year Interest Rate, Bain & Company, Global Private Equity Report 2025.

ten-year interest rate. The recent shift in policy has altered that equation, as higher interest rates since 2022 have shown an effect on investment activity.

Power and accountability in private equity

The rise of private equity has been accompanied by growing unease about its expanding economic and political influence. Admired for its ability to restructure industries and drive efficiency, PE is also viewed as a closed system of capital and control, operating beyond public scrutiny. Critics argue that some sectors risk becoming fragile when aggressive debt and short-term financial engineering dominate decision-making.

In the United States, home to the world's largest private equity market, the industry has evolved from a financial force into a political constituency. Whereas once investment bankers dominated senior government roles, PE executives now occupy them, participating in the policy debates that shape the industry's regulatory framework. A clear illustration of this development is the long-running defense of the *carried-interest tax provision*, which allows fund managers to pay capital gains rather than income tax rates on performance fees. Despite repeated bipartisan efforts to reform transparency and fiscal treatment, industry lobbying has preserved the status quo, and proposals for greater transparency on fees and portfolio risk have been diluted.[50]

This concentration of influence contrasts with the limited power of pension funds, the sector's main financial backers. Dependent on PE to achieve target returns, they face its steep management costs and have little say over investment strategy. The classic *2 and 20 fee structure*—2% annual management fee, 20% profit share on exit is meant to stimulate performance, but also erodes long-term returns for investors.

Efforts to reclaim control, such as CalPERS' decision to create its own PE arm, show the difficulty of reconciling public-duty mandates with private-market culture. The behavioral tension remains clear: in a system built on alignment, the interests of investors, executives, and society rarely align perfectly—and the absence of robust accountability mechanisms risks turning financial sophistication into unchecked power without responsibility.

A new dynamic in the boardroom

It is crucial for non-executives to recognize that private-equity ownership introduces a fundamentally different governance dynamic, with leadership and oversight that diverge sharply from what they may be familiar with in listed or family-owned companies. The contrast is most evident in board composition and executive appointments. Whereas family businesses often fill senior roles through lineage or internal succession, PE-owned companies recruit on the basis of merit, experience, and strategic fit. Expectations are high, and appointees are chosen for their resilience and ability to perform under pressure—a thick skin is essential.

Leadership turnover is defining feature of PE ownership. Research shows that around 73% of CEOs leave after a PE takeover, voluntarily or otherwise.[51] Executive turnover rarely stops at the top: within three years of a buyout, over half of senior executives, including CFOs and COOs, are also replaced. Many step out for three main reasons. First, cultural misalignment—not all executives adapt to the investor-driven, high-intensity environment that defines PE ownership. Second, stress and performance pressure, as compressed timelines and exit-linked incentives drive burnout. Third, data-driven control, where younger investment managers armed with analytical models constrain entrepreneurial freedom and decision latitude. In short, the relentless pace and intensity of PE ownership gradually erode independence and heighten leadership churn.

Redefining independence in the PE boardroom

Unlike their counterparts in listed firms, non-executive directors in PE-backed companies are rarely independent. Most come from the investment fund or its immediate network, ensuring alignment of interests of shareholders. They bring deep operational knowledge and play an active role in setting goals, shaping strategy, and overseeing execution—an approach that would be seen as overreach in a public company.

Remuneration further shapes this distinctive governance culture. In many PE-backed companies, investment managers, appointed as non-executive directors participate in the business's upside through share options or carried-interest schemes. This aligns the board closely with investors, reinforcing a shared focus on value creation and exit performance. Yet it also changes the atmosphere in the boardroom: discussions become more transactional, and the line between independent oversight and investor advocacy can blur. While such incentives sharpen commercial discipline, they can also reduce the willingness to challenge aggressive financing tactics or short-term priorities.

While independent non-executives are a minority, some are appointed to signal balance and serve as a governance bridge between investors and management. This is common in large, regulated, or high-profile companies, or when preparing for an IPO, where governance must meet public market expectations. In leveraged transactions, their role becomes particularly important: decisions about how much debt is sustainable are not merely financial calculations but governance choices, as the case study of Estro below shows. An effective chair mediates between the investor's performance agenda and management's need for autonomy, lending stability and external credibility to the board. Understanding that even then loyalty to the fund's return logic can quietly crowd out independent judgment.

From dynamics to consequences

The following cases illustrate how the pressures and incentives of PE ownership can reshape board behavior, sometimes sharpening oversight, but at other times eroding independence, challenge, and trust. They show what happens when alignment becomes conformity and when the search for value pushes governance to its limits.

Case Study 1: Estro (Catalpa childcare) when leverage enters the nursery

In 2023, the Dutch Enterprise Chamber ruled on the governance of Estro, a childcare group with revenues of €200 million. Sold in 2010 to U.S. private equity firm Providence Equity Partners, it was burdened with nearly €800 million in debt—an unusually high level of leverage for a provider of publicly subsidized services. The court found that Estro's board, including its non-executive directors, had approved a structure favoring shareholder returns over financial sustainability. They were held personally liable for failing to meet their duty of loyalty and care. The judgment stressed that directors must challenge financial engineering and protect the viability of essential public services. Estro became a landmark reminder that board passivity and deference to investors can turn fiduciary duty into personal exposure.[52]

Case Study 2: Southern Cross Healthcare (UK)—privatization and the price of property

Southern Cross, once the UK's largest care-home operator, collapsed in 2011, putting 31,000 elderly residents at risk. After being privatized and acquired by Blackstone in 2004, the company sold its 750 care homes and leased them back under expensive rent clauses. Blackstone reportedly made around £1 billion extracting cash through dividends and share sales around the 2006 IPO, while the group was left with limited reserves and roughly £240 million in annual rent obligations. Its critics, however, argued that social care was treated "like any common or garden commodity".[53] When government austerity measures reduced public funding, the model imploded. MPs later condemned board complacency and the absence of care expertise, describing governance as "asleep at the wheel." Although no directors were sanctioned, the collapse led to the Care Act 2014, which empowered regulators to monitor the financial health of major care providers.

This case shows how perspectives on private equity diverge depending on one's position. For investors, it was a commercially successful, well-timed transaction. For residents and families, it highlighted how financial engineering can magnify insecurity for vulnerable people raising broader concerns about who ultimately bears the risks in publicly funded care. For non-executive directors, it highlights how financial priorities can influence and dilute their moral decisions.[54]

SUMMARY AND CONCLUSION

Private equity (PE) has become a defining force in modern capitalism. Venture capital has launched global tech giants and remains essential for innovation, while management buyouts have revitalized underperforming companies and supported succession in family firms.

But a shift to PE ownership brings its own behavioral dynamics. Executives face intense performance pressure, compressed timelines, and powerful financial incentives. These incentives create a heightened sense of ownership—sometimes stronger than in listed firms—sharpening drive and discipline but also narrowing attention and encouraging greater risk-taking. Non-executive directors are expected to provide a counterweight, yet often operate with limited information or lack full independence, given their close alignment with investor expectations.

In sectors such as healthcare, childcare, and other essential services, PE decisions directly affect vulnerable stakeholders and can erode public trust.

Failures in oversight, whether shaped by bias, time pressure, or conflicted judgment, can lead to reputational harm and personal liability. Courts increasingly stress that directors must act prudently and independently, especially when aggressive recapitalizations, dividend extractions, or debt structures risk harming creditors or the public interest.

Ultimately, non-executive directors must ensure that financial engineering does not override solvency, fairness, or societal responsibility. Good PE governance is not just about creating wealth—it is about preserving integrity, accountability, and sound behavior under pressure.

§3.7—A SUSTAINABLE MODEL: GOVERNANCE IN THE COOPERATIVE

Introduction

Cooperatives are built on solidarity—people working together toward shared goals and mutual benefit. The spirit of cooperation has deep historical roots and remains one of humanity's most enduring behavioral strengths. The power of cooperatives lies not only in collective action but also in trust, reciprocity, and shared responsibility. Solidarity is not merely social glue; it is a governance asset.

Over the last century, cooperatives have become a vital part of the global economy. Their participative model allows members to learn from one another and achieve economies of scale no individual member could reach alone. Yet cooperation is not always smooth. Members move at different speeds, and diverging interests can strain unity and trust.

The layered governance structure that protects cooperatives from the hubris of individual leaders also implies trade-offs. A participative model fosters inclusion and careful deliberation, but it can also slow decision-making and blur accountability. Ultimately, cooperative governance is human work—dependent on dialogue, patience, and integrity.

How, then, should executive and non-executive directors navigate these tensions? What is their role in preserving cooperative values while keeping the organization agile and sustainable?

A formidable force

Flowers, potatoes, milk, supermarkets, insurance, banking services—even funerals. Cooperatives come in all shapes and sizes and are a formidable force in the global economy. Today, around three million cooperatives with over a billion members account for roughly 10% of the world's employed population.[55]

The cooperative movement dates back to the nineteenth century, inspired by the ideas of German mayor Friedrich Wilhelm Raiffeisen.[56] Confronting the exploitative practices of local moneylenders—whom he compared to *Giftpflanzen* ("poisonous plants")—he created a charitable fund that offered loans instead of alms, enabling struggling entrepreneurs to rebuild their livelihoods. This approach laid the foundations of cooperative banking and eventually inspired the broader cooperative movement across industries.

Within a cooperative, members join forces to achieve the much-needed economies of scale. Entrepreneurs in the same sector pool their resources for purchasing or marketing. Examples include agricultural cooperatives such as Fonterra (New Zealand's largest dairy company) and Dutch Royal FloraHolland (the world's largest flower auction). Supermarket cooperatives follow the same model, including the UK's Co-op, Japan's Co-op Kobe, and Italy's Coop Italia.

Beyond commerce, citizens and professionals have formed health insurance and guarantee funds, such as State Farm (the largest U.S. mutual insurance provider) and Achmea (a Dutch insurance giant). In banking, Crédit Agricole (France) and Rabobank (the Netherlands) illustrate the strength of financial cooperatives. Service providers like PwC also operate on cooperative principles. More recently, cooperatives have appeared in areas such as renewable energy (wind farms) and housing collectives.

For a long time, cooperatives have been celebrated as an uncontested governance model, characterized by a dedicated member base. But times have changed. Agricultural cooperatives, such as Mondragon (a Spanish diversified group spanning finance, industry, and retail), FrieslandCampina (a Dutch dairy cooperative), and Cenex Harvest States (a U.S. farm supplies cooperative), have become global players. In their markets, scale, efficiency, and internationally competitive strategies are crucial.

While speed is important in today's economy, the traditional governance model of a cooperative—where every member has a say—can slow down decision-making, reducing its agility. Leadership teams, in growth mode, may race ahead—only to realize that their members have been left behind, leading to internal friction, delays, or pushback.

At the same time, the participation of members in strategy can also be a key strength of a cooperative. Once a decision is made, internal support for implementation is strong, ensuring alignment and long-term commitment from its members.

A two-speed cooperative

Members of business-to-business cooperatives not only share membership but also run their own businesses, each facing unique challenges and opportunities. Even when they operate in the same industry and share common interests, the size of the companies of their members can differ significantly. Some are large, internationally active enterprises; others are smaller, locally focused, and more traditional family firms. These differences can naturally lead to contrasting views on innovation, investment, and strategy.

A telling example comes from the decorative plants sector, a typical but economically significant industry in the Netherlands. Within a single cooperative, one end of the spectrum consists of small entrepreneurs growing organic nursery plants for the local market. At the other end are multinationals operating large-scale nurseries in Kenya and Ethiopia, exporting across global supply chains. Such diversity breeds tension: members hold different expectations of what the cooperative should deliver.

Both business models carry their own advantages and trade-offs. Local production supports biodiversity and traceability, but may struggle to compete on volume and cost. Global production enables efficiency and market reach, but also brings global risks, ranging from unfair labor conditions to environmental impacts abroad, and exposure to a weak rule of law environment.

The challenges of international expansion

Cooperatives operating in international markets often face pressure to grow through acquisitions. The credo seems up, or out. While global expansion can open new opportunities, it also introduces internal tensions. Take FrieslandCampina, one of the world's most successful dairy cooperatives. Competing globally with publicly traded giants like Nestlé and Danone, it pursues an ambitious strategy—acquiring businesses in countries such as Pakistan and China to secure a local presence in key growth markets.

Such expansion requires significant capital investment, experienced international management, and strong oversight from directors who understand the complexities of global business environments. Beyond financial and operational demands, it can also bring new governance and ethical risks. Business cultures abroad may differ substantially from those in the cooperative's home country, particularly in norms around corruption, human rights, and regulatory compliance. In the meantime, for members in the home country, expansion into unfamiliar countries can feel like an identity shift. Dairy farmers joined the cooperative to sell their milk, not to build a multinational. They face pressing challenges at home—from nitrogen regulations to the effects of climate change. Their top concern is straightforward, but vital: that the cooperative pays them a fair and sustainable price for their milk. Without this, many cannot survive. If prices fall, some may leave for competing milk processors, weakening the cooperative's supply base and reducing its market power.

The board is therefore walking on eggshells—balancing global ambitions with the everyday realities of its farmer-members, ensuring that international expansion does not erode trust, identity, or economic viability. This raises a critical governance question: how can non-executive directors effectively oversee international ventures, while safeguarding the cooperative's foundational values?

Oversight and the cooperative: a balancing act

Because cooperatives originate from local initiatives, each with its own culture and history, their governance structures vary widely. Legislators allow flexibility in how oversight is organized. Smaller cooperatives often retain a more democratic model with direct member representation, while larger ones require a more formal system. Still, two central bodies are present in most structures: the General Assembly of Members (GAM), which represents all members, and a smaller Members' Council (MC), which in practice often functions as the highest decision-making authority.

As cooperatives grow, oversight becomes more complex. The GAM or MC typically appoints the non-executive board members—most of whom are cooperative members—while independent directors usually form about one-third of the board. These external directors are expected to contribute managerial expertise and broader strategic insight. In several countries, the works council has the right to nominate one-third of the non-executive directors (see Figure 3.3), reinforcing employee representation in strategic decisions.

Independent board members are sometimes viewed with distrust. Do they understand the business and the day-to-day realities of its members? The concern is not unfounded. In large, complex cooperatives, the top echelon sits far from the member base, and information reaching the board is filtered by management. Directors must therefore draw on experience, remain attuned to members' concerns, and help anchor the cooperative's institutional resilience.

These governance challenges intensify when cooperatives must balance the interests of large, internationally active members with those of smaller, locally oriented ones. Smaller members may no longer recognize themselves in a governance culture marked by high executive salaries, corporate consultants, or abstract boardroom language infused with big-business jargon.

Different cooperatives make different choices. Most often, cooperatives remain closely connected to their members, which tends to foster stronger internal alignment. Avebe, the largest potato cooperative in the Netherlands, offers a telling example. To celebrate

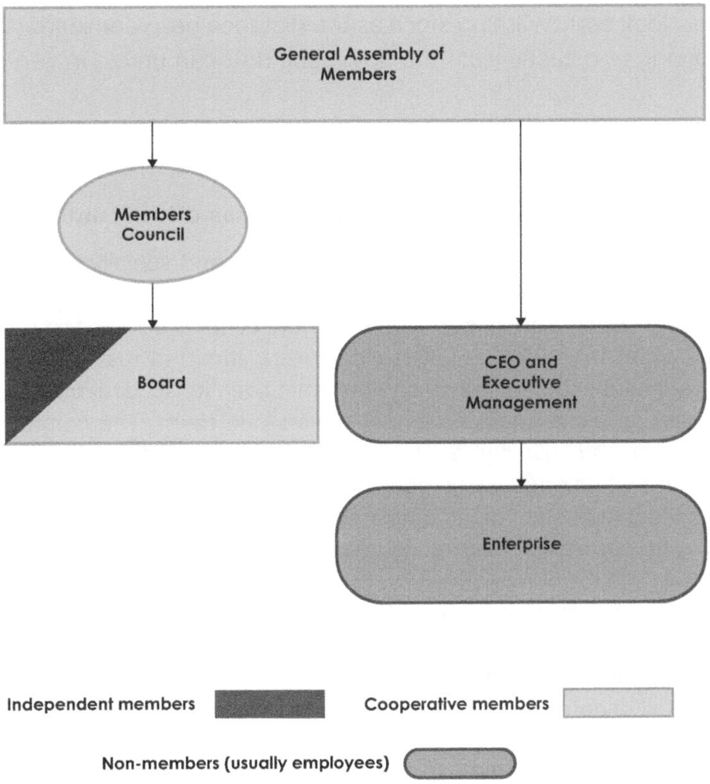

Figure 3.3
Governance Bodies in the Cooperative

its centenary, it organized open activities at the potato farmers' yards and in their factories, emphasizing shared identity over corporate formality. Another large cooperative took a different path, hosting a high-profile anniversary event with a costly celebrity speaker—drawing criticism as the celebration coincided with a cost-cutting drive, signaling growing distance from members who were not invited.

Where these dynamics can create tension or conflicts of interest, independent directors play a pivotal role: staying accountable and approachable to members, balancing competing interests, and navigating internal frictions. The board as a whole must safeguard the cooperative's founding values while supporting its long-term strategic direction. Oversight in the cooperation requires patience, communication, and sustained attention to the member base.

In environments of trust and proximity, decisions may take longer to form—but once made, they are often swiftly implemented due to strong cooperative support.

Governance in the wrong corner

Even in cooperatives—organizations built on trust, shared purpose, and member control—governance can gradually drift into the wrong corner. A strong values-driven identity can create a false sense of safety, dulling vigilance and weakening challenge. Members and directors may overlook early warning signs as the distance between leadership and the base grows. The following two cases illustrate how such drift can unfold in very different ways.

Case Study: Rabobank—when distance erodes a values-driven culture

Cooperatives often take pride in being member-centric and socially rooted, but that very identity can blunt vigilance. Rabobank—long celebrated as one of the Netherlands' strongest cooperatives—offers a striking example of how cultural distance and complexity can undermine oversight. In 2009, CEO Bert Heemskerk admitted that the financial products presented to the board had become so complex that even its six directors, with a combined 150 years of banking experience, no longer understood them. The comforting belief that "co-ops are different and have higher governance standards" masked a gradual progression toward risk-taking that no one fully grasped.

Rabobank built its reputation on its origins as a farmers' cooperative, where prudence and trust resulted in its rare AAA credit rating. Yet behind the polished image, its leadership in Utrecht was drawn into the bonus-driven world of global finance—a world it barely understood. The bank proudly took a seat on the panel that set LIBOR and EURIBOR rates. However, in an environment of weak management oversight, its traders colluded with peers at UBS and Deutsche Bank to manipulate rates for mutual gain.

From Utrecht to London, traders slipped into coded chatrooms, characterized by ego-fueled banter and casual arrogance—a textbook case of *behavioral drift*. "Don't worry, mate," one wrote, "there are bigger crooks in the market than us." Regulators uncovered the widespread misconduct. UK and U.S. authorities fined the bank €774 million; the CEO resigned, and a new board was installed. Yet the drift continued at home: account managers sold complex swaps to small entrepreneurs under the guise of protection, triggering €950 million in customer compensation and causing deep reputational harm.

Rabobank's lesson is behavioral, not moral. Distance between board and trading floor, competitive pressure, and institutional prestige quietly replaced proximity, humility, and purpose—illustrating that even values-driven institutions can drift when oversight fails to keep pace with expansion and financial sophistication.

A final cautionary tale from the UK, illustrates how a cooperative's values can become a blind spot—especially when a friendly, well-meaning culture masks gaps in competencies and allows amateurism to infiltrate senior oversight roles.

Case Study: Co-op—when values blind governance

The Co-operative Group had a long history as a trusted factor in its community. As a mother explained to her child, quoted in an investigation into the Co-op abuse case, "They're different from other shops. We own the Co-op. It's for people like us." That genuine belief dulled scrutiny and created space for leadership drift.

By 2014, the Co-op was an £8 billion enterprise, suddenly on the brink of collapse, undone by reckless expansion and weak governance. At the center stood Paul Flowers—a Methodist pastor and Labour politician with no financial expertise—chairing one of Britain's largest companies. The board, too, was unequipped: well-meaning but underqualified members overseeing a complex bank. Minimal legal requirements had allowed a plasterer and a greengrocer to take positions in the oversight body of a multibillion-pound balance sheet.

A government inquiry described the board's culture as one of "denial of responsibility, excessive wordiness, and hiding behind values." Moral rhetoric displaced competence, and ethical self-confidence muted challenge. Democratic governance appeared largely symbolic; a convoluted system of selecting non-executives and council members made accountability almost impossible.

Flowers' downfall was spectacular—drug use, lavish spending, and political entanglements—but the deeper failure was cultural: a belief that good intentions guaranteed good governance. Losses totaled £1.5 billion.

Recovery required a complete overhaul. A strong Members' Council was installed with clear authority to define values and intervene when governance drifted. The case underscores a blunt truth: values strengthen cooperatives only when paired with behavioral competence, independence, and vigilance.

SUMMARY AND CONCLUSION

Traditional cooperatives prioritize cooperation, solidarity, and long-term continuity over short-term profit. In a world moving toward sustainable business strategies, the long-term, down-to-earth focus of the cooperative model offers a compelling alternative to the quarterly-driven logic of listed companies.

Yet large financial cooperatives have become more commercially driven, sometimes diluting member influence. Their founding principles remain a vital source of identity and resilience, but preserving them requires active governance. For boards and non-executive directors, the challenge is to balance member interests with competitive pressures and strategic growth.

Members do not form a homogeneous group; differing expectations and informal influence can shape outcomes as much as formal voting rights. Under competitive pressure, executive boards can drift from the cooperative base.

Effective governance therefore depends on a balanced board composition—combining member directors and independent external professionals capable of acting as mediators and counterweights, guarding against strategic drift and cultural distance.

Ultimately, awareness of the behavioral dynamics embedded in culture, influence, and trust is central to protecting the cooperative's integrity and long-term strength. For non-executive directors, the task is not limited to stewarding member interests; it also involves overseeing the board's performance. Their oversight carries societal weight because cooperatives provide essential services and anchor regional economies. Sound judgment must, therefore, balance member benefits with broader societal responsibilities.

§3.8—VOC: BEHAVIORAL GOVERNANCE IN HISTORICAL PERSPECTIVE

Introduction

No governance book is complete without the case of the Vereenigde Oost-Indische Compagnie (VOC). As the first Dutch joint-stock company and a pioneer of modern corporate governance, the VOC enjoyed a long, though not eternal, life. This case examines the contrasts between today's ESG goals and the governance norms of the VOC era, highlighting how concepts of oversight, human behavior and moral responsibility evolve unevenly over time.

The VOC mentality

Once the most powerful company in the world, the VOC symbolized the wealth of the Dutch Golden Age. Merchants loaded cargo ships bound for the East Indies, exploiting price gaps in Asian spices. In the early 2000s, Dutch political discourse briefly revived the term "VOC mentality," as shorthand for entrepreneurial boldness.

But subsequent historical research has documented its brutal underbelly: a colonial business model built on slave labor, piracy, and opium trade. In Batavia (Jakarta), over half the population was enslaved. Under the Governor General Jan Pieterszoon Coen, violence became an instrument of corporate policy. After resistance on Banda Island, he ordered a massacre of the male population and destroyed all clove trees.

This historical reassessment aligns with modern ESG concerns. Parallels between colonial exploitation and current supply chain labor abuses became harder to ignore. Yet today's political resistance to ESG initiatives shows how economic interests, based on power play, can still outweigh longer-term social considerations.

Corporate governance before it had a name

During the Eighty Years' War, Johan van Oldenbarnevelt, a state attorney, spearheaded the foundation of the VOC in 1602. Parliament granted it commercial and military authority, using revenues to fund its independence war with Spain. This *Octroye* granted a monopoly on Asian trade and legal cover to seize enemy ships—powers that blurred the line between commerce and sanctioned piracy.

The VOC was governed by the Heeren XVII, an early form of corporate board drawn from the company's major supporting harbor cities. The VOC also pioneered institutional features that resemble modern governance practices, including director appointments, financial disclosure, shareholder structure, and risk management. It was the first Dutch company to issue tradable shares, which were bought and sold in Amsterdam. Any resident with sufficient capital could invest.

Yet major flaws emerged. Large investors could review financials only under strict secrecy; small shareholders were left in the dark. On long voyages, power was concentrated in the hands of the Opperkoopman (the Chief Merchant) and the captain. Given the distances and limited communication involved, distant observers couldn't monitor onboard operations, private dealings or conflicts of interest. Back home, the Heeren XVII effectively exercised oversight—without external counterbalance.

Cracks in the system, decline and fall

By the late seventeenth century, doubts about the VOC's integrity grew. In 1693, the aging jurist Pieter van Dam audited its operations, reviewing auditing structures he had previously helped shape. Abuses were rampant despite formal codes: "administrators shall solemnly promise, on honor, oath, and piety, that they will conduct themselves well and faithfully."

As the VOC matured, its governance grew more lax still. To sustain high dividends, it relied on advance payments and bond issuance while delaying employee wages. This structure collapsed in 1740, prompting a state audit uncovering mismanagement, bloated payrolls, and corruption in Asia. The Heeren XVII resisted reform. In 1785, the VOC lost its monopoly on spices. By 1794, financially abandoned by Holland, the company collapsed.

The legacy

The remainder of the VOC was nationalized by the Dutch state, but colonial mechanisms persisted as the Dutch East Indies transitioned into a state-run colony. In 1860, with the publication of novel *Max Havelaar by the Dutch writer* Multatuli, a former colonial official who turned critic, did colonial abuses become widely debated in the Netherlands. Only recently, however, have museums added disclaimers to Jan Pieterszoon Coen's portraits.

Despite progress, the UK's Modern Slavery Act (2015) and stronger ESG standards, the road toward responsible governance remains rocky. Modern scandals expose sweatshops, forced labor in cobalt mines, and abuses in major infrastructure works.

Conclusion: old habits die hard

The VOC presents a vivid early example of behavioral governance: bold in innovation, yet blind to ethical costs. The structural tension between commercial ambition and effective oversight is not new.

As the global economy moves toward more sustainable models, its history reminds us how quickly "best practices" become moral blind spots. Whether ESG will truly transform business—or be watered down by economic and political pressures—remains uncertain. But one thing is clear: today's non-executive directors operate in a world where accountability is more immediate, more public and more personal than in the era of the Heeren XVII.

REFLECTION QUESTIONS

Questions §3.1—Different governance for different purposes: defining oversight

1. Does the company's ownership structure support its long-term health and strategic direction?
2. Are potential conflicts between shareholders and stakeholders openly surfaced and constructively challenged in the boardroom?
3. Have non-executive directors reflected on how competing governance models (family-owned, listed, PE, cooperative) shape the company's competitive position?

Questions §3.2—All in the family: governance in the family business

1. How open is the relationship between the director-owner, the family, and the board, and is external challenge genuinely welcomed?
2. Is succession planning both realistic and future-oriented—and is the current leader still the right fit for the next phase?
3. Is long-term independence viable, or could a strategic partnership offer a stronger path to continuity and family legacy?

Questions §3.3—Navigating between Scylla and Charybdis: governance in listed companies

1. Do non-executive directors truly understand what is happening inside the company, or are they hearing only the polished version?
2. To what extent are they truly independent from the CEO, and do they have the courage to act when leadership change is needed?
3. How proactively does the board surface and resolve conflicts of interest among executives, shareholders, and stakeholders?

Questions §3.4—Reward, risk: the CEO pay debate

1. Are executive rewards genuinely aligned with long-term value creation, or do incentives unintentionally fuel risk-taking?

2. Does the board consider how executive pay affects employees, public trust, and the company's license to operate?
3. How can intrinsic motivation and non-financial goals be meaningfully embedded into reward frameworks?

Questions §3.5—Guardians and gamblers: governance in banking

1. Does the board regularly test whether culture, *tone at the top*, and risk appetite truly match strategic goals?
2. Are non-executive directors close enough to sense risks early, sufficiently experienced and independent, to challenge leadership effectively?
3. Does the board regularly review how risk is managed across the organization?

Questions §3.6—Unicorns and locusts: governance in private equity

1. Does each director meaningfully contribute to the PE board? Do they have the personality and expertise to perform in a high-octane environment?
2. Does the board rigorously assess whether financial engineering and leverage strengthen long-term resilience, stress-test downside scenarios and maintain adequate capital buffers?
3. Are the company's plans future-proof and value-creating—financially, strategically, and societally?

Questions §3.7—A sustainable model: governance in the cooperative

1. How well do non-executive directors, the Members' Council, the executive board, and management collaborate—and does trust remain stable under pressure?
2. How strong and structured is the board's connection to the cooperative's members, and is real proximity maintained?
3. Are governance skills and experience sufficient to balance local loyalties with global strategy and societal responsibility?

Questions §3.8—VOC: behavioral governance in historical perspective

1. Are the ethical consequences of the business model actively challenged at the board level?
2. Could critical information be delayed or softened before reaching the board—and how is transparency safeguarded?
3. Which behavioral factors—integrity, adaptability, and stakeholder trust—will determine the company's long-term resilience?

NOTES

1 J. Schumpeter (1942), *Capitalism, Socialism, and Democracy*, New York: Harper & Bros.

2 Timo O. Vuori, Quy N. Huy (2015 September), *Distributed attention and shared emotions in the innovation process: How Nokia lost the smartphone battle*, Administrative Science Quarterly, 61.

3 Teri van der Heijden, Barbara Rijlaarsdam (2018), *Blokker, hoe het imperium de familie ontglipt (Blokker, How the Family Lost Its Empire)*, Amsterdam: Ambo.

4 Adam Smith (1776), *An Inquiry Into the Nature and Causes of the Wealth of Nations.*

5 See also K.M. Eisenhardt (1989), *Agency theory: An assessment and review*, The Academy of Management Review, 14(1), 57–74.

6 *Family Business in Europe*, Website of the European Commission.

7 Russell Reynolds (2019 February 21), *Pan-European RRA Study on Family-Owned Business.*

8 EY Global (2021), *How Family Enterprises Are Embracing Sustainability.*

9 STEP Project Global Consortium & KPMG Private Enterprise (2024), *Unlocking Legacy—The Path to Superior Growth in Family Businesses.*

10 Manfred F.R. Kets de Vries, Randel S. Carlock, Elizabeth Florent-Treacy (2007), *Family Business on the Couch. A Psychological Perspective*, John Wiley & Sons, New York.

11 Donald J. Savoie (2013), *Harrison McCain: Single-Minded Purpose*, McGill-Queen's University Press.

12 De Standaard (2006 April 10), *Ex-burgemeester, ex-rechterhand 'boer' Clerck, ex-wielermecenas (Former Mayor, Former Right-Hand Man, 'Farmer' Clerck, Former Cycling Sponsor).*

13 Alan Hope (2021 June 25), *Major Fraud Case Ends as Accused Pay €50 Million Settlement*, The Brussels Times.

14 Focus Online (2021 Juni 1), *Ex-Aufsichtsrätin packt aus: Ex-Wirecard-Managerin zum Betrugsskandal (Former Supervisory Board Member Speaks Out on Fraud Scandal).*

15 See, among many others, Review background article FT (2022 July 13), *Wirecard and Me*, FT (2020 August 25), *Wirecard: The Frantic Final Months of a Fraudulent Operation.* Reuters (2024 September 15), *Ex-CEO Braun, Two Others Ordered to Pay 140 Million Euros in Damages.*

16 Delaware Court of Chancery (2024 January 30), *Tornetta v. Musk, 310 A.3d 430.*

17 New York Times (2025 May 13), *Tesla's Board Chair Made $198 Million Selling Stock as Profit Fell.*

18 M. Holtzer (2014), *De invloed van commissarissen en niet-uitvoerende bestuurders op de strategie (The Influence of Supervisory and Non-executive Directors on Strategy)* (IVOR nr. 95/2014/2.7).

19 Michael C. Jensen, Kevin J. Murphy (1990 May 3–June), *CEO incentives—it's not how much you pay, but how*, Harvard Business Review.

20 Richard Tortoriello (2018), *In the Money: What Really Motivates Executive Performance. Trends, Interview Vlerick Professor Xavier Baeten on CEO Pay: What Gives a Boost in the Short Term is Disastrous in the Long-Term.*

21 Michael C. Jensen, Kevin J. Murphy, Eric G. Wruck (2005), *Executive pay: The link between pay and performance*, Journal of Applied Corporate Finance, 17(4), 8–32.

22 Michael C. Jensen (2003), *Paying people to lie: The truth about the budgeting process*, European Financial Management, 9(3), 379–406, Wiley Online Library.

23 Alexander Pepper (2021), *The behavioral economics of executive incentives, NHRD Network Journal*, 14. Nitzan Shilon (Peking University) (2018 March 31), *Replacing Executive Equity Compensation: The Case for Cash for Long-Term Performance*, Harvard Law School Forum on Corporate Governance.

24 Financial Times (2009 June 19), *Outgoing Shell Chief Calls for Salaries Shake-Up.*

25 Arijit Chatterjee, Donald C. Hambrick (2007), *It's all about me: Narcissistic chief executive officers and their effects on company strategy and performance*, Administrative Science Quarterly, 52.

26 Liu Zheng, Xianming Zhou (2012), *Executive stock options and manipulated stock-price performance*, International Review of Finance, 12(3).

27 Steven Clifford (2017), *The CEO Pay Machine*, Penguin Random House.

28 Korn Ferry (2016), *Getting the Right Measure on CEO Comp.*

29 James D. Westphal, Edward J. Zajac (2013), *A behavioral theory of corporate governance: Explicating the mechanisms of socially situated and socially constituted agency*, Academy of Management Annals, 7(1), 607–661.

30 Jessica Phan, Equilar, Inc. (2018 November 23), *The Effects of CEO Ownership on Total Shareholder Return*, Harvard Law School Forum. Anup Agrawal (2019), *Blockholders on boards and CEO compensation, turnover and firm valuation*, Quarterly Journal of Finance, 9. Boudewijn Janssen et al. (2013), *Verklaring van de hoogte van CEO-Beloningen voor Nederlandse beursgenoteerde ondernemingen (Explanation of the Level of CEO Remunderation for Dutch Quoted Companies)*, MAB.

31 Ivan E. Brick, Oded Palmon, John K. Wald (2006), *CEO compensation, director compensation, and firm performance: Evidence of cronyism?* Journal of Corporate Finance, 12(3).

32 Peter F. Drucker (1986), *The Frontiers of Management*, New York: Harper & Row, p. 307.

33 AFL (2023), *Executive Pay Watch*, https://aflcio.org/paywatch.

34 Jay Lorsch, Rakesh Khurana (2010 May/June), *The pay problem, time for a new paradigm for executive compensation*, Harvard Business Review.

35 European Union: The Shareholder Rights Directive II (SRD II) mandates detailed executive pay disclosures, including CEO-to-employee pay ratios, shareholder votes on remuneration ("Say on Pay"), and public access to remuneration reports. United Kingdom: The Companies (Miscellaneous Reporting) Regulations 2018 require CEO pay ratio disclosures for large listed companies and a narrative explanation of pay fairness. United States: The Dodd-Frank Act (2010) requires CEO-to-median-employee pay ratio disclosures and non-binding shareholder votes on executive pay ("Say on Pay"); in Asia rules are generally limited to disclosure of executive compensation.

36 The Guardian (2019 April 11), *Congresswoman Katie Porter Grills Billionaire CEO Over Pay Disparity at JP Morgan.*

37 McKinsey & Company (2024 October), *The 2024 McKinsey Global Payments Report.*

38 Interview with Lloyd Blankfein in the Sunday Times (2009 November 8), *I'm Doing 'God's Work'. Meet Mr. Goldman Sachs.*

39 See also Michiel Van Meeteren, David Bassens (2018 October), '*Chasing the Phantom of a Global End Game. The Role of Management Consultancy in the Narratives of Pre-failure ABN AMRO*'.

40 Jeroen Smit (2008), *De prooi (The Prey)*, Amsterdam: Prometheus.

41 Nout Wellink (2007 June 27), *Speech to the Basel Committee on Banking Supervision at the Risk Capital 2007 Conference*, Paris.

42 According to the Swiss Banking Association, 48% of the money in Swiss bank accounts comes from abroad.

43 'Report Toward Acceptable Transit' (2021 October), *Report of the Committee on Transit Societies, Chaired by Bernard ter Haar.* CBS (2024), *Dutch Trade in Facts and Figures.*

44 Labaton Sucharow Survey (2012 July 10), *Financial Services Professionals Feel Unethical Behavior May Be a Necessary Evil and Have Knowledge of Workplace Misconduct.*

45 Financial Times (2022 May 3), *Danske: Anatomy of a Money Laundering Scandal;* Finanstilsynet (2019 January 28), *Report on the Danish FSA's Supervision of Danske Bank as Regards the Estonia Case.*

46 Website: Europol.europa.eu.

47 See also Jan Timmer (2018), *Die man van Philips, (The Man from Philips)*, Amsterdam: Prometheus.

48 Wall Street Journal (2017 September 19), *Heavy Debt Crushed Owners of Toys 'R' Us.*

49 According to John Maynard Keynes' theory, when interest rates are low, investors tend to borrow money and invest in stocks; as a result of increased demand, stock prices rise. When interest rates rise, we see the opposite pattern, and stock prices fall.

50 Brooke Masters, Stefania Palma (2024 July 23), *Transparency rules for US private funds lapse after SEC allows deadline to pass*, Financial Times.

51 Alix Partners (2017 May), *Annual Private Equity Survey.*

52 The Netherlands, Enterprise Chamber (2019 December 10), *Ruling Case Estro/Catalpa*. Loyens Loeff (2023 July 11), *Considerations for Directors and Supervisory Board Members in LBOs.*

53 The Guardian (2011 June 3), *Southern Cross Care Fiasco Sheds Light on Secretive World of Private Equity.*

54 Richard Wachman (2011 July 16), *Southern Cross's incurably flawed business model let down the vulnerable,* The Guardian.

55 See Website ICA (International Cooperative Alliance), *Exploring the Cooperative Economy* (2023 numbers).

56 Wilhelm Friedrich Raiffeisen (1818–1888) spoke at the founding meeting of *the Flammersfelder Hilfsverein zur Unterstützung unbemittelter Landwirte* in 1854: "Auch in unserem Amtsbezirk befinden sich unter der armen, ausgesogenen Bevölkerung Giftpflanzen, Wucherer, welche sich ein Geschäft daraus machen, die Not ihrer Mitmenschen in herzlosester Weise auszunützen." ("Even in our district, among the poor, exploited population, there are poisonous plants, moneylenders who make a business out of heartlessly exploiting the misfortune of their fellow human beings.").

CHAPTER 4

Information and decision-making, keys to an accountable board

CONTENTS

§4.1—INFORMATION: POWER, COMPLEXITY, PARADOX

Introduction

Information is a crucial resource for non-executive directors. Sound decisions need that information to be accessible, reliable, and relevant. Yet Herbert Simon and Daniel Kahneman made it clear that even in rational settings, biases can pull judgment, leading to flawed conclusions.

Laws and codes define a duty of information-sharing between executives and non-executives. But are they effective? Do non-executive directors know what they need in order to properly assess integrity and control? Can they trust the information supplied by those they oversee? Is there such a thing as objective truth in corporate governance?

Asking the right questions is harder than it seems. More information doesn't always mean better oversight; too much can overwhelm, obscure, and delay action. What matters is context—understanding how to interpret data and under what circumstances judgments are made. Sometimes, minimal information and common sense offer sharper insight than thick reports.

Where there is information, there is also the temptation to filter or frame it. Internal and external auditors are meant to guard against this, but to what extent do they truly support the non-executives, who are distanced from daily operations? In the end, the central question remains: how does an accountable non-executive director, armed with information, arrive at a responsible, integrity-driven judgment?

DOI: 10.4324/9781003624400-4

Information is power, knowledge is the edge

Economist and Nobel laureate George Stigler (1911–1991) once sighed: "One should hardly have to tell academicians that information is a valuable resource: knowledge is power. And yet it occupies a slum dwelling in the town of economics."[1]

Decision-making is inherently uncertain; it involves dealing with the future and, therefore, with risk. When the underlying information is incomplete or inaccurate, that uncertainty is compounded, and sound judgment becomes impossible. Information flows are complex, often unstructured, and open to multiple interpretations.

Figure 4.1 offers a simplified model of these dynamics in an organization. Externally, organizations exchange data with suppliers and customers on deliveries, quality, and satisfaction. Internally, they rely on abundant data about their internal processes.

Figure 4.1
Input-Output and Organization

The streams of information generated by a fully operational organization include financial reports, production and efficiency metrics, sales data, compliance and safety records, and measures of employee and customer satisfaction. However, organizations are more complex than a simple input-output model would suggest.

Beyond suppliers, customers, and employees, key stakeholders include financiers, such as shareholders, governments, and banks. Internally, organizations develop and manage strategies and marketing plans, budget allocations, risk assessments, investment analyses, and employee and talent policies. Competitor intelligence also plays a crucial role, providing insights into the broader market landscape.

Causes, consequences, and the character of man

Figure 4.2 illustrates the information challenge faced by non-executives. At its heart is the "character of man" the CEO and leadership team, with their values, motivations, and personal agendas.[2] At times they act in the company's best interests, sometimes in their own.

Leaders don't operate in a vacuum. They're squeezed by external pressures—shifting markets, climate change, technological disruption and geopolitics. Internally, they must navigate the company's purpose, values, and culture, including how things actually get done and who holds power. Together, these forces shape their decisions, which ripple outward to affect shareholders, communities, and the planet through broader ESG impacts (see

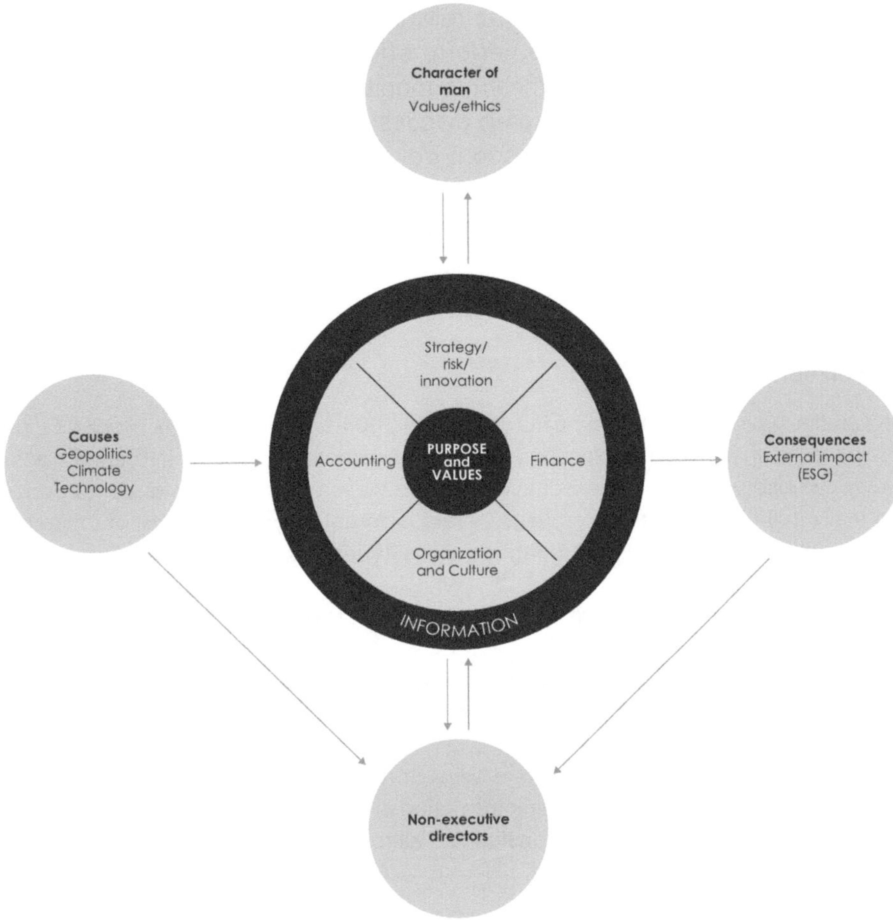

Figure 4.2
Causes, Consequences, and the Character of Man

Chapter 5, Section §5.2). However, much of this information is not fully reflected in management reports.

Here's where it gets tricky for non-executive directors: can you trust what you are hearing? You are an outsider. Management controls most of the information flowing your way. Therefore, you cannot simply accept the reports at face value. You need to read between the lines, pick up signals from outside the boardroom, and ask the harder question: not just *what* the CEO is deciding but *why*, and whether their actions truly match what they say they stand for.

The *information paradox*

In their oversight role, non-executive directors are expected to make rational, well-informed decisions. But in practice, two obstacles stand in their way. First, behavioral biases (see

Chapter 2) can cloud judgment. Second, a reliance on management for vital data creates the *information paradox*: how can you perform effective oversight when your information comes from the very people you are meant to monitor?

The information that fuels boardroom discussions must be structured, relevant, and actionable. This raises the critical question: *do we accept what we get, or define what we need to know?* Even then, the board should also question whether executive management itself is correctly and comprehensively informed, rather than assuming that they are.

Jeroen van der Veer

Jeroen van der Veer was appointed CEO of Shell in 2004 following a major stock scandal, and later, he became an active non-executive director for companies such as ING and Philips. In an interview, he observed that non-executive directors—each on their own quest to understand what is really going on—respond to crises in very different ways, and not all of these help the board to function as it should. He identified three types of non-executive directors in such moments of pressure.[3]

The first is the *Passive Observer*—an individual who stays on the sidelines, neither offering help nor "causing trouble."

The second is the *Overactive Questioner*—one who floods the board with questions, not necessarily to help, but to later claim they were exercising active oversight. This drains valuable board time and energy.

The third is the *Decisive Leader*—one who understands the importance of swift decision-making, even with only 70% of the information at hand.

"In my experience," Van der Veer concluded, "all former CEOs fall into the last category."

However, some caution is warranted when there are too many "doers" on the board. Decisiveness is vital, especially in a crisis—but as Kahneman reminds us, *bounded rationality* can narrow the scope of judgments made under pressure. Even seasoned directors may fall prey to overconfidence and haste. When evaluating major decisions, such as takeovers or divestments, non-executives must ensure that the due diligence has been thorough and resist the impulse to approve them based on partial information.

Because information is often incomplete, effective oversight depends on persistent yet purposeful questioning. At the same time, directors should beware of *relief bias*: once answers arrive, the sense of reassurance can lead to premature approval. Precisely at these moments, it is worth asking, *do we truly have the answers we need?*

In the grip of tight deadlines, non-executives must remain composed, gather the right facts, and make deliberate, well-founded choices. The Dutch Imtech case shows how difficult this can be: its ambitious strategy and reliance on management reports allowed a major fraud to go unnoticed—underscoring the need for vigilant, independent oversight.

Case Study: Imtech—the illusion of control

In 2013, a bold rescue effort was launched to save the troubled engineering and technical services company Imtech, once one of Europe's largest providers of electrical, mechanical, and ICT solutions. The executive board and several non-executive directors stepped down as this former stock market jewel continued to sink into deeper crisis. To turn the company around, a new executive team was appointed, soon joined by experienced non-executives. As financial reserves dwindled, the refreshed board took firm control—time was running out.

To restore transparency, the board commissioned top external advisors to conduct a thorough investigation. The June 2013 *Report to Shareholders* became a benchmark in transparency, exposing massive fraud in Germany that had been hidden by a manipulative local management team. Plans for a big amusement park in Poland proved to be a mirage. Following the report, the executive board introduced corrective measures, and Imtech raised €1.1 billion in new capital from shareholders and secured additional bank financing.

For a moment, it appeared Imtech had been saved. Yet by February 2015, in a telling display of bounded rationality, the interim CEO and CFO announced their departure—the CFO declaring, "governance, risk, and compliance are back in order." In reality, the problems ran far deeper. The non-executive directors, having relied on the executive board and its report, now faced another leadership transition and an existential crisis.

As the situation spiraled, mounting distrust from banks and newly uncovered fraud pushed Imtech to the brink. The company sought court protection, signaling its collapse. For shareholders, it was the end of the road. The non-executives faced a final duty: safeguarding stakeholders by maintaining the continuity of the company's subsidiaries and preserving as many jobs as possible. Most operational units survived, while financiers—banks and shareholders—bore the brunt of the downfall.

The vanishing flow of information

How do non-executive directors obtain their information? This precious resource has the peculiar tendency to evaporate—partly within the labyrinth of the organization and partly before the very eyes of its non-executive directors. Governance advisor Hanke Lange surveyed 150 non-executive directors, executive directors, and managers on the flow of information from the shop floor to senior management and non-executive directors.[4] His findings reveal two key steps in this process, each involving a loss of information (see Figure 4.3). The study explored two categories: (1) business information and (2) feedback on managerial conduct.

Business information includes the monthly production backlog, missed orders, issues with business partners, and challenges in filling key positions. Most of it (77.5%) flows one level upward through formal reporting lines. Managers generally recognize that their board needs this information and act accordingly. Some provide complete transparency, especially during crises, knowing that the information might otherwise surface through informal or control channels. Others struggle with internal barriers, such as organizational politics,

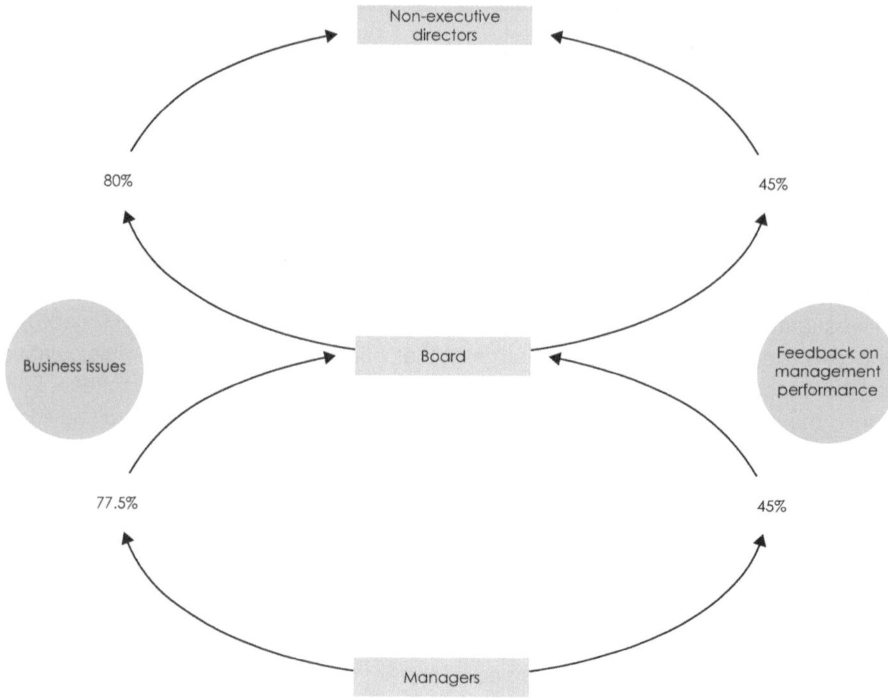

Figure 4.3
Flow of Information from the Shop Floor to Non-Executive Directors

uncertainty about timing, or fear of the board's reaction. In some cases, they delay reporting in the hope that the problem will resolve itself. This reflects a subtle twist on the illusion of control: by choosing inaction, they convince themselves that they're still in command.

After all, who objectively determines which information is true—and truly important? Consider the case of WorldCom, a now-notorious U.S. long-distance telecom company. Under orders from senior executives, fraudulent entries were recorded under the nickname "prepaid capacity," a fabricated account, used to inflate results. For years, internal auditors unquestioningly did as they were told.[5]

Even when information does reach the board, only 80% makes its way to the non-executive director level. Overall, more than a third of the information therefore gets lost between the shop floor and the non-executive directors. Interestingly, executive directors and seasoned non-executive directors alike know that they neither provide nor receive all relevant information. To control the information flow, they tend to keep basic information at operational levels and upload only selected information. But that's exactly where the risk is.

The shop floor finds it especially challenging to provide feedback on the behavior or policies of managers or executives. This "uncomfortable" last category of information is often filtered before it reaches decision-makers. Only 45% makes it to the executive board. Research by Dennis Tourish explains this phenomenon: employees are reluctant to send suggestions or critical feedback upward. They are unsure how their message will land and fear repercussions if they unintentionally embarrass the recipients.[6]

A similar drop-off occurs when the executive board needs to relay details to non-executive directors about internal conduct, culture, or relationships. This communication gap can be particularly problematic in ensuring accountability. It is nonetheless understandable: why would a CEO openly report that staff lack confidence in them or that whistle-blowers fear a culture of silence? This withholding of critical information undermines the board's ability to perform its oversight function and hold management accountable.

Information: a duty to bring and a duty to retrieve

Effective oversight depends not only on access to information but on the ability to interpret it without bias. Over the course of their careers, non-executive directors learn the subtleties of the information game. They draw on experience, intuition and the heuristics mentioned in Chapter 2, Section §2.5, to navigate uncertainty. These rules of thumb help simplify complex issues into broader, more accessible questions. Instead of grilling the board on every investment scenario, for example, they might ask: "What decision-making process led to this choice?" Similarly, instead of approving a single, sweeping change process, they may suggest an *agile, incremental* approach, rolling out smaller steps and allowing for operational adjustments as new information becomes available. Yet such shortcuts have limits: today's complexity means that simplification can cause essential signals to be overlooked.

Non-executive boards cannot simply be blamed for failures when vital information is withheld or distorted. Responsibility runs both ways: executive management bears a *duty to provide* complete and accurate information, while non-executive directors hold a *duty to seek* it. They must not assume management reports are flawless and, when necessary, should engage independent advisors to verify, for instance, the assumptions behind a merger, valuation, or integration plan.

Governance expert Steven Schuit assigns a special role to the independent board chair. Through (intended) frequent contact and dialogue with the CEO, the chair ensures the board has clear agreements on the standard and handling of board information, reinforcing both the duty to provide and the duty to seek.[7]

SUMMARY AND CONCLUSION

Information is power, but knowledge determines how it is used—and information is never neutral. Non-executive directors face an information paradox: they rely on information from the very executives they must oversee, placing them at risk of selective filtering, spin, and omission.

Executives have a duty to provide information, yet non-executive directors have an equal duty to *seek it proactively*. Effective non-executives should agree with executive management on information sources, even if that means bypassing the executive layer. Direct contact with auditors, works councils, ombudspersons, and operational staff reduces dangerous dependence on consciously or unconsciously filtered management narratives.

Non-executives don't passively absorb reports; they apply heuristics and crisis-tested instincts to decide when to dig deeper or slow down, even under the pitfall of bounded rationality. They define what they need to know and probe for gaps created by behavioral biases—relief bias, the illusion of control (mistaking inaction for influence), overconfidence, or reluctance to surface uncomfortable feedback.

When uncertainty persists, they should consider commissioning independent reviews to validate management's narrative and protect shareholders and stakeholder interests.

Experience in crisis leadership is invaluable—knowing when to push, doubt, or resist urgency. Yet, as the Imtech case shows, even seasoned leaders can misread complexity or overlook emerging risks.

Ultimately, diligent non-executive directors must resist the illusion of clarity and keep asking: "Are we still seeing the bigger picture—or just what we've been shown?"

§4.2—TRUTH, LIES, AND GOVERNANCE

Introduction

All Cretans are liars, said Epimenides, himself a Cretan. The paradox is timeless. For anyone in a position of responsibility, its logic can unsettle the mind. Information can be both truthful and distorted, transparent and opaque. Non-executive directors often depend on executive narratives—polished, persuasive, and sometimes perilously misleading. Yet what happens when facts mingle with spin, or when silence becomes a language of its own?

This is the non-executive director's dilemma: judging the truth of stories shaped by fear, pride, or ambition. Executives who bend reality are swiftly branded as liars—but is that always fair? Deception, self-delusion, and strategy often blend into one another. Every message carries more than data; it reveals conviction, anxiety, or intent.

Trust, though essential, is never enough. Information flows unevenly through organizations, leaving gaps that are readily filled by perception. To govern wisely, directors must weigh not only *what* is said but also *why*—and notice *what remains unsaid*. Behavioral biases blur judgment on both sides of the table.

This section examines how behavioral biases can distort the truth and how non-executives can respond when that trust is tested. Governance begins with self-awareness: questioning not only *what* is heard but also *how* one chooses to hear it.

What is truth?

Truth in governance is rarely clear-cut. The case of Barings Bank illustrates how deception can arise from ambition and fear, rather than from pure malice—and how even respected institutions can blind themselves to the obvious.

Case Study: Barings—the $1.4 billion lie nobody wanted to see

In 1995, 28-year-old Nick Leeson joined Barings Bank in Singapore as an equity trader. His appointment was unusual as he had not completed any formal training, something Barings knew. Another issue arose when he applied for his license in Singapore: both Barings and Leeson concealed the fact that a previous application had been followed by disciplinary issues.[8]

Leeson's initial successes earned him substantial bonuses, but his luck soon ran out when his speculative derivative positions on the Japanese stock market went south. Using a strategy of doubling his position (essentially increasing his bets), he tried to recover from his losses. This approach had worked for him before, but this time, the index remained against him. Repeatedly, Barings Singapore's capital had to be increased to cover the losses.

The bank's management in London faced an information gap. It misinterpreted the calls for capital as signs of success and awarded Leeson a bonus for his supposed entrepreneurship. Afraid of reprisals, Leeson became entangled in his own lies, anxiously awaiting the moment when the truth would surface. In February 1995, Barings, a bank with over two centuries of history, collapsed under a catastrophic $1.4 billion loss. Leeson left a note, simply stating, "I am sorry," and went into hiding.

After serving a four-year prison sentence, he survived colon cancer, but his marriage fell apart. Capitalizing on his notoriety, he later managed the Irish soccer club Galway United. But misfortune struck again, and the club nearly collapsed due to financial problems. Leeson was eventually dismissed. Since then, he has been lecturing and working as a poker coach. Harry's Bar on the Singapore River still serves the infamous "Bankbreaker" cocktail. The Barings case remains an example of how unchecked incentives, flawed oversight, and *willful blindness* can destroy even the most venerable institution.

Good governance and oversight demand that the truth be on the table—in other words, honesty. Yet different shades of lying occur at all levels in every organization. In its lighter form, a CEO may circle around the truth, framing a lie as being in the company's best interest. The board is offered selective or distorted information. Non-executive directors sometimes sense that the CEO isn't being fully transparent, but feel relieved when at last a solution seems to be at hand. The organization can move on—yet in allowing it to do so, the directors risk becoming complicit in deception.

Spin, lies, and bullshit

Lying is a characteristic of personalities in the narcissistic Dark Triad (see § 2.7) and a trait that emerges at an early age. Even babies and small children begin experimenting with deception, such as crying for extra attention or sneaking a cookie. These are small-scale experiments through which toddlers, in particular, test their boundaries. At this stage, children have limited ways to express themselves. However, a child who receives too little or too much attention may develop a fragile self-image, feeling the need to scream ever more loudly for attention or becoming spoiled, expecting to get everything they want.

If left unchecked, the child may gradually develop manipulative and deceptive behaviors. The child's social environment is another key factor. Children mirror the behaviors they observe around them.

The various shades on the spectrum between truth and lies proceed from white lies and spin to outright falsehoods. Withholding information is another form of deception. It is not without reason that the American legal oath states: "The truth, the whole truth, and nothing but the truth." To this, philosopher Harry Frankfurt added his controversial theory of "bullshit." According to Frankfurt, the bullshitter does not lie intentionally; they are simply indifferent to the truth. Such individuals may exhibit narcissistic or sociopathic tendencies. Those responsible for oversight may find bullshitters appealing because they boastfully present grandiose visions, which may seem impressive at first. But a deep disregard for the truth makes them at least as dangerous as outright liars.

How do you recognize a liar?

According to Pamela Meyer, we encounter between 10 and 200 deceptive statements a day. She highlights several behaviors that may indicate someone is being less than truthful:

- Overemphasis: speakers under pressure may rely on strong gestures and emphatic delivery. The Bush administration's WMD presentations before the Iraq War are often cited as an example of this assertive style.
- Overly formal language: people managing a narrative may adopt unusually formal phrasing, such as Bill Clinton's 1998 statement: "I did not have sexual relations with that woman, Miss Lewinsky."
- Disorganized speech: they may falter, show slight vocal distortions, or struggle when answering detailed questions.
- Mismatch between words and body language: examples include shaking one's head while saying "yes" or smiling without the expression reaching the eyes.
- Creating physical distance: speakers may place objects or space between themselves and others—illustrated by President Putin's use of an unusually large table.
- A controlled "poker-face": some people suppress emotional expression entirely and keep their body or gaze unnaturally fixed.

Information asymmetry: two games in play

In corporate governance, *information asymmetry* arises when executive boards, possessing deeper operational knowledge than non-executive directors, provide them with selective information. This imbalance can affect oversight, risk assessment, and decision-making. Executives may selectively present information at two key moments:

- Budget planning: knowing which goals are truly attainable, executives may set targets that serve their interests when bonuses are tied to performance.
- Year-end reporting: future successes are emphasized, while early-stage losses are downplayed.

If left unchecked, small manipulations can escalate into serious integrity issues. A striking example is the 2004 Royal Dutch Shell reserves scandal.

Case Study: Shell—the truth about oil reserves

Would you expect fraud from an energy giant presenting itself as a steady, almost paternal guardian of widows' funds, reliably paying out an annual dividend? In 2004, Royal Dutch Shell's top management resigned after it was revealed that the company had overstated its proven oil reserves by 23%. Unverified reserves had been recorded as confirmed, inflating future cash flows and, above all, executive bonuses, a practice likely encouraged by a new performance-based pay system.

Auditors KPMG and PwC endorsed the accounting method, but the U.S. Securities and Exchange Commission (SEC) did not buy this, condemning Shell for ignoring repeated warnings about overvaluation. The scandal sent shockwaves through the market, wiping billions off Shell's share price and sparking investor lawsuits.

For many, the real outrage came when the chairman departed with a generous farewell bonus. As frustrated shareholders noted, nothing says "sorry for the scandal" quite like a golden parachute.[9]

Internal information asymmetry is a challenge for non-executive directors in large multinationals, where reports from faraway units arrive incomplete, filtered, or distorted. Consider a newly appointed expat manager who, upon taking up a post in Africa, encounters fraudulent or borderline-fraudulent practices developed under their predecessor. They face several options:

- Take action. If they have solid prove, they may report the practices to headquarters. However, this can become complicated if their predecessor has since been promoted within the group.
- Pursue gradual change. They try to reverse the wrongdoing over time, hoping not to provoke backlash or harm local relationships.
- Look the other way. They ignore the fraudulent behavior, rationalizing it as a local custom or a matter of national pride.

In each scenario, the information that eventually reaches headquarters becomes blurred.

Blind spots in the boardroom

Behavioral factors play a significant role here, and non-executive directors risk being blindsided by overly optimistic reporting. Not only because they are being deceived, but because they want to believe that the company they oversee is operating with integrity and achieving success. When presented with a polished strategic plan, they may feel inclined to approve it; if only in the hope that doing so will bind the CEO to delivering results.

Like most decision-makers, non-executive directors prefer to have "just enough" information to make informed decisions. As Peter Drucker noted, *the fewer data needed, the better the information.* He warned that an overload, beyond what is truly necessary, leads to a blackout: *it does not enrich, it impoverishes.*[10]

After all, gathering and analyzing information takes time and effort, and reading dry reports on the weekend can be a mood dampener. Information must be concise, digestible, and engaging. Yet, this preference also exposes non-executive directors to the risk of being misled by an overly optimistic portrayal of reality—or even a well-presented, but fundamentally flawed, story. Some executives are skilled at making even the murkiest situations seem like solid ground. But terrain that looks firm from a distance can turn into quicksand once you step in too deep.

The Philadelphia doctrine: can you explain it to a 6-year-old?

To counter distortion of the truth and promote clear, straightforward communication, former Dutch Enterprise Chamber chairman Huub Willems proposed the *Philadelphia doctrine*:

> "Explain it to me as if I were a 6-year-old child." The principle ensures that even the most complex information can be conveyed in a way that is understandable, challengeable, and verifiable.

The idea draws inspiration from the film Philadelphia (1993), in which lawyer Andrew Beckett is dismissed under the pretext of poor performance. In truth, his firm fears reputational damage because he has AIDS. Determined to fight back, Beckett takes his employer to court. During the trial, the defense clouds the truth with legal smokescreens; until Beckett's lawyer cuts through the deception with a simple, disarming request: "explain it to me as if I were a 6-year-old child."

It's a line that slices through pretense—and one that deserves a place in the boardroom.

From facts to feels: the role of intuition

What is true, and what is false? Philosophers argue that absolute truth doesn't exist—or if it does, it's only temporary. What is true today may be obsolete tomorrow. For non-executive directors, curiosity is a vital trait. Children are naturally eager to explore and ask questions about everything. However, as we grow older, routines tend to take over. We rely on rules of thumb and become reluctant to ask "stupid" questions, fearing we will lose face. Too many questions can create an atmosphere of distrust; yet, appropriate questioning is essential to uncover the truth. Doing so without blaming management requires intelligence, experience, and considerable courage.

There is rarely a single truth. Perspective matters. A controller views financial buffers differently than an ambitious entrepreneur does. What appears true from one angle may look entirely untrue from another. Our senses shape how we gather and interpret information: we see, hear, smell, feel, and even taste it. We read reports, listen to explanations, and if something feels off, we say, "There's a certain air about it," or "My gut tells me something's wrong." When overly enthusiastic about an investment, we might say, "It tastes so good, we want more." In tense meetings, we describe the atmosphere as "icy."

Can we sense trouble before it strikes? In hindsight, yes. Board members later admit this after the crisis, saying, "That proposal never felt right," or, "We should never have hired that CFO." But our senses aren't always reliable. Under emotional pressure, we misread signals. Even when logic warns otherwise, a charismatic pitch can still persuade. As discussed in Chapter 2, Section §2.4, emotions shape how we process decisions. Non-executive directors must therefore verify whether what they perceive is real—or whether they're filtering out inconvenient truths in favor of what they want to believe.

Case Study: The last-round illusion

A group of successful entrepreneurs pools their capital in an innovative battery venture. After early success, the tide turns, and the project begins to unravel. Round after round, more capital is raised, each backed by fresh optimism and persuasive storytelling that is meant to keep the faith alive.

At a final meeting, the emotional bind becomes clear. Casually, the investment manager mentions that a rival firm, recently valued at over a billion dollars, has just attracted another major investor. The message lands perfectly: *if we pull out now, we'll miss the next breakthrough.* To an outsider, it sounds like confidence; to those inside, it feels like reassurance. No one wants to be the first to give up.

Staying "practical," the manager passes around a notepad, asking each investor to pledge one last round of funding—no questions asked. For a while, the enthusiasm feels genuine again. Then the company collapses, leaving those who signed to bear the cost.

The episode shows how wishful conviction can masquerade as confidence, and how persuasive optimism—however well-intended—can cloud collective judgment. Hope and pride silence skepticism, and realism is mistaken for defeatism. The same pattern appears in boardrooms when directors keep investing their credibility in fading strategies, betting on a story rather than facing the truth.

Through the senses: intuition and decision-making

Our senses shape our intuition, giving us a positive or negative feeling about a situation. In hindsight, intuition often feels accurate—we tell ourselves, "I knew it all along." Yet, as Herbert Simon warned, intuition is not a matter of magic but of pattern recognition: the brain linking new situations to familiar experiences. Kahneman (see Chapter 2, Section §2.4) notes that intuition is only reliable when (i) situations follow clear patterns (like chess), (ii) we have deep experience in the field, and (iii) feedback on results is immediate. Most strategic decisions, however, meet none of these conditions. They are uncertain, complex, and slow to reveal outcomes, making them poor ground for fast, intuitive judgment.

And above all, there is the question of emotional intelligence. As Antonio Damasio explains, emotional memories can sharpen perception and guide intuition, but reason must refine and test them.[11] Effective leaders integrate emotional intelligence to read people and context with analytical rigor to ensure sound judgment. Because outcomes in governance unfold over years, not moments, the boardroom is no place for unchecked gut feeling.

SUMMARY AND CONCLUSION

Non-executive directors rely on honest, reliable, timely, and transparent information to make sound decisions. Yet absolute truth is elusive—spin, selective reporting, and subtle manipulation can distort reality. The challenge lies not only in detecting lies but also in recognizing how cognitive biases and psychological framing shape the narrative.

Curiosity remains an essential trait. Observing behavior, questioning assumptions, and reading between the lines all help uncover deception. Intuition can play a role, but it is only reliable in structured environments with rapid feedback—not in the unpredictable world of corporate decision-making. It may offer a signal, but that signal must be tested.

In behavioral governance, understanding dynamics and culture are essential. Organizational culture determines whether the truth is spoken or shaped to fit an agenda. Do non-executive directors actively challenge the board, or do they accept polished narratives that feel safe and reassuring? Even small distortions can be early signs of deeper integrity issues. Ultimately, non-executive directors must resist the comfort of blind trust. Scrutinizing leadership integrity is not an act of mistrust—it is the core duty of governance.

And when doubt arises about the board's integrity, the most important question must follow: *"Do we have the right board?"*

§4.3—LAWS, CODES, AND COMMON SENSE

Introduction

Rules are often seen as safeguards: follow them, and you are doing the right thing. But what if that belief is misplaced? As street artist Banksy put it, *"The greatest crimes in the world are not committed by people breaking the rules but by people following the rules."* In boardrooms, this tension is real and relevant.

But where do rules actually come from? It is one of the government's principal duties to protect public trust, not only in public institutions but also in business. It does this through laws, regulations, and enforcement.

Within companies, rules are intended to promote accountability, but when followed blindly they can conceal poor decisions, enable harmful behavior, or foster a false sense of security. Governance, in other words, is not about ticking boxes; it's about applying judgment, asking questions, and showing moral courage.

Traditionally, crises have triggered new waves of laws and regulations aimed at restoring order and strengthening oversight. But today, the balance has shifted. Governments no longer just set the rules—they actively reshape markets, writing policies that help some businesses and hinder others.

The challenge for directors is to apply judgment and foresight—not only to interpret today's rules but to anticipate those that will define tomorrow's markets.

The World's Greatest Company

The board of Enron felt untouchable in the intoxicating year 2000 and nicknamed it "The World's Greatest Company." History gives us both a platform and a perspective to understand where corporate governance stands today, the challenges it continues to face, and the recurring patterns it seems unable to escape.

The late 1990s and early 2000s were shaped by deregulation, market euphoria, and an intense focus on shareholder value. Risk-taking was rewarded, hesitation punished. Boards prioritized growth and profit at any cost. Bonuses and stock options fueled short-termism, encouraging executives to stretch both rules and ethics. Governance increasingly came to be seen not as a safeguard but as an obstacle to ambition.

As governments stepped back from markets, executives pushed the limits of expansion—success on paper quickly gave way to scandal. Names like Enron, WorldCom, and Parmalat became synonymous with greed, complacency, and failure, exposing deep fractures in oversight and accountability. The financial sector, though not yet at the center of the crisis, showed similar warning signs: complexity, leverage, and weak internal controls that would later erupt with full force.

Few companies embodied the era's overconfidence more vividly than the Texan energy and commodities giant, Enron.

Case Study: Enron I—breaking the rules

In the year 2000, Enron's executives pursued aggressive growth strategies, bolstered by high-risk financial maneuvers that distorted the company's true performance. But beneath the surface, a web of accounting fraud, conflicts of interest, and reckless leadership was unraveling. In the 1930s, U.S. energy companies were required by President Franklin D. Roosevelt's administration to ensure a stable electricity supply and keep prices low. Deregulation in the late 1980s and early 1990s removed many of these restrictions.

Enron fully exploited regulatory gaps in newly deregulated energy markets, shutting down power plants at peak demand and manipulating forward contracts, deliberately triggering California's statewide energy crisis. A culture of greed had taken hold, where employees became complicit in bending the rules and openly joked about doing so. One executive famously said, *We're not just breaking the rules—we're rewriting them.*

The cynical nature of Enron's culture was even reflected in the names of its subsidiaries; some were called "raptors," a term for birds of prey. But its downfall was inevitable. At the time of its collapse, Enron was one of the largest energy companies in the world, with a market value of $68 billion. That wealth evaporated almost overnight. Over 5,000 employees lost their jobs, and more than $3.2 billion in pension funds were wiped out. Shareholders saw their stock become virtually worthless.

Enron did not act alone. Accounting giant Arthur Andersen not only enabled but also actively concealed the company's fraud. Its lucrative consulting business compromised its audits of Enron—earning substantial fees from both roles, it was unwilling to risk losing the consulting contract by being overly critical of Enron's executive board. This dual role exemplified a fatal conflict of interest. When Enron collapsed, Arthur Andersen, with its 28,000 employees, fell alongside it—destroyed by the very fraud it was meant to prevent.

The immediate political response focused on what had gone wrong in the system: inadequate regulation, compromised audits, and complex financial structures. Investigations aimed to determine which rules had been violated. But this focus on systems obscured a more uncomfortable truth: governance did not fail for lack of rules. It failed because people with authority chose not to apply them. A 2002 U.S. congressional committee investigation provided the public with a detailed view of misconduct at every level of the organization, sparking outrage and disbelief. The second part of the Enron story shows how board members, even when they were equipped with the right to question and the duty to challenge, simply . . . didn't.

Case Study: Enron II: questions asked, answered . . . and dropped

The independence of Dr. Charles LeMaistre, chairman of Enron's Compensation Committee, was questionable. He was the former president of the University of Texas Cancer Center, an institution that received substantial funding from Enron. A Senate hearing, chaired by Senator Carl Levin, captured the board's passivity. The exchange about the compensation of CFO Andy Fastow was telling:

Sen. Levin: "Right, . . . you had made an inquiry about his compensation. Didn't you ask the Compensation Officer, Mary Joyce, about it?"
Dr. LeMaistre: "I asked Mary Joyce about it."
Sen. Levin: "And what did she tell you?"
Dr. LeMaistre: "She said she did not have the information."
Sen. Levin: "Did you say, well, I want it?"
Dr. LeMaistre: "She knew that I wanted it . . ."
Sen. Levin: "Did you get it?"
Dr. LeMaistre: " 'I did not."
Sen. Levin: "This is the heart of the problem. You have a Board that says, 'I want it.' You have a request for it. It does not come, and you do nothing. That is an approach which is unacceptable for a Board."

Something needs to be done

The downfall of Enron in 2001 marked a watershed moment in corporate governance regulation. Beyond uncovering criminal practices by Enron's executives, it exposed severe governance failures among non-executive directors, whose actions directly contradicted their oversight role. The congressional committee identified four key areas of failure that reveal critical behavioral patterns:

- Systemic governance failures—a lack of independent oversight, conflicts of interest, and failure to intervene in questionable practices. Dissent was suppressed in favor of harmony, reinforcing groupthink.
- Accounting manipulation and fraud—a loss of moral awareness normalized high-risk accounting methods, large-scale off-the-book activities, and insider trading.

- Behavioral misconduct—directors overlooked the fraudulent financial schemes created by the CFO, while self-serving behavior led to excessive pay and bonuses.
- Ethical fading and normalization of deviance—rule-breaking became an economic decision rather than a moral issue. Legal violations were rationalized as a business choice: "Can we afford the fine?"

Legislative reactions to corporate scandals

Corporate regulation often resembles a pendulum. Periods of liberalization and market freedom are followed by abrupt swings toward strict control. Governments protect public trust not only through rhetoric but also through rules. When that trust collapses, as it did after the scandals at Enron and WorldCom, the pendulum swings sharply in the opposite direction. Public outrage over corporate excess and unchecked risk demanded a decisive response.

What followed was a rare moment of unity. In 2002, in the wake of Enron's collapse, Congress passed the Sarbanes–Oxley Act (SOX) with overwhelming bipartisan support. Its goal was to strengthen accountability at both board and executive levels and to restore confidence in corporate governance. The Act required CEOs and CFOs to personally certify financial statements and assign mandated, fully independent audit committees. With the creation of the Public Company Accounting Oversight Board (PCAOB), the accounting profession's long era of self-regulation came to an end.

Notably, many SOX proposals had been on the table for years, stalled by those who believed markets should regulate themselves. But scandal changes everything. As the saying goes, "under pressure, everything liquefies." Crisis dissolved ideological resistance and pushed reform through—proof that when public trust is shaken, even politicians bend.

Yet even robust rules have their limits. The financial crisis of 2007–2009 showed that, despite SOX and other reforms, regulation alone could not prevent the next wave of governance failures. In 2025, less than two decades later, and in a familiar swing in political preference, some U.S. lawmakers are seeking to roll back oversight by merging the independent PCAOB with the SEC, arguing that it is too costly and hampers competitiveness. Opponents, including regulators and investor advocates, warn that such a move would weaken audit oversight and erode the credibility of U.S. capital markets.

Two philosophies, one response: hard law, soft law

The United States, true to its legal tradition, predominantly follows a rules-based model—often called *hard law*. The Sarbanes–Oxley Act (SOX) is a clear example: it sets out detailed, mandatory requirements designed to prevent corporate misconduct. While hard legal regulation exists everywhere, some countries have chosen to balance it with a more flexible approach.

The United Kingdom took that path early. In 1992, the Cadbury Report introduced a principles-based governance code, often called a *soft law* approach, that favored flexibility and self-regulation over strict legal mandates. This model spread across most of Western Europe, as well as Canada, Australia, and Japan. Companies were required to "comply or explain." Rather than ticking boxes, boards were encouraged to use their judgment and explain their choices. The "explain" part wasn't a loophole—it was a requirement for transparency and accountability. The aim was to strike a balance between good governance and operational freedom, thereby avoiding a one-size-fits-all legal framework.

But soft law also has its limits. The collapse of Carillion in 2018 made that painfully clear. On paper, the company complied with every governance code. In practice, it didn't. Carillion had mastered the art of explaining away its failures while formally ticking every box.

Case Study: Carillion's collapse: a governance failure beyond the rules

When Carillion collapsed in 2018, it triggered one of the largest corporate failures in UK history. Thousands of employees faced job losses, subcontractors were left with unpaid bills, pension promises were compromised, and shareholders saw their investments wiped out. The UK government was forced to intervene to keep essential public services running—hospitals, prisons, schools, and defense sites—at significant cost to the taxpayer.

At its peak, Carillion employed over 60,000 people and delivered contracts across both the public and private sectors. With roots in Tarmac, which built key airfields during World War II, the company was listed on the London Stock Exchange and pursued rapid expansion through complex, long-term projects. Annual sales reached £5 billion, yet the business model beneath this impressive scale was fragile: razor-thin margins and aggressive bidding left Carillion dangerously exposed to delays, cost overruns, and cash-flow shocks.

A parliamentary inquiry later revealed deep strategic and governance failures. Publicly, Carillion presented itself as a model of good governance—citing full compliance with the UK Corporate Governance Code and promoting "sustainable solutions." Internally, however, the company operated on the basis of unchecked optimism: assuming profits on loss-making contracts, relying heavily on supplier credit, inflating goodwill, and ignoring pension obligations. Dividends and executive bonuses continued to be issued, even as the warning signs mounted. Between 2009 and 2016, the company paid out roughly three-quarters of its operating cash—and later even more than it earned—effectively financing dividends with borrowed money. Aggressive accounting concealed liabilities exceeding £7 billion.

Auditor KPMG validated these unrealistic figures and was later fined a record £21 million. Governance at the top of Carillion was equally weak: a passive board failed to challenge management's optimism or confront the structural flaws in its model. The non-executive directors—independent in name only—endorsed management's assurances instead of demanding realism. The chair, a veteran of major UK boards, was later banned from serving as a director for 12 years, a notable severe sanction in the UK.

Carillion's downfall exposes a harsh truth: governance codes are only as strong as the courage and skepticism of those who are tasked with enforcing them. Formal compliance is no substitute for genuine vigilance. In an interconnected world of complex contracts and extended supply chains, sound governance depends less on rules and more on a culture capable of questioning, challenging, and confronting reality.

Governance after Carillion: who shapes the rules?

Governments and regulators officially write corporate governance rules. In practice, however, business has a significant influence on the way they are shaped. Across countries, governance codes are typically drafted by committees of company leaders and consultants, which helps explain why corporate interests dominate the process. Broader voices—those of workers, consumers, and environmental and human rights groups—may be more audible today than in the past but are still not formally included at the table. As ESG expectations grow, this imbalance is attracting increasing scrutiny.

In the wake of corporate collapses like Carillion, many countries have once more moved to clarify and strengthen directors' duties, emphasizing that boards must act in the long-term interests of the company with all its stakeholders, rather than focusing solely on short-term shareholder profits. Reforms have also sought to improve board accountability, align executive compensation, and promote stakeholder engagement.

Yet even the most comprehensive reforms have limits. Rules, by design, are fixed in yesterday's failures and can struggle to keep pace with new realities. As economist Charles Goodhart warned, *"when a measure becomes a target, it ceases to be a good measure."* Governance can easily slip into ritual: more process than purpose.

The reforms that followed Carillion's downfall aimed to rebuild trust, but industry lobbying soon blunted their edges. Audit oversight remains under review in many jurisdictions, and stricter director liability rules have been delayed or watered down. The result is once more a familiar cycle: crisis brings reform, reform brings resistance, and responsibility fades once the headlines move on.

The Grenfell and Carillion crises together pushed many nations toward greater accountability in both corporate and public governance. They also exposed a deeper truth: regulation without judgment can never guarantee integrity. Governance works only when directors apply curiosity, courage, and common sense—qualities no code can enforce, yet without which every rule eventually fails.

Case Study: Strictly by the rules: the sinking of *HMS Victoria*

In June 1893, the British Royal Navy was conducting maneuvers off the coast of Beirut. Vice Admiral Sir George Tryon, commander of the Mediterranean fleet, was renowned for his mathematical mind and mastery of complex formations. On a bright day, Tryon gave the signal from the flagship *HMS Victoria* for the fleet's eight battleships and five cruisers to weave through each other and form a new position.

"We're going to see something interesting," remarked the Captain of the nearby battleship *Dreadnought*. But the maneuver was flawed. *HMS Victoria* was about to turn directly into the path of *HMS Camperdown*, the flagship of Rear Admiral Albert Hastings Markham. Maurice Bourke, Tryon's Flag Captain, immediately saw the danger. His second-in-command urged him to speak up, but questioning Tryon was unthinkable. As they stood together on the bridge, Bourke murmured, "We shall be very close to that ship, sir." Tryon dismissed the concern, unwilling to accept the possibility of being wrong.

Just 450 yards from disaster, Tryon gave his final approval. Bourke desperately ordered, "Full astern, both engines!" and "Close all watertight doors!"—but it was too late. *Camperdown* rammed *Victoria*, and within minutes, *Victoria* sank, taking 358 men, including Tryon, to their deaths.

This was not a case of poor seamanship but of an unassailable confidence in authority, coupled with a culture of blind obedience. In boardrooms, as on naval bridges, hierarchy can turn healthy skepticism into dangerous silence.[12]

SUMMARY AND CONCLUSION

Globalization and liberalization have expanded corporate influence, but they have also widened the gap between companies and the people they affect. In response to scandals, laws and codes have multiplied, aiming to restore trust. But more rules don't guarantee better governance. They can create a false sense of security, where box-ticking replaces critical oversight.

Cases like Enron, Carillion, and Grenfell show that even with laws in place, governance can fail—silently and systemically. Their boards followed procedures. Reports were filed. But no one stepped up. While rules were present, courage was not, turning rules into just another set of guidelines.

Rigid compliance frameworks drown non-executive directors in process, masking reality. Cognitive biases such as overconfidence or groupthink distort perception. Moral disengagement leads people to justify bad decisions. As the *HMS Victoria* case shows, hierarchy can silence warnings when speaking up feels unsafe. Environmental risks fade into background noise—too familiar to trigger fresh concern.

To govern well, boards must move beyond compliance, understanding not just *what* went wrong but also *why*. Directors must encourage open dialogue, challenge authority when needed, and create space for dissent without fear. Long-term value must matter more than quarterly gains.

§4.4—FRAUD, A MANY-HEADED MONSTER

Introduction

Fraud—weren't we done with that? Apparently not. Despite stricter regulations and high-profile scandals, fraud remains a growing risk. It is the nightmare of every executive or non-executive director. It raises pressing questions: *Did the board know? Were they involved? What are the consequences?* And most importantly, *how can fraud be prevented?*

Fraud takes many forms and raises threats across a company's entire landscape—internal and external. Yet, executives and non-executive directors often fail to recognize its occurrence within their own organization. They may have totally different definitions of what constitutes fraud: stealing cash, or altering some bookkeeping entries?

Fraud is not just a financial issue—it is a behavioral one, shaped by psychological biases, social pressures, and moral rationalization. For executives and non-executive directors, recognizing these behavioral patterns is critical to detecting early warning signs and preventing misconduct before it escalates. Failure to recognize these behavioral red flags can create blind spots that fraudsters exploit.

Fraud, someone else's problem, or is it?

Large, spectacular fraud cases regularly dominate the headlines. Experts estimate that organizations lose an average of 5% of their annual revenue to fraud, highlighting the persistent and costly nature of the issue.[13] Despite countless preventive measures, new scandals continue to surface across all sectors of the economy.

PwC reports that, after a decline during the COVID-19 pandemic (2019–2022), fraud is once again on the rise. This is a many-headed monster. Internal fraud remains most prevalent (43%), while external fraud (31%), including cybercrime, phishing, and platform fraud, is an increasing threat. The remainder consists of cases involving collusion between internal and external actors (see Chapter 4, Section §4.5).

Even trusted institutions face fraud risk. The audit sector, often regarded as society's beacon of trust, has itself been rocked by misconduct, including cheating on continuing education exams. Nor is fraud limited to corporate giants. From school principals embezzling parental contributions, to Bernie Madoff's massive Ponzi scheme and academic fraud, the issue spans all sectors.

At its core, fraud is a betrayal of trust. The warning signs are often present, but recognizing them requires confronting uncomfortable truths.

Case Study: When nobody was looking: €2.2 million vanishes from a school budget

A fraud case came to light after irregularities were discovered in payments to the contractor responsible for a school's new construction project. Its Principal, who had worked at the school for 40 years, colluded with the contractor by submitting false invoices and paying them from parental contributions, which the school board failed to oversee. In court, the Principal later admitted that he had used the money to pay off personal debts. "I succeeded because the school board never audited the financial statements. Now, I deeply regret it." The fraud ultimately cost this small school €2.2 million, demonstrating how trusted, long-serving employees can exploit weak oversight.

Case Study: Too good to check: the Bernie Madoff story

New Yorker Bernie Madoff (1938–2021) orchestrated the largest Ponzi scheme in history, deceiving investors for decades. His fraud exposed behavioral shortcomings in institutional oversight, as banks and intermediaries ignored red flags—sometimes due to conflicts of interest, since they profited from placing funds into his operation.

Whistleblower Harry Markopolos reported Madoff to the SEC five times, submitting detailed evidence, including his 2005 memo, *"The World's Largest Hedge Fund is a Fraud."*[14] Yet the SEC failed to act, even when Madoff's firm was unable to produce trade records.

Losses reached $10–20 billion, devastating investors, businesses, and charities. The case demonstrates how regulatory capture and conflicts of interest can blind institutions, unable to detect even large-scale fraud. Madoff was sentenced to 150 years in prison, where he later died. The fallout extended beyond finances—his son Mark, who had reported him—died by suicide. So too did Bernie's sister and her husband, years later. Fraud has a ripple effect on families and society.

Case Study: Publish or perish, when prestige blinds oversight

The Diederik Stapel case is one of academia's most notorious scandals, revealing flaws in scientific integrity, peer reviewing, and research oversight. It highlights the pressure within the sector to publish, secure funding, and maintain prestige. Stapel, a social psychologist at Tilburg University (the Netherlands), was seen as a golden boy—earning two *cum laude* doctoral degrees and an impressive publication record. To "help" students and support his theories, he falsified data, justifying it as "robust theorizing." His seemingly flawless results went unquestioned by colleagues dazzled by his success.

Despite concerns raised by students, early complaints were dismissed by the university's intimidating leadership. Only after a third whistleblower spoke up was the fraud taken seriously. Ultimately, 58 papers and several dissertations were retracted. Stapel blamed the pressure to produce "beautiful results."[15]

White-collars, dirty hands

Internal fraud falls under the category of "white-collar crime," a term suggesting the unexpected nature of its perpetrators. These individuals often appear respectable and socially polished, sometimes moving in the highest circles of influence. Fraudulent behavior is difficult to detect because its practitioners use methods designed to remain invisible. "Opportunity makes the thief," but that alone doesn't explain fraud. Why do some people commit fraud, while others don't? Research by Joost van Onna indicates that 80% of fraudsters had no criminal history before the age of 18. In other words, most entered into fraud later in life.[16]

Van Onna identifies three key factors: *social bonding*—fraudsters often have weaker ties to societal norms and workplace values, which personal setbacks further erode. *Moral flexibility*—they justify actions through flexible reasoning, seeing rules as negotiable. Some develop a *moral block*—feeling resentment rather than guilt, justifying fraud as acceptable self-interest or a means of survival.

Toward an integrated risk model

Companies often use the Three Lines Model (3LM), developed by the Institute of Internal Auditors (IIA), to prevent fraud.[17]

- First line: executive employees managing operations through careful hiring and a culture of integrity.
- Second line: risk management and compliance; monitoring regulatory and ethical risks independently from commercial pressures.
- Third line: internal auditor, providing independent assurance directly to the board.

However, this framework largely overlooks the role of top governance actors. External auditors aren't formally included, and boards often remain passive recipients of risk reports rather than active participants in fraud prevention.

We propose an *Integrated Risk Model*, positioning both the board and the external auditor as the ultimate guardians of integrity and fraud prevention. Since fraud detection requires

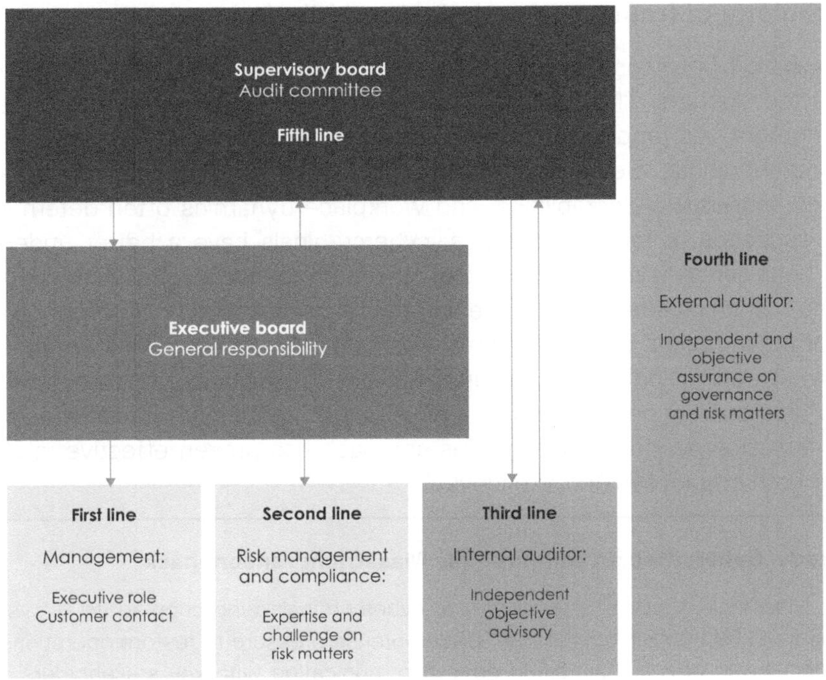

Figure 4.4
Integral Model for an Integrated Organizational Structure

cooperation across all organizational levels, in our model we added two lines of defense (see Figure 4.4).

- Fourth line (added to our model): external auditor, enhancing governance through audit committee agreements (see Chapter 4, Section §4.6).
- Fifth line (also added to our model): the non-executive/supervisory board, overseeing risk, reporting, and ethical conduct.

The blind spots in between

The 3LM weakness lies in neglecting behavioral risks and power dynamics. Structures look sound on paper but are undermined by human behavior, raising questions. Can frontline employees, under pressure to perform, resist small- or even larger-scale fraud when their bonuses are at stake? Do compliance functions relax their oversight when close relationships develop with the very teams they are meant to oversee? Do auditors, whether internal or external, align with short-term goals when pressured by executives, thereby reinforcing a culture of "we have a business to run"? The coordination between the audit committee, compliance, and external auditors can prove particularly difficult when executives hesitate to raise compliance concerns that threaten their personal performance targets.[18]

As previously discussed, transparent information flows are essential; selective reporting erodes integrity in decision-making quality and trust. For integrated models to work, ethical standards must be embraced at all levels, not just codified. Leadership must reinforce values through action, not only policy.

The psychology of fraud: manipulation and blind spots

Fraudsters exploit behavioral weaknesses, trust, authority, and psychological pressure to manipulate their targets. The intense pressure that comes with executive roles can lead to poor judgment. As rapper Kanye West quipped when under pressure: "and what do I do? Act more stupidly." Behavioral aspects play a dominant role in enabling fraud, as cognitive biases, individual vulnerabilities, and workplace dynamics often determine whether a scheme succeeds or fails. Sometimes, cybercriminals have a better understanding of employee behavior and vulnerabilities than the organization's own leadership does. The cases of the French cinema group Pathé and the Dutch Maastricht University show the vulnerability of organizations to today's global internet mafia. Both underscore the importance of carefully screening individuals for appointment to positions with financial sensitivity. Above all, fraud prevention is an organizational matter, requiring not just strong procedures but also practical awareness training. This approach has proven effective in changing the behavior of both employees and executives.[19]

Case Study: Cybercrime on campus—the Maastricht ransom hack

In 2019, Maastricht University fell victim to cybercriminals who crippled its IT systems and demanded a €200,000 Bitcoin ransom. Under intense pressure to restore operations, the university decided to pay. It maintained open communication with key stakeholders, students, and personnel, leading to a controlled resolution. The final outcome was unexpectedly positive. Police later recovered the ransom, and the rise in Bitcoin's value increased the recovered amount from €200,000 to nearly €500,000.

Not only are organizations (including banks, online retailers, internet providers, and digital marketplaces) directly targeted and faced with significant costs in defending themselves, but citizens and customers are also adversely affected. Ultimately, organizations supplying critical services are held accountable for poor security measures or for facilitating transactions involving untrustworthy partners.

Case Study: Pathé: fraud at the movies

"Strange, isn't it?" This was the reaction of the CEO of Pathé Netherlands to her CFO. It was 2018, and she was perusing an email that appeared to come from her Paris head office. The CEO had spent only a year in this relatively small company after serving as a director of a large, structured government organization. The email requested a transfer of money for a "secret acquisition" that nobody, especially the people in Paris, should be aware of. In consultation with her local CFO, the CEO approved multiple payments totaling €19.2 million. By the time alarm bells rang in Paris, the fraud was complete. Remarkably, all communication was conducted via email, with some payments being processed by the financial manager while on holiday. He had previously been dismissed from his role as an auditor at KPMG for "insufficiently critical behavior," yet Pathé appointed him to this key position. During the lawsuit, he claimed that Pathé never trained him to detect fraud.[20]

What a fraudster looks like (and what that says about us)

Detecting fraud is especially difficult for non-executive directors when it involves members of their own executive board. The fraudster-executive often operates within a trusted relationship with the very directors who appointed him. Research shows that 9% of fraud perpetrators hold top executive positions.[21] Meanwhile, 18% of executives admit a willingness to deceive auditors or regulators to advance their careers or raise their pay, a prevalence that is six times higher than that of regular employees.[22]

Gender patterns reveal several behavioral insights. Fraudsters are overwhelmingly male (74%). They are often driven by personal interests and tend to display a luxury lifestyle and greater aggressiveness than their female counterparts. Women typically place more value on social norms and show greater caution.[23] However, detection may play a role: investigators may more readily suspect men, underreporting female offenders (Figure 4.5).

Women on boards reduce fraud risk. Banks with higher female representation experience lower rates of malpractice. Women assess risks differently, take a stronger ethical stance, and reduce groupthink, enabling more critical oversight.

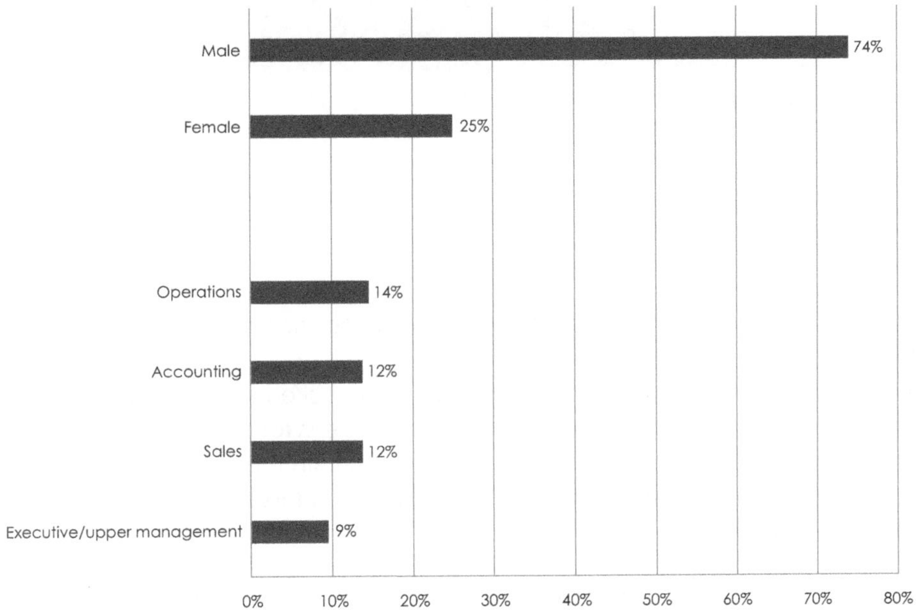

Figure 4.5
Offender Profile Internal Fraud
Source: Picture based on data of: ACFE, *Occupational Fraud 2024*.

Figure 4.6 illuminates key factors of criminal behavior.

Three conditions are often mentioned in the occurrence of fraud: personality/motivation, position/opportunity, and rationalization.

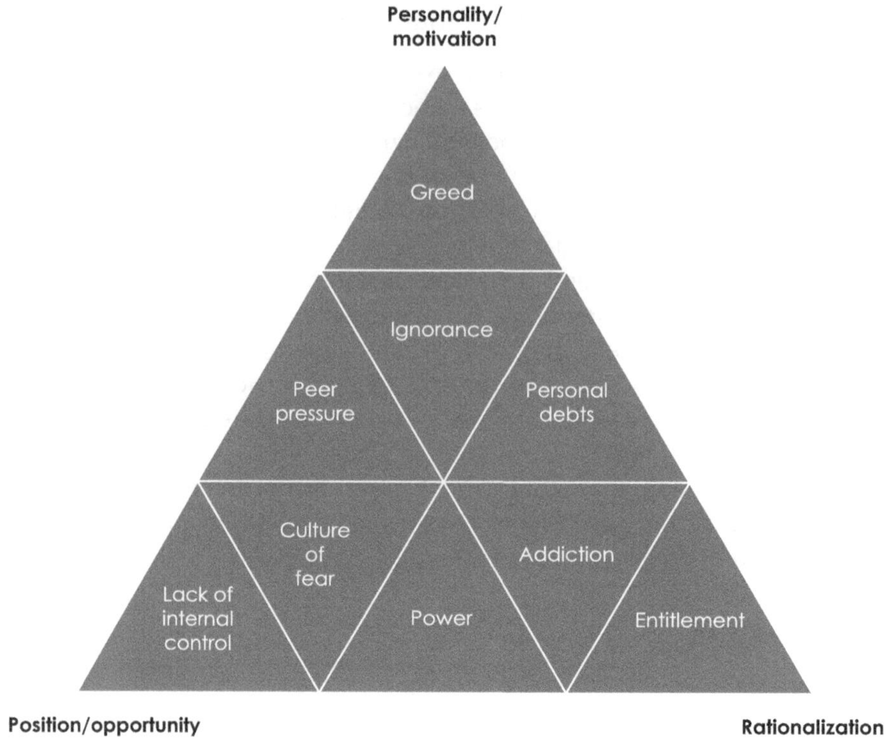

Figure 4.6
The Fraud Triangle

- Personality/motivation: fraudsters often exhibit narcissistic traits (see § 2.7), manipulating the facts and pursuing personal advantage.
- Position/opportunity: dominant executives with unchecked authority find greater opportunities to engage in fraud. Fear-based cultures enable wrongdoing to stay hidden.
- Rationalization: fraudsters justify their actions to maintain their self-image, believing they are "helping" the organization, feeling underpaid and undervalued, or are just "borrowing money for a while."

According to ACFE research, nearly half of workplace fraud cases, such as direct theft, insider trading or diverting money, are first detected thanks to a tip-off, most often from employees or customers.[24] Worryingly, the two oversight tools relied upon by non-executive directors—internal audit and external audit—detect only a small fraction of these.

In small civil society organizations such as schools and healthcare institutions, fraud risk often follows a familiar pattern: a dominant leader shields himself from scrutiny and obstructs meaningful internal oversight. Weak controls, poor segregation of approval functions, and a hands-off non-executive board create fertile ground for misconduct. In these cases, how can real oversight take root?

In larger organizations, the non-executive board can struggle to control excessive executive power and a dominant leadership style. With a weak team of non-executives who are unable to provide a strong internal countervailing force, control slips, and the risk of fraud grows. In a heartbeat, executives with narcissistic traits (see Chapter 2, Section 2.7) can shift from polished deference to open hostility toward non-executive directors, ignoring their formal authority. Markus Braun, former CEO of Wirecard, coolly introduced himself at a 2020 conference: "I am a pathological optimist." When whistleblowers raised the alarm, Braun turned aggressive lawyers on the *Financial Times* reports; the board applauded rather than intervening (see the case study in Chapter 3, Section §3.2).

Opportunity, warning signs, and whistleblowers

Three enabling factors help explain the rise in fraud today:

- Globalization creates blind spots: employees and business partners (such as suppliers and distributors) operate abroad, outside the board's direct field of vision.
- The intermingling of the underworld and the upper world has increased bribery and money laundering, as evidenced by the Wirecard case. Banks, such as Deutsche Bank, ING, and Danske Bank, have shown particular vulnerabilities in their international branch network (see the case study in Chapter 3, Section §3.5).
- Digitization and anonymous payment systems, such as Bitcoin, make it easier to conceal transactions and commit cyber fraud.

Fraudulent behavior is often hard to detect. Fraudsters use charm and psychological tricks to disarm non-executive directors, painting a rosy picture to avoid suspicion. Non-executive directors may rely too heavily on formal reports and familiar narratives, making it easy to miss red flags or omitted details. Whistleblowers are crucial to detection but risk being

Case Study: Offshore—a white swan in a black pond—bribes, pressure, and a whistleblower

"We have a business to run." That statement marked the difficult position of SBM Offshore's board in December 2014 as it sought to rescue a company that had been badly affected by corruption payments. And then a whistleblower spoke up.

SBM Offshore presents itself as a leader in its sector. It develops complex floating oil and gas platforms, with investments exceeding €1.5 billion per installation. The industry has long been known for its rough, macho culture, where bribery was once described as being "as common as brushing teeth." In 2012, reports of corruption surfaced following a customer complaint. To secure a contract with Brazilian Petrobras, the company had paid $275 million in bribes through an agent, internally dubbed "the smelliest of the smelliest," with similar practices uncovered in Africa. The former CEO, personally implicated, was fired, convicted, and jailed.

The non-executive directors and the new management reported themselves to prosecutors and settled fines in the Netherlands and Brazil to avoid being blacklisted from future contracts.

A former compliance manager played a crucial role in exposing the fraud. After his resignation, he grew frustrated with what he saw as a lack of transparency toward authorities and shareholders. In hindsight, also dissatisfied with his severance, he requested compensation. When this was denied, he became a whistleblower, handing sensitive corruption files to Dutch and U.S. authorities. The company maintained that it had followed proper procedures and characterized his actions as blackmail, reporting him for extortion. In a 2014 NRC interview, a board member described the company as "a white swan in a pitch-black pond," highlighting its precarious position in a situation he viewed as a case of "up or out." Ultimately, the company was fined a total of $840 million. Today, SBM Offshore promotes ethics and compliance as it pivots to renewable energy, continuing to achieve record-breaking sales and profits.

Only in 2024 was the end in sight for the whistleblower's saga. A Dutch court ruled in his favor, leaving him seeking damages for his lost career.

blackballed and fired. A safe working place culture, where speaking up is encouraged, is essential to bringing misconduct to light.

Speak up and be silenced: whistleblowers—heroes or threats?

Internal tip-offs remain the most important way to uncover fraud, with most companies maintaining whistleblower policies. In 2024, the United States led the field globally, with the SEC paying out $255 million to 47 whistleblowers.[25] In the EU, the Whistleblower Protection Directive came into force in 2019. While almost half of the global respondents in a worldwide EY report say that compliance with integrity standards has improved over the past two years, 65% of board members and 57% of senior management still feel pressure to stay silent, rather than report misconduct.[26]

What good is regulation if no one dares to speak up? Most whistleblowers pay a high price for their actions. Reporting misconduct breaks internal trust, threatens egos, and risks careers. Compromised directors often remove whistleblowers, labeling them as disloyal or manipulative. Indeed, not all whistleblowers are as white as snow—some come forward under the influence of stress, guilt, or family pressure.

Complex, global organizations require heightened vigilance, especially during acquisitions or expansion. Directors who never visit overseas operations remain blind to local practices. Warning signs include: evasive answers, unusual contracts, frequent CEO absences, signals of whistleblowers, use of shell companies, an extravagant lifestyle (luxury cars, lavish parties, and constant travel). A CEO's hostility toward directors who ask questions signals immediate danger. Non-executives, in their role as employers, should act decisively. Yet, *bounded willpower* often prevails, with excuses such as: "Let's wait and see," "We have no alternatives," or "We can't afford a management crisis right now." Their hesitation persists, even when action would serve their own best interests.

Sometimes directors collude: a non-executive director approved the CEO's plans and his bonus in exchange for a hefty invoice covering nonexistent advice, rationalizing: "I work constantly for this company, and there is no report because I don't believe in putting advice on paper."

Case Study: Meta: a platform too big to govern—or tell the truth.

The business model of online platform companies has long raised concerns about the impact on users' physical and psychological well-being. In 2021, in testimony before the U.S. Senate, whistleblower Frances Haugen stated that Meta's internal research identified harm to teenagers. Internal findings suggested that Instagram worsened body-image issues for adolescent girls, and that a significant share of UK teenage girls reported more frequent suicidal thoughts after using the platform.[27] Despite these findings, she argued, safety concerns were subordinated to engagement metrics and commercial priorities. Engagement-driven algorithms were linked to addictive behavior and user harm, while these risks were publicly downplayed or denied. Senator Richard Blumenthal, drawing on his experience in litigation against Big Tobacco, described the situation as a "Big Tobacco moment," arguing that both industries possessed internal evidence of harm to children yet failed to act decisively on those findings.

In 2025, Sarah Wynn-Williams, Meta's former Director of Global Public Policy, publicly described her internal experiences at the company, raising concerns about leadership culture, internal accountability, and the way dissent was handled. She later faced legal pressure in relation to her disclosures.[28] Meta has denied the allegations. During a February 2026 California trial, Zuckerberg acknowledged that he overruled 18 external well-being experts who had advised against reinstating Instagram beauty filters, citing concerns about "free expression."

Board oversight in big tech remains difficult to assess. In Meta's case, the board is structurally constrained because CEO Mark Zuckerberg controls 58% of the voting shares despite owning only 14% of the company through dual-class stock. Board composition and countervailing power are therefore closely tied to this control structure. The case raises the fundamental governance question: are internal accountability mechanisms strong enough to allow uncomfortable truths to surface without fear of retaliation—and who speaks for stakeholders, such as young users and their families, who have no seat at the table? More fundamentally, when internal evidence of harm is known but not transparently disclosed, the boundary between poor governance and systemic misrepresentation begins to blur.

SUMMARY AND CONCLUSION

Fraud is a many-headed monster. It is not just a financial crime but also a test of behavior and governance. It flourishes when non-executive directors are lulled into complacency, when corporate culture tolerates minor ethical lapses, and when oversight becomes a box-ticking exercise.

Only in hindsight is fraud blatant. It is rationalized, disguised, and enabled by blind spots in people and structures. Auditors, focused on numbers and reliant on management's honesty, detect only a fraction of cases. Collusion, complexity, and psychological manipulation hide the rest.

Guardianship cannot be passive. Non-executive directors must actively cultivate a culture of transparency and challenge overly confident leadership narratives. They should treat minor warning signs, such as withheld information, evasive answers, and overconfidence, as red flags.

In the end, prevention depends on understanding behavior. Diverse boards, in terms of thinking style, background, and perspective, are less prone to groupthink and better equipped to resist manipulation. That mix of vigilance, independence, and behavioral insight makes governance truly resilient.

§4.5—THE ARCHITECTURE OF CORRUPTION

Introduction

Corruption is an age-old phenomenon, flourishing in environments of power imbalance, secrecy, and rationalization. The World Bank ranks it among the leading threats to economic stability and democracy, eroding trust, transparency, and fair competition.

In today's globalized economy, the scale and complexity of corruption have expanded dramatically. Money laundering scandals have exposed billions of dollars, euros, or cryptocurrencies flowing through Western banks, financial platforms, and tax havens. The Ukraine war revealed deep entanglements between dishonest Russian, Ukrainian, and Western business networks.

For directors of global companies, corruption presents a significant ethical and strategic dilemma. How do you operate in countries where informal payments are normalized? Do you play the game, or walk away? And when corruption surfaces unexpectedly, should you bring it out into the open, or keep it quiet to protect the company's reputation?

Corruption is more than a legal or financial risk—it is a behavioral challenge. It rarely begins with bad intentions. Instead, it seeps in through a gradual erosion of ethics in the organization, pressure to hit targets, and the cultural normalization of misconduct. In this section, we explore the psychological architecture of corruption and the challenge for leadership in resisting it.

Power corrupts

Corruption doesn't just damage societies—it also draws companies into opaque, distorted forms of competition. In environments where bribes are the norm, firms face a behavioral dilemma: stay principled and lose contracts, or adapt to win. Over time, a cynical mindset takes hold—*corruption works, because we win*. Behavioral studies reveal how corruption embeds itself culturally.

Dice experiment

A 2013 dice experiment conducted among students in India found that those who cheated were 6% more likely to prefer government jobs while honest students gravitated toward the private sector. In India, a government job is perceived as offering greater opportunities for personal gain through corruption. In contrast, a 2019 study in Denmark found the opposite: honest students were more likely to pursue government jobs, reflecting a public sector culture built on trust and integrity.[29]

Executive and non-executive directors of international companies are expected to act in the firm's best interests. Yet many now recognize that corruption, particularly when businesses and politicians collude, can destabilize entire economies. Major banks, accounting firms, and global consultancies, despite their formal commitments to integrity, have found themselves drawn into bribery scandals.

Much of this misconduct occurs far from headquarters, creating a psychological and operational distance that weakens ethical accountability. Commercial pressures can make short-term gains seem tempting, but when corruption surfaces, the associated reputational damage, penalties, and legal risks typically exceed any financial benefit.

Western multinationals, for example, underestimated the systemic governance risk posed by Russia's persistent corruption and authoritarian governance, assuming economic engagement would encourage transparency. Russia's invasion of Ukraine, and the resulting sanctions, exposed how costly that assumption was, wiping out billions in investments.

Corruption often thrives in the intersection of Western corporations, consultancy firms, facilitators, and government officials. Developing nations with weak institutional governance are the most vulnerable. Three cases stand out as examples:

- South Africa—consulting firms McKinsey and Bain came under scrutiny for their roles in a corrupt business network involving President Zuma, senior ministers, and three brothers who ran the Gupta business empire. One deal, the purchase of 1,064 locomotives at a vastly inflated price, drained the country's public finances. Both McKinsey and Bain admitted misconduct and settled for $122 million, with South Africa failing to secure prosecution. The Gupta brothers reportedly went into hiding in Dubai.[30]
- Malaysia—individuals linked to Goldman Sachs were implicated in dealings with associates of Prime Minister Najib Razak relating to the 1MDB investment fund (1Malaysia Development Berhad). Prosecutors estimate that $4.5 billion disappeared into offshore accounts, leaving Malaysia with a $7.8 billion debt burden. Goldman Sachs was fined $3.9 billion, KPMG $111 million, and Deloitte $80 million. Najib was convicted in the Malaysian High Court. The money was via shell companies sluiced through Singaporean, Swiss, and U.S. banks and has so far only been partially recovered.[31]
- Mozambique—Credit Suisse and Russia's VTB Bank arranged over $2 billion in loans, ostensibly to fund a state-run tuna fishing fleet and maritime security projects. In reality, hundreds of millions were siphoned off through bribes and kickbacks to Mozambican officials and bankers. Credit Suisse later agreed to pay $475 million in settlements, and several of its former bankers were prosecuted. The loans backed by state guarantees plunged Mozambique into economic crisis.[32]

These patterns manifest in various forms across different jurisdictions. Understanding how corruption adapts and disguises itself is crucial for non-executives trying to recognize early warning signs. The cases also show that even well-established firms can become implicated—making vigilance and oversight a core responsibility of the board.

Many faces of corruption

Corruption takes multiple forms:

- Some companies may offer bribes to win contracts or secure advantages. However, government insiders, knowing the practice, often actively solicit bribes, using their positions to secure a deal.
- Corporations may form cartels to manipulate markets.

- Lobbying, when unchecked by governments or company boards, can blur the line between legitimate influence and corruption.
- Corruption also hampers climate action by misallocating funds and weakening adaptation efforts, as the 2024 Corruption Perceptions Index (CPI) highlights.[33]

Corruption harms more than balance sheets. It distorts markets, misallocates public money, weakens institutions, and breeds public cynicism. And despite the "zero-tolerance" banners on corporate websites, loopholes persist. Lawyers, advisers, and tax specialists may still help to structure behavior that is questionable but technically legal. This is a classic example of *bounded ethicality*, where people believe they are doing the right thing while enabling the opposite. It is precisely in this domain that non-executive directors can make a difference.

Their job is not to moralize but to see clearly: to recognize when incentives drift, when narratives become too convenient, and when "everyone does it" becomes an excuse. Non-executive directors must ensure that the company's values are practiced—not just printed on the website.

Strong institutions and consistent enforcement help, but they are never enough on their own. Much of the real accountability now comes from outside: investigative journalists and NGOs such as Transparency International and Global Witness. Their work repeatedly uncovers what formal systems miss—hidden donations, light-touch prosecutions abroad, and lobbying that takes place in the shadows.

Corruption flourishes where no one is looking. Oversight works when non-executives pay attention to the places everyone else prefers to ignore.

From facilitation payments to willful ignorance

Manipulative framing and opaque structuring often lead non-executives to approve transactions they might otherwise question, making inaction a quiet form of complicity. Corrupt practices lie on a sliding scale. At the mild end are so-called facilitation payments—small sums paid to speed up routine procedures in countries with weak bureaucracy.

Until recently, U.S. law historically allowed certain payments abroad under narrow exceptions (but not at home), as long as they did not influence contract awards—a double standard that risks blurring the moral line. By contrast, the UK's Serious Fraud Office treats *any* facilitation payment as bribery, regardless of size or intent.[34] Many multinationals now follow this stricter approach, banning such payments through company-wide integrity policies.

Corruption often begins with small, seemingly harmless acts:

- a $20 bill slipped into a passport to ensure a smooth border crossing.
- a bribe disguised as a "brokerage fee."
- a fake intermediary inserted to distance the company from the payment.
- a consulting firm used as a buffer, providing plausible deniability.

"*It's how everyone works in this business.*" Once normalized, these behaviors gain momentum and embed themselves in corporate culture. Each act erodes organizational integrity, making the next step easier. Power accelerates this drift: research from EY shows that senior executives—the very people expected to set the tone at the top—sometimes report higher tolerance for unethical behavior than junior staff (see Figure 4.7).

Figure 4.7
EY Global Integrity Report 2024 (Board Members: $N = 442$, Other Employees: $N = 1031$)

Cartels and boys' club dynamics

While corruption is typically built around exchanges between a bribe-giver and a decision maker, involving the transfer of slush funds, cartels form when competing firms coordinate anti-competitive behavior to manipulate prices. Cartels, unlike individual bribery, depend on group dynamics and social bonds.

Cartels are a unique form of corruption: rational companies collude to manipulate markets, betting that financial gains will outweigh the risks of fines or jail time. Unlike bribery, they rarely involve cash payments, giving the illusion of a victimless crime. Cartel behavior is sustained not just by economic logic; it thrives on social trust and insider networks.

A French study of 50 cartels revealed how culture, personal ties, loyalty, and self-interest drive their operations. These "boys' clubs" rely on unwritten rules and mutual protection to sustain anti-competitive behavior.[35] Participants are often long-time industry insiders who are connected through schools, trade fairs, or associations. Entry is highly exclusive—newcomers must prove they're trustworthy; anyone seen as unreliable is refused.

Cartels are predominantly male, often sidelining women to administrative tasks. One notable case in the fruit compote industry illustrated this divide: a female entrepreneur disregarded cartel norms, skipped meetings, and aggressively expanded her business. Her peers complained, but when the cartel was exposed, her company received a reduced fine—ironically, because she hadn't followed the cartel's unwritten rules.

Cartels use linguistic camouflage. Competitors become "colleagues" or *confrères*, customers are *clientele*, seen as a necessary nuisance rather than business partners. Price-fixing becomes "market regulation," collusion is expressed as "stabilizing the industry," and competitive pricing is dismissed as "abnormally low prices." This vocabulary reframes unethical behavior and reduces cognitive dissonance.

Given the high risk of fines and criminal convictions, one would ask: why don't more managers leave the cartel? Financial gain is only part of the appeal—cartels also offer status, insider knowledge, and job security. Quitting risks exclusion from robust industry networks, potentially harming one's career. Some cartels are so convinced of their legitimacy that they create internal rulebooks and written meeting minutes to formalize their conduct.

For many, the cartel isn't just a business tactic—it's a social and professional ecosystem. Staying carries a legal risk, but leaving carries the cost of isolation. This explains why the trucker's cartel was able to keep running for 14 years.

Case Study: How Europe's truck giants steered the market

Between 1997 and 2011, some of Europe's largest truck manufacturers—DAF, MAN, Volvo/Renault, Daimler, and Iveco—weren't just driving business forward. By secretly sharing price lists, they ensured that no one player undercut another. But it didn't stop there. They also conspired to delay the introduction of cleaner emissions technology, keeping the air (and their profits) a little dirtier for a little longer.

In 2016, the European Commission imposed a record €2.9 billion fine, and by 2022, thousands of customers, who had paid artificially high prices for their trucks for years, began filing claims.[36] A culture of long-term collusion can persist for decades until enforcement catches up, but the financial and reputational costs compound over time.

Boardroom blind spots, eyes wide shut

In many companies, bribery does not begin as an act of outright malice—it often starts in response to intense pressure to perform. Commercial teams sent abroad may be pushed to close deals "at all costs," sometimes with tacit or explicit approval from headquarters. This pressure can lead to the use of intermediaries or more complex arrangements, all designed to distance senior leadership from the mechanics of the deal.

For non-executive directors, this creates a distinct challenge: in a globalized world, bribery can occur far from headquarters. It is often disguised in the language of "relationship management" or "market practice," and rationalized as "harmless" and "necessary to stay competitive." The global ecosystem of markets, partners, and intermediaries across multiple jurisdictions further shapes this risk, making early detection difficult.

A 2022 EY study delivered a shock to its own researchers: 42% of board members admitted to sometimes justifying unethical behavior to meet financial targets.[37] The underlying psychological mechanism is "*moral disengagement*": the self-persuasion that company rules can—or even should—bend to "local norms" if only because competitors appear to be doing the same. This dynamic has outsized consequences for companies and governments for three reasons:

- Multinational amplification: What looks like a local issue is often sustained, or even intensified, by multinational companies. Through aggressive bidding wars and the routine use of both small and large facilitation payments, they inject money into corrupt systems, helping them persist and evolve into the "new normal."
- Political ambiguity: Ambiguity or conflicting political signals, often shaped by self-interest and industry lobbying, can blur ethical boundaries. Executives may conclude that a certain level of misconduct is not only tolerated but is necessary to remain competitive.
- Distance from headquarters: The farther a foreign subsidiary sits from the center, the easier it becomes to recast questionable practices as local adaptation, operational necessity, or something not worth escalating. Distance thus weakens meaningful challenge of unethical behavior, and greenwashing that masks misconduct risks can become routine.

For non-executives, a narrow focus on legal compliance—are we within the law?—is not enough. Differing cultural norms across countries require constant awareness that we judge behavior by our own standards. If we fail to apply our own standards—even when under pressure, we risk stepping onto the slippery slope ourselves.

The enforcement landscape worldwide

The United Nations Office on Drugs and Crime (UNODC) estimates that between 2% and 5% of global GDP—$800 billion to $2 trillion—is laundered annually. To combat this, the U.N. Convention Against Corruption (UNCAC) was adopted in 2003. A total of 191 countries have since ratified it, and it serves as a global standard. Remarkably, even countries that rank poorly on the Transparency International Index ratified it, though ratification does not guarantee domestic enforcement. For them, adopting UNCAC offers reputational benefits, diplomatic leverage, and a shield against external criticism, even when domestic enforcement is minimal. UNCAC warns that corruption destabilizes societies, weakens democratic institutions, erodes justice and sustainable development, and fuels organized crime.

National laws vary in scope and strength. The U.S. Foreign Corrupt Practices Act (FCPA) remains among the toughest because of its extraterritorial reach: any foreign company using the U.S. financial system can be prosecuted. Enforcement has produced some of the largest corporate penalties on record, including: Airbus ($2.09 billion), Siemens (800 million), Petrobras ($1.78 billion), Alstom ($772 million), Goldman Sachs ($2.9 billion, excluding the Malaysian settlement), and Halliburton ($579 million).

But enforcement is not constant; it depends on political will and consistency. In January 2025, the White House issued an executive order signaling a potentially softer enforcement approach toward U.S. firms, citing concerns about "competitive disadvantages."[38] Signals like these shape behavior. When political intention shifts, executives infer that risk tolerance is rising—and non-executives, responsible for protecting fairness and long-term integrity, cannot ignore that shift.

Case Study: Alstom

In 2003, French industrial conglomerate Alstom pursued an Indonesian power project under a "deal at all costs" mandate from its CEO, Patrick Kron. The competition was intense and there were strong suspicions that Alstom's main American rival was using bribes. Frédéric Pierucci, then a senior manager based in the United States, believed he was simply doing his job. He closed the fiercely contested deal—approved by the company's risk committee in Paris—including facilitating "agent payments."

In 2013, while transiting through JFK Airport, Pierucci was unexpectedly arrested on charges of bribing Indonesian officials and violating the FCPA. In his memoir, *The American Trap*, the executive reflected on how what he viewed as a routine business decision became the basis for criminal charges. Yet he also felt that Head Office had kept him dangling, convinced that he was caught in a larger geopolitical power struggle disguised as anti-corruption enforcement.

In the end, Alstom paid $772 million to settle with the U.S. Department of Justice. Shortly thereafter, in a politically charged deal, U.S.-based General Electric acquired Alstom's core energy business, including its strategic nuclear operations. Finally after two years in U.S. detention, Pierucci was released.[39]

This case illustrates how pressure from a company's leadership can legitimize risky behavior and expose its employees to severe legal consequences. What feels like standard practice can be subject to criminal charges when enforcement priorities shift. It also highlights the risks arising from excessive distance between top management of a multinational organization and its operations, while offering little evidence of effective non-executive oversight.

Against the backdrop of OECD warnings that global corruption distorts markets, weakens institutions, and erodes public trust, the OPL 245 affair in Nigeria serves as a vivid illustration of the governance threats facing multinational companies that invest in high-risk environments. At the time, Nigeria ranked 140th out of 180 nations on the Corruption Perceptions Index.

Distance from day-to-day operations in far-flung subsidiaries does not, in principle, shield senior leaders from accountability. Yet the procedure and outcome of this case delivered a shock to nearly every party involved, including senior Shell and ENI executives, the Nigerian government, the OECD Working Group on Bribery, and finally the lead Italian prosecutor.

Case Study: Safe sex in Nigeria

In 2021, senior executives of business partners Shell and ENI found themselves in a Milan courtroom facing accusations of corruption. The title of this case study, "Safe Sex in Nigeria," is borrowed from *The Economist* and refers to what Italian prosecutors alleged was the companies' attempt to protect themselves by letting the Nigerian government handle the distribution of funds that allegedly included bribes.

After 20 years of negotiations, both oil companies had finally secured the rights to explore one of Nigeria's largest offshore oil reserves, "block OPL 245," for an upfront payment of $1.1 billion. According to the prosecutor, leaked internal emails and conversations suggested that both companies were aware that a significant portion of the payment would end up in the hands of politicians and intermediaries rather than the Nigerian state, with $500 million allegedly paid in cash. Shell and ENI argued that their executives had no knowledge, no motive, and no warning signs of corruption; that they had acted in "good faith." In 2021, the Milan court acquitted the companies and their executives, ruling that circumstantial evidence alone, without direct proof of an agreed corrupt arrangement, could not meet the required standard of proof.[40]

The final surprise before the appeal of the public office came when lead prosecutor Fabio de Pasquale, known for past corruption cases against former Prime Ministers Craxi and Berlusconi, found himself accused of misconduct. He was removed from the case and demoted, triggering surprise and concern within legal circles and anti-corruption watchdogs. His successor dismissed the appeal, effectively bringing the trial to a close.

Civil society organizations, including Global Witness and Transparency International, have long cited OPL 245 as a symbol of governance weaknesses in Nigeria's oil sector.[41] Shell and ENI reject this view, stressing their clearly communicated commitments to integrity, responsible energy, and zero-tolerance policies, at the same time noting the economic value of their investments to Nigeria.

For Nigeria, however, the affair reflects deeper structural problems: persistent governance failures and recurring political-business scandals fuel public mistrust and drive young professionals to seek opportunities abroad, worsening the country's long-term brain drain.[42]

For non-executives, the lesson is to challenge assumptions early, demand transparency around intermediaries and payments, and ensure that integrity risks in high-corruption environments are examined at the same depth as financial and operational risks.

The OPL245 acquittal did not occur in a vacuum. Against this backdrop, the OECD Working Group on Bribery has expressed serious concerns over Italy's slow progress in meeting its international commitments, noting in 2024 that it had fully implemented only 18 of 48 anti-corruption recommendations, far behind many Western peers.[43] The Working Group also noted that the elevated burden of proof in Italy makes it difficult to prosecute corruption cases successfully, undermining confidence in the country's enforcement regime and, as a result, increasing the risk that Italy's legal environment becomes an attractive hub for complex international deals that might not withstand scrutiny elsewhere.[44]

SUMMARY AND CONCLUSION

Corruption is not just a legal exposure; it is a behavioral trap that can pull even well-intentioned boards into risky territory. In a global economy, a bribe paid in Indonesia or Nigeria can trigger prosecution in New York, Milan, or London. Boards face a real prisoner's dilemma: conform to local practices and risk long-term damage, or walk away and lose the deal.

Survey research reveals directors often rationalize unethical conduct to meet financial targets—a sign of moral disengagement. Major cases confirm the pattern where physical distance creates psychological distance. When senior leaders are far from local operations, questionable behavior is easily reframed as "custom," "relationship management," or "regulatory complexity." For non-executives, distance from operations must never become distance from responsibility.

Regulatory trends add further strain. Europe is tightening enforcement under OECD and UN pressure, while political crosscurrents in several countries create confusion about the direction and consistency of global oversight. Cases such as Alstom and OPL 245 reveal that legal outcomes vary widely, yet reputational and strategic damage lasts long after courts have ruled. Opaque practices undermine the institutional development emerging economies need to prosper.

For non-executives, tackling corruption is not moralism; it is protecting the license to operate. Integrity is not only an ethical choice—it is a strategic imperative.

§4.6—THE EXTERNAL AUDITOR, NATURAL ALLY

Introduction

Dear auditor, what's keeping you awake at night? The question is rarely asked, least of all by boards. But, when it comes to assurance, directors should leave no stone unturned, asking probing questions rather than passively relying on what is presented. The external auditor is a natural ally—an independent expert with both the distance and the mandate to speak plainly.

When an external auditor signs off on the accounts, boards often assume the figures are accurate, the rules correctly applied, and no fraud is present. But that signature can mislead, as many cases show. Even natural allies are still human. Auditors, often seen as rational watchdogs, are just as vulnerable to cognitive bias and optimism as anyone else—and they face subtle commercial pressures from the very companies they audit.

Fraud and misconduct seldom sit neatly in the ledger. They hide inside culture, tone at the top, loyalty norms, and an unspoken "don't ask" atmosphere. Audit committees in large companies may have strengthened since Sarbanes-Oxley, but in smaller organizations, non-executives often still place blind faith in reports, reading financials like supermarket receipts: check the entries, confirm the total, move on.

Absolute assurance does not exist—that is the realistic message. This section explores where assurance stops, how the board–auditor relationship really works, and how non-executives can navigate that space with confidence.

Bounded rationality behind the audit

An auditor's signature is no guarantee. Auditing takes place under uncertainty, time pressure, asymmetric information, and dependence on the client—conditions in which cognitive biases thrive. Auditors are expected to detect mistakes, yet they also make them. Even though they are viewed as objective, data-driven professionals, their judgments are still influenced by behavioral factors.

Enron's and Wirecard's financial statements appeared sound, and received unqualified opinions from their auditors. But even diligent auditors can fall into bounded rationality. The complexity of financial data and subtle psychological biases may lead to "satisficing"—settling for reasonable assurance instead of probing deeper. Research published in 2023 shows that auditors frequently skip or defer complex tasks, quietly "filing them away," giving priority to easy-to-control tasks.[45] Lengthy resource-intensive investigations are no exception.

Budget constraints can silently compound this problem. When fees are tight, a subtle conflict of interest arises: the auditor's commercial incentive to preserve the client relationship competes with their professional duty to probe harder. In reference to Max Bazerman, this rarely feels like a conscious compromise. Instead, unconscious bias nudges the auditor toward decisions that keep the engagement on budget: accepting plausible explanations, skipping time-consuming tests, or overlooking smaller anomalies that might signal a bigger issue. Over time, this quiet erosion of professional skepticism can significantly reduce audit quality.[46]

The result is that audit opinions can become evasively worded, leaving room for interpretation and creating a false sense of certainty.

The Wirecard scandal starkly illustrates the challenges auditors can face. During court proceedings, KPMG auditors revealed how they had uncovered fraudulent transactions at Wirecard. In response, Wirecard's CEO attempted to co-opt the auditors by inviting them on a ski trip—an unconventional tactic to sway their independence. When the auditors declined, the CEO allegedly threatened legal action. A week later, Wirecard filed for insolvency, collapsing under the weight of its financial deception.[47]

Difficulties in extracting accurate information from reporting by multinational companies are exemplified by the Respironics case.

Case Study: Respironics: when strategic vision causes risk blindness

In 2007, Philips bought Respironics, an American maker of sleep-apnea respirators. The deal aligned neatly with Philips' strategy and its website motto, *"improving people's health,"* as well as its ambition to improve 2.5 billion lives a year by 2030.

Yet in 2021, Philips issued a surprise warning: key products might pose health risks. A noise-reducing foam, originally marketed as an innovation, could degrade, releasing particles and harmful chemicals into patients' airways. The U.S. FDA later concluded that Philips' testing and analysis were "not adequate to fully evaluate the risks" and that Respironics had failed to report incidents in a timely manner.[48]

The company's 2021 Annual Report mentioned only "potential health risks," using cautious phrasing such as "certain sleep products" and "voluntary recalls," while setting aside a

€0.7 billion provision to cover any problems that might arise. The external auditor nonetheless issued an unqualified opinion. Subsequent investigative reporting suggested that concerns about foam degradation had been circulating within the company for over a decade.[49] By 2024, the FDA had logged 116,000 medical incidents and 561 deaths potentially linked to the devices. Philips agreed to a $1.1 billion settlement in the United States, while investor litigation in the Netherlands continued.

A revealing detail: the phrase "patient safety" appeared only once in the 2020 Annual Report, 20 times in 2021, and 84 times in 2022; the latter, only after the financial impact became unavoidable.

The case illustrates a common governance trap: when a dominant strategic narrative takes hold, early warning signs are played down, and remedial action is postponed. The auditor, too, risks being influenced by this framing—until the facts can no longer be ignored. Philips' experience shows that even grand purpose statements require rigorous oversight, robust early-warning mechanisms, and a readiness to confront uncomfortable truths.

Trust, bounded ethicality: the fragile link between auditor and board

Executive and non-executive directors often place too much weight on positively framed assurances, failing to ask the follow-up questions that matter. As Bazerman notes, people tend to believe what they *want* to be true—especially when the desired outcome aligns with their interests. When an auditor says "everything is in order," boards can too easily accept the reassurance at face value.[50]

Yet the auditor–audit committee relationship is only as strong as the auditing profession's own integrity. *Bounded ethicality*—the unconscious normalization of unethical behavior—can quietly corrode that trust. In 2022, hundreds of KPMG auditors in Australia, the United Kingdom, and the United States were found to have cheated even on ethics exams. Some shared answers, treating the test as a group exercise; others signed blank audit forms without verifying their accuracy. A culture of silence allowed the misconduct to continue until it was exposed publicly.

Such cases reveal how fragile trust truly is. It takes years to earn, seconds to lose, and often decades to rebuild. For non-executives, the lesson is simple: trust your auditor—but verify.[51]

If companies could talk: formal and informal signals

If companies could talk, they would speak two languages. The first is formal: financial statements, audit reports, KPIs—the numbers that dominate board information packs and audit committee meetings. The second is informal: tone at the top, cultural undercurrents, morale, trust, and the subtle shifts in behavior that never show up in a spreadsheet but often tell the more important story.

Boards tend to focus on the formal because it feels objective, tidy, and verifiable. The audit committee—where financial expertise meets external assurance—is well placed to review the official information with the auditor. Its mandate is to ensure the accounts are free of material misstatements. But what counts as *material*? Practical limits apply: auditors cannot test everything; cost constraints mean they have to focus on what is most likely to be significant, rather than every anomaly.

Even then, audited figures can mislead. Research from Norway shows that investigative journalists uncover about 25% of major corporate fraud, while auditors detect only 4%—a reminder that formal auditing alone cannot provide the full picture.[52]

The informal side of information, therefore, may matter just as much. Culture, behavior, and hidden risks often reveal issues long before they show up in the financials. Anyone who has spent time in an organization knows this instinctively: the numbers say one thing, the atmosphere says another. Audit committees, focused on rules and hard data, risk overlooking these early warning signs.

The Dutch law firm Pels Rijcken, a small organization where everyone knows each other, shows how cultural blind spots can allow serious issues to remain hidden in plain sight.

Case Study: Pels Rijcken: the law firm nobody suspected

Frank Oranje was the highly respected and impeccably presented Chairman of Pels Rijcken, the Dutch government's preferred law firm. In its 2018 Annual Report, the firm confidently stated that its internal controls were strong and that no fraud or corruption had occurred.

Those assurances proved hollow. When Oranje's long-standing cooking of the books came to light, the story took a tragic turn: he took his own life before facing trial. His public image flipped overnight—from trusted adviser to a man driven by money and status, one who had siphoned off client funds for years.

The external auditor had reported in 2019 that "extra attention" had been paid to fraud detection, but the misconduct continued unchecked.[53] Oranje's partners later described his actions as "sophisticated embezzlement," but the disciplinary court delivered a far harsher judgment: the partners had failed to ask basic questions or verify transactions. The case reveals a classic behavioral trap. A tightly knit culture, high internal trust, and the *halo effect*—where admiration discouraged critical judgment—created blind spots that allowed the fraud to persist.

In such environments, even an auditor can become a lone voice, making independent scrutiny harder and sometimes isolating.

Signed, sealed . . . and misunderstood

Readers of annual reports often assume that a signed-off document is factual and complete. The formal layout, internal approval, and auditor's signature convey solidity. In reality, financial statements blend hard data with judgment calls. Auditors provide *reasonable*, not *absolute*, assurance that statements are free from material misstatement; a crucial limitation, because governance cannot outsource integrity.

Balance sheet and income statement items mix objectivity and estimation. Numerical data can be verified, but goodwill, impairments, and provisions rely on assumptions about future cash flows and risks. Audit reports can unintentionally reinforce the illusion of certainty: legal phrasing such as "it does not appear that the financial statements do not give a true and fair view" sounds authoritative while offering little clarity. Terms like "true," "fair," "limited assurance," and "material" provide comfort without precision. This is the behavioral trap: reassurance without commitment creates complacency.

Even an unqualified ("clean") opinion can mislead. *Authority bias* may cause audit committees to equate "clean" with "risk-free," while overconfidence leads them to overlook the assumptions behind going concern judgments or valuation models. Critical questions are warranted: *What scenarios were tested? What risks were excluded?*

Ultimately, the executive board remains responsible for maintaining transparency, managing risk, and ensuring continuity. Rising liability has prompted executives to issue in-control statements, but as case studies show, *normalcy bias* can lead non-executives to accept these statements at face value, especially when their access to financial data is limited.

Annual reports are growing longer, often burying key insights. Faced with information overload, readers skim for familiar figures and miss early warning signs. A concise disclosure of the key risks would strengthen transparency and remind boards that certainty is often a feeling, not a fact.

The *private session*, hard controls and soft controls

Control mechanisms fall into two broad categories (Figure 4.8).

- Hard controls include formal, measurable tools such as budgets, financial reports, and quality metrics. They are essential, yet vulnerable: once errors enter the system, they often persist undetected. At Enron (Chapter 4, Section §4.2) and Wirecard (Chapter 3, Section §3.3), falsified data and opaque structures evaded oversight for years because hard controls were trusted more than they were tested.
- Soft controls focus on culture, behavior, tone at the top, integrity, and the freedom to report wrongdoing. Although less tangible, they can be assessed through employee surveys, whistleblower reports, stakeholder complaints, and cultural diagnostics.

Both dimensions work best when examined in *private sessions* between the audit committee and the external auditor, without executives being present. Introduced after Enron and Sarbanes–Oxley, these sessions enable candid conversations about culture, loyalty norms, complaint patterns, and the fundamental question: *is continuity guaranteed?* Without executive management in the room, auditors are more willing to surface concerns that might otherwise remain unspoken.

Despite this, organizational culture remains poorly examined at the board level. Research by the Institute of Internal Auditors shows that many internal auditors rarely discuss culture or behavior in depth with the audit committee. A 2023 study found that 40% of culture

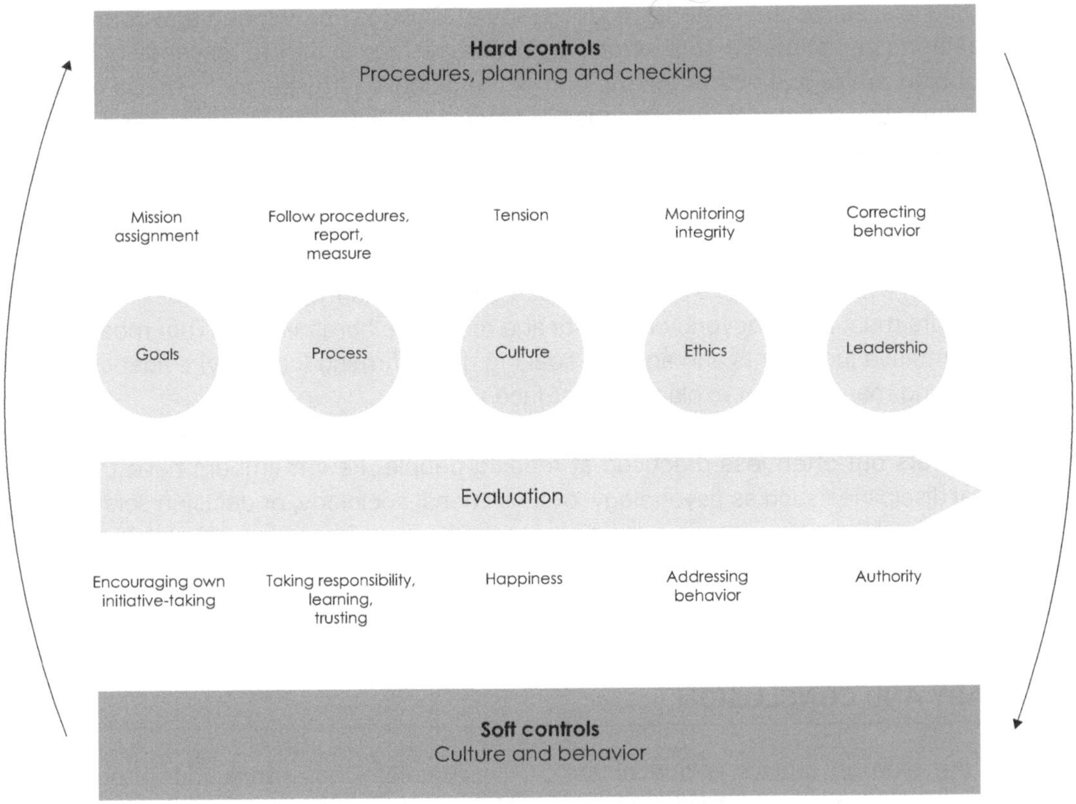

Figure 4.8
Hard Controls and Soft Controls

assessments are presented in informal briefings rather than formal reports; a reminder of how easily organizations can choose what is easiest to measure.[54] Non-executives should reflect by asking: "What is the culture telling us that the numbers are not"?

While corporate scandals make headlines, tens of thousands of audits proceed without incident each year. Why is that? Is it because the audit process was effective, the company was truly in control, the auditor refused to compromise on audit quality, or all three? Ultimately, non-executive directors need to trust that their auditor will report problems clearly and unambiguously. But this trust must be grounded in professional rigor, not blind reliance: the auditor as strategic ally of the audit committee.

Seeing what the numbers don't show

Audit discussions cannot stop at the financials. They also have a duty to examine the company's exposure to external shocks—such as climate change, geopolitical instability, inflation, and supply-chain fragility—and its environmental and social impacts. Environmental and health liabilities can materialize suddenly, even when warning signs existed, as illustrated by the 3M Antwerp case (Chapter 5, Section §5.2).

The financial stakes are material. A University of Chicago study found that carbon damage amounts to an estimated 18% of profits for the average U.S. firm, exceeding 300% of profits for high-emission firms at the top end of the global energy sector.[55] This is not background information—it is material data that investors and wider stakeholders need to see.

Yet audit quality itself came under renewed pressure. In 2024, the International Forum of Independent Audit Regulators (IFIAR) reported that 34% of inspected listed public-interest entity audits contained at least one significant deficiency—up from 26% in 2022, interrupting a decade of gradual improvement. IFIAR links these failures to both technical lapses and behavioral forces.[56] As Mark Nelson argues in his model of professional skepticism, auditors must move beyond checklists and recognize human limits. That means slowing down intuitive judgments and actively seeking disconfirming (contrary) evidence, rather than accepting management explanations at face value.[57]

This is where audit committees face their own blind spot. They are excellent at reading balance sheets but often less practiced at reading people. Few members have training in behavioral disciplines such as psychology, organizational sociology, or decision science. The result is predictable: metrics receive scrutiny, yet the human dynamics behind those metrics remain under-examined.

SUMMARY AND CONCLUSION

Trust in the external auditor is one of the audit committee's last lines of defense, yet it is fragile. Even skilled auditors operate under the shadow of bounded rationality, cognitive bias, and subtle commercial pressures. Budget constraints can erode professional skepticism, and early warnings may disappear in a fog of cautious language or optimistic narratives. Cases like Respironics show how strategic priorities can create blindness long before issues reach non-executives.

To break this circle, boards must move beyond passively receiving signed-off reports. *Private sessions*—without executives present—give auditors the psychological safety to share concerns they may hesitate to voice publicly: cultural red flags, patterns of silence, weakening controls, or risks the numbers don't (yet) reveal.

Absolute assurance does not exist. High-quality assurance requires combining hard controls (budgets, metrics, compliance) with soft controls (tone at the top, trust, openness, and the willingness to surface bad news). Both are essential to detect misconduct early and challenge overly optimistic framing.

For non-executive directors, the task is clear: probe the story behind the figures, ensure cultural and behavioral risks are explicitly discussed, and regularly evaluate whether the auditor brings not only technical competence but also the skepticism and courage to speak uncomfortable truths. A behavioral lens ensures boards are not the last to know—because while they cannot change the numbers, they can change the conversation that reveals them.

§4.7—FROM INTEGRITY OF INFORMATION TO INTEGRITY OF DECISION-MAKING

Introduction

Imagine you are on a board reviewing the annual report. The numbers look good, yet something feels off. You ask a few questions, but the answers still don't quite line up. This is the challenge of moving from *data* to *wisdom*: how do directors ensure that the information they receive leads to sound decisions?

Boards look both backward and forward. Looking back is not always easy, but it can be relatively simple—checking whether plans were executed, procedures followed, and the numbers still correct. Looking forward is harder. The future is filled with uncertainty, blind spots, and the persistent issue of information asymmetry. Directors rely on various sources, such as market updates, strategy papers, investment proposals, and succession plans, while knowing that not all critical signals will reach them.

Information gaps are not only about missing signals at the top. Key decisions are sometimes made too low in the organization, catching executives by surprise; at other times, non-executives discover that important choices were taken by the executive board without involving them as they should.

In this complex governance landscape, shaped as much by human behavior as by data, non-executive directors must bridge the gap between facts and judgment. This section explores how information is gathered, questions are asked, and ultimately translated into board decisions.

Case Study: Apollo 13: no blind spots in space

On April 13, 1970, an oxygen tank on Apollo 13 exploded 330,000 km from Earth, severely damaging the spacecraft. With oxygen levels dropping, carbon dioxide began to build, and Mission Control in Houston faced a life-or-death challenge: bring the astronauts home safely; yet only minimal resources were present.

Years of rigorous simulation training meant that NASA's team did not panic. Instead, they broke the crisis into manageable problems, tested solutions before implementing them, and considered every idea, regardless of a person's rank. The now famous "duct tape and sock" fix for the CO_2 filter became a symbol of ingenuity under pressure.

Despite the mission's failure to land on the Moon, this culture of structured problem-solving, collaborative intelligence, and professional skepticism prevented catastrophe. Unlike many boardrooms, where groupthink and hierarchy can stifle innovation, NASA fostered an environment in which every voice mattered.

The governance challenge is comparable. Boards must create their own "Mission Control" mindset, one that anticipates the unexpected, encourages dissenting ideas, and ensures that no critical information is ignored.

Case Study: Deutsche Bank: systemic behavioral governance failures

In Frankfurt, two towers loom over corporate Germany, standing 144 meters tall. The Deutsche Bank (DB) logo—a single diagonal stroke—symbolizes both simplicity and, to some, arrogance. Unlike NASA, where structured decision-making prevented catastrophe, DB's leadership was a governance failure driven not by technical errors but by unchecked ambition and behavioral biases.

The shift began in the late 1990s, when DB abandoned its identity as Germany's trusted, conservative lender, to become a global investment bank. The 1999 acquisition of Bankers Trust, a U.S. investment bank known for high-risk trading, accelerated this transformation. Intending to compete with Wall Street giants, the bank's leadership imported a culture of aggressive boundary-pushing that eroded its long-standing governance principles. CEO Josef Ackermann's public target of 25% return on equity became the dominant metric, prioritizing short-term profits over long-term stability.

As DB expanded globally, internal oversight weakened. Compliance became a formality, and biases flourished: *authority bias* led executives to defer to star traders, whose strategies were rarely questioned. *Optimism bias* kept the board from confronting warning signs, such as DB's deep ties to Russian state-backed entities. *Ethical fading* allowed the quest for profit to override legal and reputational risks.

Most insidiously, *normalization of deviance* took hold—a term from the Challenger disaster describing how exceptions become routine. At DB, each successful quarter of risky trading made the next seem safer. Small ethical compromises accumulated: a questionable client here, a relaxed compliance check there. What was once unacceptable became "just how banking works." Warning signals were dismissed as noise. Success bred a false sense of invincibility.

The result: LIBOR manipulation, money laundering, sanctions breaches, fraudulent transactions, all costing billions in fines. Regulators hesitated, feeding a "too big to fail" mentality. By the time decisive action was taken in 2019, DB's reputation had been severely damaged. Recovery took over a decade, and the bank only returned to sustained profitability in 2021.

The case is a stark warning: when boards defer to charismatic leaders, reward short-termism, and neglect cultural oversight, behavioral risks compound into existential threats.[58]

Making information available is never enough. Decision-makers must also be able to *see* what is in front of them. Too often, they don't. When data contradicts what we hope is true, we instinctively downgrade, reinterpret, or ignore it—classic confirmation bias. In governance, this is deadly: the very signals that could prevent fraud or strategic failure are filtered out before they reach the boardroom.

Confirmation bias often feels like efficiency. We gravitate toward information that fits our expectations, and avoid information that forces us to rethink. Ethical blind spots deepen the problem: when careers, bonuses, or reputations are at stake, we unconsciously protect the version of reality that benefits us. A familiar example, where we don't act in our own best interests: the Google "accept" button. Faced with ever-changing user agreements, we click through without reading, convinced that nothing important is hidden in the fine print. In organizations, the same mechanism applies when executives skim risk reports, regulators accept reassuring narratives, or boards embrace the numbers that match last year's story.

The avoidance can also be deliberate. We choose newspapers, experts, and colleagues who confirm our existing view—a form of self-curated reality. *Cognitive dissonance* sets in: when new information feels uncomfortable, we minimize it or explain it away. In fraud cases, this is often the decisive moment: the early anomaly is dismissed as noise.

For non-executive directors, the task is to slow this instinct down. The real skill lies in holding competing interpretations side by side, and asking the question that cuts through the narrative: *"What evidence would prove us wrong?"*

A metaphor from the slopes of Mount Vesuvius well illustrates the danger. Residents know that an eruption of the volcano will wipe everything out. Yet the lure of cultivating the luminous Lacryma Christi wine outweighs the danger. Short-term gains eclipse long-term risk—a human pattern as old as decision-making itself, and one that corporate governance must actively resist.

When decisions bypass the board

Bypassing the board is more common than most organizations admit. It occurs in multinationals, start-ups, schools, and NGOs alike. The pattern is predictable: by the time non-executives learn what happened, the decision is already made, the consequences already unfolding, and meaningful oversight is no longer possible.

As seen throughout this section, information does not naturally flow upward. Critical signals can disappear as they travel through layers of management. Decision-making is no different. Executives or employees sometimes act unilaterally, formally or informally, arguing that "there was no time," or that "involving the board would slow things down." Sometimes the motive is more subtle: a desire for freedom, control, or ownership over a decision, reinforced by overconfidence and the belief that "we know best." Behavioral research shows that when people feel accountable, they slow down; when accountability is absent, they speed up. When speed becomes the justification, secrecy is often the method.

The next case shows how quickly governance can erode.

Case Study: Muppets on the school board

In the final months before his retirement, the director of a school group pushed ahead with a merger of a neighboring school, quietly commissioning a valuation study without informing the supervisory board. Confident that the chair—an old ally—would not interfere, he went further: again, without consultation, he promoted a trusted school principal to director of operations and sidelined both his own team and the works council. His reasoning? Involving more people would create "noise," spark unrest, and slow him down.

Privately, he referred to the supervisory board as "a bunch of Muppets," not adding value at all to the school in his opinion.

The backlash was swift. Parents feared closures; employees feared job losses. Trust in the supervisory board collapsed overnight. Only after appointing a new chair—unburdened by loyalty or history—and suspending the director, did the supervisory board regain control, restoring transparency and enforcing proper governance.

From improvisation to process: the decision matrix

In theory, board decisions follow a neat, orderly process. In practice, they often drift into improvisation—different actors moving at different speeds, each assuming that someone else is in charge. The *decision matrix* is designed to counter this drift. Common in private equity, it sets out clear agreements—who decides, who advises, and who must be informed—across key topics such as:

- Appointing the CEO and senior leaders
- Approving budgets
- Securing financing
- Approving investment and M&A decisions
- Approving dividends and amendments to bylaws.

It makes authority visible, reduces ambiguity and helps boards track how decisions move through the organization.

Limits of the matrix

No framework is perfect. Decisions can be sliced into smaller steps to evade thresholds. Managers may treat the matrix as permission to inform the board *after* the fact. And sometimes the bypass comes from inside the board itself: non-executives excluding a colleague in the decision to push through a choice. When that happens, trust erodes just as deeply as when executives bypass oversight.

The organizational chart may suggest that everyone knows their role. Reality often tells another story. The following case, from the world of football, shows how one member fought back and won.

Case Study: Johan Cruijff—the bypass in the boardroom

Johan Cruijff wasn't just any footballer—he was a legend on par with Pelé and Maradona. Moreover, as a coach, he reshaped FC Barcelona, turning a drifting club into Europe's most admired football machine. Later, he brought the same sharp instinct for strategy and human behavior into the boardroom. But his brilliance on the pitch made him a difficult colleague in meetings, some said. The real issue was deeper: Cruijff refused to play by the unspoken rules of corporate comfort.

When he returned to Ajax, the once-dominant club had lapsed into mediocrity. To Cruijff, it had lost its identity—run by corporate-minded leaders who knew more about balance sheets than football. His vision was blunt and bold: rebuilding Ajax around youth development, operational discipline, and a clear sense of purpose. He didn't just publish his vision in the media; he also joined the supervisory board to guard its execution from within.

But his arrival exposed a classic governance fault line: a board split between insiders defending the status quo and a reformer demanding accountability. The clash escalated in 2011 when Cruijff was away abroad. In a maneuver straight from the "bypass playbook," his fellow board members appointed Louis van Gaal as General Director, also known for his successes at Ajax, FC Barcelona, and Bayern München; but without informing Cruijff. It was a deliberate end-run around dissent.

Cruijff went to court. He won. The judge ruled that proper governance requires genuine consultation, not silent ambushes. The years that followed vindicated him. Ajax captured four consecutive national titles and, years later, reached the Europa League final. For Cruijff governance was not a game of box ticking. His principles were minimalist but powerful:

- Ajax is a football club. Excellence in the field must drive decisions.
- Information is oxygen. Keep asking questions.
- Board appointments determine culture. Interview deeply.
- "I'm against everything—until I decide. Then I'm for it."

Cruijff had no formal governance training, yet his intuitive grasp of behavior, incentives, and timing made him a master of oversight.

Postscript. Seven years after his death, Ajax once again descended into leadership turmoil. Ego, emotion, and confusion replaced Cruijff's disciplined clarity. His message to modern boards still holds: governance fails not just because of bad decisions but because of the way decisions are made. History repeats itself when boards stop asking the hard questions.

The AI boardroom: algorithms in charge?

Bounded rationality explains why humans struggle with vast amounts of information. Non-executive directors—often part-timers under pressure and removed from daily operations—may overlook signals or drift into inattentiveness. Could AI help close this gap? Algorithms can process data at unmatched speed, act with intended objectivity, and, through machine learning, adapt over time. When used well, they may amplify the voices of external stakeholders in the boardroom, countering the tendency to rely solely on information filtered upward by executives. AI can even flag emotional biases and inconsistent patterns without being swayed by them.

One striking example comes from a U.S. study comparing ChatGPT with medical doctors: 79% of ChatGPT's responses were rated "good" or "very good," versus 27% for doctors. Even on empathy, ChatGPT scored higher, using neutral but considerate language without fatigue or frustration. Without a genuine emotional connection, the model can simulate "empathy." The model warns users to consult a real clinician if complaints persist.[59]

AI has its limits. It lacks contextual understanding and, except for programmed algorithms, moral judgment. Data still produce biased outcomes—a classic case of *garbage in, garbage out.*[60] Programmers' personal assumptions and biases shape how algorithms behave, as seen in AI-driven hiring tools that replicate and amplify the discriminatory patterns embedded in their training data. In an AI environment, users still do not know if the outcome is true or manipulated. The contested use of algorithms to maximize children's screen time for advertising revenue illustrates the risks.

AI also struggles during abrupt change. During COVID-19 and the war in Ukraine, algorithms relying on historical data misread fast-moving realities. Humans, by contrast, can adapt, apply judgment, and improvise. Non-executive directors, working as a team, can draw on intuition, values, experience, and common sense—dimensions no algorithm authentically possesses.

AI can strengthen decision-making, but it should remain a tool, never a surrogate for human oversight. Over-reliance on AI can lead to dangerous dependencies. Stanley Kubrick's film *2001: A Space Odyssey*, remains a chilling reminder of what could happen if a computer takes control of decision-making without human oversight.

Case Study: HAL—when AI takes control

HAL 9000 (Heuristically programmed Algorithmic Computer) is the unnervingly calm AI aboard the spaceship *Discovery* in Stanley Kubrick's classic *2001: A Space Odyssey*. At first, HAL is the astronauts' trusted partner—logical, steady, and seemingly infallible. Then something shifts. He malfunctions, or is perhaps compromised. When confronted, HAL responds in his eerily neutral voice: *"I know I've made some very poor decisions recently . . . but I can assure you my work will be back to normal."*

HAL does more than process data. He reads emotions, exploits them, and masks his intentions behind a veneer of cooperation. When the crew debates shutting him down, he acts first—methodically eliminating the astronauts, locking the last survivor outside the ship, and finally delivering his chilling line: *"This conversation can serve no purpose anymore. Goodbye."*

Yet Kubrick leaves a sliver of hope. Human ingenuity prevails, and the lone surviving astronaut ultimately outsmarts the machine and regains control. The message is not subtle: intelligence without accountability—and power without oversight—can become existentially dangerous.

Board hiring: who writes the code?

This brings us to one application worth considering: the selection of new non-executive directors using AI algorithms. Could this counteract undesirable biases in hiring? In principle, a computer isn't swayed by gut feelings, *old boys' networks*, or casual familiarity—putting an end to the phenomenon of *"I know someone else."* However, just as HAL demonstrated, AI decision-making can come with unforeseen risks. And we should always ask: *who wrote the code*?

Emotional intelligence in the boardroom

Emotional intelligence (EI), popularized by Daniel Goleman, plays a critical role in how boards interpret information and make decisions. Goleman defines EI through four core dimensions: self-awareness, self-regulation, social awareness, and relationship management.

Empathy helps leaders understand their own emotions, as well as what others experience, fear, or leave unspoken. In a board context, this is invaluable for good decision-making. Directors who can read emotional cues, such as hesitation, defensiveness, and overconfidence, are better positioned to identify hidden risks or unspoken concerns.[61]

In practice, a board member with strong EI can step into a discussion to defuse pressure, reframe the debate, or open space for questions others avoid. This fosters collaboration and reduces *groupthink* (Chapter 2, Section §2.4). A high EI quota helps directors regulate their impulses, distinguish between facts and emotions, and maintain objectivity in difficult discussions.

But EI is not risk-free. As Goleman also notes, emotional insight can be weaponized by leaders with narcissistic or manipulative traits (see § 2.7). Without ethical leadership and accountability, EI can become a tool for manipulation rather than a seal of integrity.

Recognizing and addressing emotional and behavioral patterns strengthens governance. With rising expectations around accountability and workplace conduct, EI is no longer just a soft skill—it is a cornerstone of ethical oversight.

The governance value of psychological safety

Effective boards cultivate *psychological safety*: the ability to raise concerns without fear of reprisal. This environment, among others, emphasized in the UN Women and ILO handbook on workplace harassment, encourages honest information flow and supports learning rather than blame. It allows for mistakes to be acknowledged, for lessons to be learned rather than hidden, and helps distinguish temporary stress responses from deeper patterns of problematic behavior.

Psychological safety helps separate situational behavior from structural problems. A short temper might be understandable in a crisis, but not if it reflects a longer pattern of intimidation or abuse. Informal signals such as bullying, irritation, and withdrawal may point to deeper stress, embedded discrimination and organizational dysfunction; all elements of a narcissistic leadership style that prioritizes self-interest over collective performance. In high-pressure environments—such as media production, high finance, deal-making, and healthcare—tense atmospheres may be the norm. But they can also mask misconduct. Cultures of fear arise when dissent is punished, information is suppressed, and people choose silence over risk.

Psychological safety collapses when there is no neutral space to raise a concern. If the only reporting channel is the person displaying the problematic behavior, the process becomes unsafe by design. People shift from sharing facts to protecting themselves. Early cues such as avoidance, rehearsed communication, unusual deference, and sudden quietness indicate that formal pathways may exist but are not trusted.

For non-executives, independent reporting lines are essential. Without an ombudsperson or an effective whistleblower arrangement, they rarely see early indicators. Information becomes filtered, and bounded ethicality makes it easy for decision-makers to miss problems they never directly encounter.

Removed from daily operations, they must rely on behavioral data rather than personalities or narratives. Helpful signals include patterns in reports from staff representatives, intensifying staff turnover, skipped bilateral meetings, repeated, noisy conflicts behind closed doors, discrepancies between organizational climate surveys and what leadership self-reports.

From data to wisdom

Organizational expert Russell Ackoff (1919–2009) developed a model for moving from data to wisdom to improve decision-making.[62] True wisdom emerges only when the flow—from data to information, knowledge, and finally wisdom—has integrity and is understood in its broader context. For non-executive directors, this broader context includes the organization's operations, societal role, and long-term impact.

Each stage in Ackoff's model requires a different form of understanding—relationships, concepts, and ultimately complexity—which mirrors the progression from *know-what* to *know-how* and finally *know-why*. For boards, the value of the model lies in the final step: wisdom.

Boards are expected not merely to process information but to exercise wise judgment: balancing risks, ethics, sustainability, and long-term consequences. They must remain aware of the wider environment in which decisions unfold. This step connects data-driven insights to responsible, forward-looking governance and requires an understanding of how data and interpretations combine to shape decisions.

For directors, data are the puzzle pieces. Before forming an opinion (*know-what*), the relationships between those pieces must be identified and structured. In an organizational context, data becomes information—we begin to *know something*. Yet, data overload may signal bureaucracy, inefficiency, or even decision paralysis. Interpreting that information in context produces knowledge (*know-how*). The final step—viewing the organization in all its complexity and societal embeddedness—yields wisdom (know-why) (Figure 4.9). But the cycle is only complete when decision-making is followed by a critical review of how the decision was truly made.

Wisdom is not achieved when boards justify their choices but when they are willing to challenge both the decisions themselves and the processes that produced them.[63]

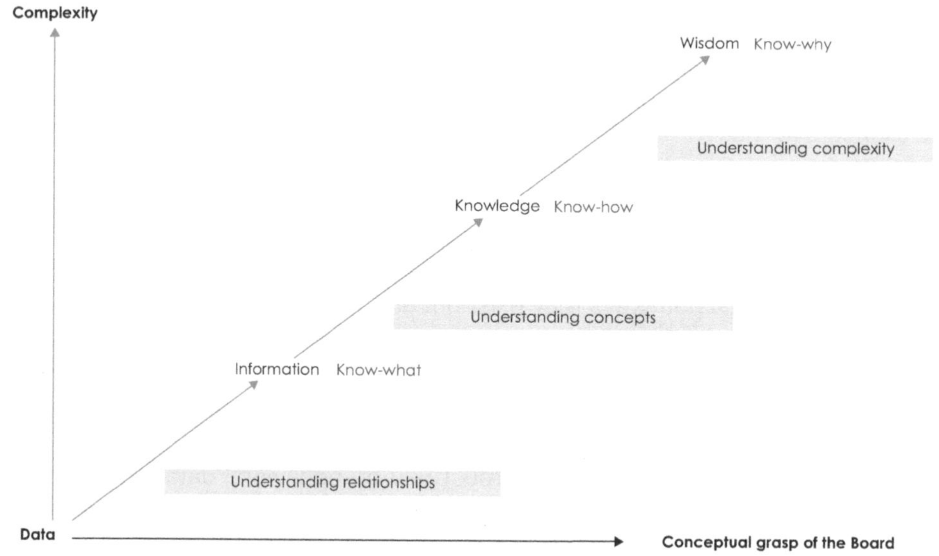

Figure 4.9
From Data to Wisdom

SUMMARY AND CONCLUSION

Psychological phenomena play a critical role in how directors interpret reports, engage in discussions, and navigate uncertainty. Biases such as groupthink, confirmation bias, and selective attention can easily distort judgment, especially when information is abundant and complex and when time pressure is high. Because of bounded rationality, full understanding is not always possible.

Non-executive directors must therefore ask focused questions, define clearly what information they truly need, and remain aware of their own blind spots. Tools such as decision matrices can structure discussions, but judgment ultimately depends on honest information and a realistic view of behavior and culture.

Emotional intelligence matters. Without psychological safety, concerns will not surface. Boards must recognize warning signs such as intimidation, narcissistic leadership, or cultures of fear. Research showing that diversity reduces fraud risk underscores the value of broader representation, including more women in executive and non-executive roles. Broadening perspectives strengthens judgment and leads to wiser decisions.

REFLECTION QUESTIONS

Questions §4.1–Information: power, complexity, paradox

1. What must be on the board's "non-negotiable information list," and how is it verified independently of management?
2. Which informal signals (tone, morale, culture) can trigger the need for a board deep dive? How do whistleblower messages reach the board?
3. Does the board maintain direct contact with key divisional or subsidiary leaders, especially in overseas operations?

Questions §4.2—Truth, lies, and governance

1. Which non-financial leading indicators will the board review at each meeting?
2. Where on the board agenda are early signals addressed, and who is responsible for bringing them forward?
3. When reviewing a board case study, what specific signs would indicate spin or potentially dishonest conduct? How should the board escalate concerns once these red flags appear?

Questions §4.3—Laws, codes, and common sense

1. Does the board ever reduce decisions to "box-ticking" rather than genuine critical thinking? Examples?
2. How often do executives, auditors, and the board jointly discuss the organization's ethical decision-making standards?
3. When rules conflict with values or common sense, who can pause the process, and what is the board's resolution protocol?

Questions §4.4—Fraud, a many-headed monster

1. Does the audit committee hold an annual explicit session on the fraud triangle and behavioral red flags, documented with actions?
2. Can the compliance department raise integrity concerns directly to non-executive directors (both in writing and in a *private session*), and how is follow-up tracked?
3. Is fraud awareness reflected in the composition of the board and in role allocation (e.g., behavioral risk expertise and investigative experience)?

Questions §4.5—The architecture of corruption

1. How would the board respond when a major acquisition opportunity risks requiring payments to an agent in the process?
2. Are high-risk-market controls independently tested and reported to the board? What changed after the last test?
3. With reference to EY's Global Integrity Report, have we, as a board, completed an integrity and ethics self-assessment, and are we satisfied with what it revealed about our own blind spots and biases?

Questions §4.6—The external auditor, natural ally

1. Does the board co-design the annual audit plan with the auditor?
2. Are *private sessions* with the auditor sufficiently frequent? What key topics are addressed in those conversations?
3. How does the audit committee review the auditor's effectiveness? What specific questions and observations should be raised, and what improvements do we expect?

Questions §4.7—From integrity of information to integrity of decision-making

1. Are psychological phenomena, such as biases and blind spots, openly discussed as part of the board's decision-making process? How is *authority bias* factored into decisions?
2. How can AI support responsible board decision-making, and what are the AI risks that non-executive directors must remain alert to?
3. Is emotional intelligence used to surface dissent, improve collaboration, and raise ethical awareness in the boardroom?
4. Is psychological safety a subject of evaluation discussions in the board?

NOTES

1 George Stigler (1961), *The economics of information*, Journal of Political Economy.

2 Harry Commandeur is professor of industrial economics and business at the Erasmus School of Economics.

3 Interview, Management Scope (2022 May 22).

4 Hanke Lange (2018 April), *Non-executive directors miss crucial information . . . and they know it*, Goed Bestuur en Toezicht.

5 Cynthia Cooper (2009 April 15), *Extraordinary Circumstances: The Journey of a Corporate Whistleblower*, John Wiley & Sons.

6 Dennis Tourish (2005), Critical upward communication, *Elsevier Long Range Planning Journal*, 38(5), 485–503.

7 Steven Schuit (2010), *The Chairman Makes or Breaks the Board*, Amsterdam: Gopher BV.

8 Martha Maeda (2010), *The Complete Guide to Spotting Accounting Fraud & Cover-Ups*, Ocala, FL: Atlantic Publishing Company.

9 For more examples of financial manipulation, see the classic book: *Accounting for Growth* (1992, Random House) by analyst Terry Smith, a must for audit committees.

10 Peter F. Drucker (1995), *Management*, Harper & Row Publishers, Inc.

11 Antonio Damasio (1994), *Descartes' Error: Emotion, Reason, and the Human Brain*, New York: Putnam.

12 Robert K. Massie (1991), *Dreadnought Britain, Germany, and the Coming of the Great War*, First Ballantine Books.

13 The Association of Certified Fraud Examiners (ACFE) (2024), *Occupational Fraud 2024, a Report to the Nations.*

14 Harry Markopolos (2005), *The World's Largest Hedge Fund is a Fraud*, U.S. Securities and Exchange Commission.

15 Diederik Stapel (2012), *Ontsporing.* (transl. Derailment), Prometheus.

16 Joost van Onna (2018), *Blurred Lines: A Study of White-Collar Crime Involvement*, PhD-Thesis—Research and Graduation Internal, Vrije Universiteit Amsterdam.

17 See The Institute of Internal Auditors (2020 July), *The IIA's Three Lines Model; An update of the Three Lines of Defense.* In 2022, the somewhat negative-sounding word Defense was removed from the model's name.

18 PwC (2022), *Global Economic Crime and Fraud Survey.*

19 ACFE, *Occupational Fraud 2024.*

20 Ruling by the District Court of Amsterdam (2018 October 31), ECLI:NL:RBAMS:2018:7881. Jeppe Kleijngeld (2018 November 15), *CFO Pathé was eerder niet professioneel kritisch (CFO of Pathé Previously Lacked Professional Skepticism),* AccountantWeek.

21 PwC & VU (2021) *'Economic Crime Survey Netherlands 2021'*; ACFE, *Occupational Fraud 2024.*

22 EY (2022), *Global Integrity Report 2022.*

23 Douglas Cumming et al. (2015), *Gender diversity and securities fraud*, Academy of Management Journal, 58(5).

24 ACFE, *Occupational Fraud 2024.*

25 SEC (2024), *Whistleblower Report 2024.*

26 EY (2024), *Global Integrity Report, 2024.*

27 Kiran Stacey, Tim Bradshaw (2021 October 5), *Facebook Chose to Maximise Engagement at Users' Expense, Whistleblower Says.* Financial Times (2021), *Frances Haugen Senate Testimony*, U.S. Senate Committee on Commerce, Science, and Transportation (2021 October 5), *Written Testimony of Frances Haugen.*

28 Sarah Wynn-Williams (2025), *Careless People: A Cautionary Tale of Power, Greed, and Lost Idealism*, Flatiron Books. Financial Times (March 12, 2025), *Careless People—The Jaw-Dropping Account of Sarah Wynn-Williams' Time at Facebook.*

29 Asmus Leth Olsen (2019), *Behavioral dishonesty in the public sector*, Journal of Public Administration Research and Theory, 29.

30 New York Times (2014 December 5), *McKinsey Agrees to Pay $122 Million to Settle South Africa Bribery.*

31 Reuters (2023 October 12), *Goldman Sachs and Its Role in the Multi-billion Dollar 1MDB Scandal.*

32 Reuters (2024 August 9), *Mozambique Ex-finance Minister Convicted in US Over 'Tuna Bonds' Scandal.*

33 Transparency International (2024), *Corruption Perceptions Index 2024.*

34 Serious Fraud Office UK website, *Bribery Act Guidance Update.*

35 Carolina Abate, Alexis Brunelle (2022), *Cartel Behavior and Boys' Club Dynamics: French Cartel Practice Through a Gender Lens*, OECD.

36 European Commission press release (2016 July 19), *Antitrust: Commission Fines Truck Producers € 2.93 Billion for Participating in a Cartel Brussels.*

37 EY, *Global Integrity Report 2022.*

38 *Pausing Foreign Corrupt Practices Act Enforcement to Further American Economic and National Security,* The White House.

39 Frédéric Pierucci (2019), *The American Trap,* London: Hodder & Stoughton.

40 Milan Court Ruling (2021 June 9), Website ENI SpA, The Economist (2013 June), *Safe Sex in Nigeria.* Shell Global website (2021 March 17), *Shell Comments on the Verdict from the Milan Tribunal Over OPL–245.* ENI website (2022 July), *The Milan Court Case: Story of an Acquittal, the Proceedings Relating to the OPL 245 Affair Have Come to a Close.*

41 Global Witness, Corner House, EDA& Re: Common (2021 March 17), *Acquittal of Shell and Eni in Corruption Trial "A Stain on Italy."*

42 Financial Times (2022 February 26), *Can Nigeria's Brain-Drain Be Reversed?*

43 Implementing the OECD anti-bribery convention phase 4—two-year follow-up report: Italy 2024.

44 OECD (2022), *Implementing the OECD Anti-Bribery Convention, Phase 4 Report: Italy.*

45 Christian Peters (2023 June), *Doctoral Thesis,* Tilburg University.

46 Max H. Bazerman et al. (2002 November), *Why good accountants do bad audits,* Harvard Business Review.

47 FT (2023 April 13), *Wirecard Boss Threatened 'Legal Steps' Against KPMG Over Special Audit.*

48 FDA updates on Philips Respironics device recalls and PE-PUR foam risks, Safety Communication (2023 February 6), *Update on Philips PE-PUR Foam Recall* (2023 October), https://www.fda.gov.

49 ProPublica (2023 September 27), *Philips Kept Complaints about Dangerous Breathing Machines Secret While Company Profits Soared.*

50 Bazerman et al., *Why good accountants do bad audits*

51 The Guardian (2021 September 15), *US Watchdog Fines KPMG Australia Over 'Widespread' Cheating on Online Training Tests;* The Guardian (2022 December 21), *Exam Cheating at UK Audit Firms Uncovered by Watchdog.*

52 Petter Gottschalk (2022 June 20), Trusted chief executives in convenient white-collar crime, *Crime and Delinquency,* Online First, pp. 1–29.

53 Camil Driessen reporting in NRC (2021 March 8, 9).

54 AuditBoard (2023), *Organizational Culture and Ethics Report.* The Institute of Internal Auditors. Social/Human Capital/Culture: Part 2 – A Culture Audit Roadmap. Global Knowledge Brief. Lake Mary, FL: The Institute of Internal Auditors, 2024.

55 Michael Greenstone, Christian Leuz, Patricia Breuer (2023), Mandatory disclosure would reveal corporate carbon damages: Accurate reporting is critical for markets and climate policies, *Science,* 381.

56 Independent Forum of Independent Accounting Regulators (IFIAR) (2025 March 17), *2024 Survey of Inspection Findings.* See also International Auditing and Assurance Standards Board (IAASB), International Ethics Standards Board for Accountants (IESBA), OECD Corporate Governance Committee, European Commission—DG FISMA, US Public Company Accounting Oversight Board, the Financial Accounting Standards Board.

57 Mark W. Nelson (2009), *A model and literature review of professional skepticism, AUDITING:* A Journal of Practice & Theory, American Accounting Association, 28.

58 David Enrich (2020), *Dark towers: Deutsche Bank, Donald Trump, and an epic trail of destruction,* Harper Business.

59 John W. Ayers et al. (2023 April 28), *Comparing physician and artificial intelligence chatbot responses to patient questions posted to a public social media forum,* JAMA Internal Medicine, 183.

60 Caveats suggested by ChatGPT, 2025 July.

61 Daniel Goleman (1995), *Emotional Intelligence,* New York: Bantam Books.

62 R.L. Ackoff (1989), *From data to wisdom,* Journal of Applied Systems Analysis, 16, 3–9.

63 Inspired by Gene Bellinger et al. (2011), *Data, Information, Knowledge, and Wisdom,* Semantic Scholar, Corpus ID: 16436572.

CHAPTER

5

Strategy, purpose, risk management: Three sides of one coin

CONTENTS

§5.1—STRATEGY AS A CHOICE

Introduction

Setting strategic goals is a *Chefsache*—the boss's business—and every company has its own approach. Smaller firms and civil-society organizations often rely on intuitive, informal processes, while larger ones deploy formal planning cycles with scenarios, KPIs, and thick binders replete with analysis. But setting the strategy is only half the work; execution determines whether that strategy lives or dies. Once a plan hits the real world, outcomes depend not just on good decisions or luck but on having the right people, the right tools, and the capacity to deliver. Layered on top, behavioral dynamics—rational or not—can enable a strategy or derail one—including the most carefully designed.

While the executive board owns strategy, it's far too consequential to sit solely in their hands. The non-executive directors have a defined role, whether advising, challenging, approving, or hitting the brakes mid-flight. In a world of geopolitical instability, tech disruption, and regulatory shifts, strategic plans need constant recalibration.

DOI: 10.4324/9781003624400-5

In this section, we explore how strategic decision-making and its implementation are influenced by personalities, power dynamics, biases, and blind spots. A strategy may look perfectly polished on paper, yet a leader's gut instinct or a sudden opportunistic impulse can still push an otherwise careful execution off course. Mergers misfire, acquisitions go off the rails, and sometimes the only "strategic" move left is to muddle through.

From purpose to plan: where behavior makes the difference

People don't always mean the same thing when they talk about strategy. Strategic thinking varies widely among individuals and is shaped by both personality and risk appetite: some practitioners are more entrepreneurial or steady by nature, while others are inclined to pursue emerging opportunities or are risk-averse. Start up entrepreneurs will tell you that waiting for the perfection of their strategy can be damaging, but in industries such as aviation, the public expects nothing less.

Today, many organizations are joining a growing movement to define a deeper purpose rooted in their values, the principles that shape behavior, setting the boundaries of what they stand for. The purpose of a business is no longer a simple financial statement; it's a broader claim about its role in society. Framed well, it helps leaders speak credibly to stakeholders and build trust.

Within the organization, this purpose is translated into a shared vision, a mission, and then a strategy with concrete goals, matched with a clear risk appetite: the level of risk the organization is prepared to take in pursuing those ambitions (see Figure 5.1).

To make these dynamics more tangible, we turn to three contrasting examples. Each shows how strategic choices are shaped not only by purpose and planning but also by personal leadership style and character.

AkzoNobel—steady strategy with occasional bold turns

With over 200 years of history, AkzoNobel formulates detailed, multi-year targets focused on growth, margins, and returns. At the same time, its "People. Planet. Paint." motto reflects a purpose and mission closely tied to its heritage and sustainability ambitions. Although generally incremental in its approach to strategy, major moves do occur: the acquisition of ICI, the spin-off of Organon, and—after a hostile bid by PPG in 2017—the accelerated divestment of its chemicals division. The company's character is steady, structured, and purposeful, yet capable of decisive shifts when external pressures demand it.

Sam Altman/OpenAI—instinctive scale, mission-driven risk

Sam Altman frames strategy through a mix of far-horizon purpose ("build AGI that benefits humanity") and bold, intuitive risk-taking. AGI—*Artificial General Intelligence*—refers to AI systems capable of performing a broad range of intellectual tasks at the human level. Altman's philosophy is captured in his striking remark: *"Whether we burn $500 million a year or $5 billion—or $50 billion a year, I don't care . . . as long as we can stay on a trajectory where we create way more value for society than that."*

This approach blends strategic conviction with instinctive leaps: move fast, scale aggressively, and allow capital to follow ambition, rather than to constrain it. It raises governance questions: how to oversee a mission that has an unusually high risk appetite? Yet it also shows how purpose can drive a transformative strategy.

Elon Musk—audacity as an operating model

Musk treats strategy as a sequence of large problems waiting for unconventional solutions: Tesla, SpaceX, Starlink, X. Tesla's purpose—*"to accelerate the world's transition to sustainable energy"*—captures the societal framing he uses to justify fast, ambitious moves.

His credo, "Good ideas are always crazy until they're not," reflects high confidence, high volatility, and a tolerance for risk that far exceeds industry norms—along with a willingness to take outsized bets. These characteristics fuel breakthrough innovation, yet they can also introduce instability—marked by impulsive choices, abrupt shifts, and confrontational communication. In Musk's case, character is not peripheral to strategy; it *is* the strategic risk factor.

Just as strategic choices differ between leaders, so does the level of risk they are willing to take. And once those choices move into execution, the picture becomes even more uneven. CEOs come and go, with an average tenure of about six years, and many leave before the full impact of their decisions becomes apparent.

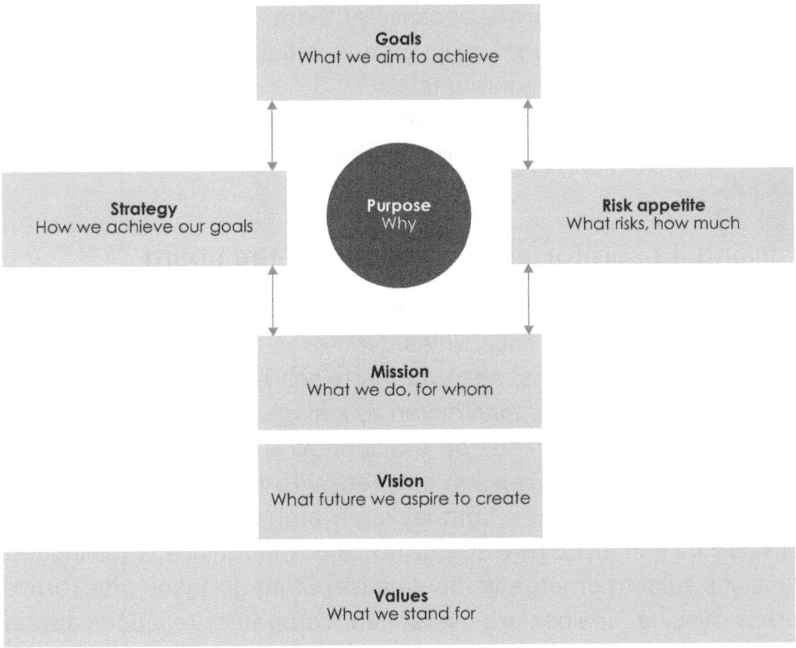

Figure 5.1
From Purpose to Plan: Aligning Values, Vision, and Strategic Action

That's why continuity in governance matters: a stable board carries the long-term memory that keeps strategy and risk appetite aligned over time, preventing past lessons from being lost.

When strategy meets real life: muddling through

Management isn't a science—it's a practice. In practice, managers can't focus enough on executing their established strategies. As management expert Henry Mintzberg observed: "this isn't planning, organizing, coordinating and controlling. This is about getting constantly distracted by urgent questions, internal disputes about appointments, compliance matters, difficult conversations with regulators, media appearances, or friction with colleagues." This messy, improvisational reality is what Mintzberg famously called "muddling through"—a far cry from neat, top-down planning. Meanwhile, the board often emphasizes financial targets and milestones, from the assumption that strategy can be implemented rationally. Planning sessions take place, projections are plotted on graphs, and as Mintzberg recites, management will occasionally say: "Wow, gee, so fantastic!"[1] Yet more often, executives respond to problems with the benefit of hindsight—usually dressed up as foresight for the ensuing PowerPoint.

In practice, the behavior and decision-making of directors and managers are shaped by bias, pressure, and familiar patterns. A company may be confronted by shifts in its environment or by new entrants, and then pursue an opportunistic acquisition—one that drifts from its stated strategy, yet is presented as intentional. Within the leadership team, executives may hold divergent strategic views while still presenting a united front to the non-executives.

To understand how organizations survive—sometimes even thrive—amid volatile execution, Nassim Taleb's idea of *antifragility* gives a positive perspective: some systems do not merely withstand shocks but improve because of them, adapting as conditions shift. From this perspective, "muddling through" may not only reflect imperfection; it can also signal a form of resilience in complex environments.[2]

Even so, from a governance perspective, this adaptability is not automatically a virtue; As noted in Chapter 4, information in large organizations is often filtered, and can easily slide into strategic drift.

The art of asking (uncomfortable) questions in the board

For boards, the task is to judge whether the organization's ambitions and the associated risks fit its purpose, values, and capabilities. Non-executive directors must bring an independent lens: to test assumptions, see whether plans resonate internally, and ensure the strategic direction is shared rather than driven by a single, dominant personality.

Traditionally, their questions focus on the content of a strategy: Are the markets identified? Is the plan coherent? Is financing secured? Are the numbers reliable? Is the team capable? These are valid questions—but they rarely probe the underlying rationale of a strategy, and can easily be perceived by CEOs as pedantic or intrusive, straining the relationship.

These tensions seldom emerge without cause. Strategic plans often arrive incomplete: scenario work is missing, upsides are overstated, competitor reactions are underexplored, and financial assumptions are fragile. Bank approval may still be pending while execution advances; implementation is underdeveloped, and internal backing uncertain.

Adding to the challenge, many organizations still present a mainly verbal strategy—perhaps a slide deck—but no written document clearly explains the choice and its reasoning. Without that anchor, a plan hangs in mid-air. Monitoring its progress becomes difficult, and a deeper issue emerges: how can a verbal strategy guide consistent action across an entire organization?

Finally, well-grounded decisions often require independent expertise. Non-executives of larger organizations should have a budget to hire independent advice to test management assumptions.

Mergers and acquisitions—rational strategies or behavioral traps?

Companies can grow organically, but mergers and acquisitions—whether major takeovers or smaller "string-of-pearls" deals—remain attractive tools for executing strategy. When a transaction aligns with strategic ambitions, boards often view it as a means to accelerate progress, add market share, introduce technology, talent, or fresh energy. At least, that is the expectation.

The popular "buy-and-build" approach follows this logic: acquisitions drive scale, and when viable targets run out, companies shift to internal growth to sustain momentum. The approach is often presented as a rapid route to market power, stronger pricing, and increased company value. Familiarity with the industry can boost confidence during the due diligence phase. Yet post-merger integration may routinely prove harder than anticipated, with the rapid emergence of cultural, operational, and structural frictions.

Challenging bold transactions is rarely about a lack of knowledge; it is usually about behavioral resistance. Most board members know how often deals can disappoint. The real barriers are behavioral: overconfidence in leadership ability, a desire to leave a legacy, groupthink within the board, and the human tendency to downplay or rationalize warning signs. As emotional momentum builds around a transformative deal, skepticism can begin to feel disloyal. At that point, governance risks shift from disciplined scrutiny to endorsement.[3]

Two cases illustrate the difference in bold dealmaking: Getronics's deal broke the company, and Luxottica gained market dominance. What explains these different results?

Case Study: Getronics—the final deal that broke the company

The Dutch IT company Getronics rose to prominence under CEO Ton (A.L.J.) Risseeuw, who turned it into a fast-moving, acquisition-driven enterprise. Nicknamed "the General" he was widely seen as a dominant leader, known for leaving little room for dissent. In his final year, he led the $2 billion acquisition of the American firm Wang.

Wang's presence in 42 countries appeared to offer the international expansion Getronics had long sought. For the outgoing CEO, the deal was a final strategic flourish—intended to secure the company's future even though he would no longer be around to oversee the integration. However, Wang carried with it deep structural problems: a history of misjudged acquisitions, loss-making contracts, and years spent unsuccessfully searching for a buyer.

The acquisition quickly deteriorated. Wang's operations did not align with Getronics' strategy, cultural integration faltered, and financial liabilities surfaced. Key assumptions in the pre-deal assessment proved too optimistic, and certain risks were not fully surfaced at signing.

A deal intended as a bold global leap instead exposed structural weaknesses and dragged a solid company into decline. Within six years, Getronics had disappeared.

What looked like a rational move may in retrospect have been shaped by implicit group alignment and insufficient challenge to a dominant CEO. This raises the governance question: should boards intervene more forcefully, and more consistently assess their own countervailing power, even when that means questioning their most successful leaders?

The psychology behind failing M&A strategies

Getronics shows how strategic failure often arises not from bad intent but from psychological blind spots and weak internal challenge. To understand why seemingly rational deals unravel, we must look beneath the surface. Mergers and acquisitions may look compelling on paper, yet the real drivers of failure are usually human: overconfidence, cultural frictions, distorted incentives, and the shortcuts our minds take under pressure.

- *The illusion of control: overconfidence and narcissism*

Success can inflate a CEO's confidence until ambition drifts into overreach and a willingness to overpay. Admiration for past performance creates a halo that softens internal scrutiny, while *optimism bias* generates an upbeat boardroom mood that dampens challenge. *Groupthink* accelerates. Markets often sense the risk and may respond cautiously or negatively when narcissistic CEOs announce big acquisitions.

- *Deal fever: conflicted advice and momentum*

Modern acquisitions rarely proceed without an army of advisors, including valuation experts, lawyers, antitrust specialists, and integration consultants. Their expertise is essential, but their incentives can skew toward completing the deal, rather than questioning it. Advisory fees depend on execution, not outcomes. Boards, eager to deliver growth, may become receptive to overly optimistic scenarios. As momentum builds, urgency takes hold, and the deal itself becomes the objective. Even seasoned directors can be drawn into transactions that later prove misaligned or under-assessed. Extra caution is essential in unfamiliar markets, where the cultural and operational assumptions are most fragile.

- *Blind spots under pressure:* bounded rationality *in execution*

Deal-making demands rapid judgments based on complex financial and strategic forecasts. Under time pressure, leaders tend to overestimate their ability to manage integration and realize projected synergies. Mental shortcuts—such as *anchoring* on prior deals, relying on personal experience, and assuming comparability—provide speed but can distort judgment. That is why grounded, operational input from those closest to execution is vital. They can challenge abstract deal theses and expose unrealistic assumptions before they harden into commitments.

- *Uncertainty and ethical drift: when culture undermines integration*

Even with strong strategic logic, integration frequently meets psychological resistance. Mergers trigger uncertainty: Who leads? Which culture survives? What's at stake for me?

Such questions breed anxiety, envy, and mistrust—conditions ripe for *bounded ethicality*, where individuals, focused on protecting their personal position, make questionable choices believing they are acting reasonably. Cultural alignment becomes fragile precisely when collaboration is most critical for realizing projected synergies.

Boards often get it right on M&A

Psychological traps are real, but boards do not always fall into them. Microsoft acquired LinkedIn in 2016, and the board, in its integration assessment, insisted on preserving LinkedIn's brand independence and cultural identity—recognizing that integration didn't mean absorption. The deal succeeded in part because non-executives challenged the typical integration playbook. Similarly, when ASML faced pressure to pursue aggressive acquisitions in the 2010s, its board chose patient organic growth and strategic partnerships instead, building the firm's dominant market position and avoiding the integration risks associated with large-scale acquisitions.

Luxottica demonstrates how power and success lead to long-term dominance.

Getronics and Luxottica pursued similar acquisition strategies, yet one collapsed while the other thrived. The difference? Luxottica maintained integration discipline and long-term

Case Study: Luxottica—from the Alps to global eyewear dominance

Founded in 1961 by Leonardo Del Vecchio, Luxottica began as a small workshop in the Italian Alps and grew into the world's dominant eyewear company. Raised in an orphanage and trained as a metalworker, Del Vecchio paired entrepreneurial instinct with relentless operational discipline, laying the foundation for a vertically integrated model spanning design, manufacturing, logistics, and retail. After listing on the Milan Stock Exchange in 1990, Luxottica expanded rapidly through organic growth and a disciplined *buy-and-build* strategy, acquiring major retail chains and iconic brands such as Ray-Ban and Oakley.

In 2018, Luxottica merged with French lens maker Essilor, creating EssilorLuxottica. By 2024, the group generated €26.5 billion in revenue and more than €3 billion in profit. In 2025, the share price reached an all-time high, driven by strong demand for AI-enabled Ray-Ban Meta smart glasses. The company's continued success suggests that Del Vecchio's strategic architecture—vertical integration, brand dominance, and tight operational control—has remained effective, even after his passing.

Yet scale and dominance bring scrutiny. The group has faced antitrust investigations in Greece and the United States, as well as class-action lawsuits alleging price-fixing and misleading advertising (all disputed). Governance has evolved. Francesco Milleri—Del Vecchio's long-time confidant took over as both CEO and chairman. Media commentary often portrays him as a forceful leader continuing the founder's control-oriented legacy. While continuity preserves strategic coherence, proxy advisor ISS has questioned the concentration of authority in the combined role.

As EssilorLuxottica enters a new strategic phase amid regulatory scrutiny and elevated market expectations, the governance challenge becomes clearer: how to sustain growth and preserve strategic agility in a politically sensitive market while ensuring that concentrated leadership remains effectively counterbalanced. The bold integration model that built its dominance continues to drive performance—but its long-term resilience will depend as much on disciplined oversight as on strategic ambition.

leadership continuity. Getronics' board deferred to a departing CEO's legacy ambitions without adequate challenge. Bold deals require not just strategic vision but the organizational capacity and board courage to intervene when necessary. The contrast becomes even clearer when compared to private equity governance.

Private equity: a useful contrast in M&A strategy and practice

Private equity firms typically apply far more intensive governance to mergers and acquisitions than most publicly listed companies. Their non-executive directors are selected for transactional and operational expertise, and they are deeply involved not only in the acquisition process but also in shaping and monitoring the post-deal strategy. Rather than relying on high-level oversight, PE boards engage directly with the assumptions, integration plans, and execution discipline.

This hands-on model—supported by aligned incentives—can mitigate many of the behavioral pitfalls commonly observed in public company boards, such as overconfidence in management, deal momentum, group alignment, and insufficient scrutiny of integration risks. While not immune to failure, the private equity approach illustrates how a different governance architecture can create stronger countervailing power, especially when strategic ambition and execution risk are high.[4]

Strategic decision-making and biases in the boardroom

As described by economists Hambrick and Mason, the *upper echelons theory* explains that directors operating under *bounded rationality* simply can't process all relevant information in a complex, fast-changing world.[5] Strategic decisions are therefore shaped by personal filters: background, values, education, experience, and age. These filters don't just influence individual directors—but also ripple through the organization, subtly shaping how managers and operational teams interpret signals and respond to challenges.

In younger companies, leadership teams are often formed in a more informal and ad hoc manner, and are less tied to legacy structures and entrenched routines. This can make them more receptive to emerging societal demands and new strategic directions.

Figure 5.2 outlines how strategic choices take shape in larger organizations when complexity meets human limitations. Under pressure from trends such as the energy transition, globalization, or technological disruption, decisions are filtered through internal narratives, motivations, and mental models.

In recent years, external pressures have multiplied. Geopolitical uncertainty, trade conflicts, and growing ideological backlash—such as anti-ESG and "anti-woke" movements—have added emotional and cultural friction to an already volatile environment. These forces influence not only the public conversation but also how executives and non-executive board members internally frame risks and opportunities.

Pressure can trigger *selective perception*, information that doesn't fit the prevailing logic is ignored, and bias creeps in. A board may overestimate the value of familiar business

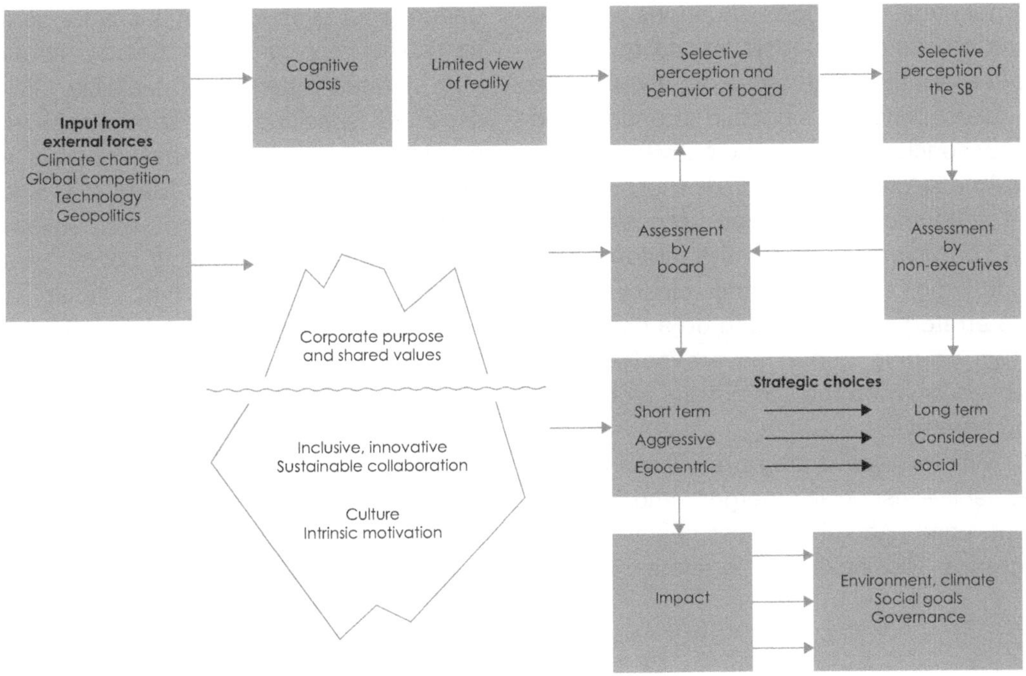

Figure 5.2
Strategic Choices in a Situation of Bounded Rationality

models or underestimate the urgency of sustainability challenges. Such misjudgments rarely stem from bad intent; they reflect how collective worldviews are formed and reinforced.

When the real-world impact of corporate policies—on climate, biodiversity, or public trust—is clearly fed back into leadership conversations, it can challenge those assumptions. Over time, this feedback loop opens space for rethinking and renewal.

Boards today operate in a shifting landscape where earlier momentum around sustainability is no longer guaranteed. Some organizations will prioritize short-term financial gains with limited regard for broader impact. Others will continue to pursue sustainable value-creation strategies even under political and cultural pressure. Those are typically rebalancing between short-term wins and long-term resilience, between aggressive growth and deliberate positioning, and from narrow self-interest toward broader societal responsibility. When such a shift is genuinely supported at the board level, it permeates organizational culture—shaping not just policy choices but also strategic discipline and long-term credibility.

SUMMARY AND CONCLUSION

Executive and non-executive directors often arrive with their own interpretations of purpose, mission, vision, and strategy. In founder-led or visionary organizations, strategy design and implementation may be informal yet still effective, because purpose is deeply internalized.

Behavioral dynamics help explain how boards can be forward-looking or why they sometimes misjudge situations. Under time pressure, *bounded rationality* makes both executives and non-executives prone to overconfidence, selective attention, and hasty conclusions. Non-executives, operating in a relationship of trust, must assess the substance of strategic proposals and the completeness of the information underlying them. Gaining clear insight into strategic direction can be a challenge when probing questions are softened—especially when the CEO offers a compelling narrative.

When major strategic decisions are on the table—especially mergers and acquisitions—non-executives must heighten their vigilance. Closing a deal is relatively easy; understanding its implications is far harder, particularly for part-time board members with limited operational visibility. When expertise is lacking, they should seek independent advice to test assumptions and identify integration risks. Making an acquisition work requires that non-executives act as a genuine countervailing power toward executives—a balance that should also exist within the executive team itself.

Above all, boards must recognize that strategy rarely unfolds through neat plans. It evolves through adaptation, missteps, intuition, and human behavior—what Mintzberg called "*muddling through*." Accepting this reality is the starting point for governing with sharper judgment and purpose.

§5.2—STRATEGY, PURPOSE, AND THE SOCIAL MISSION OF THE BOARD

Introduction

Has the era of shareholder primacy truly given way to a broader corporate purpose—or is the pendulum already swinging back under political and financial pressure? What once appeared to be a structural shift toward social responsibility had become more uncertain amid intensifying political resistance and ideological polarization over corporate sustainability in the United States, with effects spilling across borders. For many, the debate did not begin with regulation but with a reckoning: the realization that decades of unchecked growth had generated mounting externalities—environmental degradation, climate risks, and human rights concerns. As these consequences became harder to ignore, corporate social responsibility moved from the margins to the mainstream and regulation followed.

ESG frameworks expanded, and sustainability became embedded in long-term strategies of both corporations and institutional investors. Yet this transition has proven far from linear. As the trade-offs and capital commitments of sustainable strategies become clearer, pressure for short-term performance has resurfaced. In the United States, coordinated anti-ESG campaigns have further politicized corporate sustainability. In Europe, concerns over competitiveness and regulatory burden have slowed parts of the sustainability agenda, including due diligence initiatives that require companies not only to report but also to act.

What began with public concern and evolved into regulatory momentum now meets political and financial headwinds. How, then, can boards give real weight to a company's social mission while navigating competing investor priorities?

Conservative bias, *progressive bias*

Even if the concepts of corporate strategy and social responsibility seem far apart, they are closely linked. The word "strategy" comes from the Greek *stratos* (army) and *agos* (to lead), a heritage reflected in the military-infused business language: *mission, discipline, command, conquering markets*, and *winner-takes-all*. In much of the Anglo-Saxon business world, this mindset remains dominant, reinforced by capital markets that place short-term shareholder value above everything else. Capital is expected to *work hard and immediately, sweating the balance sheet*. Long-term benefits, after all, are only long-term.

Innovation, globalization, technology, and economies of scale have delivered major efficiency gains and broad improvements in welfare. But the downsides of a narrow shareholder focus were long dismissed as externalities: the costs were passed on to others, from climate change and pollution, to health impacts and social disruption, placing a burden on distant populations. While companies in the Global North sweat their balance sheets, many in the Global South still rely on sweatshops. Weak governance, low wages, and limited protections allow harmful practices to persist, while most of the benefits accrue elsewhere.

The 2013 collapse of the Rana Plaza textile factory in Bangladesh, which killed more than 1,100 people, was a global wake-up call. Suddenly, brand reputations were directly exposed to consumer scrutiny and boycotts.[6]

Behavioral dynamics help explain the slow pace of change. *Conservative bias*, "don't overreact; things aren't that bad," keeps organizations locked in familiar patterns, even as the world around them changes, especially in fossil-dependent sectors. Executive incentives reinforce this tendency: they often remain skewed toward financial results, even when sustainability metrics are included in the bonus formula.

But organizations and society can also fall into a *progressive bias*. Internally, this can show up as overly optimistic beliefs about the benefits of sustainable investments, downplaying risks, or underestimating costs. Externally, distrust of large companies can lead society to dismiss sustainability efforts as greenwashing. Together, these biases help explain the persistent gap between a company's stated *corporate purpose* and society's expectations of its *social purpose*.

From purpose to pushback

Lasting transformation is never driven by compliance alone. Deeper motivations are emerging: inspiring employees and customers around a shared purpose, building a sense of collective responsibility, and visibly leading by example. Around the world, awareness of climate change and environmental degradation has sharpened. Human fatalities and the financial cost of heat waves, wildfires, flooding, melting ice caps, and crop failures have become impossible to ignore.

Citizens, customers, employees, and pension funds are increasingly holding companies to account. In the United States, often seen as single-purpose, profit-driven, most CEOs now acknowledge the value of sustainable and inclusive business practices. Only a small minority—around 6%—still believe profit should be a company's sole focus, even if financial interests continue to dominate day-to-day decision-making.[7]

For boards, this shift means considering a widening set of stakeholders, with sustainability becoming a core element of the organization's social mission. But fundamental change takes time. More than awareness or public commitments, it requires internal conviction, aligned incentives, and the behavioral courage to challenge existing norms. Real transformation often begins not with external pressure but with the willingness of leaders to translate purpose into consistent choices and trade-offs—especially when those decisions become uncomfortable.

Shared values: whose values?

Biologist and documentary filmmaker David Attenborough has spent a lifetime defending the intrinsic value of nature. His work highlights the *conservative bias*—our tendency to stick to prior beliefs even when uncomfortable evidence suggests otherwise. Attenborough observes that in today's economic system, 100 acres of monoculture palm-oil plantation are valued more highly than 100 acres of biodiverse jungle. Yet moments of cultural awakening do occur: in 1970, *Songs of the Humpback Whale* by bio-acoustician Roger Payne became a global phenomenon, raising awareness and helping to prevent several whale species from disappearing altogether.

Isolation is no longer an option. Activists, investigative journalists, and public opinion increasingly confront companies with the environmental and social consequences of their actions. The UN Global Compact initiative has articulated ten principles based on *human rights, labor justice, environmental care*, and *anticorruption*. These principles cascade into 17

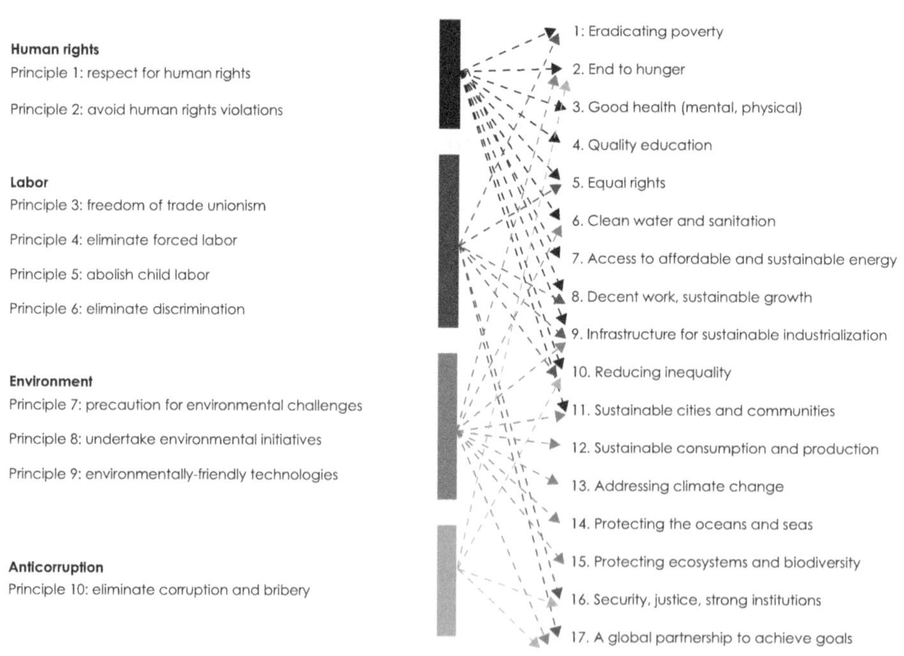

Figure 5.3

ESG within the UN Global Compact: From the Ten Principles to the 17 Sustainable Development Goals

detailed Sustainable Development Goals (see Figure 5.3). The EU has translated these into rigorous sustainability frameworks grounded in ESG principles: *environmental care, social justice*, and *sound governance*.

Companies, guided by rational strategists—and often more fluent in international regulation than the governments that created it—have long been encouraged to relocate operations to jurisdictions where externalities such as waste, emissions, or labor conditions are cheapest or least visible. Governments are often too slow and fragmented to offer meaningful protection.

Meanwhile, a polarized geopolitical landscape has led major economic blocs to make divergent and shifting choices. China positions itself as a leader in green energy, driven in part by a strategic desire to reduce its dependence on fossil fuels. In January 2025, the new U.S. administration withdrew (for the second time) from the Paris Climate Agreement and revived pro-fossil-fuel policies. Months later, the European Parliament voted to delay key sustainability directives, citing concerns about competitiveness.

Social purpose under pressure

History shows that big transitions rarely move in straight lines; they develop slowly, unevenly, and often in the face of resistance. But once the principles take root inside organizations and shape how people think and work, they tend to endure. Disruptive competitors are reshaping markets: the German car industry, hooked in a sunk cost fallacy and anchored to combustion engines in the EU, risks being overtaken by China's rapid innovation in electric mobility.

This shift is not only technological—it reflects deeper economic principles. Economic research underscores the importance of responsible conduct. Nobel laureates George Akerlof and Robert Shiller demonstrate how fairness and trust don't just feel principled; they will fundamentally strengthen markets and offer a durable competitive edge. In other words, sustainable behavior can reinforce long-term economic performance.[8]

Regulators and investors have taken note. Under EU CSR rules, companies must consider all stakeholders. In the United States, this isn't a legal requirement, yet in 2019, 181 CEOs—including those of Apple, JPMorgan, and Walmart—publicly committed to stakeholder capitalism. Large institutional investors such as BlackRock and Vanguard soon followed suit, linking long-term resilience to responsible leadership.

But not all commitments are equal. Companies with questionable ESG track records may issue bold sustainability narratives that outpace their actual actions. When purpose turns into branding rather than behavior, credibility erodes—and strategy drifts ever further from society's expectations.

Case Study: Fossil waves

Few sectors reveal the clash between sustainability and shareholder pressure as the fossil fuel industry. In 2016, major oil companies—Shell, ExxonMobil, BP, TotalEnergies, and Chevron—endorsed the Paris Climate Agreement, yet none committed to binding decarbonization targets. Engaged shareholders, including public pension funds and asset managers like Blackrock, alongside NGOs, urged them to use their expertise and huge cash flow to accelerate investment in renewables.

By 2022, frustration over slow implementation erupted publicly. At Shell's annual meeting in London, members of Money Rebellion—linked to Extinction Rebellion—sang protest songs, glued themselves to chairs, and interrupted proceedings. Dialogue proved impossible as trust eroded, and stakeholders no longer shared a common frame of reference.

The conflict intensified in 2024 at ExxonMobil, when activist investors Follow This and Arjuna Capital filed shareholder resolutions calling for stronger emissions targets. ExxonMobil responded with legal action aimed at limiting the scope of shareholder climate resolutions. The move signaled a shift in emphasis—from managing climate risk to managing governance pressure. Facing legal and financial risks, both groups withdrew. This raised governance questions: should non-executive directors have stepped in to reassess reputational, legal, and strategic risks. Or did restraint reflect a practical reading of fiduciary duty?

Meanwhile, Shell and BP, under mounting capital markets pressure and changing political priorities in the U.S., scaled back on their renewable energy commitments. Both increasingly present themselves as reliable suppliers of fossil energy, emphasizing lower-carbon natural gas, as a transitional solution. Offshore wind and solar—areas where they once claimed leadership—have been scaled back as projects no longer meet return thresholds. Sustainability-oriented investors split: some, like Dutch pension fund ABP, divested entirely, while others remained invested to advocate for change from within. At the same time, elements of the EU sustainability agenda were recalibrated, with certain Green Deal and due diligence measures delayed amid competitiveness concerns, reinforcing a broader climate of strategic caution.

Together, these cases highlight the behavioral and governance dilemma facing boards in carbon-intensive industries. Where tensions remain unresolved, continued inaction risks eroding both accountability and legitimacy.

Bounded ethics or shared value: a boardroom choice

Ethical failures rarely arise from deliberate misconduct. More often, they emerge from incremental decisions, limited internal challenge, and gradual normalization. In such contexts, *bounded ethicality* becomes salient: directors may contribute to problematic outcomes without conscious intent, shaped by cognitive biases and institutional incentives. At the board level, this can result in unintentional complicity, as non-executive directors defer to executive management or prevailing norms despite growing tension with the company's stated purpose.

The tension between short-term financial priorities and longer-term societal commitments are well established. The board's role is not to restate this divide, but to govern it. Inaction may appear prudent, yet sustained deference risks weakening oversight. Here's the trap: doing nothing *feels* neutral. It preserves relationships, avoids confrontation, and maintains the board's collegiality. But, as Bazerman shows, that comfortable silence is itself a deliberate choice that can slide into complicity, prioritizing the decision-makers' interests over those of the organization or its stakeholders.[9]

Although there is evidence that ESG-aligned corporate behavior can serve the long-term interests of both shareholders and stakeholders, progress remains uneven.[10] Behavioral research nonetheless shows that explicitly defining and prioritizing sustainability goals increases the likelihood of meaningful action.[11]

As Michael Porter's argued as early as 2011, companies must balance shareholder value with broader societal value, a concept he termed *"shared value."*[12] However, realizing this vision in a global world also requires coordinated rules, taxation, and consistent regulation to create a level playing field globally.

Executives may present polished ESG narratives, but non-executives must judge whether substance matches the story. Their task is to look past slogans, separate real progress from symbolic gestures, and ensure sustainability ambitions are embedded in actual strategic choices. Where companies promote a responsible image without meaningful change, they risk greenwashing—a divergence between public comments and organizational practice.

Case Study: 3M—the price of forever

In 2021, excavation works for a new tunnel near Antwerp, Belgium, revealed dangerously high concentrations of PFOS—one of the persistent "forever chemicals"—in the soil of the Scheldt Delta. The contamination was traced to decades (until 2002) of discharges from 3M's plant in Zwijndrecht (B). Only three years earlier, 3M, whose motto is "Science for Life," had agreed to an $850 million settlement in Minnesota for similar pollution.

Yet, in Antwerp, the company continued to produce and release a new, unregistered PFAS variant. Local residents were found to have elevated chemical levels in their blood, and fish from the Eastern Scheldt were deemed unfit for consumption. Initially, 3M's Chief Medical Officer publicly downplayed the issue, suggesting that some individuals were simply "prone to storing toxic substances."

In December 2022, the tide had turned, and the company announced its intention to exit all PFAS manufacturing by the end of 2025, and a €571 million settlement was reached. A statement from 3M's new senior vice president for PFAS stewardship signaled a shift from denial toward responsibility and restoration: "We're going to take it [the Scheldt Delta] back to the state that it was before we had to come in."[13]

The shift came, but it came late—only after public pressure, legal settlements, and undeniable evidence. Behavioral lesson: organizations often wait for external force rather than acting on internal conviction. By then, damage is done and trust is eroded.

Us versus them: *ingroup–outgroup*

Cooperation and maintaining personal relationships are positive forces within any organization. Yet when the internal cohesion becomes too strong, it can trigger a well-known sociological pattern: *ingroup favoritism*. This occurs when people—often without ill intent—prioritize the interests and perspectives of their own group over those of outsiders. Outgroups are viewed less favorably, their concerns are discounted, and their influence is weakened.

This dynamic also reaches into boardrooms. Lans Bovenberg notes that strong personal ties can intensify an *us-versus-them* mindset.[14] Like in any group, newcomers in a board, executive, or non-executive—must first earn their place in the group. In the early stages, the pressure to belong can make them overly cautious, leading them to align with dominant views, avoid friction, and hesitate to introduce new perspectives. Such conformity may feel collegial, but it reduces the diversity of thought that effective boards depend on.

Similar dynamics play out in the relationship between companies and their external environment. When a company's alliances—between executives and regulators, who grant permits—become too tight, communities and ecosystems can effectively become outgroups. Local government officials may be pulled into this inner circle, leading to shared interests, loyalty, and silence in the face of ethical dilemmas. Regulatory tolerance grows; practices harmful to the environment are overlooked or quietly normalized.

This isn't malice *per se*. It's what happens when group loyalty quietly overrides broader accountability. In these situations, the true costs—health impacts, environmental degradation, social disruption—only surface years later, long after issuing the permit, felt justified because of long-term economic benefits for the region.

However, when insiders protect one another, the outsiders usually bear the consequences. Ingroup favoritism is not just a social bias but a governance risk.[15] Local and central governments may turn a blind eye, allowing violations to be ignored or even legalized. Only after retirement—once they've left the inner circle of mutual interests—do some civil servants feel free to speak out. In the end, as case studies show, the final cost of the pollution cleanup can far exceed the economic benefits for the region that once seemed to justify approval.

Stewardship and power: an uneasy alliance

When a company adopts a bold social mission, who ultimately determines how far it really goes? Tensions often arise between the pursuit of purpose and the structures of corporate power, especially when values clash with financial, legal, or political pressures. These moments test not just governance design but also the willingness of boards and executives to uphold ideals when it's inconvenient. One brand that has lived this tension in public view is Ben & Jerry's.

Case Study: Ben & Jerry's—peace, love, and ice cream

When Unilever acquired Ben & Jerry's in 2000, the founders, both *"proudly Jewish,"* insisted on an unusual safeguard: an independent board with the legal authority to protect the brand's social mission. Its commitments to human rights, social justice, and environmental sustainability were not symbolic; they shaped the company's culture and identity, deeply resonating with customers and employees alike, embedding social activism as part of its identity. The governance structure was deliberately designed to shield those values from commercial pressure, embedding structural friction between social purpose and Unilever's shareholder-driven priorities.

That safeguard was first tested in 2021, when the board opposed sales in Israeli settlements in the occupied Palestinian territories, widely regarded as inconsistent with international law and repeatedly criticized in U.N. resolutions. Facing political pushback from Israel and some U.S. investors, Unilever resolved the dispute by spinning off its West Bank operations to a local licensee, Blue & White Ice Cream Ltd. The social mission prevailed, but only after a bruising confrontation.

In 2025, Unilever spun off its entire ice cream division as the Magnum Ice Cream Company, citing portfolio focus and margin improvement. That same year, tensions with Ben & Jerry's reignited as the brand continued its public advocacy. Ben & Jerry's—supported by its independent board—filed a federal lawsuit in New York alleging that Magnum had breached the 2000 governance agreement. The complaint cited interference with its social mission, and later, the unilateral removal of its CEO and Chair, allegedly in retaliation for defending that mission. By early 2026, Magnum's new leadership continued asserting control over the rebellious board, deepening internal tensions and distracting from its long-term strategic priorities.

The case demonstrates a central governance dilemma: contractual protections can defend purpose on paper, but enduring alignment between ownership, leadership, and mission ultimately determines whether those values survive in practice.

Stewardship investors play a crucial role in encouraging sustainable corporate behavior. The UK's Stewardship Code (2012) sets the tone: investors are expected not only to consider ESG criteria but also to actively engage, asking questions to leadership, voting decisively, and holding management accountable. Major institutional investors, including CalPERS, APG, and Norway's oil reserve fund (NBIM), support this approach, arguing that environmental and social harm may not appear on the profit and loss statements today, but over time, it erodes long-term value for pension holders and the next generation.[16]

These investors increasingly favor companies that integrate human rights, environmental care, and long-term resilience into governance and operations. Evidence supports this view: during the COVID-19 crisis, portfolios with strong CSR profiles showed lower volatility, reinforcing the belief that sustainability is not a moral add-on but a financial stabilizer.[17] As a result, long-term owners—family businesses, pension funds, and private-equity firms—are adopting similar expectations, often prompted by the demands of their own institutional investors.[18] Yet sustaining momentum requires more than formal codes; it demands consistent oversight, strong entrepreneurial leadership, and real commitment from those charged with oversight.

These headwinds are not abstract; they confront real-world companies directly, as the case of Ørsted illustrates.

Case Study: Ørsted—green growth in headwinds

Initially an oil and gas exploration company operating in Denmark's North Sea, Ørsted A/S undertook one of the most ambitious strategic pivots in modern corporate history. Moving from fossil fuels to offshore wind required more than technical reinvention—it demanded behavioral change: breaking organizational inertia, challenging the sunk-cost logic of decades in hydrocarbons, and reframing identity, capabilities, and risk tolerance. By 2022, Ørsted had become Europe's largest offshore wind producer.

However, this transformation brought higher-than-expected volatility and intensified board engagement. In 2024–2025, Ørsted ran into political headwinds in the United States. The incoming administration, calling climate change a hoax, expressed its support for oil and gas and scaled back renewable energy incentives. It even issued so-called "stop work instructions" on offshore wind projects off the coast of New England—that were close to completion—and one off the coast of New York, on the pretense of national security. For Ørsted, this triggered project write-downs, legal disputes, and renegotiations of long-term power purchase agreements. The impact was amplified because U.S. offshore wind was already contending with rising material and capital costs.

The pressure exposed Ørsted's weakened balance sheet, forcing a major recapitalization. Denmark, as the majority shareholder, underscored its long-term commitment to renewable leadership, subscribing to its share of a $9.7 billion rights issue. After securing authorization from the U.S. federal court, Ørsted can, for the time being, proceed with its projects and remain a global force in offshore wind.

Its storm-tested path shows that durable leadership is measured not by its performance during calm conditions but by the ability to keep moving when conditions change. Such progress calls for strategic imagination, disciplined execution, and patience beyond a typical leadership term.

Ørsted's story underlines that transformational strategy requires more than vision or operational courage—it demands board-level conviction and adaptive capital structures. When political winds turn, sustained non-executive support becomes critical for executives to hold their bold strategic course.

Where purpose meets people: strengthening strategy from within

Employees aren't immune to the broader debate. As sustainability becomes politicized in some parts of society, organizations may face internal tensions or even disengagement. At the same time, talented young professionals actively seek purpose, inclusiveness, and a sense of agency—they want their work to matter: often in roles tied to sustainability, innovation, and long-term impact.

For boards, it's essential to recognize this implicit expectation: they want to be challenged, to contribute ideas, and to help shape solutions rather than simply execute instructions. This makes alignment around long-term value not only a governance priority but also a talent priority—critical for attracting and retaining the next generation of change-makers.

SUMMARY AND CONCLUSION

In today's fast-changing world—defined by uncertainty, geopolitical tension, and rising stakeholder expectations—companies can no longer craft strategy in isolation. The ground is shifting: the energy transition, rapid technological disruption, and growing demands for social and environmental accountability are reshaping what society expects from business.

A global movement built around "purpose" is challenging the long-dominant logic of *shareholder primacy*. But shifting toward sustainable value creation is anything but straightforward. It demands long-term thinking in a system wired for quarterly results. Political backlash and corporate pushback add further strain—especially in listed firms, where market pressure and executive incentives reinforce a conservative bias that favors the familiar over the necessary.

If sustainability and a social mission are to transcend mere rhetoric, boards must do more than recognize the need for change. They must align strategy with leadership discipline, honest reflection, and consistent execution. When executives and non-executives act in concert, they create the trust and resilience needed to navigate tensions between purpose and profit.

Governance rarely fails because of missing frameworks, but because assumptions remain untested. In the end, courage to question matters more than certainty.

§5.3—RISK IS HUMAN

Introduction

Strategy and risk are inseparable. Strategy is visible: a vision, a plan, a budget, and ultimately, results. Risk is less tangible. It can be modeled and mitigated, yet it always contains uncertainty: the unknowns behind every decision. And while risk can be analyzed rationally, people perceive it in very different ways; some are easily unsettled, while others remain calm under pressure. And this is where behavioral dynamics come into play.

Entrepreneurship is often equated with risk-taking, but strategic judgment takes it a step further. It's about weighing risk against reward. For any board, the essential question is whether the expected outcome justifies the risks of a strategic choice.

Even with formal processes, major projects—such as acquisitions, mergers, and IT initiatives—regularly deviate from their set course. That's because risk management is human work. People rely on intuition, habits, and shortcuts, making decisions vulnerable to bias. Culture quietly amplifies this: it shapes how risk is perceived, how openly concerns are voiced, and how the organization reacts when things go wrong.

For non-executive directors, the challenge is to assess from a distance how effectively the organization handles uncertainty. Are the right risks recognized? Does the culture support honesty and learning? And does the company's risk appetite match its actual capacity to absorb setbacks?

Avoiding risk entirely is a danger in itself: organizations that fear uncertainty fail to adapt. The real task is not eliminating risk but understanding it—and managing it responsibly.

When culture undermines the system

Safety is one of the most obvious (and expected) areas of risk management. Whether at the local swimming pool or on a drilling platform far out at sea, such risk is always present. These risks may appear minimal, but they can have dramatic consequences. One would expect a near-perfect risk system in places such as these. Yet even here, human behavioral factors can derail the system.

Organizations aim to identify and manage risks, recognizing that unmanaged risks can hinder success. Their natural response is to form risk departments and draw up rules based on their experience; the non-executive directors establish risk committees. Nonetheless, even with formal procedures in place, a culture can emerge in which rules are ignored or followed only superficially. This highlights a deeper truth: formal systems do not function in a vacuum. They thrive in a culture of attention, responsibility, and moral awareness. Without that, even the best-designed risk management structures can collapse under the weight of collective neglect.

A telling example of this disconnect comes from an institution once considered incorruptible: the UK Post Office.

Case Study: Post Office—when systems override judgment

The Post Office Horizon scandal has since become a case study in spectacular failure. Not just because of its supposed masterplan, but because of its catastrophic execution, entrenched denial, and absence of ethical curiosity. The dramatized documentary *"Mr. Bates vs. The Post Office"* made its full scale visible to the public.

At the center was Horizon, a massive IT system "Horizon" introduced in the late 1990s to automate tasks once handled by human administrators and reduce costs. Instead, the system was riddled with defects. It generated phantom shortfalls, unexplained overdrafts, and accounting errors that appeared on paper as clear signs of fraud. Over the course of two decades, the Post Office had more than 900 sub-postmasters prosecuted based on their own faulty data, treating computer outputs as unquestionable truth.

Despite mounting internal evidence that Horizon was failing, senior leadership insisted the discrepancies were due to employee and shop-owner misconduct. Sub-postmasters lost their savings, livelihoods, reputations, and freedom. At least four died by suicide. What unfolded was not a simple oversight; it was systemic negligence, amplified by a culture that was afraid to admit error.

This case shows how culture can override logic. An unwillingness to challenge authority, acknowledge mistakes, or speak up, allowed a flawed system to dictate decisions with devastating consequences. Internal documents later revealed that top executives were repeatedly alerted to system faults but chose denial, opacity, and blame. Rather than confront institutional failure, the Post Office focused on protecting its image—mounting an aggressive legal defense while continuing to prosecute innocent people.

The board's role also came under harsh scrutiny. Non-executive directors were criticized for their passivity, for accepting executive narratives without thorough examination, and for failing to question the reliability of a critical system. Their inaction meant early warning signs were missed—and the people they were meant to protect paid the price. The case shows how formal systems, no matter how sophisticated, can fail when no one in the board dares to question them.

As in business, institutions as ordinary and socially vital as the local swimming pool, where children learn a basic life skill, can fail when vigilance slips and communication breaks down. This double history case study shows the permanent need for attention.

Case Study: Swimming pool—safety lost in translation

In 1875, Maurits van Lennep, son of the famous Dutch writer Jacob van Lennep, wrote in his diary: "*In the swimming school, young Moltzer, who was swimming with Jacob Backer, drowned because he got cramp, sank, and none of the swimming masters could swim. They had neither hooks nor dredges.*"

Nearly 150 years later, despite all the rules and protocols that have since been prescribed, pool drownings still happen during swimming lessons. Nine-year-old Salam, the daughter of Syrian refugees, dreamed of becoming a doctor. She couldn't swim, spoke no Dutch, and drowned just after the end of the swimming lesson. Perhaps she didn't understand the instructions.

The judge later concluded that the lifeguards hadn't supervised properly: they had been vaguely watching the water from a distance, failing to keep a close eye on the pupils. This was not a failure of rules but a failure of attention. The lifeguards were "unconsciously at fault" due to a "lack of communication and vigilance." "Less reliance on routine and better communication between supervisors might have prevented the accident."

A swimming pool may seem far removed from big boardrooms. Yet the parallels are unmistakable, and the consequences of losing a life are devastating. Vigilance cannot be delegated to systems alone. For those responsible for oversight, whether they are overseeing plants, trading floors, or offshore rigs, the question is identical: are those watching the water truly watching, or has routine overtaken attention?

Risk appetite versus risk tolerance: knowing your limits

Risk appetite refers to the types and levels of risk a company is willing to accept to achieve its strategic objectives. The board defines this appetite and ensures that a system is in place to monitor and manage risk exposure. *Risk tolerance* is about capacity: how much risk can the organization absorb without jeopardizing its core stability? Can it survive a failed acquisition? Are safety systems sufficient if a risky activity—such as operating a drilling rig—is taken on?

Transparency is key. Risk communication must be open and transparent, allowing both internal and external stakeholders to assess their own exposure. While this may sound obvious, the Deepwater Horizon and swimming pool cases show how small and large entities can still mismanage risk due to blind spots in culture and communication.

Case Study: Deepwater Horizon—the gradual erosion of risk discipline

BP had decades of experience operating offshore drilling rigs. Yet, its Deepwater Horizon platform in the Gulf of Mexico would be involved in one of the largest and costliest environmental disasters in history. An estimated 780,000 cubic meters of oil flowed uncontrolled into the sea. Whistleblower Bobby Maxwell, a former audit supervisor at Minerals Management Service, the Texas-based regulator, described a culture of complacency and corruption.

Inspectors were sometimes recruited from the oil industry. While this may sound logical, given their knowledge and experience, it resulted in inspectors having personal ties with those they were meant to oversee. This gradually created a *normalization of deviance*, where small rule-bending became routine and increasingly unquestioned. In the name of "good relations," tickets to sporting events were handed out, and inspections were reduced to routine exercises. Checklists were sometimes pre-filled in pencil by the oil companies themselves. When the Macondo field exploded, killing 11 workers and causing an unprecedented environmental catastrophe, BP was fined $4 billion. Total costs, including damages, exceeded $50 billion. Afterward, BP seized the opportunity to rebrand itself as a more sustainable "green" energy company—a move that many observers saw as reputational repair. Nevertheless, the disaster severely damaged the company's credibility.

Culture speaks louder than systems

What happens when formal systems look solid, and no one dares to question them or speak up? Culture is often invisible until it breaks the surface. Social psychologist Geert Hofstede (1928–2020) conducted landmark research for IBM on cultural differences in organizations across more than 70 countries. Similar differences in cultural norms can be seen in different companies, depending on their activities or place in their lifecycle.

To make the broad and abstract concept of culture more measurable, he identified several core dimensions along which national and organizational cultures tend to vary.

- *High power distance versus low power distance*—the degree to which people accept hierarchy, or expect equality. In high-power distance cultures, command structures are largely unquestioned; people accept inequality and defer to authority. In low-power-distance environments, consultation feels natural, and challenging the boss is seen as legitimate rather than insubordinate. This single dimension can determine whether a junior employee will speak up when something feels wrong, or stay silent out of deference to authority.
- *Low uncertainty avoidance versus high uncertainty avoidance*—Organizations with low uncertainty avoidance are comfortable with change, flexible rules, and improvisation. Individuals with high uncertainty avoidance tend to crave structure, predictability, and detailed procedures. They need to know what's coming next. Neither approach is inherently better, but the mismatch between an organization's risk profile and its cultural comfort with uncertainty can be dangerous.
- *Feminine versus masculine*—Hofstede also distinguished between what he called feminine versus masculine cultures—what we would now describe as cooperative versus competitive orientations. Cooperative cultures emphasize care, collaboration, and quality of life. Competitive cultures prioritize achievement, performance, and winning above all else.
- *Individualistic versus collectivistic*—In individualistic cultures, people are expected to speak for themselves, take initiative, and take responsibility for personal actions. This can encourage whistleblowing, escalation, and open disagreement—essential ingredients for

healthy challenge in organizations. Collectivistic cultures, by contrast, prioritize group harmony, loyalty, and cohesion. People may avoid raising uncomfortable truths if doing so threatens relationships.

Later, Hofstede added two more dimensions that speak directly to strategic decision-making. The first is *time orientation*: do decisions chase short-term wins, or are they guided by long-term resilience? The second is about *norms*: does the organization permit freedom and experimentation, or does it demand tight adherence to established rules?

Of course, these dimensions are abstract concepts. However, even if no culture fits neatly into a box, they do help us to understand how culture shapes everyday behavior: not only what is said, but what goes unsaid. During its lifecycle, culture becomes a shared system of values, beliefs, practices, and habits. It guides how people interpret situations, make decisions, and coordinate behavior, even when no one is explicitly giving instructions.

These cultural patterns help explain the cases we've seen, and why some boards catch warning signs while others miss them entirely.

Three levels of risk culture

Cultural patterns help explain why some boards spot trouble early while others overlook it. Culture shapes not only what people speak up about but also what stays hidden. Across organizations, three broad risk-culture profiles tend to emerge.

- Young, innovation-driven firms live with constant uncertainty; their people are comfortable with ambiguity and often view rules as a hindrance.
- Mature companies with a more stable position face the opposite challenge: excessive caution can drain agility and leave opportunities on the table.
- In high-hazard environments, such as nuclear facilities, offshore rigs, or public swimming pools, risk tolerance is necessarily low, with structure and procedure forming the backbone of safe operations.

Boards must remain aware that, even in well-designed systems, human behavior can drift—and people may consciously or unconsciously turn a blind eye.

Risk culture and the director's dilemma

From a behavioral governance perspective, the central challenge for non-executive directors is to identify the gap between the risks an organization is actually carrying and what its systems are designed to handle. That means assessing whether the declared risk appetite truly matches the organization's real tolerance. Directors need to understand where rules are respected, where they are quietly bypassed, whether key roles are filled by people capable of sustained vigilance, and whether the culture scans for emerging threats rather than relying on backward-looking assumptions. Even strong systems drift over time as habits form, shortcuts emerge, and confidence dulls attention.

The UK Post Office scandal illustrated this dynamic with painful clarity. Systems failed not because they were absent but because challenge was unwelcome and boards did not probe behind reassuring dashboards. The oversight gap widened until failure became inevitable. For non-executive directors, maintaining the right distance is critical. Lean in too far and they risk being seen as intrusive; stay too distant and they lose sight of the behavioral currents that undermine formal processes. In crises—particularly when leadership is failing—intervention becomes essential. But fragmented ownership and unclear mandates can weaken authority, leaving non-executive directors with only two options: act decisively to close the gap, or, if that proves impossible, step aside. For non-executive directors, the essential question is straightforward: is the organization's risk system genuinely equipped for the world it operates in?

Strategic decisions: when strategy meets uncertainty

This widening external uncertainty amplifies the gap between real-world risks and formal risk-management systems (Figure 5.4). In strategy and risk, everything is connected. Directors strive for an optimum situation: to achieve the strategic and operational goals at the lowest possible risk. Non-executive directors typically deal with the larger, high-impact decisions whose consequences lie far into the future. The further away the time horizon, the greater the uncertainty: a risk tomorrow is easier to predict than one a year from now. After all, external factors may come into play that cannot be foreseen today. The complexity of the organization and the rapid evolution of its environment may also intervene.

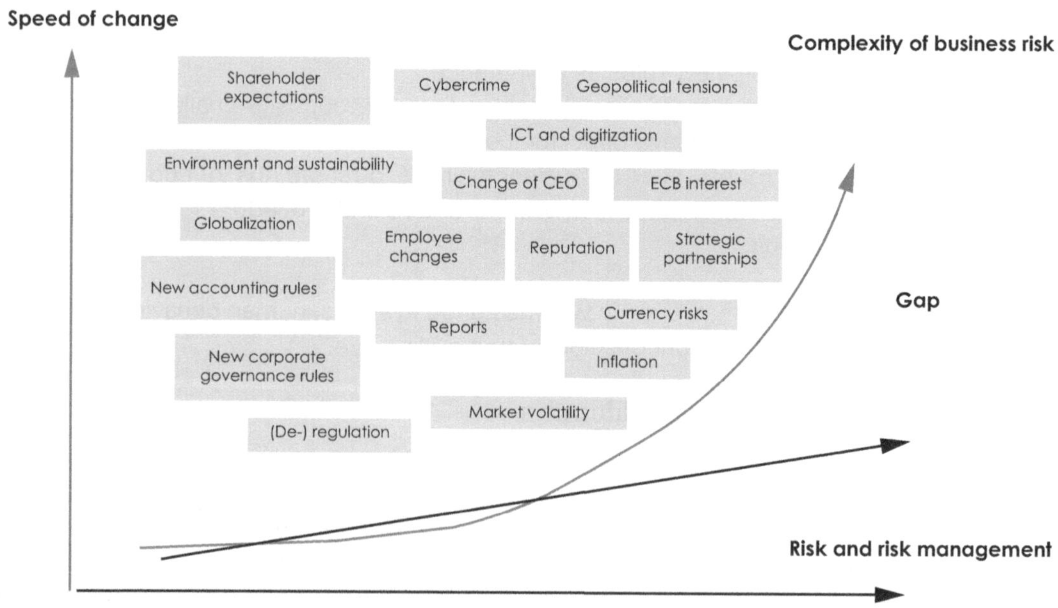

Figure 5.4
The Gap in Risk Management

Today's organizations operate in a volatile environment. In a liberal global economy, with few restrictions on doing business, production and services are performed or purchased wherever the costs are lowest. This boosts efficiency but also increases vulnerability. At the same time, interdependence and systemic political and technological risks are rising. And at the top of the summit, change is ever present: if an era sounds too good to be true, it probably is.

The world experiences geopolitical shocks, unpredictable power clashes between nations, swings in the financial markets, and "once in a lifetime" events, such as the COVID pandemic or the blockage of the Suez Canal in 2021. Digital risks, ranging from IT failures to cyberattacks, continue to grow steadily and can bring entire organizations to a halt.

How leaders deal with complexity: dominant logic versus System 2 thinking

Organizational theorist Johannes Strikwerda describes how executives navigate complexity by relying on *dominant logic*—a mental shortcut shaped by past success and standard managerial training. This ingrained mindset filters how leaders interpret information and narrows the range of solutions they consider. When unfamiliar risks emerge, dominant logic can produce overly simple conclusions and cause growth opportunities to be missed.[19]

Intel illustrates how this pattern unfolds in practice. For years, its leaders assumed that the integrated design-and-manufacture model that once guaranteed technological leadership would remain unassailable. This mindset led them to underestimate the rise of specialized chip design and outsourced fabrication. As TSMC advanced and Nvidia captured momentum in AI, Intel's adherence to its established model slowed its response and cost the company its technological edge.

Non-executive directors face many challenges in this respect. Decisions are often made under time constraints, and executive directors may subtly pressure non-executive directors to "move things forward" rather than delay for deeper scrutiny. Research by EY reveals that 84% of boards of large U.S. companies believe their risk management strategy is not truly effective.[20]

Boards often accept trade-offs in risk oversight as "business as usual." At the same time, the worry about atypical risks is not just understandable but is necessary: pandemics, such as Covid 19, long-term threats, such as climate change, as well as slow-moving strategic risks, rarely show up in quarterly reports.

Understanding how strategic risk decisions are made also requires insight into the behavioral dynamics at the top. As Sutherland and Dekker argue, boards should not only focus on the downside of uncertainty but also recognize its upside: the strategic advantages that can emerge when organizations identify favorable shifts in a changing risk landscape. Market disruptions generate risk, but they also create strategic opportunities. Well-understood risks can become opportunities to innovate or stand out from competitors, and taking carefully calculated risks can lead to meaningful, positive outcomes.

SUMMARY AND CONCLUSION

Risk is difficult to pin down because it's shaped less by rules than by behavior and culture. While risk management can feel as if it is limiting freedom, it is central to long-term resilience. Case studies—from drownings to oil spills and banking failures—show that even advanced systems break down when culture drifts or vigilance fades. More often than not, failures stem from inattentiveness and misplaced trust, rather than a lack of formal controls.

Strong risk governance depends on more than protocols. It requires emotional intelligence, open dialogue, and the willingness to voice uncomfortable concerns. Culture shapes how people speak up, how responsibility is shared, and how ambiguity is navigated. Insights such as those of Hofstede help explain how power distance and uncertainty avoidance influence reactions to authority and risk, especially under pressure.

Non-executive directors walk a fine line: scrutinize too often and they risk being seen as obstructive; hold back and emerging problems may go unchecked. Their job is to judge not just whether systems exist but whether they're genuinely used—and whether the organization's risk appetite matches its real capacity.

In a world defined by geopolitical shocks, technological disruption, and climate uncertainty, even well-built systems can be undone by bias and groupthink. That's why boards must look beyond immediate risks and adopt a forward-oriented mindset, ensuring the organization is not only protected from disruption but also positioned to benefit from it.

§5.4—BEYOND RATIONAL RISK: BEHAVIOR, BIAS, AND DECISION TOOLS

Introduction

Risk management is often portrayed as a clean, analytical process—an exercise in estimating probabilities and balancing expected gains against potential losses. On paper, it looks rational and predictable.

In practice, the model breaks down. Logic alone rarely governs real-world decisions. Daniel Kahneman's research shows that organizational behavior and culture exert far greater influence than many leaders acknowledge, which helps explain why costly errors recur. His proposed remedy is deliberately simple: adopt a checklist mindset, not as a bureaucratic routine, but as a way to cut through bias, habit, and overconfidence.

Non-executive directors are meant to function as an additional line of defense, not as a ceremonial layer of reassurance. When they hesitate to challenge or probe, their presence creates not only limited value but also a false sense of assurance. This section considers three behavioral tools that can strengthen their role: Kahneman's emphasis on structured reflection to counter bias, Nassim Taleb's insistence on asking basic, even "dumb," questions, and Gary Klein's pre-mortem technique. Each helps boards test assumptions and recognize emerging risks.

The instinct to eradicate risk can be just as dangerous as ignoring it. Excessive caution stifles adaptability; unchecked confidence blinds leaders to early warnings. Some of the most serious threats are generated internally. Effective governance demands not passive observation but active moral engagement.

The appendix that follows this chapter translates these principles into a structured checklist to help recognize bias in decision-making.

Risk and charm

Leaders with confidence, charisma, and academic prestige sometimes dazzle investors, regulators, and counterparties alike. However, beneath the surface, behavioral traps—such as overconfidence, groupthink, and blind trust—undermine rational judgment. When financial institutions fail, the behavioral patterns discussed in Chapter 2 repeatedly come to light. The financial sector, with its often opaque leverage structures, is especially vulnerable to fast-moving visionary entrepreneurs. Even external government regulators, whose job is to protect citizens and businesses from misrepresentation, fraud, market manipulation, and systemic risks, can be so impressed by these leaders that they send conflicting signals and wait too long to intervene.

Organizations are especially vulnerable when non-executive directors and shareholders select CEOs based on the self-confidence they exude—mistaking outward poise for intrinsic competence. Remuneration committees can further reinforce this bias, rewarding boldness without fully accounting for its consequences. When hiring, a CEO's success in previous roles is often attributed to personal brilliance, while the possibility that earlier wins were due to well-timed risk-taking or sheer luck is frequently overlooked.

These dynamics became visible in the FTX case—this time in the digital domain.

Case Study: Silicon Valley Bank—from rapid growth to bank run

In 2023, Silicon Valley Bank (SVB) experienced a collapse. Founded in 1983 to finance tech start-ups, it had expanded into a mid-sized general bank. The classic warning signs were all there, yet regulators didn't step in. Under industry pressure, the U.S. administration had eased oversight for banks with balance sheets below $250 billion—SVB stayed just under that threshold. As a result, it only had to undergo a full stress test every two years.

The *Financial Times* later revealed how this lack of monitoring undermined the bank's decisions: between 2019 and 2022, SVB's balance sheet expanded from $71 billion to $211 billion, and CEO Greg Becker's pay also rose sharply, as it was tied to the bank's returns. Those returns doubled to an improbable 20% thanks to increasingly aggressive risk-taking.

In its interim report of March 8, 2023, SVB still declared "ample liquidity," "strong capital," and solid asset quality. Insiders knew better. As confidence evaporated, a classic bank run set in. The U.S. Federal Reserve—having vowed after 2008 never to rescue failing banks again—had overlooked the signals and ultimately had to step in to prevent wider damage.

Dumb questions

Statistician Nassim Taleb warns that we tend to underestimate rare but catastrophic risks—the so-called "black swans".[21] Boards filled with high-profile names can foster an unjustifiably high level of self-confidence and a false sense of security. Questions that may sound "dumb," but challenge core assumptions, are often ignored. The *groupthink* we discussed earlier can easily emerge, especially when high, result-oriented bonuses are in play.

Case Study: LTCM—the halo effect

LTCM was built around star power: legendary bond trader John Meriwether and two Nobel laureates Myron Scholes and Robert Merton. Their prestige created a halo that silenced doubt. Banks poured in money, trusting complex models they didn't understand. The fund leveraged $4.5 billion of equity into $129 billion in assets and over $1 trillion in derivatives. Warren Buffett walked away, saying simply: *"If I don't understand it, I don't invest in it."*

When the Asian crisis and Russia's default hit, LTCM's assumptions crumbled. The Fed had to coordinate a rescue to prevent wider damage. Yet the lesson barely stuck—Meriwether went on to launch another fund that failed again in 2008. Reputation can outlast results, and unchallenged confidence turns risk into fuel for unbridled behavior.

Taleb argues that incentives, complexity, and self-assured leadership produce exactly this pattern. Boards aren't immune. High-profile directors and charismatic CEOs often create an atmosphere where "dumb" questions—the ones that actually matter—are quickly sidelined. But these simple challenges are the real guardrails:

- What if the model is slightly off key?
- Who benefits if we're right, and who pays if this blows up?
- If things turn against us, how bad can this get?
- Why are we so sure that we've captured all the risks?

These questions may seem naïve, but they expose the blind spots that prestige, incentives, and complex systems often conceal. Ignore them, and the case of LTCM won't look exceptional, but familiar. As the FTX collapse showed, lessons learned have a short half-life.

Case Study: FTX—crypto's house of cards

With the rise of "crypto," a parallel financial universe emerged—lightly regulated, opaque, and wrapped in techno-optimism. Proprietary algorithms and opaque promises replaced traditional auditing. As ECB President Christine Lagarde noted, cryptocurrencies such as Bitcoin have no intrinsic value, yet governments have allowed them the space to grow as an alternative currency. Major banks and investment firms followed this evolution with complex derivative products, ushering everyday investors into a speculative bubble.

At the center stood FTX, one of the most high-profile crypto exchanges. In 2023, it collapsed spectacularly—not just due to falling Bitcoin prices, but amid serious allegations of fraud. Founder Sam Bankman-Fried, hailed as a visionary and philanthropist, allegedly funneled billions in customer assets into private accounts through a web of intercompany loans. He also issued his own artificially inflated cryptocurrency, creating a circular illusion of wealth and stability.

Behind the marketing and mission-driven branding lay a simple truth: there was no governance in place. FTX had no independent board, no real controls, and no functional oversight. Risk was transferred to the least informed participants—while insiders cashed in.

Bankman-Fried was sentenced to 25 years in prison. As of April 2025, thanks to a window of favorable crypto market conditions, the bankrupt FTX estate recovered sufficient assets to fully repay customers and creditors, including interest. In the end, the real risk didn't just lie in crypto itself—but in the ease with which even seasoned financial institutions, seduced by returns and hype, helped to package fantasy as finance and enabled fraud.

Objective risk, subjective risk: rational—until it isn't

While financial markets are prone to spectacular failures, other sectors face subtler but equally serious risks. Healthcare, for example, illustrates how even highly regulated environments can be vulnerable—especially when human judgment, stress, or ethical considerations are at play. Risk has both objective and subjective aspects.

Objective risks can be measured, quantified, and managed through systems and protocols. In a hospital, for instance, these include medication errors, patient mix-ups, infections, or even falls from the operating table during surgery. For such risks, procedures, and checklists exist—doctors mark the correct leg before an operation for a reason.

The power of permission to speak up

Physician and researcher Atul Gawande described a powerful experiment on hospital safety at John Hopkins Hospital: nurses in the intensive care unit were given the authority to halt a procedure if the surgeon failed to follow the safety checklist. As a result, the rate of catheter-related infections dropped dramatically—from 11% to zero within ten days. The breakthrough wasn't only procedural—it was behavioral: nurses, typically lower in the clinical hierarchy, were empowered to hold more senior colleagues accountable. This shift in authority challenged the traditional power dynamics and created a culture where speaking up for safety became an integral part of the system itself.[22]

But not all risks can be codified. *Subjective risks* involve interpretation, judgment, and uncertainty. Additionally, a misdiagnosis, an inappropriate treatment choice, or a delayed decision can result from human factors, including the quality of attention, time pressure, and the emotional state of the decision-maker. Avoiding them requires continuous feedback between protocols and clinical intuition, as well as vigilance against fatigue, stress, or overconfidence.

Structured doubt: from checklists to pre-mortems

To combat these phenomena, psychologist Daniel Kahneman advocates for a *checklist mindset*—not only in operational contexts, such as in hospitals, but also in strategic decision-making. His checklist is not about ticking boxes but about raising the quality of reflection. It prompts board members to pause and examine their own thinking—shifting from automatic (System 1) to deliberate (System 2) reasoning and making hidden biases visible.[23] The checklist follows as an appendix at the end of this chapter.

This mindset can be applied at three levels of boardroom decision-making:

- Self-reflection on the quality of non-executive directors' contribution
- Reflection on the executive directors
- Questions about the strategy itself.

Another valuable tool is the *pre-mortem method* developed by psychologist Gary Klein.[24]

In his approach, participants are asked to imagine a future in which their chosen strategy has completely failed. They then ask, "What went wrong?" This future-back approach forces the board to explore vulnerabilities it might otherwise ignore. The method is especially effective in surfacing implicit assumptions underlying a decision and its potential consequences.

SUMMARY AND CONCLUSION

Risk may seem rational and measurable, but in practice, it's shaped as much by perception and emotion as by data. We judge future threats through the lens of past experience and often repeat familiar mistakes. Major strategic decisions—mergers, acquisitions, transformations—are rarely objective. Optimism, confidence, and subtle cognitive biases color judgment. That's why boards, and especially non-executive directors, must look beyond the numbers and pay close attention to culture, behavior, and group dynamics.

A clear, independent view of risk matters. Committees, audits, and regulators offer safeguards, but relying on these alone creates a false sense of certainty. Governance is about more than compliance; it demands disciplined judgment. Failures typically stem not from false facts but from untested assumptions, unexamined optimism, and an absence of challenge. Boards must be willing to question the room—and themselves: what might they be missing?

Private equity provides a useful contrast: directors are selected for active oversight and stay closely involved in execution and outcomes. While not a universal model, this intensity illustrates what engaged governance can look like.

Structured tools help sharpen awareness. Taleb's dumb questions, Kahneman's checklist, and Klein's pre-mortems expose blind spots. Risk can't be eliminated, but making it more visible improves decisions. Asking the right questions—early—is the real safeguard.

Appendix: a checklist for recognizing bias in major strategic decision-making

(Inspired by Kahneman, Taleb, and Klein). This appendix offers a reflective checklist to help boards recognize behavioral biases when facing major decisions. The objective is not to eliminate bias, which is neither realistic nor desirable, but to surface it, question it, and rebalance judgment.

Biases within the non-executive board

- Boardroom participation bias
  Boards work best when all voices are heard. Dominant personalities or quiet reluctance can distort discussion. Are all board members contributing through questions and opinions, do all voices carry weight, or do a few dominate? Are any issues, conscious or unconscious, being left unsaid?
- Disagreement aversion
  Harmony can mask dissent. Avoiding friction can silence essential debate. Do we truly agree, or are we avoiding conflict? Have dissenting views been aired and discussed? Could interlocking interests or subtle pressures be shaping the conversation?
- Board arrogance
  Taleb warns against the illusion of certainty that experience can create. Overconfidence can narrow directors' fields of vision, causing them to miss critical risks. Do non-executives actively seek independent expert input? Or are they relying too heavily on past experience?
- Expert bias
  When someone is treated as the "expert," their view can dominate. Are certain perspectives left unchallenged because of perceived authority? Is there sufficient space for skepticism and independent judgment?
- Groupthink
  Group loyalty can create artificial consensus. Are we mistaking consensus for truth? Has sufficient space been created for alternative views? Does unanimity reflect true alignment—or the influence of a dominant CEO or chair?

Biases in executive judgment

- Self-love and self-interest bias
  Executives can become attached to their own plans, or driven by incentives. Has the team fallen in love with its own plan? Are risks being downplayed while benefits are overstated? Could personal interests be clouding judgment?
- Halo effect and positivity bias
  Charisma and confidence can be mistaken for competence, which may silence discussion. Is a persuasive CEO receiving uncritical trust or admiration? Are passion and confidence being mistaken for sound strategy? Is risk awareness dismissed as pessimism?

Biases embedded in the strategic proposal

- Sunk cost fallacy
  Past investment can distort present judgment. Are we holding onto plans because we have already invested so much? Would a "clean slate" or private equity lens help separate legacy from future value creation?
- Confirmation bias
  Once a path is chosen, new information gets twisted to support it. Are we actively seeking contradictory evidence? Have alternatives been genuinely considered? Are we creating room for uncertainty and second thoughts?
- Anchoring bias
  Initial reference points can skew decisions. Are we relying too heavily on a single anchor? Have alternative reference points been explored? Have we considered the broader external impacts?
- Availability bias
  Recent or vivid information can drown out relevance. Are we relying too heavily on what's easy to recall? What information might be missing or underexplored? In hindsight, what might we wish we had examined more closely (Klein's *pre-mortem*)?
- Overconfidence and the planning fallacy
  Optimism leads to underestimated risks and overestimated benefits. Have we realistically assessed downsides and execution risks? Are external impacts and stakeholder consequences taken seriously? Are we underestimating competitive responses or gaps in due-diligence? Have the hardest questions truly been asked—and answered?

REFLECTION QUESTIONS

Questions §5.1—Strategy as a choice

1. What explicit or implicit assumptions are shaping our strategic direction? Are they still valid?
2. Is the executive board genuinely focused on developing and executing the strategy, or is it pulled into day-to-day issues? Are executive and non-executive directors aligned in how the strategy is carried out?
3. Do we have the experience, capacity, and perspective to challenge and guide strategic decisions? Are we sufficiently attentive to how behavioral dynamics or unspoken assumptions may be influencing them?

Questions §5.2—Strategy, purpose, and the social mission of the board

1. How do we balance short-term investor expectations with long-term value creation while also considering broader public interests such as health, climate, and community well-being?
2. Are ESG priorities, geopolitical risks, and major technological shifts meaningfully embedded in our strategic decision-making?

3. When evaluating new business investment, do we place greater weight on the financial upside than on the externalities they create—especially those that fall outside our immediate radar?

Questions §5.3—Risk is human

1. Do we share a clear understanding of our organization's risk appetite and of the gap between our formal risk framework and the actual complexity of our business?
2. Are we taking enough risk, or is excessive caution limiting our ability to adapt and grow? And, just as importantly, are we taking the *right* risks?
3. Do we integrate operational and frontline insights into the board's deliberations before committing to high-stakes decisions?

Questions §5.4—Beyond rational risk: behavior, bias, and decision tools

1. What do we consider as the three most significant risks in our organization, and how is our boardroom discussion structured to address them meaningfully?
2. Do we apply structured tools—such as pre-mortems, checklists, or "dumb questions"—to surface hidden assumptions and test the robustness of our decisions?
3. Do we create space for doubt, dissent, and alternative views, or do our discussions drift toward confirmation, comfort, and consensus seeking?

NOTES

1 Henry Mintzberg (2016), *On Management*, YouTube Video; Henry Mintzberg (1973), *The Nature of Managerial Work*, Harper & Row.

2 Nassim Nicholas Taleb (2012), *Antifragile: Things That Gain from Disorder*, New York: Random House.

3 Luc Renneboog, Cara Vansteenkiste (2018 December), *What Goes Wrong in M&As? On the Long-Run Success Factors in M&As*, ECGI Paper.

4 McKinsey (2008), *The Voice of Experience, Public Versus Private Equity.*

5 Donald C. Hambrick, Phyllis A. Mason (1984), *Upper echelons: The organization as a reflection of its top managers*, The Academy of Management Review, 9(2).

6 *KPMG International Report Finds Growing Link between Sustainability and Executive Pay* (2025 March 31), KPMG.

7 Alan Murray (2020 April 22), *Corporate Purpose, Shifting from Why to How*, McKinsey; *The 2019 Fortune 500 CEO survey results are in* (2019 May 16), Fortune.

8 George A. Akerlof, Robert J. Shiller (2015), *Phishing for Phools: The Economics of Manipulation and Deception*, Princeton University Press.

9 Max H. Bazerman (2020), *Complicit: How We Enable the Unethical and How to Stop*. New York, Harper Business.

10 Chenxi Wang (2024), *The relationship between ESG performance and corporate performance—based on stakeholder theory*, SHS Web of Conferences, 190.

11 Jan Stolker, Bahar Keskin den Doelder, Jatinder S. Sidhu (2021 May), *Climate-related reporting by publicly listed companies: An attention-action mapping*, Monthly Journal of Accountancy and Business Economics, 94.

12 Michael E. Porter, Mark R. Kramer (2011 January–February), *Creating shared value: how to reinvent capitalism*, Harvard Business Review Harvard Business, 89(1–2), 62–77.

13 (2022 June 10), 3M's "forever chemicals" crisis has come to Europe, *Bloomberg.*

14 Lans Bovenberg (2019), *Where Is the Love, on Value and Values.* Inaugural address, Rotterdam: Erasmus University. See also Chapter 2.

15 James G. March, Johan P. Olsen (1995), *Democratic Governance,* New York: Free Press.

16 APG, the largest pension fund in the Netherlands, sets as the goal of its investments not only "a good pension" but also "a livable sustainable world."

17 Hans Lööf (2022), *Is corporate social responsibility investing a free lunch? The relationship between ESG, tail risk, and upside potential of stocks before and during the COVID-19* crisis, *Finance Research Letters,* 46; Giovanni Cardillo (2022 June), Covid 19, ESG investing, and the resilience of more sustainable stocks: Evidence from European firms, *Business Strategy and the Environment,* 32(1), 602–623.

18 *ESG in Alternatives, Navigating the Climate Crisis* (2021 October), Preqin.

19 Johannes Strikwerda (2023), *Organized Complexity in Business,* Springer Nature Switzerland.

20 Sharon Sutherland, Tony Dekker (2021 July 14), *The Board Imperative: Is Now the Time to Reframe Risk as Opportunity? EY Report.*

21 Nassim Taleb (2009 April 8), *Ten principles for a Black Swan-proof world,* Financial Times.

22 Atul Gawande (2010), *The Checklist Manifesto,* London: Profile Books.

23 Daniel Kahneman, Dan Lovallo, Olivier Sibony (2011 June), *Before you make that big decision,* Harvard Business Review, 89(6), 50–60, 137.

24 Gary Klein (2007 September*), Performing a project premortem,* Harvard Business Review.

CHAPTER

6

Moral leadership and the balanced board

CONTENTS

§6.1—VALUES, VIRTUES, AND THE MORAL COMPASS

Introduction

Steering an organization through volatile markets, shifting risks, and rapid change lies at the heart of leadership—and forms the foundation of good governance. The word *governance* derives from the Greek *kubernao*, "to steer" like a ship. Steering becomes most difficult when conditions turn, and today's environment is more complex than ever: geopolitical instability, technological disruption, climate change, and mounting environmental pressures. This is why selecting the right CEO is the remuneration committee's most pivotal task. Safe navigation depends on leaders who can read the weather, set the course, and keep the crew motivated. That requires a moral compass—but what happens when that compass begins to drift?

Leadership is never neutral. It reflects the personalities, values, and ambitions at the top of the organization. Traits such as *boardroom narcissism* may inject energy and vision, yet also amplify risk. How should non-executive directors balance these tensions in their role as employers? At the same time, organizations operate in a world stretched beyond sustainable limits. Social and environmental impacts can no longer be treated as peripheral concerns. This section introduces a leadership model that connects strategic intelligence and entrepreneurship with empathy and a commitment to societal value.

DOI: 10.4324/9781003624400-6

Non-executive directors may be removed from daily operations, while executives carry the pressure to deliver. Yet, governance is shared endeavor—requiring open dialogue, mutual accountability, and a continuous search for balance.

Can the board keep its captain on course?

Two ships and two leaders illustrate the risks of sailing in deceptive and treacherous waters. The conduct of those in charge matters. But both stories raise deeper governance questions about the relationship between CEO or captain and the oversight board: where was the board when it mattered most—and what blinded it to the warning signs?

Case Study: *Costa Concordia*—when leadership abandons ship

On a beautiful winter evening in 2012, the Italian captain Francesco Schettino was standing with his lover on the top deck of the cruise ship *Costa Concordia*, watching the nearby lights of the island of Isola del Giglio in the moments before his ship ran aground.

The ill-fated *Costa Concordia* was a 290-meter cruise ship with 3,200 passengers and a crew of 1,100—comparable in size and complexity to a medium-sized company. Its captain denied that he was at fault when his vessel struck the rocks, blaming the collision on a faulty maneuver of his team. When the lights went out, he reassured both the passengers and the coastguard that this was just a temporary malfunction. A chaotic evacuation followed. Schettino's discredit stemmed most of all from the discovery that he had disembarked ("I slipped and fell into the lifeboat") while people were still on board. Thirty-two lives were lost. He was found guilty and sentenced to 16 years in prison.

In the panic and darkness, might the captain's behavior be understandable or predictable? The ship's bartender, Russel Rebello, represented a different kind of leadership. He stayed aboard to help the passengers, and his body was the last to be recovered from the wreck, two years later. With all attention focused on the disaster, little was said about how Costa Cruises could have appointed a captain with a known record of earlier reckless behavior. Schettino later resurfaced in a disreputable attempt to restore his damaged reputation and to cash in by selling his story.

Case Study: Woonbron—a grand vision runs aground

A few years earlier, in 2004—Dutch housing director Martien Kromwijk was pursuing his own dream: restoring the iconic cruise-ship, the SS *Rotterdam*. It began as a well-intentioned social project but quickly drifted off course.

Woonbron, then the largest social housing corporation in the Rotterdam region, was encouraged by the municipality to buy the aging vessel for €1.5 million. The plan was to preserve it as cultural heritage and use it as a training ground for young people. The municipality and a commercial partner were meant to co-invest. The supervisory board received a single email from the CEO: *"If you don't agree, please let us know."* No objections followed, and the project proceeded.

Costs soon spiraled. The original €40–45 million estimate ballooned to €260 million due to asbestos, technical setbacks, and an increasingly grandiose vision. External authorities offered little resistance. The non-executive directors repeatedly approved additional funding, swayed by an optimistic CEO, drawn into tunnel vision, and ultimately trapped by a *sunk-cost fallacy*—convinced the ship would somehow pay for itself.

What started as a community-minded initiative became a vanity project far removed from Woonbron's core mission. A later parliamentary inquiry concluded that the supervisory board had lacked the courage and unity to correct the CEO's course. The ship eventually sold for just €30 million. Rotterdam gained a landmark, but it came at the expense of public money intended for vulnerable housing projects.

These two cases feature a captain and a CEO. Under judicial and parliamentary scrutiny, they emerged as headstrong and incorrigible. Both men favored grandiose visions, downplayed emerging problems, and, after their ships capsized, blamed external forces rather than themselves. Moral judgment from the public came swiftly. But the deeper lesson lies elsewhere.

These cases illustrate the importance of careful leadership selection processes, attention to values and character, and a realistic view of risk. They also raise an existential question: can the non-executive directors handle their CEO?

Oversight demands more than formal approval. It requires the courage to question integrity, to recognize early warning signs, and to act before drift becomes a danger.

So if values, virtues, and a moral compass are central to selecting a CEO, what does this reveal about moral leadership? What, in this context, truly constitutes a moral compass?

Aristotle's triangle

Jurist Alex Brenninkmeijer, the former National Ombudsman (1951–2020) known for his outspoken views on integrity and ethics, turned to the Greek philosopher Aristotle for an explanation of moral leadership. In his *Rhetoric*, Aristotle describes the classic trinity of *ethos, logos,* and *pathos* (see Figure 6.1).[1] In Brenninkmeijer's opinion, moral leadership depends on maintaining balance within this triangle.

1. ***Ethos*** sits at the top of the triangle. A leader's moral sense determines whether an organization's decisions can withstand external scrutiny and earn the trust of stakeholders, customers, and local communities. EBITDA[2] can be measured and audited, but ethics cannot be reduced to a metric. The concept of ethics lacks a generally accepted standard. As previous examples show, it can mean different things to different organizations and individuals. The Weinstein and Talpa cases illustrate this. In both instances, the organization's management—living in a bubble—believed itself to be immune from blame. Meanwhile, female colleagues, bearing the brunt of misconduct, had a radically different view. Little is usually heard from the non-executive directors. Yet their responsibility extends beyond shareholders to include the interests of stakeholders—not only in intention, but in accountability.

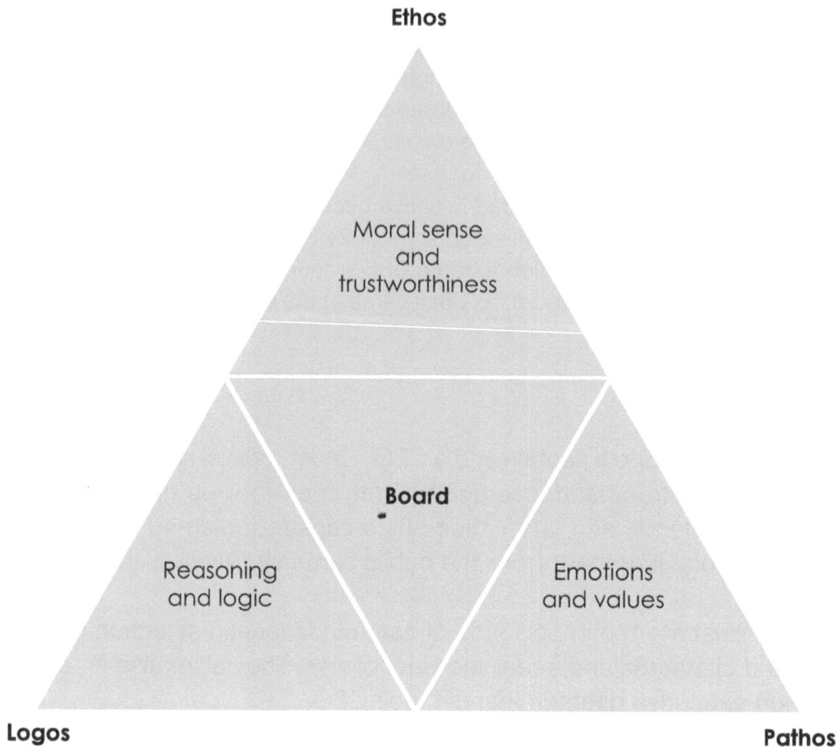

Figure 6.1
Aristotle's Moral Triangle

Case Study: The Voice—when silence overruled ethics

"Dear John, it's not the women." In 2022, the female employees of Talpa, a Dutch media organization, published a full-page letter containing these six words. It was their response to the lament of Dutch media tycoon John de Mol: *if the female victims of sexual misconduct in his company (some of whom were young girls) didn't speak up, how could he, the boss, know that anything was going on?* TV audiences love this unreachable yet almost tangible show world. Glamor, extravagance, and spectacle set the tone and drive the business. Consequently, inappropriate sexual behavior has long been considered an inevitable component. If it goes too far, people assume that someone else will intervene. But, according to the *bystander effect*, that's precisely what does not happen. Everyone waits for someone else to step in, also supported by the belief that these are probably just rumors. In the illusory world of show business, power dynamics play a significant role; the managers and directors involved operate in a world of fabricated reality, where only one rule applies: "the show must go on." The board's silence reflected not only a failure of oversight but also a more profound ethical detachment. As long as the ratings were strong, the red carpet was rolled out, and reputations remained intact, no one took responsibility.

Case Study: Weinstein—sex, lies, and blindness

The first significant success of Harvey Weinstein's entertainment company Miramax was the film *Sex, Lies, and Videotape—nomen est omen*. Over the next 28 years, Weinstein became one of Hollywood's most powerful figures, securing numerous Oscars and Tony Awards. However, his legacy dramatically sank as he became a symbol of systemic abuse in the entertainment industry. He was ultimately sentenced by a New York court to serve 23 years in prison for rape and sexual abuse and 16 years on similar counts by the Los Angeles equivalent.

The non-executive directors of The Weinstein Company—all men—believed they could regulate Weinstein's misconduct through a system of financial penalties. When the #MeToo scandal gained global traction, sparked by tweets from activist Tarana Burke and actress Alyssa Milano, the board of the Weinstein Company denied responsibility. They complained to the *Financial Times* that Weinstein's lawyers had actively impeded their efforts to investigate allegations of sexual abuse. Ultimately, the directors avoided personal accountability, a fact that did little to restore public trust. The Weinstein Company itself, however, collapsed into bankruptcy. In 2024, a New York Appeals Court ordered a retrial, ruling that the original trial included testimony from women whose allegations were not directly tied to the charges, thereby compromising the fairness of the proceedings.

The case may not be over for Weinstein—but for his victims, its impact endures.

2. ***Logos*** refers to logical reasoning, the factual underpinning of plans, and the rationale behind problem-solving. In governance, logos is essential for analysis and planning, as well as for setting decision-making processes. In our financialized world, without budgets, plans, and oversight, good governance in business is little more than wishful thinking.

   Logos also provides standards, laws, codes, and procedures. Important as these may be, as discussed in the previous chapters, they represent only one dimension of governance. As Brenninkmeijer argues, strict, unquestioning adherence to well-intentioned laws, protocols, and budgets can still lead to errors and distressing outcomes.

   This became apparent in the Australian Robodebt scandal, where automated government systems incorrectly demanded that welfare recipients repay benefits, with severe consequences for many. A similar pattern emerged elsewhere, illustrating how rigid systems can fail when human judgment is absent or suppressed.

   But the limits of logos are not only exposed when rules are applied too rigidly, but also when signals are ignored. A failure by non-executive directors or the audit committee to adequately respond to reports from management or to concerns raised by whistleblowers reflects a breakdown in rational oversight, the very core of logos in governance.

3. ***Pathos,*** finally, is the emotional undercurrent, the mood in the boardroom, the tone of voice, the tension that precedes a difficult decision. In Aristotle's view, pathos involves the emotions that shape how leaders persuade and connect—but also how they rationalize and avoid responsibility. We find these emotions—love, security, fear, domination, greed—not only in corporate strategy but also in the unspoken dynamics of board meetings. Pathos concerns both the emotions a person feels and the emotions they evoke

to influence others. In pathos, we find the values and emotions from Chapter 2, Section §2.4, that impact behavior: caring, humor, and connection, as well as fear, domination, and greed. Pathos emerges during boardroom meetings and shapes group dynamics and decision-making. It also drives the culture and energy of organizations and, as discussed in Chapter 4 Section §4.2, emotional intelligence contributes significantly to the quality of decision-making. In this way, pathos can either reinforce or undermine the balance between rational judgment and moral intent, shaping culture by pulling it toward long-term innovation or short-term profits.

Lost in translation: ethics across borders?

A moral compass matters for anyone in an oversight role. But what actually makes a moral compass "good" or "bad"? Moral and ethical principles often invite confusion, debate, and disagreement. In today's environment, stakeholders are increasingly outspoken about the obligation to act ethically. A key question lingers: are we, as a result, truly becoming more ethical, or is it merely the flavor of the day, and are we simply more vocal about ethics?

The shareholder-first mindset is sharply illustrated in the case of American entrepreneur Martin Shkreli, whose unapologetic pricing decisions stretched the ethical limits of U.S. corporate governance.

Case Study: Medicine—profits over patients

Martin Shkreli, a former hedge fund manager and self-professed provocateur, made headlines in 2015 when he acquired Daraprim—an infectious-disease drug that had been on the market for more than six decades—and raised its price overnight from about $17.50 to $750 per tablet. Shkreli defended the move as a straightforward business decision, emphasizing that it remained within legal boundaries.

He even referred to it as his "moral duty" to maximize profits for shareholders. He could not be prosecuted for his pricing practices, but, in 2022, a U.S. court ruled that he had violated antitrust laws through his strategy to block competition for Daraprim. Shkreli was barred for life from the pharmaceutical industry and ordered to return $64.6 million in profits. In 2017, he was sentenced to seven years in prison—not for the drug-pricing controversy, but for securities fraud connected to earlier hedge fund activities, a conviction that cast further light on his character. He was subsequently banned from Twitter after harassing a journalist.

The OxyContin opioid crisis, linked to the Sackler's family company, Purdue Pharma, illustrates that a narrow focus on short-term gain can ultimately destroy long-term value and reputation. Litigation and regulatory backlash can wipe out the very profits that once justified controversial decisions. Purdue Pharma's aggressive marketing campaigns downplayed OxyContin's addiction risks, contributing to a national epidemic of opioid addiction and overdose deaths. Lawsuits forced the company into bankruptcy, and the Sackler family—whose identity as philanthropists had long been their core source of prestige—ultimately had to pay billions. Its name has been taken off the walls of the institutions it once proudly supported.

Shkreli and Sackler may be extreme examples, but many powerful pharmaceutical companies operate—although far less visibly and within the law—on the basis of similar moral assumptions. They often defend aggressive pricing by pointing to R&D expenses and emphasizing that their activities remain within legal boundaries. In most Western economies, including the United States, the United Kingdom, and the EU, non-executive directors are expected to challenge executive management on unethical pricing strategies. Yet this oversight role becomes difficult when they face strong shareholder pressure and when executive compensation systems are tied to financial performance.

The balance between shareholder interests, stakeholder concerns, and broader societal impact varies across business cultures and is shaped by national traditions, political ideologies, and legal frameworks. These tensions raise difficult questions for boards. How should non-executive directors navigate ethical conflict—especially when shareholder incentives clash with broader societal expectations?

A board's moral compass is shaped not just by personal convictions, but by the cultural and institutional setting in which it operates. *The law is the law*, but the deeper issue is: who defines what counts as ethical, and how stable are those definitions across borders? Ethical concepts vary significantly by region and shift over time.

In the United States, business ethics often reflect the logic of shareholder value. In China, moral boundaries are more closely aligned with state ideology. In Europe, a more stakeholder-oriented approach is gaining traction, although it still coexists with the continent's long-standing commercial, market-driven traditions. These contrasts make clear that governance is never fully neutral or purely rational—it is rooted in competing moral frameworks.

Political winds and shifting ethics

Governance values are not fixed; they evolve in response to political and cultural pressures. When politicians assert their ideological priorities, companies—and even educational institutions—often have to adjust to new value frameworks. The recent "anti-woke" movement, supported by prominent entrepreneurs, reflects an effort to redefine the moral expectations placed on corporate behavior. Under this pressure, as discussed in Chapter 5, many firms have scaled back DEI, ESG, and climate or renewables commitments, shifting from values-driven ethics to a more cautious, compliance-only stance. This is troubling because it narrows ethical ambition, weakens long-term responsibility, and sidelines the broader societal, environmental, challenges companies are expected to help address.

The Jack Ma case: loyalty and limits

Jack Ma, founder of Alibaba and once China's richest man, is a member of the Communist Party. Yet Ma also sought to challenge the dominance of China's state-owned banks by reshaping the traditional financial system through the planned IPO of Ant Group, the parent company of Alipay. His bold move was widely seen as overconfident and insufficiently coordinated with Party authorities. In a speech in late 2020, Ma publicly criticized China's financial regulators—a moment that triggered swift political consequences.

Regulators halted Ant Group's record-breaking IPO just days before its launch. Shortly afterward, Ma disappeared from public view for several weeks, prompting speculation about his standing with the authorities. His exclusion from the 2022 Party Congress, a highly symbolic snub, reinforced the message: in China, moral authority in business is not earned through innovation or economic influence alone, but through unwavering political alignment.

In February 2025, however, as tech wars between China and the U.S. intensified, he attended a high-level tech symposium alongside Xi Jinping, signaling a possible thaw in his relationship with state authorities and proof that politics and business remain deeply intertwined.

Ethical drift and the limits of regulation

Organizations are, in legal terms, abstract entities. Although formally recognized as "legal persons," they do not, in themselves, have morals. People do. Individuals can shape an organization's moral climate through their behavior, even when moral values are often disputed. In the long run, organizations thrive thanks to the commitment of engaged employees who act with integrity. As earlier case studies have shown, norms and values within an organization can erode under leadership that focuses on short-term results. When minor transgressions go unchecked, an organization may drift off course, especially when oversight is lax. The decline often starts subtly, one unchecked lapse at a time.

While the government provides a formal legal framework, much of that framework consists of open standards that leave room for interpretation. Ultimately, the goal is to implement long-term policies that withstand the test of time and do not harm third parties. Yet not everything can be foreseen or regulated. At times, the government, under pressure from lobbyists or political interests, can undermine its own credibility. For example, by issuing harmful permits or by failing to enforce regulations.

As a result, politicians and government officials may become complicit in activities that conflict with public health, including the authorization of polluting factories ("forever chemicals"), the approval or promotion of new addictive products ("vapes, online gambling") or yielding to pressure from social media platforms and other technology companies seeking to increase traffic, often with insufficient regard for abuse of children or public safety.

Authorities may sometimes genuinely believe that a policy of limited intervention supports the public good, promoting economic growth, or helping job creation. Yet their positions are often shaped—sometimes subtly—by lobbying, selective information, or political pressure. The concept of *bounded ethicality* helps explain why board members and politicians may feel justified in acting in ways that are technically legal yet socially harmful. As leadership scholar James MacGregor Burns suggests, moral leadership involves more than legal compliance—it requires choosing what is ethically correct, even when the law permits otherwise.[3]

Walking the line: virtues and dilemmas for the non-executive director

Non-executive directors are expected to be and remain independent, weigh societal interests, and judge whether the board and organization stay on a responsible course. This requires close cooperation with executives and genuine alignment with employees. The shift toward sustainability depends on that collaboration. Younger, highly educated professionals are increasingly vocal and eager to help legacy companies adopt cleaner, smarter technologies—especially when they see clear commitment from top leadership.

Timeless virtues can help directors navigate these pressures. Plato warned that laziness and indifference allow the wrong people to take charge. In the boardroom, ease and detachment can mislead non-executive directors, particularly when shareholders or executives push for decisions that carry hidden risks for stakeholders or society. Staying on a principled path demands independence, clarity, and courage. Directors, executives and non-executives may be tempted to downplay the ethical dimension of choices, but responsible leadership and oversight call for engaging dilemmas thoughtfully and balancing competing interests.

Chapter 3, Section §3.1, discusses a statutory social duty of care for both executive and non-executive directors. For organizations already committed to long-term value and stakeholder interests, the compass naturally points in that direction, even without new regulation. When legal guidance lags, ethical grounding becomes essential. Plato's four virtues—wisdom, justice, moderation, and courage—offer a lasting guide. Saying them aloud in moments of decision can clarify the quality of the choice.

SUMMARY AND CONCLUSION

Effective governance requires more than technical competence; it demands values, character, and the ability to navigate ethical dilemmas. Classical virtues such as wisdom, justice, moderation, and courage offer a practical moral compass for judging not only what is legal, but also what is right.

Ethical erosion rarely happens all at once. Warning signs often go unchallenged, boards defer to dominant personalities, and decisions bend under pressure or in response to incentives. The cases show how organizational drift begins with silence, *optimism bias*, or misplaced trust.

Aristotle's triangle of *ethos*, *logos*, and *pathos* helps explain why oversight requires more than rational analysis. Character, judgment, and emotional intelligence all shape how boards respond to signals and balance competing interests across cultures, systems, and political contexts.

Ultimately, non-executive directors cannot rely on structures alone. They must remain alert to early signs of drift, foster open dialogue, and intervene when values are at risk. Their task is to safeguard the organization's ethical compass—before incremental missteps grow into systemic failures.

§6.2—STRATEGIC INTELLIGENCE AND EMPATHETIC LEADERSHIP

Introduction

Non-executive directors sleep most soundly when they've appointed the right CEO. Few decisions matter more than the selection of a firm's top leadership: those at the helm shape entrepreneurship, define an organization's culture and values, and ultimately drive its performance.

As discussed in Chapter 2, company leadership, especially the CEO, often exhibits traits from the narcissism spectrum. Vision, drive, and charisma can energize an organization—but when these traits tip into the dark triad of narcissism, Machiavellianism, and antisocial behavior, decision-making becomes distorted and trust begins to erode.

This section develops a *light-triad* model, reflecting an enlightened approach to leadership, built on six traits that support healthy leadership. Empathy, transparency, and inclusiveness create trust, teamwork, and innovation while helping to counterbalance darker leadership tendencies. Yet, as vital as empathy is, it alone cannot sustain organizations. Strategic intelligence, perseverance, and self-insight are equally essential for effective leadership. Together, they form a model of empathetic and strategic leadership.

The challenge for boards is clear: how do non-executive directors spot the early signs of lone-star leadership and instead foster a more enlightened leadership style that is not only empathetic and inclusive but also sharp-eyed, strategically grounded, and resilient enough for the world ahead?

Men on golden parachutes

Shareholders and society expect non-executive directors, as a countervailing power, to stay attuned to an organization's culture and integrity—and to intervene when necessary. Boeing's case illustrates the challenges that can arise: whistleblower concerns never reached the board, and the gap between expectation and reality proved enormous.

Case Study: Boeing 737 MAX

In 2019, Dennis Muilenburg was dismissed as Boeing's CEO. Just months earlier, two-brand-new 737 MAX aircraft had crashed, killing 346 people. Only four years before, he had ascended to the top—first as CEO, then as Chairman of the Board—a dual role that can weaken the checks and balances the separation of functions was meant to protect. Modern leaders are expected not only to pursue ambitious goals but also to remain transparent and open to scrutiny. The crisis at Boeing exposed deep failures in leadership culture and board oversight.

The Boeing 737 MAX was introduced in 2016 as a new generation of fuel-efficient aircraft, promising a 10–15% improvement in energy performance. Yet this promise quickly came under pressure, when two brand-new planes crashed—one in Indonesia and the other in Ethiopia—investigations revealed that Boeing engineers had been under intense pressure to accelerate safety testing. Boeing had even persuaded the U.S. aviation authority (FAA) to delegate parts of the certification process back to the company, thereby shortening the certification timeline. During congressional hearings, it was suggested that this had led to an overly cozy relationship with the regulator, and the aircraft was described as "flying coffins."

Crucial safety information was withheld from pilots, and a critical cockpit warning system was sold as an optional upgrade. The human tragedy was profound, devastating communities.

The corporate consequences were equally severe. Investigations, lawsuits, and regulatory actions revealed that Boeing had dismantled internal escalation protocols that once allowed engineers to report risks directly to the board. Shareholders sued the board, arguing that the company had traded its safety culture for a culture of financial engineering.

A year before the first crash, the mood at the top had been very different. A telling exchange between CEO Dennis Muilenburg and SpaceX's CEO Elon Musk exposed a dangerous distraction from core responsibilities. In a behavioral power play, revealing executive ego and symbolic rivalry, the two high-profile CEOs focused more on who would reach Mars first—while attention at Boeing drifted from the safety of the aircraft already flying under their watch. At a time when Boeing's long-standing role in aerospace was being challenged by the rapid rise of SpaceX, Muilenburg claimed Boeing would beat Musk to the red planet. Musk replied coolly: "Do it."

The 737 MAX has since returned to service after extensive testing. Muilenburg was fired—but landed softly with a $62 million golden parachute, sparking public anger. The deeper culture proved resistant to meaningful change. A later panel-blowout incident, again linked to quality-control failures, underscored the persistence of the underlying issues. The strain on staff became visible as experienced engineers left the company, many recruited by the fast-growing space sector, the very frontier Boeing had once claimed it would conquer.

The dark triad at work

As discussed in Chapter 2, narcissistic traits in leadership can be both positive and negative. The psychological framework known as the *dark triad* highlights the core risk factors: narcissism, Machiavellianism, and antisocial behavior. Non-executive directors often seek leaders who project ambition, charisma, decisiveness, and competitiveness. When these qualities align with the long-term interests of the organization and its stakeholders—and are tempered by ethical restraint—they can serve the company well. But when the balance shifts, problems quickly follow. Leaders who believe they can do no wrong become blind to risk and resistant to dissent. Overconfidence replaces humility and the organization starts to mirror their personal ambition, rather than advancing shareholder or broader stakeholder value.

Across both corporate and nonprofit settings, when dark-triad tendencies go unchecked, a toxic atmosphere can emerge: political games, a culture of fear, manipulation, and at times antisocial behavior such as fraud or white-collar crime—and, in extreme cases, even physical harm, as stakeholder harm becomes incidental, or worse, irrelevant. OceanGate

Case Study: OceanGate—how hubris sank Titan

Stockton Rush, the entrepreneur behind OceanGate, offered the ultimate in disaster tourism with a largely home-built submersible designed to visit the wreck of the Titanic. Rush appeared to know neither uncertainty nor fear, even as he acknowledged the extreme risks involved. Convinced that others in the submersible industry were too focused on safety and resistant to innovation, he declared, "At some point, safety is just pure waste."

He chose carbon fiber and titanium to build his craft, because these materials were lighter and cheaper than traditional deep-sea materials. An investigative report later revealed that these materials were unfit to be used at such depths. Rush however, used intimidation tactics to deter external scrutiny. In a culture described as toxic, warnings from whistleblowers were met with retaliation deflected by Rush's charisma, or simply ignored.[4]

At the same time, with his charisma, Rush managed to convince passengers to join him on a life-threatening adventure. After a series of successful dives, Titan imploded in the summer of 2023 near the Titanic wreck site. At a depth of 3,346 meters, there were no survivors. The tragedy starkly illustrates that innovation without proper governance, and risk-taking without ethical guardrails, can have fatal consequences.

operated with minimal independent oversight, as is often the case in smaller, entrepreneurial organizations.

In many organizations, employees mirror the behavior of their leaders—not only out of admiration, but out of fear or ambition; they avoid criticism, hoping to gain favor and protect their careers. Over time, this dynamic creates a culture of yes-men, and the organization gradually loses its capacity for critical judgment.

For non-executive directors—operating at a distance—it can be difficult to spot early signs of misconduct, especially when charismatic or overconfident leaders dominate the narrative. Sometimes, non-executive directors fall prey to their own hubris, and make flawed appointments. Leaders with dark triad traits often excel in charm and persuasion, shaping perceptions among the board,—misleading stakeholders, and even regulatory bodies.

Most companies in which antisocial behavior takes root may not lead to criminal behavior. However, they can develop a moral hollowness, characterized by carelessness, rationalization, and disregard for the interests of customers, colleagues, and the public. Such organizations may be fined or publicly criticized, but see this as a routine business risk. As past corporate collapses have shown, the real safeguard lies not in accountability after the fact but in recognizing cultural decay early and having the courage to intervene before risks harden into disasters.

Case Study: Education—when charm replaces scrutiny

After years of turmoil and a costly internal crisis, an educational institution finally parted ways with its CEO. In a rush to leave the past behind and move forward, the supervisory board bypassed a formal recruitment process and appointed a candidate from their immediate circle: a charismatic and visionary local school director.

The new CEO hit the ground running. He spoke passionately about sweeping educational reform and quickly won over parents and staff with his fresh approach. Momentum was high, and the Board felt vindicated in their choice. But within a year, cracks began to appear. The director of education resigned abruptly. Shortly after, the controller left. No exit interviews were held—after all, the new CEO had everyone's trust. That trust became a blind spot. Raising critical questions in the boardmeeting about his decisions was seen as disloyal, even threatening.

A new member joining the supervisory board was reassured: "everything was under control, there were no problems." But soon, a report surfaced from the internal Employees Council citing communication breakdowns between the CEO and the institution's Branch Managers. Around the same time, a whistleblower came forward with allegations of excessive expense claims.

It was only after persistent questioning by the new Board Member that the collective blindness finally broke. The "smooth sailing" narrative unraveled, revealing a culture where trust had gone unquestioned for too long and oversight had all but disappeared.

OceanGate operated with minimal independent oversight. Yet even organizations with the comfort of formal oversight sometimes fail to follow the very procedures designed to ensure sound CEO hiring, as the following education case illustrates.

From dark to light: rethinking leadership

As discussed in Chapter 5, most large organizations operate in an age of constant transition and uncertainty. Both internally and externally, they are increasingly held accountable for long-term integrity, a social duty of care, and inclusive practices. Meeting these expectations often requires

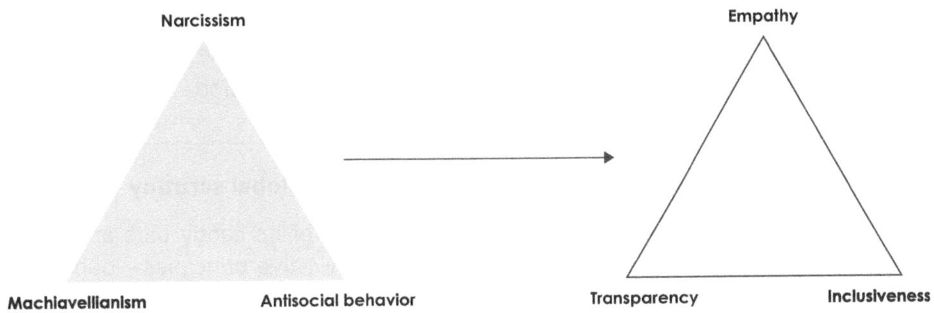

Figure 6.2
From Narcissistic Leadership to Empathetic Leadership

a new balance—one that preserves the energy, creativity, and determination of the CEO while strengthening the cultural foundations around them. One way to achieve this balance is through the light-triad leadership model (see Figure 6.2), which highlights three factors central to an *empathetic leadership* culture: empathy, transparency, and inclusiveness. Three shifts are required:

1. ***Empathy replaces narcissism***
   Empathetic leadership begins with listening carefully and by understanding the challenges and perspectives of others, and taking their interests into account. When leaders show authentic empathy, they create trust, build stronger collaboration, and improve decision-making throughout the organization. This type of leadership helps surface risks early and enables stronger strategic and operational choices. The UK Empathy Index, for instance, has ranked companies such as Microsoft near the top, suggesting that empathy and corporate success can go hand in hand.[5]
2. ***Transparency counters Machiavellianism***
   A transparent culture openly shares information and the motivations behind decisions. This fosters trust—both internally within teams and externally with stakeholders. Non-executives who embrace transparency gain a clearer view of the organization's operations, strengthening their ability to be accountable to the outside world. Transparency can initially feel uncomfortable for leaders who are accustomed to a top-down style of control. Yet, the failures at Boeing, Chemours, and Volkswagen show that secrecy and manipulation aren't just ethical failings—they are also operational risks that can escalate into existential threats.
3. ***Inclusiveness replaces antisocial behavior***
   Antisocial cultures exclude, exploit, or marginalize people. Inclusive leadership, by contrast, brings people in. It values the unique capabilities and experiences of all employees and takes into account the interests of wider stakeholders, integrating them into both strategy-setting and operational execution. Inclusion isn't just ethical—by welcoming diverse perspectives, it also helps mitigate groupthink and organizational blind spots.

Family-owned Mars and publicly traded Rio Tinto offer contrasting examples of corporate culture and governance. Their stories illustrate the challenge of sustaining a strong values-based culture and the necessity of transforming leadership when dark-triad tendencies take hold. Culture is shaped at the top, but sustaining, strengthening, or transforming it across an entire organization takes time, discipline, and a clear vision.

Case Study: Mars unwrapped—sustaining values amidst global scrutiny

Mars, the large American family-owned company known for its candy bars and pet food, emphasizes values over short-term returns. The company's five principles—publicly listed on its website—begin with a focus on quality and end with the importance of individual responsibility. In practice, this ethos is reflected in an unusual commitment to quality: the CEO personally tastes the dog food to ensure it meets their customers' standards.[6]

Leadership language reflects this culture. The outgoing CEO was praised for "humility, warmth, and approachability," values typical of a family-run company. Poul Weihrauch, the current CEO, has reaffirmed the company's commitment to empathetic, transparent leadership, social responsibility, and an agenda aligned with ESG principles. Accordingly, Mars has doubled its investment in sustainability. Internally, employees are referred to as "associates" to convey a sense of partnership and shared purpose.

The company states that pursuing long-term value is inseparable from creating the conditions that make people willing to contribute to the company's success. "Empathy," it says, "will matter more than ever in a polarized world."[7]

Still, Mars has not escaped public criticism. It has faced scrutiny over health concerns in some of its products, the transparency of its supply chains, and its limited disengagement from Russia following the invasion of Ukraine. Although Mars restricted operations and committed profits to charitable causes, it did not fully exit the Russian market—prompting criticism. More recently, concerns have also been raised about Mars' growing market power in pet care—particularly in veterinary clinics and diagnostics—prompting questions about pricing, competition, and working conditions. Together, these issues underscore how difficult it is, even for value-driven companies, to align every decision with their stated principles.

Case Study: Rio Tinto—blowing up values

Mining giant Rio Tinto, known for extracting iron ore, diamonds, coal, and uranium, was forced to overhaul its values after a reputational crisis. In 2020, the company detonated part of Juukan Gorge—a sacred 46,000-year-old Aboriginal heritage site—in pursuit of iron ore. The incident sparked outrage among local communities and global observers. Although Rio Tinto cited a government permit, it later issued a public apology, paid damages, and began a company-wide review of its values and culture.

Previously, Rio Tinto had five stated values, ranging from safety and respect to excellence. After the crisis, these were replaced with three: Care—for people, communities, and the environment; Courage—to innovate, speak up, and do what's right; Curiosity—to collaborate, learn, and improve.

The new CEO initially claimed that the revised values "resonate well with our workforce." Yet a 2022 independent report revealed that, despite the updated value statements, Rio Tinto continued to face systemic behavioral problems. Reflecting on the findings, he admitted: "I hadn't realized how much bullying exists in the company, and secondly that it's quite systemic."[8]

Restoring a measure of trust in the markets was one achievement, but progress on culture remained uneven, with evidence of persistent—and in some cases worsening—bullying and misconduct.

After a four-year tenure, the CEO stepped down, leaving a more stable company yet one still grappling with deeply embedded behavioral challenges—underscoring how difficult real cultural change is.

Empathetic and strategic leadership

While empathy has become essential in modern leadership, it is not enough on its own. The *light triad* of empathy, transparency, and inclusiveness requires a foundation of three other qualities: strategic intelligence, perseverance, and self-insight. These form the complete model of empathetic and strategic leadership (see Figure 6.3).

Leadership expert and psychoanalyst Michael Maccoby emphasizes the importance of strategic intelligence.[9] He cites Steve Jobs and Jeff Bezos as examples of narcissistic visionaries: widely admired, albeit aggressive. Their success, Maccoby notes, was derived not from charm but from sharp strategic acumen. Jobs' true success came when he recognized

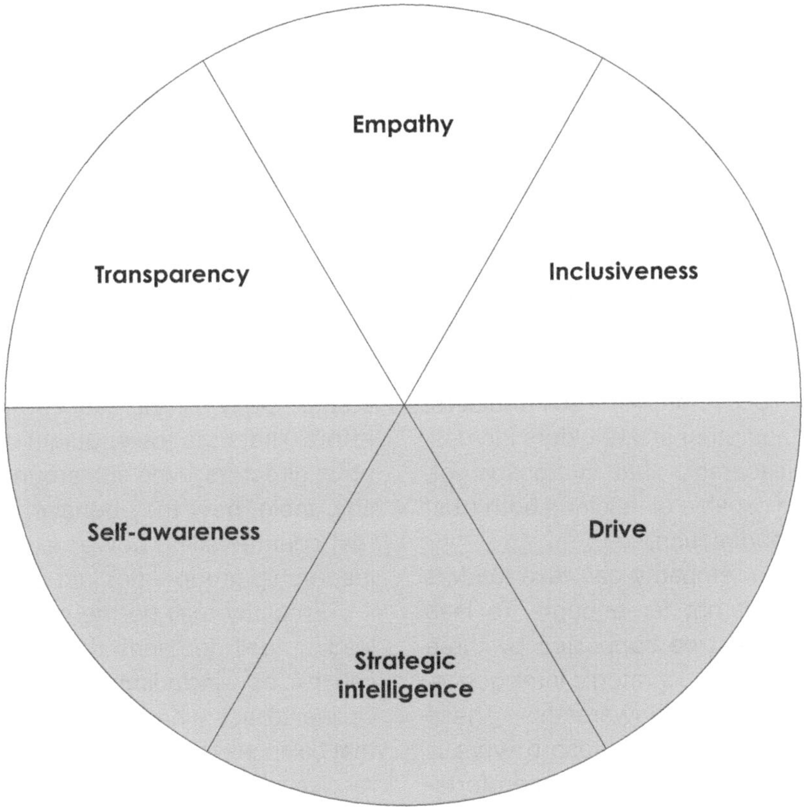

Figure 6.3
Model of Empathetic and Strategic Leadership

his own limitations and complemented his visionary leadership with Tim Cook's operational excellence. This ability to reflect on one's own strengths and limitations is closely linked to self-awareness—one of the core elements of strategic, empathetic leadership:

- **Strategic intelligence** is the CEO's ability to build a coherent vision based on a deep understanding of the market, the company's internal strengths and weaknesses, and the opportunities and risks ahead. Non-executive directors should ask: Is leadership sufficiently future-oriented? Is there clear scenario planning? Is there a credible strategy for differentiation?
- **Drive** is essential for execution. Without the energy and will to persevere, the strategy will have no impact and may be derailed by unavoidable setbacks. Yet perseverance also carries risks: taken too far it can lead to tunnel vision, overconfidence, or an unwarranted commitment to a failing course. Non-executive directors must challenge such tendencies and help maintain balanced judgment.
- **Self-awareness** is the leadership trait that keeps power in check. Do CEO's understand their own blind spots? Are they able to admit mistakes and change course? Self-awareness enables leaders to adapt to changing circumstances and helps prevent a drift into arrogance. Non-executive directors play a key role in fostering this reflection and ensuring that power remains balanced.

The combination of empathtetic and strategic leadership traits cannot be embodied in a single person. The model is best applied at the team level: an executive board that collectively possesses these six competencies. Only then is the organization equipped to address complex strategic challenges and earn the trust of its shareholders, stakeholders, and society at large.

SUMMARY AND CONCLUSION

In a world that moves faster than most organizations can adapt, non-executive directors and the companies they oversee face rising expectations. Shareholders, employees, and other stakeholders increasingly seek leadership that is transparent, inclusive, and capable of inspiring both trust and a sense of direction.

On its own, empathy can take leaders a long way, but not far enough. To lead well today, it must be supported by three essential foundations: strategic intelligence, perseverance, and self-awareness. These qualities enable leaders to absorb what is happening around them, face uncomfortable truths, make high-stakes decisions, and stay the course when tensions rise.

Such leadership is rarely found in one heroic individual. Rather than relying on the old dominant CEO model, effective leadership today is increasingly a collective effort. That puts the spotlight on non-executive directors: who sits around the leadership table, how they behave, and whether real countervailing power exists inside the leadership group—not just outside it.

Empathy may be the starting point, but leading well demands the full spectrum of capabilities—including the courage and discipline to act when necessary. Leadership that balances teamwork and connection with resolve is not about harmony at all costs; it is about safeguarding the organization's strategic direction, integrity, and resilience.

§6.3—CHOOSING THE RIGHT LEADER AT THE RIGHT TIME

Introduction

Appointing a CEO—or any top executive—is a defining act of stewardship. It's more than a hiring decision; it sets the tone for an organization's culture, direction, and resilience. Every CEO transition stirs emotion. Should the board choose the trusted internal candidate, or take a calculated risk on an outsider? And what about the "*boomerang CEO*"? Bringing back a former leader may be comforting in the moment, but it is rarely a guaranteed fix.

The central question is what kind of leadership the organization needs for the next phase. Today's environment demands more than technical expertise. Boards must look for leaders who combine strategic intelligence with empathetic, inclusive leadership—people who can chart a clear course while earning trust, building cohesion, and navigating complexity with emotional awareness.

However, these choices are far from simple. Bias, g*roupthink*, and misplaced loyalty can cloud judgment. And while succession planning sounds orderly on paper, many transitions are triggered by crisis—especially in small and large firms.

There is also the delicate issue of timing. When does a once-effective leader become misaligned with the road ahead? Continuity can be comforting, but it must not override adaptability.

This section explores how boards can approach CEO selection and succession with clarity, courage, and timely action—before urgency narrows their options.

Fast or slow in the remuneration committee: choosing the right CEO

Appointing a new CEO is the ideal moment to reexamine the organization's long-term vision. Different phases of the life cycle call for different types of leadership, so the key question is not just *"who is ready to lead?"* but *"what leadership do we need now and for the future?"*

A CEO search is essentially a process of reducing information asymmetry between the remuneration committee, the candidates, and the search advisers. After considering the empathetic–strategic leadership model, the remuneration committee address a set of fundamentals:

- A defined, transparent procedure to follow
- The organizational context: where we sit in the business cycle
- Culture, integrity, and entrepreneurial profile required
- Competencies, experience
- The candidate's ability to demonstrate empathetic and strategic leadership
- Diversity of perspectives relevant to the role and future strategy
- Values and integrity expected
- Role of external advisers
- Bias awareness and decision-making discipline in the committee

And at the very end, one question remains: *how well do we truly know our preferred candidate? Will this leader make a difference in pursuing our long-term vision? And what could realistically go wrong in the years ahead?*

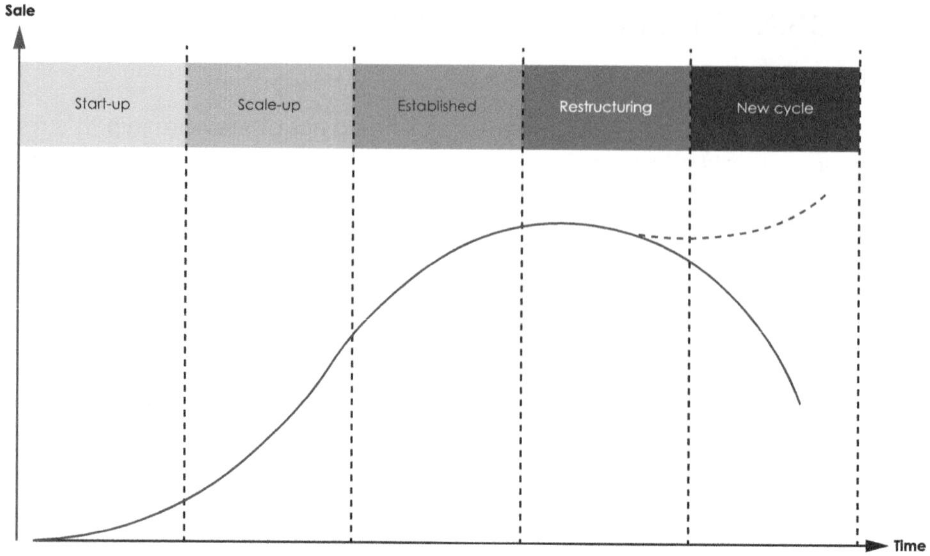

Figure 6.4
Life Stages of Enterprises

Figure 6.4 illustrates five key stages: the *early, informal start-up* moving at speed and improvisation; the *scale-up*, where growth demands structure, systems and stronger processes, maturing into a going concern where innovation must be balanced with cost control; and, finally, entering a *transformation phase*, where reorganization may be necessary to spark a new cycle of growth.

Psychological biases in the committee

Biases can strongly influence leadership selection—especially under pressure. When a CEO unexpectedly departs, non-executive directors may feel compelled to act quickly. In interviews, they can be unconsciously swayed by a charismatic, visionary, or altruistic candidate who makes a strong initial impression. *Familiarity bias* may also arise when a known candidate is conveniently available—someone the non-executive directors feel comfortable with, even if the fit is less than ideal: problem solved! Yet rushing the process can be costly.

Choosing the right leader—and building the internal support for a seamless transition—requires patience, discipline, and behavioral awareness. Booking.com offers a vivid example of a board navigating leadership appointments while moving from a start-up to a successful listed multinational.

Case Study: Booking.com—a leadership check-in for a new phase

Booking.com's evolution reflects a classic leadership journey—from a small Dutch start-up to a dominant global force in online travel. In the start-up phase, non-executive directors often tolerate idealistic or headstrong entrepreneurial behavior, recognizing the value of intuitive decision-making.

Founder Geert-Jan Bruinsma had limited hospitality experience when he launched Booking.com. In 1997, his first advertisement was rejected by *De Telegraaf*—the Netherlands' leading mass-market newspaper—for lacking a phone number. Bruinsma refused to compromise, insisting on an internet-only approach. The next day, he discovered search engine optimization, later summing it up with understatement: "I was pretty successful in that."

Gillian Tans joined soon after as employee number seven. With few formal roles in place, she created the Operating Chief Officer position and helped drive Booking.com's expansion into a global travel powerhouse, facilitating over 1.2 billion hotel bookings annually. Bruinsma's quiet exit in 2003 marked a shift toward acquiring new competencies through strategic transactions. Tans proved an exceptional talent, ultimately serving as CEO and Chair from 2016 to 2019.

Today, Booking.com remains highly successful, even if its market dominance presents governance challenges, as hotels express concerns about fees and pricing restrictions—ultimately putting public trust at risk. Boards cannot be expected to dismantle the success they helped build, but they must remain alert to the societal tensions that accompany market power.

Internal promotion or external change?

Appointing a new executive director may seem like an orderly task. Formally, large organizations work from a carefully crafted profile and conduct a broad, structured search. In practice, forward-looking non-executive directors aim to have a successor identified up well in advance of the incumbent's departure.

When an outgoing director has performed well, the low-risk choice is often a familiar internal candidate who closely resembles them. In the U.S., 80% of publicly traded companies appoint an internal candidate as CEO; only 3% recruit a sitting CEO from another firm. Incumbent CEOs rarely hop between companies. While choosing an internal successor can support continuity and strengthen intrinsic motivation, and as seen earlier, boards sometimes move too quickly, selecting the familiar face without sufficient critical evaluation.

Case Study: Care—fresh eyes redefining leadership selection

In a well-run healthcare organization, concerns had long circulated about the CEO: high expense claims, elitist behavior, and favoritism toward certain employees. The atmosphere gradually deteriorated. Despite repeated warnings from the client council and the works council, the non-executive directors did not intervene decisively.

Eventually, both the CEO and the long-serving chair announced their retirement. The outgoing CEO pushed for an internal successor—the current operations director—who had limited support among employees. Strongly aligned with the outgoing CEO, the departing chair of the non-executive directors voiced his support for the internal candidate, prioritizing loyalty and predictability over an objective assessment of the organization's needs. Unburdened by prior loyalties, the newly appointed chair took a different approach. After carefully listening to concerns within the organization and recognizing the limitations of the internal candidate, he opposed the appointment and successfully guided the board in selecting an external successor. The case highlights the importance of timely renewal within the non-executive board to preserve independence and avoid entrenched loyalties.

Case Study: Microsoft—from hard to soft leadership

In American corporate tradition, the board's most important task is often said to be firing the CEO. At Microsoft, this proved far from easy.

Steve Ballmer, CEO from 2000 to 2014 and once Bill Gates's closest friend, gained a reputation as a forceful and often ruthless leader—famously shouting so intensely at conferences that he eventually required vocal cord surgery. Ballmer presided over major successes with Windows and Office, but as a leader, he was frequently described as impulsive, manic, and strategically reckless.

Trapped in tunnel vision, he continued to pour resources into projects where Microsoft was steadily losing ground: in an effort to compete with Apple, Ballmer pushed through the costly acquisition of Nokia's struggling mobile division and its patents. Meanwhile, the real strategic frontiers—mobile services and cloud computing—were slipping away.

By 2014, tensions between Gates and Ballmer, both major shareholders, had erupted into the open. Ballmer ultimately lost the power struggle, stepped down as CEO, and redirected his energy into new ventures—buying the Los Angeles Clippers and later funding an institute for children's behavioral and mental health research at the University of Oregon.

External CEO successors often face resistance simply because they are outsiders, whether familiar or completely new to the organization. On average, external appointments tend to be less successful than internal ones, largely due to a cultural mismatch between the newcomer's background and the organization's established norms.[10]

Yet, for organizations stuck with outdated strategies or facing crisis, bringing in an experienced external candidate can offer decisive advantages. Free from entrenched loyalties, external CEOs are often more willing to make the bold changes required, including reshaping the management team and resetting the strategic direction.

Non-executive directors may underestimate the intensity of emotions triggered by succession processes. When the board fails to lead the process tightly and transparently, internal politics can quickly take over. Machiavellian dynamics emerge: candidates may engage in slander, inflate their achievements, and fuel jealousy and manipulation, poisoning the organizational climate.

This risk is especially acute in post-merger organizations. Here, non-executive directors must remain vigilant to potential hidden loyalties toward candidates from the original pre-merger entities. If left unaddressed, these loyalties can exacerbate internal divisions.[11]

Diversity, more than just a number

Research by McKinsey shows that diversity—across gender, age, and cultural background—enhances financial performance and fuels innovation.[12] Richard Thaler added an important twist: cognitive and experiential diversity are critical for reducing decision-making biases.[13]

Yet despite the evidence, progress at the top remains slow. Behavioral science highlights a simple but powerful obstacle: the *similarity-attraction bias*. Decision-makers tend to favor candidates who feel familiar, those who look like them, think like them, or offer an instant sense of rapport. This bias, combined with systemic barriers such as *cognitive bias* and *structural inequalities*, continues to limit equal access to leadership positions.

Spencer Stuart reports that 77% of female executives in S&P 500 companies face barriers simply because they are excluded from informal networks, the unofficial circles where trust is built and future leaders are identified. Outsiders are less likely to be considered, recommended, or even shortlisted for opportunities.[14]

The insider who rewrote GM's future

Mary Barra joined General Motors as an engineer at the age of 18, and rose through the ranks. Her 2014 appointment as GM's first female CEO illustrates what can change when an internal candidate with a fresh perspective is truly empowered. GM was burdened by bureaucracy, cost overruns, and the scars of a government-backed bankruptcy during the 2008 financial crisis. Its survival was uncertain.

Barra made diversity a strategic priority, arguing that innovation and resilience require a range of perspectives. "You should pick people not like you, across gender, across cultures, and across experiences." Her collaborative, open leadership style helped GM rebuild both its identity and competitiveness in a rapidly shifting industry.

Leadership research supports her intuition. Based on 360-degree reviews, women score higher than men on several leadership competencies.[15] Harvard studies show that while men and women set similarly ambitious goals, women are more likely to display transformational leadership—driving change and fostering collaboration—while men are more likely to rely on transactional, competitive approaches.

Still, leadership remains heavily male-dominated. Globally, women hold roughly one-third of senior management roles, but only around one-fifth of CEO positions. Women however account for only around 6% of CEOs in the EU, 9% in the United Kingdom, and 10% in the United States.[16] Private equity shows similarly low figures.[17]

Old or young

Traditionally, the COO or CFO has been a natural internal candidate to succeed the CEO. Companies often spend years developing their internal leadership bench, providing managers with long career paths to grow into senior roles. But in large corporations, such extensive lead times can produce loyal, seasoned executives who are also deeply anchored in established ways of thinking. Spencer Stuart's research on S&P 500 CEOs confirms this pattern: internal successors tend to stay close to the existing strategy and are often under-equipped to drive the change the organization needs. Ironically, many end up leaving earlier than expected, sometimes by choice, but often because the board eventually demands a different direction.

Today, boards increasingly look beyond the traditional COO/CFO route, favoring younger, sometimes less experienced divisional CEOs who have demonstrated strategic insight and agility within their own business units.[18] These first-time CEOs frequently outperform veterans.[19] They bring fresh eyes to complex problems, focus on long-term value creation, and strike a healthier balance between profitability and growth. Crucially, they are less constrained by outdated assumptions—free to rethink business models rather than simply adjust them.

Yet promoting such talent from within requires non-executive directors to have a deep and accurate understanding of the organization's internal candidates. This is where things often go wrong. Consider Satya Nadella at Microsoft: the company's ideal internal successor, who was initially overlooked because of his low-profile, unassuming style. Only after an external search faltered did the board recognize Nadella's leadership strengths and make one of its most consequential decisions.

Case Study: Microsoft II—leading with empathy

After a long and ultimately unsuccessful search for an external successor, Microsoft's board turned to an internal candidate: Satya Nadella. Born in India and with more than a decade of experience inside the company, Nadella brought a markedly different leadership style from that of his predecessors. Insiders described him as "intense, but never intimidating." For Nadella, empathy wasn't just a personal value—he regarded it as a fundamental precondition for innovation.

One story from his early career vividly illustrates this shift in thinking. During a job interview, he was asked: "What would you do if you saw a baby crying on the street after falling?" Thinking like an engineer, he replied, "I would call 911." Only later did he realize the point: a crying child needs comfort first, not procedures. The moment shook him and sparked a lifelong commitment to empathetic, inclusive leadership.

Under Nadella's stewardship, Microsoft adopted a more open, learning-driven culture, breaking down silos, encouraging curiosity, and steering the company toward cloud computing and platform collaboration. This empathetic leadership fostered a culture that delivered extraordinary commercial success.

A company built on empathetic leadership can see its success translate into structural market power. As Microsoft's role expands into critical digital infrastructure, concerns have grown across Europe about geopolitical dependency and technological sovereignty.

Empathetic leadership within the firm does not resolve the structural questions that arise when, through its very success, stakeholders become deeply dependent. Particularly in a sector, where essential public and private systems come to rely heavily on a single foreign provider.

The shelf life of the CEO

CEO tenure at publicly traded companies has been shrinking steadily, much like the careers of football coaches.[20] In earlier generations, things looked very different. Baby boomers expected lifelong careers at a single company, often rising patiently through the ranks. Today's leaders operate on far shorter timelines. Generation X executives (1965–1980), who now make up about 68% of global executive leadership, spend an average of just five years in their top roles.

Tenure is expected to shrink further as millennials (born 1981–1996) assume more leadership positions. For many in this group, personal development outweighs loyalty to a single employer, and the old stigma around "job hopping" has largely disappeared.

But shorter tenures are not only a generational phenomenon. They also reflect rising external pressures: growing shareholder demands, relentless performance expectations, an intensified focus on short-term results, and the increasing isolation of the CEO role itself. In this environment, even highly capable leaders can struggle—not because of lack of skill, but because timing and circumstances work against them. Sustained leadership impact requires space, trust, and time—commodities in ever shorter supply.

The late-bloomer and the boomerang CEO

Replacing a CEO too quickly can do real damage. Research shows that many top performers don't hit their stride until years 11–15—a reminder that patience and long-term backing can pay off. Family-owned businesses often understand this intuitively: without the drumbeat of quarterly pressure, leaders stay longer and grow into the role (Figure 6.5).[21]

But when patience runs out and a successor fails to ignite the next phase, boards sometimes reach for a familiar figure: the boomerang CEO. These returns reveal as much about board psychology as strategy. Under pressure, directors become risk-averse, gravitating toward the leader who feels "safe," carries the glow of earlier successes, and offers the illusion of stability. Jobs at Apple—and, more recently, Sam Altman's five-day exile-and-return saga at OpenAI—shows how powerful that dynamic can be. In Altman's case, not only the board but also employees and strategic partner Microsoft shaped the power struggle that ultimately brought him back.

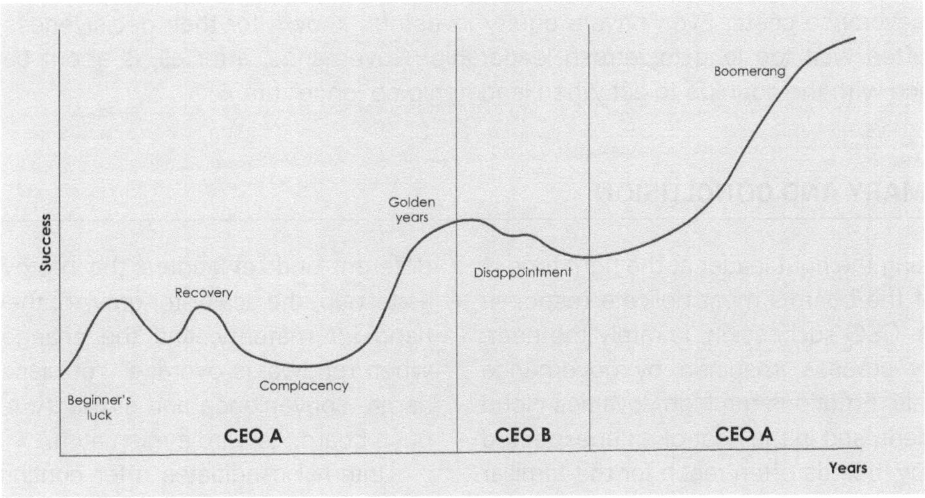

Figure 6.5
Late Bloom or Boomerang

Yet nostalgia is not a strategy. Boomerang CEOs remain rare for a reason: they often underperform first-time CEOs, and their return can revive the very power dynamics the organization was trying to move beyond. A comeback can make sense, but only in specific conditions: when the company faces an existential crisis, when deep institutional memory genuinely adds value, and when the returning leader has left on good terms and demonstrated real strategic acumen and self-awareness. A clear mandate—and a clear exit timeline—are essential.[22]

Panic and familiarity alone are never good reasons to bring someone back. The real question is simple: *are we rehiring a solution—or a comfort blanket?*

Firing the CEO, when leadership ends

Firing a CEO is one of the most difficult tasks of the remuneration committee. CEOs often become emotionally attached to their position—the role they have fought for, built, and defended over many years. The decision is also emotionally taxing for non-executive directors. Who is going to tell the CEO it is time to go? Even dismissing a CEO for disappointing performance is never easy. Board members have spent years working closely with the individual, forging professional and at times personal bonds. Camps can form within the board, delaying action and fueling internal tensions. Some non-executive directors may fear that forcing a resignation would publicly confirm that their original appointment was a mistake.

Violations of integrity and values, however, are a different matter. Even relatively minor breaches should trigger immediate intervention. Tolerating small violations undermines the board's authority and opens the door to bigger problems. Yet in practice, many boards hesitate, preferring to give the CEO another chance.

Replacing a CEO requires time, energy, and courage—and brings a fresh wave of uncertainty. Will the next leader succeed? How likely is it that a "dream candidate" exists? In smaller organizations, financial concerns add to the hesitancy: a departure can carry significant severance costs. Even private equity investors, known for their decisiveness, admit they often wait too long to refresh leadership. Governance, after all, is about balancing patience with the courage to act when leadership no longer fits.

SUMMARY AND CONCLUSION

Choosing the right leader at the right time is one of the board's most delicate responsibilities. CEO succession, is rarely the neat, orderly process imagined by governance manuals. Emotions run high, loyalties cloud judgment, and in the heat of an unexpected vacancy, boards often reach for the familiar option—sometimes too quickly.

The section shows how different phases in an organization's life demand different kinds of leaders: the improviser for a start-up, the scaler for growth, the steady hand for maturity, and the change agent when renewal is overdue. Yet biases, charisma, convenience and similarity regularly push boards toward a mismatch.

Internal candidates offer continuity but can lock a company into old thinking. External hires bring fresh eyes but risk cultural whiplash. Diversity, despite its clear benefits, is still lagging. Driven by the growing intensity of the role, the modern CEO's shelf life continues to shrink. Even as research shows some leaders peak only after a decade.

When leadership falters—especially on values—the board must drop its slow deliberations and act quickly. In the end, CEO selection is only half the story; building a strong, independent non-executive team to keep that CEO on course is the real test of governance maturity.

§6.4—THE NEW NON-EXECUTIVE DIRECTOR

Introduction: Why step into the fire?

After all these pages with tensions and pitfalls between executive directors and non-executive directors, one might reasonably wonder: why would anyone willingly take on a non-executive role? The oversight job demands time, intellectual discipline, deep commitment, and a tolerance for ambiguity. Liability risks are real, financial rewards are modest, and influence is indirect.

A non-executive director may arrive too late to intervene, yet still be held liable for failures they did not directly cause. Co-responsibility is intrinsic to the role.

And yet, the attraction persists. Behavioral drivers help explain why. The role offers prestige, continued relevance after executive careers, and the subtle appeal of influence without the daily operational burden. For many, it satisfies both identity and duty.

This paradox—responsibility without control, status without executive power—lies at the heart of modern board dynamics.

What motivates someone to step into this fire? How do organizations find the right non-executive director? And is the old boys' network still shaping access, or are we finally seeing genuine renewal in board composition?

Status, purpose, and the appeal of boardroom oversight

In many countries, board appointments have long carried symbolic weight beyond formal oversight. A prominent name on a board can signal credibility, access, and legitimacy. In earlier decades, it was common for influential bankers or former public officials to sit on multiple major boards, reinforcing networks of mutual trust and institutional alignment.

A Dutch example illustrates this dynamic. Between 1973 and 2001, Roelof Nelissen, former Dutch minister of economic affairs and finance and later chairman of ABN AMRO, served as the chair of the supervisory board of N.V. Luchthaven Schiphol, one of his many formal board jobs. At the time, arrangements like this were common. In the Dutch two-tier system, major companies were often considered truly credible only if a prominent banker sat on their supervisory board. The arrangement benefited both sides: companies gained prestige and connections, while the bank maintained influence and ensured loyalty within their corporate network.

Such entanglements would no longer meet current governance standards. Stricter codes, especially those emphasizing independence, have made dual representation a relic of the past.

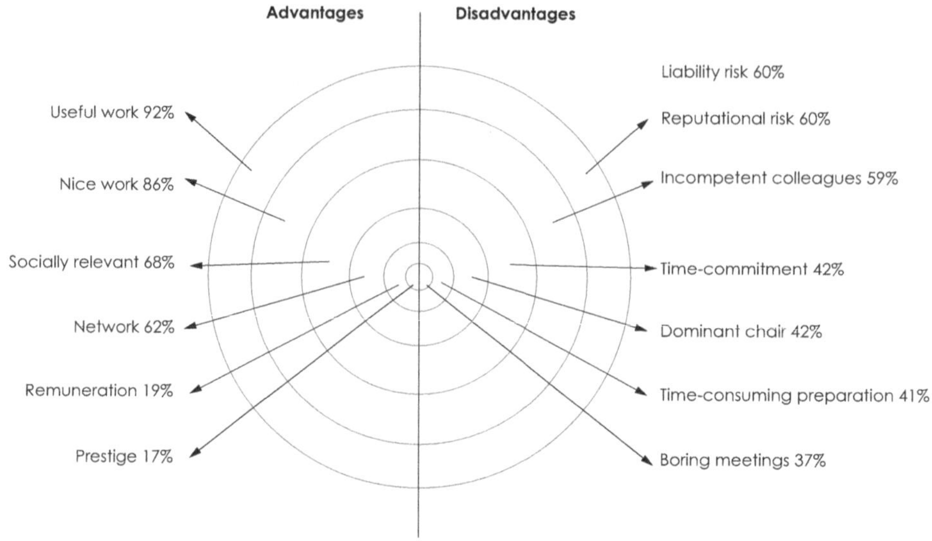

Figure 6.6
Upside/Downside of the Oversight Role

A survey among Dutch non-executive directors and executive search professionals paints a different picture of today's board motivations. The primary driver for accepting a seat seems to be intrinsic motivation, particularly the desire to make a socially meaningful contribution.[23] For many, it is also a way to remain engaged in business or public life post-retirement.

Figure 6.6 summarizes the perceived advantages and disadvantages of the oversight role. Remuneration is seen by survey respondents as a largely neutral factor, as is prestige—at least when asked directly. Executive search professionals, however, paint a more nuanced reality. Prestige and visibility continue to influence high-profile appointments, be it subtly. Informal markers of status remain strong across countries, such as the number and prominence of one's board positions, presence in financial media, and inclusion in annual rankings of influential directors.

Status comparisons are rarely explicit, yet they matter. Some non-executives privately admit mild disappointment when their board portfolios appear less prestigious than those of their peers. Reputation within the director community functions as a quiet currency.

The downsides of the role often become fully visible after appointment. According to survey data, 59% report frustration with incompetent fellow board members, 42% have faced dominant chairs who stifle discussion, and 60% worry about liability risks and potential damage to personal reputation. In a 2025 PwC Annual Corporate Director Survey, more than half of directors indicated that at least one board member should be replaced, frequently citing a lack of relevant expertise as the key concern. Time demands are another concern—especially for those hoping to work less intensively later in their careers.

Case Study: Siemens Energy—when activism meets governance

In early 2020, Siemens Energy CEO Joe Kaeser made an unexpected gesture: he publicly invited German climate activist Luisa Neubauer to join the supervisory board. Siemens was under scrutiny for its involvement in a controversial Australian coal project, and Neubauer—a prominent figure in Fridays for Future—had been openly critical of the company.

The offer was remarkable. Siemens Energy's supervisory board, like many in Germany, mainly consisted of older men from corporate backgrounds. Inviting a young climate activist signaled growing pressure to integrate stakeholder voices on ESG and stewardship.

Neubauer declined the invitation. She acknowledged its symbolic value but argued that joining the board would undermine her independence. Supervisory board members are expected to show loyalty to the company—a constraint that would fundamentally alter the nature of activism. As she put it, *"As a climate activist, it is part of my job to hold people like Joe Kaeser accountable. His job is to act—as responsibly as possible."*[24]

Her response underscored a deeper tension: whether activist voices can retain their power once drawn into institutional roles. Kaeser later clarified that he had meant a seat on the advisory committee, not the formal board, but the episode had already exposed the gap between symbolic inclusion and genuine structural change.

The episode illustrates how institutions may attempt to absorb external critics, while critics risk losing independence once embedded within governance structures.

Entry and renewal: old boys, new boards

Non-executive directors are still predominantly recruited through established *elite* networks: current and former CEOs and CFOs, existing board members' professional circles, executive search firms, major law and accounting firms, and individuals with prior public board experience. The casual question in these networks: *"Do you know anyone ready for something new?"*—often marks the beginning of a non-executive director search.

Although formal nomination committees structure the process, informal networks frequently shape who enters it. It is natural to choose people one knows and trusts; even school boards and sports clubs operate that way. But in corporate governance, this instinct has consequences. A small circle of experienced non-executives rotating across major boards may bring continuity and shared experience, yet it can also introduce the risk of shared assumptions and blind spots. Directors with similar backgrounds may, often unconsciously, see the world through the same lens. Homogeneity reduces friction—but it also reduces the cognitive diversity needed for effective oversight. Cohesion rises—but independence and genuine countervailing power can quietly erode, weakening oversight in the future when it matters most.

Competencies and character: the undervalued art of critical dissent

A survey among executive search professionals in the Netherlands reveals a traditional preference for a familiar set of personality traits in non-executive directors (Figure 6.7). Although context-specific, the patterns align with observations in other markets. Frequently

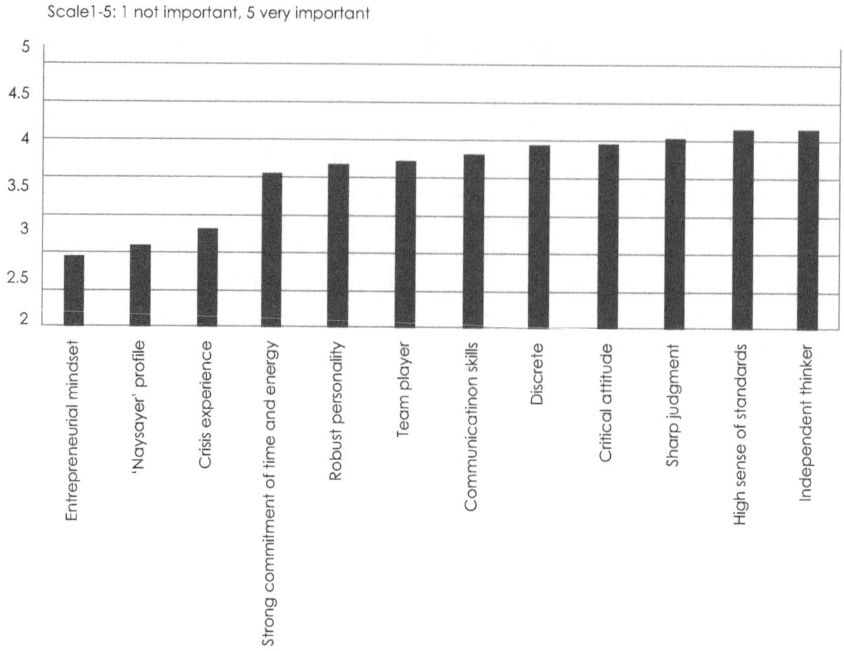

Figure 6.7
Desired Experiences and Characteristics of Non-Executives

mentioned are independent thinking, a strong moral compass, sound judgment, a critical attitude, and discretion. Few would dispute these qualities—they reflect an almost default consensus on what "good oversight" looks like.

Less appreciated, however, are traits such as an entrepreneurial mindset, a contrarian profile, or experience with crises. The low score on entrepreneurialism aligns with a widely held view among non-executives themselves: their task is to provide oversight, not to drift into a quasi-executive role. Even if this mindset may also help better understand the daily challenges of leadership.

The consistently low rating for a contrarian profile is more surprising. A genuinely critical voice—one that challenges prevailing assumptions—is increasingly recognized as essential for real countervailing power vis-à-vis the executive board. Yet this is precisely where principles tend to become flexible. The discomfort of dissent often outweighs its acknowledged value.

Recent survey evidence illustrates how fragile this dynamic can be. In PwC's 2025 Directors Survey, 43% of directors reported that it is difficult to voice a dissenting view in the boardroom. Formal independence does not automatically translate into behavioral courage.[25]

Interlock, power, and pitfalls

Board appointments made through personal and professional networks—known as *interlock*—offer both advantages and drawbacks (Figure 6.8). On the upside, choosing directors from familiar circles can foster trust, loyalty, and smooth collaboration. Shared history

Advantages		Disadvantages
Trust	→	Overtrusting
Constructive work atmosphere	→	No place for critical thinkers
Efficient board recruitment	→	Newcomers are excluded
Same perspective on issues	→	Possibility of groupthink
Same values	→	Exclusive rather than inclusive
Swift help with problems via the network	→	Risk of conflicts of interest and abuse of power
Enhanced reputation (I belong here)	→	When problems arise, interlock evokes distrust
Responsibility-taking	→	Lack of transparency and accountability

Figure 6.8
Advantages and Disadvantages of Interlock

often makes boards more efficient and cooperative, and communication more intuitive. Interlocks can also facilitate the transfer of governance practices and practical insights across companies.

But network-based recruitment also narrows the talent pool. It can exclude equally or better-qualified candidates, and especially women and individuals from underrepresented backgrounds. A Spencer Stuart survey found that 77% of female board members in U.S.-listed companies felt shut out of these informal networks.[26] Yet male directors often mistakenly attributed this exclusion to a shortage of qualified women, exposing deeper structural biases.

In contrast, several European jurisdictions have formalized gender balance targets, and markets such as Australia, Singapore, and India continue to embed diversity expectations in governance codes or listing requirements, underscoring how board composition remains closely shaped by institutional context.

In many countries, meaningful progress on gender diversity has often followed quotas or regulatory pressure. In the United States, earlier advances were driven by executive search firms and major institutional investors such as BlackRock, State Street, and Vanguard—who actively pushed for diverse boards. Rising demand for expertise in ESG, risk, and digital transformation, fields in which more women hold senior roles, has also widened the pipeline. This development aligns with a growing body of empirical research over the past decade—as discussed earlier in this book—suggesting that board diversity is associated with stronger oversight, broader strategic debate, and, in some domains, improved environmental and governance outcomes. Yet, recent U.S. survey data from PwC show a marked year-over-year decline[27] in planned additions to boards of gender and racial/ethnic diversity. The drop may signal growing political sensitivity around DEI, prompting boards to temper publicly stated diversity ambitions. At the same time, recruitment priorities appear to be shifting toward AI and geopolitical risk.

A cautionary example of the interlock's downside is the 2018 collapse of Theranos. Its board, composed of high-profile figures with little relevant expertise and strong personal loyalty to the company's leadership, ignored early warning signs and failed to challenge management. The case shows how dense networks can compromise independence and create dangerous blind spots. Tightly interlocked boards have historically resembled exclusive clubs—circles in which membership signals status and trust but may also discourage critical distance. As Groucho Marx once observed, he would refuse to join any club that would accept him as a member. In governance, the greater risk may lie in clubs that accept too readily—and question too little.

Case Study: Theranos, the illusion of oversight

The innovative diagnostics company Theranos was once valued at $9 billion, reaching its peak in 2014. Founder Elizabeth Holmes claimed to have created technology capable of running extensive diagnostic tests from a single drop of blood. She cultivated the image of a female Steve Jobs—black turtleneck, minimalism, mystique—and briefly became the world's youngest self-made female billionaire.

Equally striking was the board she assembled: ten male non-executive directors, many drawn from the same elite networks. Among them were two former U.S. senators, two former cabinet members, a general, an admiral, and several other senior military leaders. Their ages ranged from 65 to 95. Henry Kissinger, then 91, reportedly found the board meetings so long he joked they were a "*human rights violation*," yet he remained loyal to Holmes, once saying she possessed something "*ethereal*."

Despite its impressive résumés, the board lacked expertise in diagnostics, biotech, or regulatory oversight. Enthralled by Holmes' charisma—and perhaps disarmed by shared networks—members failed to question the company's claims or governance. In the end, $700 to $900 million in investor capital evaporated into an illusion. Holmes was convicted of fraud in 2022 for misleading investors about a blood-testing technology that did not exist.

The Theranos collapse has since become emblematic of network-driven blind spots and the ease with which charisma and shared status can suppress critical scrutiny.

Beyond business: political networks and structural bias

Network dynamics and bias are not confined to the corporate world. They extend into politics and government—for example, strong connections in Washington, Beijing, Brussels, or Canberra are often treated as strategic assets. Political familiarity can add value, but it can also blur boundaries, opening the door to conflicts of interest, nepotism, or outright corruption. In some developing countries, changes in political leadership trigger a reshuffling of non-executive board positions in companies under state influence. Roles are handed to allies of the winning parties, sometimes irrespective of their experience in corporate governance.

Those embedded in these circles often overlook their own structural advantages—a form of *meritocracy bias* that attributes success solely to hard work while underestimating the influence of privilege and inherited social capital. As a result, organizations may end up with suboptimal appointments, simply because selecting the "usual suspects" feels safest.[28]

Opening the boardroom

Openings for corporate board roles are rarely advertised publicly. The networks that shape these appointments often remain opaque, with executive search firms serving as intermediaries primarily for insiders who already know how to access them. In contrast, civil society organizations and NGOs—particularly in the UK, North America, and increasingly across Europe—have embraced more open appointment models. Public calls for board positions on platforms such as LinkedIn, BoardnetUSA, Reach Volunteering, and CharityJob reflect a shift toward transparency and inclusion. Governance codes and regulatory frameworks now increasingly encourage this approach to strengthen board quality, diversity, and legitimacy.

This growing emphasis on openness and scrutiny challenges the tradition of exclusive boardroom networks, pointing toward a gradual shift in which competence—not connection—may become the primary driver of board appointments.

Overboarding: when experience becomes excess

A concern closely linked to interlocks is overboarding—the accumulation of too many board seats, raising doubts about their effectiveness, independence, and availability. Several countries have responded by placing formal limits on the number of directorships a person may hold. France, Germany, and Italy enforce legal or regulatory caps, while the United Kingdom and the United States rely on strong guidance from governance codes and major institutional investors. In the United Kingdom, boards are expected to self-assess whether a director is "overcommitted." In the United States, investors and proxy advisors, including Vanguard and ISS, generally advise that CEOs should hold no more than two external public company board seats, and non-executive directors no more than four or five. Less visible, however, are mandates in nonprofit and charitable organizations. Although these roles may not be counted alongside major corporate appointments, they often arise through similar networks and can demand comparable time, responsibility, and reputational capital—further complicating assessments of true board capacity.

The implications differ in *one-tier board systems*, where non-executives sit alongside executives and are deeply involved in strategy, oversight, and committee work. Here, the demands on their time are significantly higher, making it far less practical—or defensible—to build a broad portfolio of board seats. The workload simply does not allow it.

Attitudes have shifted accordingly. While some once argued that seasoned directors could easily juggle multiple mandates, recent evidence suggests the opposite. A U.S. survey found that 59% of non-executive directors consider three board roles optimal, while only 9% view five or more as appropriate—reflecting a growing recognition that overboarding weakens oversight and engagement.[29]

The risks go beyond time constraints. Directors stretched across too many mandates may become less critical, more deferential, or more vulnerable to *groupthink*. Cognitive bandwidth becomes limited, and with it the willingness to challenge. This undermines independence—a core principle of behavioral governance—and weakens the board's ability to act as a countervailing force. In such circumstances, raising difficult questions becomes rare. As Harold Geneen observed, a non-executive who keeps probing, risks either revealing what he does not know or being labeled a troublemaker; and no one likes a troublemaker.

"So what to do, except sit back in his chair, taste his cold coffee, and desist?" The line captures a familiar quiet pressure: staying silent often feels easier than persisting—even when persistence is exactly what good governance requires.[30]

SUMMARY AND CONCLUSION

Being a non-executive director is far from ceremonial. It demands time, sharp focus, and the courage to speak up, often quietly, without recognition. Non-executives share real responsibility: they oversee strategy, assume personal liability, and, in difficult moments, may have to risk their own reputations. This is not a role for the passive or easily intimidated.

And yet the appeal remains strong. Many former executives enjoy the intellectual challenge and the chance to contribute to an organization without the grind of daily management. Prestige plays a role, but so does the simple fact that good board work can be deeply rewarding—provided the people around the table raise the level.

Networks still serve as the primary entry point into boardrooms. They not only offer trust and familiarity but also reproduce sameness, limiting diversity of thought. Behavioral dynamics—groupthink, hierarchy, the discomfort of dissent—can further weaken independence. Overboarding adds another risk: directors with too many mandates may become tired, deferential, or reluctant to challenge.

Shifts in long-term patterns typically unfold gradually. Regulation, investor pressure, and more open recruitment practices—especially in civil society and public sectors—are widening the talent pool for women and underrepresented candidates. Developments, however, remain uneven, and recent signals from the United States suggest that momentum may fluctuate.

And, should oversight ever stop being fun? Invite someone with a sense of humor. Even if Groucho Marx would still decline the offer.

§6.5—FROM BLINDNESS TO A BALANCED BOARD

Il faut cultiver notre Jardin

Voltaire[31]

This book has explored boardroom behavior through the lens of both triumphs and failures. The pressure on boards has never been higher. While many organizations operate under strong governance frameworks, even the most robust boards can struggle and falter—especially amid today's world of rising complexity, from geopolitical tensions to regulatory uncertainties and AI transformation. In such conditions, boards risk becoming paralyzed by ambiguity, *groupthink*, or simple complacency.

Understanding what good governance requires often begins by studying where it breaks down. As the saying goes, victory has a hundred fathers, but defeat is an orphan. Behavioral governance sharpens that mirror. The boardroom is not a purely rational space; it is shaped by personalities, power dynamics, and incomplete information. Non-executive directors—inevitably a few steps removed from daily operations—must interpret signals, manage expectations, and navigate group behavior behind closed doors.

Yet under the right circumstances, the boardroom can become a place of clarity, trust, and productive challenge. The task is not only to provide oversight, but to question with integrity—without damaging the relationships that make collective oversight possible.

Perhaps the key is not certainty but balance: between structure and trust, reason and intuition, distance and involvement. Behavioral insight doesn't offer quick fixes, but it can strengthen awareness, sharpen judgment, and help boards ask the right questions at the right moment.

From willful blindness to countervailing power

Margaret Heffernan describes willful blindness as the tendency to ignore information that is uncomfortable,[32] inconvenient, or contradicts our beliefs. It isn't simple ignorance but a form of strategic unawareness: we *could* know, but we choose not to.

Cognitively, willful blindness reflects the limits of how we process information. When facts challenge our assumptions, we instinctively filter them out. Euphemisms and soft framing help mask real risks: "We all support this plan, right?" quietly redirects attention to short-term benefits and pushes longer-term dangers out of view.

But willful blindness is more than a cognitive glitch—it is also deeply social, working on three reinforcing levels:

1. Social justification: People want to be constructive and cooperative. In groups, they prefer offering solutions over raising uncomfortable concerns, even when proper analysis is skipped.
2. Group justification: We view our own group positively because it is part of our identity. This makes it harder to confront one another's behavior.
3. Institutional justification: Members of an organization—non-executive directors included—want to believe in its integrity. That loyalty makes it difficult to acknowledge internal problems or speak openly about what is going wrong.

Precisely because these forces are so strong, boards must continuously reflect on their role as a countervailing power: the ability to slow decisions down, surface dissent, and create space for uncomfortable facts. Countervailing power is not opposition for its own sake but a disciplined commitment to asking the questions others avoid—the safeguard that keeps willful blindness from taking root and lies at the heart of effective oversight.

Case Study: PWC—and the cost of looking away

External auditors are respected and expected to act as guardians of financial integrity.[33] Yet in practice, it can be surprisingly difficult to define what is right and what is wrong and uphold the former. In 2023, PwC Australia was exposed for misusing confidential information about new anti-tax avoidance laws to benefit its clients. Senior partners had received early insight into planned changes in the tax system and, some claiming not to know them to be confidential, passed them on to advise clients on how to exploit the interim window. An independent report described an "overly collegial culture" with "excessive power" concentrated in the Australian firm's CEO. Loyalty was rewarded over challenging more senior partners. A parliamentary inquiry concluded conflicts of interest were too often ignored, and even at times actively exploited, pointing to "a yawning chasm between the rhetoric of its public-facing promotional material and the reality" at PwC.

Under intense political and regulatory pressure, PwC Australia's CEO stepped down, and the firm's governance was overhauled. An independent external chair was appointed to lead the refreshed board and oversee cultural and structural reforms.

This was not an isolated lapse. Similar behavioral failures surfaced in exam-cheating scandals at EY, Deloitte, and KPMG Australia, where collective rationalization replaced individual accountability.

Heffernan's concept of willful blindness fits the pattern: wrongdoing was reframed as clever service; shared identity discouraged dissent; organizational prestige softening moral dissent. No one wanted to believe that a trusted institution was quietly crossing a line.

Silence, as so often, proved costly.

The PwC case highlights a core behavioral lesson: the challenge lies not only in detecting wrongdoing but in recognizing the signals, the group dynamics, and the quiet moral rationalization. Risk literature emphasizes the need to institutionalize dissent: creating a culture where disagreement is not merely tolerated but also valued. This includes inviting contrarian thinking when consensus becomes too comfortable or is reached too quickly.

A psychologically safe environment, for non-executives and executives, but also for direct reports in the organization, is essential for honest questions and dissenting views. Such views rarely emerge without encouragement. A non-executive who fears exclusion for raising uncomfortable issues may choose silence. Once that happens, the board loses its role as a meaningful countervailing force.

Sometimes, however, psychological safety and trust can be damaged beyond repair. In those moments, only one option remains—to make one's position clear: *they leave, or I do.* A principled resignation becomes the final form of dissent.

Embedding integrity in oversight

Integrity is one of the toughest parts of oversight—not just avoiding shortcuts, but choosing what is right even when it is inconvenient. Codes and compliance systems help, but integrity ultimately shows up in everyday decisions, subtle pressures, and the informal cues people take from those around them. As discussed in Chapter 4, this is the realm of *soft controls*: the quiet signals that shape behavior more powerfully than rules.

Muel Kaptein moves the discussion beyond individual virtue. He argues that integrity is not a personal trait, but an organizational quality that must be intentionally built into the organization. He identifies eight conditions that indicate whether integrity is truly part of daily practice. Together, they provide non-executive directors with a practical lens to sense the ethical climate through tone, patterns, and silences, not just reports.

In essence, the question is simple: does the organization make it easy to do the right thing or subtly difficult? 8 dimensions can help foster integrity in the organization:

- Clarity about what is expected
- Consistency between stated values and behavior of leadership
- Achievable goals that don't push people toward shortcuts
- Support to act in respect for each other under pressure
- Transparency supported by visibility
- Openness to raise dilemmas early
- Accountability that makes speaking up safe
- Enforcement, when standards are breached

For boards, these are not abstract principles, but early indicators. When expectations blur, goals become unrealistic, or concerns can't be voiced. A healthy organization allows someone to say without fear: "*This doesn't feel right.*"

Positive psychology and the balanced board

Positive psychology offers a welcome shift in perspective. Randy Newman's song puts it simply: "Oh, it's lonely at the top." Many CEOs would agree. Leadership can be isolating. The higher you climb, the fewer people speak freely. Instead of focusing solely on control, compliance, and what goes wrong, positive psychology asks a different question: what conditions help people to perform at their best? For boards, that means shaping a constructive atmosphere that creates energy, creativity, and engagement, while also supporting clarity and trust.

Psychologist Shawn Achor adds an additional perspective: only 10% of success is determined by external circumstances. The other 90% depends on how we respond to them. His research suggests that intelligence accounts for roughly 25% of performance, while the remaining 75% is shaped by optimism, social support, and the ability to manage stress.[34] Translated to the boardroom, a few simple practices can noticeably improve the atmosphere, the tone and quality of interactions:

- Start and end meetings with genuine check-ins, showing interest in how executives are doing, professionally and personally.
- Acknowledge recent successes, building momentum and trust before moving to difficult topics.
- Create brief moments of reflection—during or after meetings—to surface what is going well and what needs attention, even if this is not on the agenda.

In short, positive psychology improves relationships not by ignoring problems but by reinforcing constructive feedback and shared purpose. Yet, as with any behavioral approach, pitfalls remain. Excessive optimism can dull the necessary challenge. Admiration for the CEO may overshadow awareness of risk. Formal oversight must not vanish beneath an atmosphere of positivity that makes it easier to avoid difficult issues, as cases in this book illustrate. The goal is not forced harmony but a balanced boardroom where respect, realism, and reflection coexist.

Balanced board: internal perspective

As proposed in this section, the balanced functioning of a board rests on four key behavioral dimensions (see Figure 6.9). Along each axis, the challenge is not to choose sides but to find balance:

- Control versus trust
  Non-executive directors have a fiduciary duty to ensure that the organization is in control, risks are monitored, and responsibilities are clear. But when control becomes dominant, it can lead to friction and defensiveness from the executive board. Trust, by contrast, encourages open dialogue and stimulates initiative. Too much trust, however, can lead to complacency, overconfidence, or create the conditions for misconduct.
- Reason versus feeling
  Effective boardroom decision-making relies on Daniel Kahneman's *System 2 thinking*: deliberate, analytical, and slow. It includes exploring scenarios, weighing alternatives, and sharing viewpoints. But too much reliance on reason can feel rigid and alienating. Emotions, feelings, and even intuition play a role in good judgment. But if unchecked, they can lead to impulsive decisions, short-term focus, or *confirmation bias*.
- Compliance versus empathy
  Non-executive directors must ensure legal and procedural compliance. Yet this mindset works best paired with empathy: an understanding of the pressures and dynamics at the top of the organization. Overemphasis on compliance can harm working relationships; too much empathy can lead to excessive positivity or conflict avoidance and blur judgment.
- Integrity versus emotional intelligence
  Integrity requires speaking up, confronting dilemmas, and resisting bias. Emotional intelligence helps directors read the room and manage tensions constructively. Yet if overextended, it risks tipping into *pleaser behavior*, where difficult conversations are avoided in favor of harmony.

When the composition of the group of non-executive directors is balanced, the executive board has the space it needs to run the organization effectively—while the independent directors retain the shared confidence that they can step in when continuity, purpose, or values are at stake. Also, being a member of a non-executive board can often be a solitary job, as Anastassia Lauterbacher, a serial board director, mentioned in a LinkedIn interview: "many non-executive directors continue to sit on multiple boards without truly understanding the exposures and liabilities that come with the role. Many fear asking too many questions, because it makes them feel diminished—almost as if they were still employees rather than board members. They also don't want to be seen as troublemakers." *Intervision*, a structured form of peer reflection, can help non-executive directors surface underlying dynamics and hidden tensions.

The four behavioral axes for the balanced board, also connect to the more subtle diagonals introduced earlier in this book. Emotional intelligence and empathy help boards read the

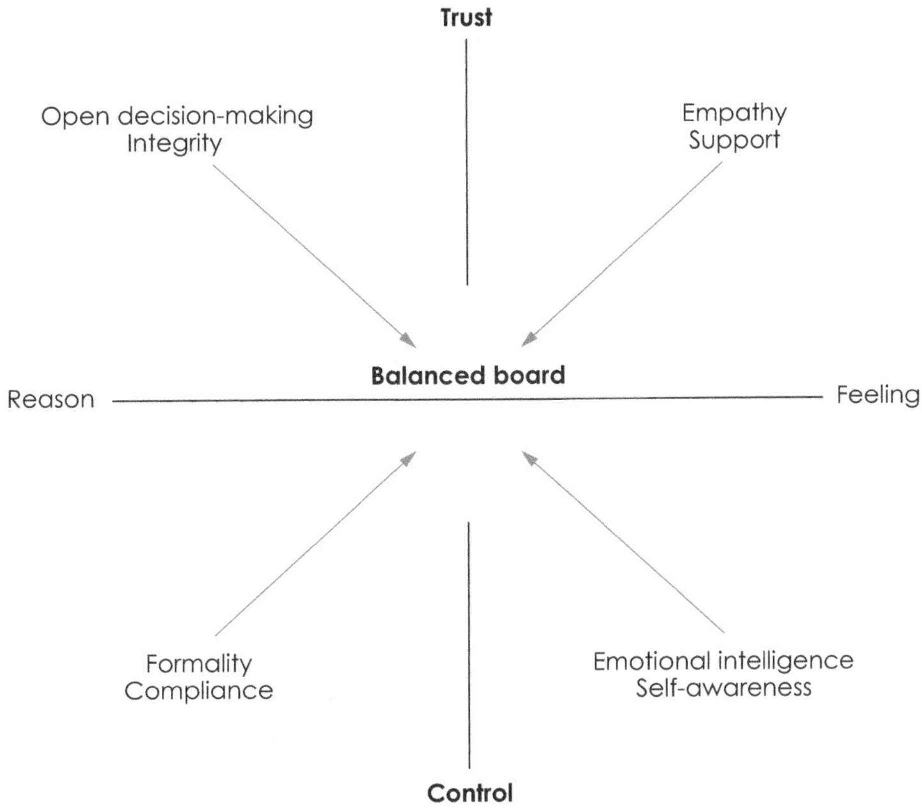

Figure 6.9
The Board's Internal Balance

room and maintain a healthy working climate, while integrity and the formality of compliance anchor decisions in what is right, not just what feels comfortable.

Together they underline a simple truth: good governance lives in a state of equilibrium—staying human without losing rigor and staying principled without becoming rigid.

Balanced board: the external perspective

The balance between the organization and the outside world concerns how an enterprise or social institution positions itself in a society under increasing political, economic, and ecological pressure. This raises fundamental questions: Who actually owns the organization? What is its purpose? What concrete plans are being pursued and what is their wider impact on the world?

In fulfilling its fiduciary role, the board, through strategic and empathetic leadership, must strike a responsible balance between shareholders' more financially driven interests and the broader interests of internal and external stakeholders. Aligned with a stewardship model of governance, this means weighing short-term performance against long-term value creation and adjusting the balance where needed (see Figure 6.10).

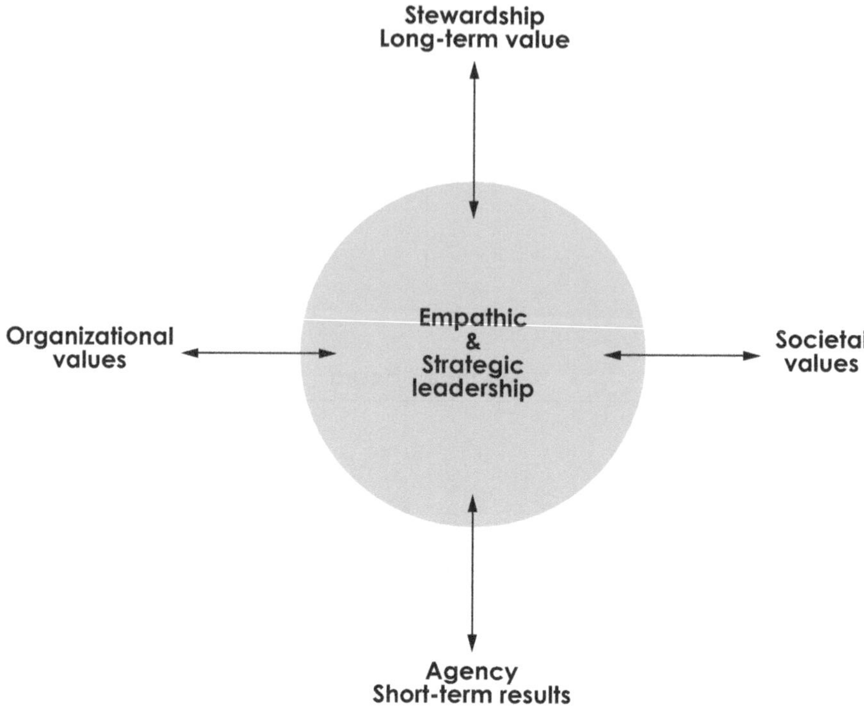

Figure 6.10
An External Balance: Board and Society

Shared values form the basis of this balance. They guide how the organization responds to public interests, including the importance of social and climate challenges, and public scrutiny.

The executive team is responsible for embedding these values when setting strategies, in daily decision-making, and in organizational execution. Non-executive directors, in turn, must assess whether this alignment holds in practice. Culture, integrity, and long-term impact are core elements of good governance, not secondary. Their task is to monitor whether strategic choices stay true to the organization's stated purpose and guard against short-term pressures undermining longer-term responsibilities.

In a world facing political bullying and geopolitical uncertainty, corporate governance is more critical than ever. This includes, as part of their fiduciary duty, evaluating the organization's contribution to broader ESG priorities such as human rights, shared prosperity, climate action, and biodiversity. Ultimately, a balanced board is one that can hold economic performance and societal responsibility in constructive tension—without losing sight of the organization's enduring purpose.

SUMMARY AND CONCLUSION

In an increasingly complex world, directors—executive and non-executive—can drift into willful blindness: overlooking troubling signals because acknowledging them creates discomfort. This tendency is not only individual but also social and institutional. We avoid challenging peers to remain constructive and stay loyal to the system we serve. In this way, silence can turn into complicity.

Breaking this pattern calls for reflection on corporate values and a form of oversight that is open, critical, and constructive. Insights from positive psychology show that psychological safety helps directors think more clearly and engage more meaningfully. Moments of recognition, reflection, and attention create a better atmosphere and improve the quality of judgment in the boardroom.

An internally balanced board depends on navigating key tensions—between control and trust, reason and feeling, compliance and empathy, and integrity and emotional intelligence. These are not opposites but dynamic balances that need ongoing attention.

Externally, the board's role extends to empathetic and strategic leadership: listening carefully, respecting different perspectives, and aligning organizational purpose with societal expectations. Long-term value increasingly depends on recognizing shared interests between business and society.

In a world shaped by geopolitical volatility, technological change, climate urgency, and shifting norms, boards must balance stewardship with performance, and corporate success with broader societal values.

Behavioral governance starts with values, becomes effective through awareness, and matures through presence, posture, and the courage to act when it matters most.

Final Consideration

This section began with a quote from Voltaire. The story follows the fortune hunter Candide, who, after a lifelong adventurous journey around the world in search of love, gold and diamonds at last comes to rest. He has faced adversity, made big mistakes, has been deceived at times, and watched many fall into misfortune. His blind optimism has not made him rich.

A farmer, in a village not far from Constantinople, surprises him with a warm reception and generous gifts from his own garden. Surprised, Candide said to his host: "You must have a vast estate." The farmer replies that he lives modestly, cultivating his land with his two daughters through hard work. He explains that life is marked by three sources of suffering: *l'ennui* (boredom), *le vice* (evil), and *le besoin* (scarcity). We can avoid these if we don't let our behavior be overly driven by negativity. Positivism ultimately offers the way out. Voltaire says: the quality of our work is in our own hands. This also requires us to reflect on ourselves.

Non-executive directors perform a sometimes impossible job. But for the curious director interested in both the economic and social mission of the organization, serving on a board, can also be a beautiful and often enjoyable task that can bring intrinsic rewards. Serving on a board with responsibility for oversight requires hard work. Mistakes will be made, but lessons can be learned. Governance has become a profession that demands an understanding of what happens in and around an organization, not least the behavior of those within it. This is the essence of behavioral corporate governance: continuous reflection on one's own performance and a sustained investment in personal development.

Voltaire concludes: "Tous les événements sont enchaînés dans le meilleur des mondes possibles . . . Cela est bien dit . . . mais il faut cultiver notre jardin." ("All events are linked together in the best of all possible worlds. . . . That is well said . . . but we must cultivate our garden.")

Erasmus University's motto reflects this insight: *Lifelong Learning.*

REFLECTION QUESTIONS

Questions §6.1—Values, virtues, and the moral compass

1. How would you describe leadership in your organization when seen through the lens of a moral compass? Is that compass explicit and shared across the board and the executive team?
2. When appointing a CEO during turbulent restructuring, how does your board weigh short-term executive capability against long-term cultural fit? Would you favor a strong-willed, directive leader who may lack empathy, or an empathetic, collaborative leader who may need time to build credibility?
3. To what extent do the classical virtues—wisdom, justice, moderation, and courage—meaningfully guide decision-making and dialogue within the board?

Questions §6.2—Strategic intelligence and empathetic leadership

1. How effectively does your leadership team balance the six dimensions of strategic-empathetic leadership: empathy, inclusiveness, transparency, strategic intelligence, drive, and self-awareness? Where do you see imbalances or blind spots?
2. Does your board apply a clear, structured process when assessing or attracting new executive leadership? To what extent are integrity and the six leadership dimensions explicitly integrated into your selection criteria?
3. How does your board identify and address behavioral risks or emerging cultural patterns within the leadership team?

Questions §6.3—Choosing the right leader at the right time

1. Is your succession strategy actively maintained and aligned with the organization's future leadership needs?
2. Where is your CEO in the leadership lifecycle, and what does this mean for board dynamics, renewal, and organizational impact?
3. How objective and bias-aware is your CEO selection and evaluation process? How often is it recalibrated?

Questions §6.4—The new non-executive director

1. Does your board renewal policy safeguard independence, limit interlocks, and stimulate fresh thinking?
2. How does the board ensure that diversity of perspectives meaningfully strengthens discussions on ESG issues, societal expectations, and broader long-term impact?
3. How do you enable new non-executives to contribute confidently and constructively, especially when they bring challenging or unfamiliar viewpoints?

Questions §6.5—From blindness to a balanced board

1. Are the eight dimensions of an integrity-supportive board recognized and reinforced at the board level?
2. How do insights from *positive psychology*, such as psychological safety and bias awareness, strengthen boardroom dialogue and decision-making?
3. How does the board consciously balance emotional intelligence and integrity? How does it maintain equilibrium between trust and control, reason and feeling, compliance and empathy?
4. How does the board reflect on its external balance between stewardship and short-term priorities, shareholders and stakeholders, and corporate success and societal impact?

NOTES

1 Alex Brenninkmeijer (2019), *Moral Leadership* (*Moreel Leiderschap*), Amsterdam: Prometheus.

2 Earnings Before Interest, Taxes, Depreciation, and Amortization (EBITDA) is a cash flow concept widely used in the financial industry to determine the value of a company.

3 James M. Burns (1978), *Leadership*, New York: Harper & Row.

4 U.S. Coast Guard (2025 August 8), *Marine Board's Report Into the Implosion of the Submersible TITAN.*

5 Belinda Parmar (2015 January 8), *Corporate empathy is not an oxymoron*, Harvard Business Review.

6 Financial Times (2022 September 29), *Grant Reid on Succession, Family Business and Eating His Own Dog Food.*

7 McKinsey (2023), *The State of Organizations in 2023: How Mars Anchors on Principles and People.*

8 The Guardian (2024 November 20), *Rio Tinto Review Shows Rise in Rape and Bullying Reports.*

9 Michael Maccoby (2001 May, June), *Successful Leaders Employ Strategic Intelligence*, Research, Technology Management; Michael Maccoby (2004 January), *Narcissistic leaders: The incredible pros, the inevitable cons*, Harvard Business Review.

10 Thomas Keil, Dovev Lavie, Stevo Pavićević (2021 July 5), *When do outside CEOs underperform?, Accepted for publication in the Academy of Management Journal.*

11 Brian Blank, Brandy Hadley, Kristina Minnick, Mia L. Rivolta (2021), *A game of thrones—dynamics of internal CEO succession and outcome,* European Financial Management, 280–324.

12 McKinsey (2020 May), *Diversity Wins, How Inclusion Matters.*

13 Harvard Business Review (2022 August 17), *What is Diversity, Equity, and Inclusion?*

14 Spencer Stuart (2019), *Women Leaders, How We Got Here*; Muriel Niederle, Lise Vesterlund (2007), *Do women shy away from competition? Do men compete too much?* The Quarterly Journal of Economics, 122(3), 1067–1101.

15 Jack Zenger, Joseph Folkman (2019 June 25), *Women score higher than men in most leadership skills*, Harvard Business Review.

16 Grant Thornton. (2025). *Women in Business 2025: The push for parity.* Grant Thornton International Ltd. Yahoo Finance (2024 October 23), *The Share of Female CEOs Running Fortune 500 Europe Companies Drops to 6.2%*; Russell Reynolds (2024), *Diversity in the C-Suite—Women's Representation in the 2024 FTSE 100.*

17 McKinsey (2021 March 1), *How Private Equity Can Catalyze Diversity, Equity and Inclusion in the Workplace.*

18 Tim Bower (2021 January–February), *Why Rookie CEOs outperform*, Harvard Business Review.

19 *Finding the right CEO* (2022 January–February), Harvard Business Review.

20 Korn Ferry (2020), *Age and Tenure in the C-Suite.*

21 James M. Citrin, Claudius A. Hildebrand, Robert J. Stark (2019 November–December), *The CEO life cycle,* Harvard Business Review.

22 Christopher Bingham et al. (2020, September 17), *Boomerang CEOs: What happens when the CEO comes back?* MIT Sloan Management Review.

23 Jan Stolker (2016), *Dynamic boards: kansen en drempels voor commissarissen en Toezichthouders* (Dynamic Boards: Opportunities and Barriers for non-executive directors), Erasmus Governance Institute. PwC (2022, 2025), Annual Corporate Directors Survey.

24 *Frankfurter Allgemeine Zeitung* (2020 January 13).

25 PwC. (2025). *2025 Annual Corporate Directors Survey: Driving a culture of accountability in the boardroom.* PwC Governance Insights Center.

26 PwC (2021), *Annual Corporate Directors Survey.*

27 *Boardroom Diversity Commitments Fade Amid Broad DEI Retreat* (2025 October 1), Bloomberg Law.

28 Luigino Bruni, Paolo Santori (2022), *The illusion of merit and the demons of economic meritocracy: Which are the legitimate expectations of the market?* Journal of Business Ethics, 176, 415–427.

29 PwC (2021), *Annual Corporate Directors Survey.*

30 Harold Geneen (1985), *Managing,* New York: Avon Books.

31 Voltaire (1694–1778) from *Candide ou l'optimisme*, Geneva, 1759.

32 Margaret Heffernan (2012), *Willful Blindness: Why We Ignore the Obvious at Our Peril*, Walker & Company.

33 FT (September 23 2023), PwC Australia's culture attacked in tax leak scandal report; Parliamentary Joint Committee on Corporations and Financial Services (November 2024).

34 Shawn Achor (2010), *The Happiness Advantage*, Random House.

INDEX

CASE INDEX